Ecumenical Directions
in the United States Today

Ecumenical Directions in the United States Today

CHURCHES ON A THEOLOGICAL JOURNEY

EDITED BY
Antonios Kireopoulos
with Juliana Mecera

NATIONAL COUNCIL OF THE CHURCHES OF CHRIST IN THE USA
FAITH AND ORDER COMMISSION THEOLOGICAL SERIES

Paulist Press
New York / Mahwah, NJ

The Faith and Order Commission of the National Council of the Churches of Christ in the USA thanks the Presbyterian Church USA for the generous contribution that made possible the publication of this book.

Copyright © 2012 by Faith and Order Commission of the National Council of the Churches of Christ

All rights reserved. No part of this book may be reproduced or transmitted in any form or by any means, electronic or mechanical, including photocopying, recording or by any information storage and retrieval system without permission in writing from the publisher.

Cover photograph: Courtesy of Lisajsh / Shutterstock.com

Cover design by Sharyn Banks
Book design by John Eagleson

Library of Congress Cataloging-in-Publication Data

Ecumenical directions in the United States today : churches on a theological journey / Edited by Antonios Kireopoulos with Juliana Mecera.
   p. cm. – (National Council of the Churches of Christ in the USA Faith and Order Commission theological series)
Proceedings of a conference held in July 2007 at Oberlin College.
ISBN 978-0-8091-4755-7 (alk. paper)
  1. National Council of the Churches of Christ in the United States of America. Commission on Faith and Order – History – Congresses. 2. Ecumenical movement – United States – History – Congresses. 3. Oberlin (Ohio) – Church history – Congresses. I. Kireopoulos, Antonios. II. Mecera, Juliana.
BX6.N2E27 2011
280′.0420973 – dc23   2011042940

Published by Paulist Press
997 Macarthur Boulevard
Mahwah, New Jersey 07430
www.paulistpress.com

Printed and bound in the
United States of America

CONTENTS

INTRODUCTION
Faith and Order: Some Ecumenical Directions for a
Theological Journey
    Antonios Kireopoulos   1

Part I
LOOKING BACK
The Significance of Oberlin 1957
and Reflections on the Last Fifty Years

CHAPTER 1
The Legacy of This Place: Oberlin, Ohio
    Barbara Brown Zikmund   15

CHAPTER 2
The Ecumenical Significance of Oberlin
    Donald W. Dayton   34

CHAPTER 3
Fifty Years and Running: Oberlin '57, Back and Beyond
    Jeffrey Gros, FSC   57

CHAPTER 4
The Apostolic Faith Study and the Holy Spirit
    Cecil M. Robeck Jr.   77

CHAPTER 5
Evaluating Faith and Order's Publishing Record:
The *Perichoresis* of Texts and Contexts
    Joseph A. Loya, OSA   103

CHAPTER 6
Faith and Order in Oberlin: 1957 and 2007
    Diane C. Kessler   130

Part II
THE PRESENT MOMENT
Visions of Christian Unity and the Postmodern Context

CHAPTER 7
Orthodoxy, Postmodernity, and Ecumenism:
The Difference That Divine-Human Communion Makes
    Aristotle Papanikolaou   143

CHAPTER 8
The Bible on Postmodern Surfaces
    Jione Havea   172

CHAPTER 9
Faith and Order in a Postmodern World:
A Response [to Havea and Papanikolaou]
    Michael Root   190

CHAPTER 10
The Search for Unity since 1957: A Catholic Perspective
    Avery Cardinal Dulles, SJ   207

CHAPTER 11
Issues Facing Ecumenism: A Perspective from
the World Council of Churches
    Sarah Heaner Lancaster   220

CHAPTER 12
Evangelicals, Ecumenism, and Emerging Questions:
Reflections on Complexity in Light of Oberlin II
    R. M. Keelan Downton   230

Part III
LOOKING FORWARD
Issues Facing Ecumenism and Interfaith Issues

CHAPTER 13
The Future of Our Journey: Issues Facing Ecumenism
John A. Radano   239

CHAPTER 14
Kingdom Chaos—The Joy of Finding Unity:
An Evangelical Perspective on the Future of Ecumenism
Kevin W. Mannoia   256

CHAPTER 15
Vision of Christian Unity on the Ecumenical Landscape
and Soundscape: A Pentecostal Ecumenical Engagement
David D. Daniels III   271

CHAPTER 16
Issues Facing Ecumenism
C. Christopher Epting   294

CHAPTER 17
How the Work of Christian Unity Relates to Interreligious
Relations and Dialogue: When Good News Sounds Bad
John Borelli   304

CHAPTER 18
Christian Ecumenism and the Abrahamic Faiths
Lewis S. Mudge   330

CHAPTER 19
The Buddhist-Christian Encounter in the United States:
Reflections on Christian Practices
Amos Yong   357

CHAPTER 20
Oberlin 2007: The Need for an Expanded Methodology?
John T. Ford, CSC 380

CHAPTER 21
The Flame of Ecumenism: Student Resurgence
and an Emerging Ecumenical Model
Juliana M. Mecera 392

Oberlin II: Contributors 404

Introduction

FAITH AND ORDER: SOME ECUMENICAL DIRECTIONS FOR A THEOLOGICAL JOURNEY

Antonios Kireopoulos

When theologians from many of our nation's Christian communities gathered together in July 2007 at Oberlin College, they engaged upon a threefold task. They looked back at Faith and Order's theological legacy that had fostered close relationships among many of their churches over the past five decades; assessed the present situation of the churches, both traditional and emerging, both growing and shrinking, and named challenges and opportunities presented by the current context; and looked ahead at how the churches, and by extension their ecumenical commitments, might develop in the coming years. It was a lot to do in just three days.

What resulted at Oberlin was not a definitive study of the past, present, and future of the churches. Instead, what resulted was a realistic appraisal of U.S. ecumenical accomplishments—from bilateral agreements bringing churches into full communion with one another to joint advocacy to remedy critical issues of injustice—and a nuanced view of ecumenism's continued ability to foster meaningful change in the life of the churches and in the society in which they are planted. This book is a collection of papers that were presented at the conference, and a few reflections that followed it. In them, the reader will see evidence of these results.

Of course, no book can capture the fullness of an experience. On the one hand, what is inevitably missing is the validation received by many of the attendees of their longtime work in ecumenical circles. On the other hand, also missing is the inspiration

FAITH AND ORDER: SOME ECUMENICAL DIRECTIONS

that motivated young attendees to now pursue ecumenical work as essential parts of their respective vocations. However, a book can give insights into these experiences, and even convey a sense of their significance and impact, particularly if its contents point to the situation in which the readers, and their communities, find themselves. This is the hope behind the publication of this volume.

Faith and Order is one of the streams that converged to form the modern ecumenical movement. Preoccupied with the theological issues that divide and unite the churches, Faith and Order is sometimes considered the "theological wing" of the movement. This characterization is not quite accurate, in that all areas of ecumenical life are theological: advocacy is based on theological convictions regarding God's justice in the world; mission is based on theological imperatives to proclaim salvation in Christ; and Christian religious education is nothing if it is not based on theological principles for faith formation.[1] Nevertheless, this characterization does point to what drives Faith and Order: the quest for theological unity among the churches, so that we may one day be truly united, and thus it is singularly focused on theological dialogue for theology's sake.

As in other settings worldwide, in the United States this dialogue is housed in the particular national expression of ecumenical conciliar life, specifically in the National Council of the Churches of Christ in the USA (NCC). Beginning as the Federal Council of Churches in 1908 and evolving into the NCC in 1950, this organization replicated programmatic initiatives found in other national settings and at the World Council of Churches. Thus in 1957, what would evolve into the Faith and Order Commission was begun—also at Oberlin College—with a conference titled "The Nature of the Unity We Seek." It was this milestone that was being commemorated with the 2007 conference "On Being Christian Together: The Faith and Order Experience in the United States."

The planning committee for the fiftieth anniversary conference was composed of a diverse group of men and women (in terms of religious tradition, race, age) who sought to provide a program representative of the ecumenical movement itself and broad enough to be representative of the growing diversity within the wider Christian community. The effort was helped immensely by Dr. Ann Riggs, a member of the Friends community who at the time was serving as the NCC's associate general secretary for Faith and Order. Reflecting on the experience, Dr. Riggs once noted the juxtaposition of traditional Faith and Order themes (apostolicity, for example) with new critiques (postcolonialism); of ecclesiological imperatives (say unity) and questions of relevance (postdenominationalism); of Christian metanarratives (born of a Christian worldview) and the reality of competing narratives (prompted by pluralism).[2] It was this juxtaposition that gave Oberlin the feel of something at once consistent with Faith and Order interests and yet an exciting edginess that came with dealing head-on with a new situation.

THE STRUCTURE OF THE BOOK

This book is divided into three sections. The first section, "Looking Back: The Significance of Oberlin 1957 and Reflections on the Last 50 Years," offers a glimpse at the legacy of Faith and Order in the life of the U.S. churches.

The first section starts with a study of Oberlin itself, a place rich in American religious history and one that was ideologically perfectly suited for both the 1957 and 2007 conferences. As religious historian and author Barbara Brown Zikmund writes, "issues of faith and order, and issues of life and work, permeated early Oberlin." Next comes an assessment of Oberlin's ecumenical significance, written by the historian of Pentecostalism, Don Dayton. In his essay he argues that both the continuities and contradictions inherent in American religious history are embedded in the history of Oberlin, and thus "Oberlin can give us new categories to think about these divisions [and] can help raise a model of the possibility of reuniting these impulses in a way that can help us transcend the non-theological debates that are tearing our churches apart."

Jeffrey Gros, a longtime director of Faith and Order at the NCC, presents a history of the commission's work in the fifty years from Oberlin I to Oberlin II. Though expanded from the paper he originally presented at the conference and now incorporating reflections on that event, it is helpful to consider what he sees as both the limitations and the potential of Faith and Order's work in the United States, even as he highlights the main accomplishments of the movement decade-by-decade during these last fifty years. This is followed by Cecil Robeck's evaluation of one of these accomplishments, the output on the theme of the apostolic faith. His essay shows how this work resulted in the expansion of the Faith and Order table to include Holiness and his own Pentecostal traditions, because of both the theme itself and the language used to articulate it.

No assessment of Faith and Order can be complete without an assessment of its texts, hence Joseph Loya's survey of many of the texts produced in the fifty years between the conferences. Going one step further, this Byzantine Catholic theologian shows the growing influence of the Orthodox and Catholic churches in this ecumenical scholarship through their participation on the commission, and thus also attests to a widening of the U.S. ecumenical table. Concluding this section, long-time ecumenist Diane Kessler's postconference reflection discusses the changes in the ecumenical arena from 1957 to 2007: different contexts bring different priorities, different personalities, different challenges, and different opportunities. "The vision of the unity we seek may be clearer to some than when the question was asked in 1957 . . . and [some] churches are reluctant to respond to the vision that has been unfolding," she writes, "yet the reconciling nature of the God we know through Jesus Christ in the Holy Spirit makes claims on Christians and our churches to which we must respond."

These essays serve to set the stage for a look at the present situation in which U.S. churches find themselves today. The second section of the book deals with issues facing these churches, individually and collectively as the ecumenical community, in today's postmodern context.

Aristotle Papanikolaou, a Greek Orthodox theologian, brings to this conversation an exploration of Orthodoxy's central belief in the realism of the divine-human communion as manifested in Jesus Christ. As he writes, "It is this particular core of the tradition that will shape Orthodoxy's response to central questions of a present situation, even beyond postmodernity, and that constitutes the single most important contribution that Orthodoxy can bring to ecumenical dialogue." In his essay, Pacific Islands theologian Jione Havea asks, "Can 'premodern' texts (which were questioned in the 'modern era') be at home in the 'postmodern world'?" In answering this question, he challenges the need for metanarratives and instead finds value in interweaving the biblical narrative with other narratives wrought in various Christian experiences. Michael Root's response to these two papers asserts the need for theologians like himself to engage the challenges to the idea of truth raised by postmodernity. In doing so, he helpfully reminds us of the distinction that "Faith and Order requires a firm sense of truth, but also must be sensitive to the social dynamics of truth, the way claims of truth relate to the assertion of power."

In the next essay, Avery Dulles questions whether ecumenical dialogue can indeed anymore be expected to successfully engage such challenges to the point of bringing about Christian unity, if the methodology is to continue to produce convergence texts that harmonize doctrinal positions of the churches. In its place, drawing on many years of observing ecumenical dialogue and particularly Catholic contributions to this engagement, he suggests a methodology that allows for "growth through mutual attestation," one that enables identification with another church's position ("receptive ecumenism") and relies on the Holy Spirit to guide the churches to such mutual identification ("spiritual ecumenism"). Sarah Heaner Lancaster, a Methodist theologian, suggests that such a shift might be necessary because in today's context "traditionally divisive questions do not always hold interest for present-day theologians, partly because those questions have not seemed to get any closer to resolution and partly because they seem misguided in the first place." Writing from the vantage point of the World Council of Churches, she notes the various trends that work against traditionally ecclesiological questions and cause the churches to consider new theological priorities. The complexity of this new reality is the topic of Keelan Downton's reflection. As a young theologian writing from the perspective of the emergent church, he suggests that the individual Christian's role is to "navigate this complexity—to find some way to live *well* amid intersecting systems" of various traditions.

The third, and last, section of the book points us to the future. What are issues that loom large on the religious horizon?

John Radano, who served more than two decades on the Vatican's Pontifical Council for Promoting Christian Unity, first lists the issues that are on the global ecumenical agenda: the nature of the church, moral discernment in the churches, sources of authority, the healing of memories, conflict and peacemaking. But most interestingly he points to what he sees as requiring even more of our attention: the reception of ecumenical achievements to date so that the degree of real unity in relationship already gained can be claimed, and the divisions that persist and continue to happen within the Christian community due to a tendency to divide rather than to commit to reconciliation. Bringing an Evangelical perspective to the task of identifying urgent issues facing ecumenism, Kevin Mannoia describes the various "differences" between churches that are typically understood as Evangelical and other churches, particularly in terms of the relevance of ecclesiological concerns raised in ecumenical conversation. After doing so, he concludes that "the unity of the church is not only possible, but is increasingly necessary as more and more Evangelicals seek deeper understanding and partnership in the cause of Christ in the world."

From the perspective of an African American, Pentecostal tradition, David D. Daniels wonders if "the ecumenical landscape and soundscape [in North America] would clearly be reconfigured by a Christian unity that transcends . . . denominationalism, overcomes institutional racism and strives for racial justice, links apostolic faith with apostolic power, and overcomes [what he calls] the orality-literacy divide." He argues that these four points identify today's ecclesiological challenges and point to how, with an intentional pneumatological orientation, the churches can achieve genuine unity. C. Christopher Epting directs his gaze upon one issue, the debate around which is tearing at the fabric of many churches, including his own Episcopal Church, specifically the issue of homosexuality. Setting his analysis against three lenses—authority of Scripture, the role of tradition, and the place of reason—he asserts that "in order for these three streams, and sources of authority, to interact, to engage one another, indeed to correct for one another, there must be an environment, a container, if you will, inside of which the conversation can take place," namely, the church itself.

Ecumenical engagement is, of course, a process among Christian churches. The next three papers take us beyond the churches' boundaries, to an issue facing all churches, that of interfaith relations. While the goal of ecumenism is unity, the goal of interfaith relations tends to center around better theological understanding, close relationships, and collaboration on issues of common concern. And while interfaith relations can be effectively pursued by individual communities, it is most effective when done collectively as the ecumenical community.

John Borelli, a longstanding participant in interfaith engagement, raises the point that even at the birth of the modern ecumenical movement (at the 1910 World Missionary Conference in Edinburgh), the matter of relating to people of other faiths was taken up, in the form of a "damaging question about the scandal of witnessing and propagating a disunited Christianity to the world of other religions." Recognizing the shifts, both in terms of ecumenical relationships and how the church looks upon other religions, he states that now is the time, not for comparative religion, but comparative theology, which "proceeds from theological conviction and with respect and care for what those of other religions have to say so that by learning well their tradition in a comparative context with one's own tradition, a deeper understanding ... of one's own convictions is reached." Focusing on the Abrahamic construct, Lewis Mudge turns to the need for Jews, Christians, and Muslims to seek peace, for the sake of the world. This is based on an ethical imperative toward "shared responsibility to one another," which in turn means "responsibility to a covenantal promise [to be a] blessing to humanity," which "members of each of the three faiths living in mutual relationships [must] recognize ... in the lives and traditions of those of the other faiths." Amos Yong takes this mutual recognition one step further, to the interaction of Christianity and Buddhism. If such engagement is genuine, according to him, "the Christian contribution to the ongoing vitality of Buddhism in America will itself be what is required to sustain the plausibility and vigor of Christianity itself in a world of many faiths."

Rounding out the identification of issues is John Ford, who argues that what has been lacking in ecumenical theological dialogue is the ability to take theology from the abstract to the practical. He thus proposes a new, or rather expanded, methodology, one that forces the interaction between the realm of "Faith and Order" and the domain of "Life and Work." Closing this section, and the book itself, is a reflection by Juliana Mecera, an emerging

Orthodox theologian. In her reflection, she takes special notice of Oberlin II's deliberate inclusion of over one hundred ecumenically engaged or interested students and considers the resurgence of student involvement in both local and national ecumenical work, with their newer methodologies, to be one important hallmark of the beginning of the next fifty years of Faith and Order in North America.

TWO STEPS FORWARD

As indicated just above, one intentional choice made by the conference planning committee was to invite young theologians to attend. Partly to introduce some of the next generation to ecumenism, and partly to learn from new participants and those already engaged about how they see the world and how ecumenical exploration must answer their questions if it is to be effective, this decision has borne much fruit. Two of the essays in this book are by up-and-coming theologians; some of those attending have deepened their involvement in the movement; many of those attending have moved into ecumenical circles locally, regionally, nationally, and globally; and the Faith and Order Commission committed resources to an online journal, *New Horizons in Faith and Order*, with the hope that it would provide another outlet for younger theologians to get their thinking into the religious marketplace.

Another choice made by the conference planning committee was to infuse the conference itself with the kind of diversity that is reflective of the Christian community in the United States. A perusal of the program would show that this was achieved on various levels, but most pertinently in the programming: paper presentations, responses, panel discussions, moderating opportunities. However, as the content of this book was being organized, one glaring omission became obvious: the relative lack of diverse voices—in terms of gender, race, and ethnicity (though not religious affiliation)—with regard to the presentations made in the form of delivered papers. Few experiencing the entirety of Oberlin II would have perceived this lack of diversity; the rotation of speakers, panelists, commentators, and others was a swirl of rich diversity. However, in trying to collect written papers that would provide a historical record of the event, this diversity could not be adequately represented. As the current director of Faith and Order, I express the regret of many of those involved in planning (including myself) with regard to this paradox.

To address the kinds of issues that would create such a paradox, the Faith and Order Commission embarked upon a new initiative to bring more diverse voices into theological dialogue. This initiative, called "Ecumenism from the Margins: Christian Unity in the Quest for Justice," is a consultation series, sessions of which take place concurrently with each Faith and Order meeting, which seeks to bring voices and perspectives from otherwise marginalized communities, or from communities that have not been part of traditional theological discussions, to the ecumenical conversation.

This series, which owes much of its inspiration to Faith and Order commissioners Rev. Dr. Young Lee Hertig (Presbyterian Church USA) and Rev. Dr. Johnny Hill (Progressive National Baptist Convention Inc.), has brought African, Latino, Caribbean, Native, and Asian American voices to the table. It has brought perspectives from communities like the Metropolitan Community Church and the Western Rite Antiochian Orthodox Church, and analyses from theologians working in the areas of postcolonialism and interfaith relations. Each presentation has sensitized the Faith and Order commissioners in new ways that have influenced the current work of the commission. And to ensure a long-lasting influence on the dialogue, it has resulted in the concretizing of these concerns in the commission through the creation of a study group that will begin its work in the next quadrennium. Most certainly, issues that come from the margins, push the churches toward the margins and even ask who defines the margins, are issues that impact the divisions—and unity—of the churches.

THE FAITH AND ORDER CALLING

A reader can tell from the above survey of the material in this book, and of two of the outcomes of Oberlin II, that Faith and Order has a particular calling among the churches. This calling is to theologically explore the issues that divide and unite the churches in order to move the churches along toward unity. As the global Faith and Order mission statement puts it, "To call the churches to the goal of visible unity in one faith and in one Eucharistic fellowship expressed in worship and common life in Christ, and to advance toward that unity that the world may believe."[3] This calling is commonly affirmed as a way to bring those who follow Christ into the kind of unity for which Jesus prayed: "I ask not only on behalf of these, but also on behalf of those who will believe in me through their word, that they may all be one" (John 17:20ff., NRSV).

Over the years, there has developed a divergence in the understanding of what this unity is for which we seek. This divergence centers on the degree of emphasis we give to what already binds us to one another as Christians or to what still separates us into disparate Christian communities. Oftentimes, the ecumenical goal of unity is stated in terms of visibly manifesting the divine gift of unity we already at least partially share through our common confession of Jesus Christ as Lord and Savior. Thus the task is to show that, despite our ecclesial differences, at our core we are really the one body of Jesus Christ. On the other side of the spectrum, the ecumenical goal of unity is stated in terms of doctrinal unity. This is not to be understood as uniformity in practice, but rather as unity in dogmatic belief. The task here, then, is to bring about ecclesiological harmony so that we might heal the brokenness in the one body of Jesus Christ.

To use an illustrative example, when we look at the Faith and Order mission statement, then, and its affirmation of the goal of "one Eucharistic fellowship," if we consider the various Christian beliefs about the Eucharist, how would the goal of unity best be served in this case? Does our common confession allow us to partake from the same Eucharistic table even though we have different views of the Eucharist? Or must we reconcile our differing beliefs about the Eucharist before we can truly become united around a common table?

Put another way, when we gather in ecumenical fellowship, do we rejoice in that together we give a more visible face to the degree of unity we already share, or do we lament the fact that we are not fully united? Different churches give different answers to this question. Nevertheless, even as we learn something from one another's perspective, what the ecumenical conversation has taught us is that, no matter which perspective one may hold, we are equally compelled to take up the theological task to explore these questions together. What we are not allowed to do is to be resigned to our divisions, and thus allow the maximal ecumenical and ecclesiological vision to be reduced to a minimal ecumenical and ecclesial exercise in cooperation.

In this book, the reader will see that this theological task has been pursued with vigor by churches in the United States (and churches globally, for that matter). It stems from the conviction that theology is at the heart of who we are as the church. Building personal relationships has allowed for honest theological exchange, sometimes difficult, and always leading to better understanding. Strengthening institutional relationships has enabled movement away from suspicion and toward genuine appreciation for what theological gifts each church brings to the ecumenical table. And indeed, this experience has revealed, and continues to reveal, that division among Christians renders less credible our proclamation of the gospel message. It is this realization, and the desire to instead proclaim salvation with full integrity, that ultimately motivates the churches to be involved in Faith and Order.

CONCLUSION

I would like to thank the many people who made this volume possible. First is Gil Stafford, the theologian from the Church of God (Anderson, Indiana), who served as the chairperson of the conference planning committee, and who presided over Oberlin II even as he was going through the illness that eventually took his life. His spirit is not only present in this volume; it guides many ecumenists who have followed in his footsteps. In addition, I thank the many people who served on the planning committee with Gil. Next, I would like to thank Rev. Dr. Sue Davies (United Church of Christ), who was chair of Faith and Order during the time of the conference, and who was a driving force not only of the conference itself, but also of the Ecumenism from the Margins consultation series that evolved from it. Further, I'd like to thank Dr. Ann Riggs, whose leadership was evident at the conference, and whose friendship and collegiality are still greatly appreciated by those who continue to dialogue at the Faith and Order table.

Thanks also goes to Rev. Dr. Michael Kinnamon, the general secretary of the National Council of the Churches of Christ in the USA, a consummate ecumenical theologian whose encouragement was instrumental to the completion of this volume, and to Dr. Anton Vrame, the current chair of the Faith and Order Commission, whose leadership has been key to helping the commission to begin living into the promise envisioned by Oberlin II. And finally, I'd like to thank Ms. Juliana Mecera, who served almost two years as the Elenie Huszagh Orthodox Intern at the NCC, and whose hard work in helping to edit this volume is the real reason it is in readers' hands today.

The Oberlin II conference took place just before the beginning of the current quadrennium, the four-year period by which we mark the work and progress of all NCC initiatives. The publication of this book comes at the end of this quadrennium. Bringing together this collection of papers has coincided with rich theological discussion in Faith and Order by current commissioners whose new work, inspired by Oberlin II, seeks to build on the profound legacy represented in these pages. It is to these colleagues that I dedicate this volume.

NOTES

1. These four streams of the ecumenical movement are clearly and concisely described in the General Introduction of *The Ecumenical Movement: An Anthology of Key Texts and Voices*, edited by Michael Kinnamon and Brian E. Cope (Geneva: WCC Publications, 1997), 1–5. A revised edition of this classic resource, to be edited by this author and Kinnamon, is scheduled to be published in 2012.

2. This summary was made in remarks on the 2007 Oberlin conference that were given at the Faith and Order Commission meeting on March 19, 2009, at the Florida Center for Theological Studies in Miami.

3. National Council of the Churches of Christ in the USA, *Faith and Order Handbook* (2008), p. 16, *www.ncccusa.org*.

PART I
LOOKING BACK

THE SIGNIFICANCE OF OBERLIN 1957
AND REFLECTIONS ON THE LAST
FIFTY YEARS

Chapter 1

THE LEGACY OF THIS PLACE: OBERLIN, OHIO

Barbara Brown Zikmund

> Following its presentation at Oberlin II, this paper was originally published in the *Journal of Ecumenical Studies* 42, no. 4 (Fall 2007): 499–510, and is copyrighted (2007) by the *Journal of Ecumenical Studies* (*JES*). It is reprinted here with the permission of the author and *JES*.

BEGINNINGS

Oberlin owed its beginning to a man named John Jay Shipherd, a Congregational minister with a keen desire to evangelize the West. Shipherd was working in Elyria, Ohio, when he began dreaming of a religious colony where, as he put it, "consecrated souls could withdraw to Christian living in the virgin forest." One of his students, named Philo Penfield Stewart, encouraged him, and together Stewart and Shipherd conceived of a plan for a utopian colony and school. They proposed to name the colony after John Frederic Oberlin, a pious European pastor who was very popular with missionary-minded American Christians, because in 1830 the American Sunday School Union published *The Life of John Frederic Oberlin, Pastor of Waldback*.

Shipherd and Stewart were dreamers. In a providential sequence of events they obtained a tract of land southwest of Elyria and began convincing families to move to Oberlin. By March 1833 a small group began to clear the woods. Oberlin's first resident, Peter Pindar Pesse, moved his family into a new log cabin a month later. By the end of 1833 approximately a dozen families called Oberlin home.[1]

About the same time Shipherd contracted with some teachers and made plans for a school. He was impressed with the success of the Oneida Institute in upstate New York, which operated on a manual labor plan. In such a school students worked the land to pay for their studies. The only other educational institution in the area, Western Reserve College in Hudson, Ohio, did not have enough land to support manual labor. Soon, what began as an innocent common school mushroomed into an ambitious plan for higher education. On February 28, 1834, the Ohio legislature granted the Trustees of the Oberlin Collegiate Institute a state charter.[2]

Things did not go well. Some teachers decided not to come; the school's president fell ill; the students did not understand the manual labor scholarship system; and Shipherd was inept at handling funds. Although classes began on December 3, 1833, with thirty students living and working in the colony, by the end of the year the financial situation was serious. Faith and luck led Shipherd to Cincinnati, Ohio, a booming metropolis at the southern edge of Ohio. In Cincinnati a drama had been unfolding that was to have major consequences for Oberlin.

LANE THEOLOGICAL SEMINARY

Lane Theological Seminary had been chartered in 1829 in Cincinnati, Ohio, to train clergy for various forms of Protestant ministry on the expanding western frontier. Its early years had been characterized by a battle between "New School" Presbyterian/Congregational leaders deeply committed to revivalism and abolition and "Old School" Presbyterian/Congregational leaders just as passionate to protect the doctrine and practices of classic Calvinism.

During these years, Arthur Tappan, a wealthy eastern abolitionist philanthropist, began talking about starting a "New School" theological seminary on the manual labor plan. He was convinced that such a work-study system was the only way to provide affordable education on the western frontier. To that end, Tappan commissioned Theodore Weld, a radical activist who had felt a call to ministry through revivalism and who had been a student at the Oneida Institute, to determine where this seminary might be located.

Weld listened to many suggestions and eventually recommended that Tappan's dream seminary build on the foundations of Lane Theological Seminary, where a "New School" takeover was already in progress. With Tappan's support, Lyman Beecher, a well-known New England "New School" Congregationalist, became president of a revitalized Lane Theological Seminary. Beecher was well-known and brought prestige to the school; he was theologically progressive and positive about frontier revivalism; and most importantly, Arthur Tappan was ready to pledge a great deal of money to Lane if Beecher was president.

After Beecher arrived in Cincinnati, so many students flocked to Lane that by 1833 it had one of the largest seminary enrollments in the country. Tappan was pleased, but wanted more. As an abolitionist he asked Weld to discuss immediate emancipation with the students. Therefore, early in 1834, although the faculty did not think it was prudent, the students held a debate on the question, "Ought the people of the slave-holding states abolish slavery immediately?" and whether the idea of repatriating slaves to Africa should be supported by the churches. Cincinnati is just across the river from Kentucky, and the debate was very controversial. At its beginning most students agreed that slavery was wrong, but they did not consider immediate emancipation reasonable. By the end of the debate most students had experienced a change of heart and fervently believed that Christians should work for immediate emancipation.[3]

Cincinnati was a river town bordering a slave state (Kentucky). Following the debate the students formed an Anti-Slavery Society and immediately began working to elevate the plight of blacks in the area. They established reading rooms, libraries, and schools. Predictably the mingling of students with the black population aroused bitter antagonism among many town citizens. Almost overnight what was happening at Lane became national news.[4]

As the school year came to an end the faculty asked the students to disband their antislavery organization and to refrain from public discussion and activities. Their principles were right and their intentions good, but "they should not move so far in advance of public sentiment." These patronizing words incensed the students, who became even more zealous in their antislavery activities during the summer break.[5]

The Lane Board of Trustees became increasingly alarmed. In August a committee reported to the board that "no seminary should stand before the public as a partisan, on any question upon which able and pious Christians differ." It proposed a set of regulations forbidding students to organize societies without faculty permission and to not hold meetings except for worship or study purposes.[6]

The students were outraged. When the seminary reopened in the fall the students refused to cooperate and were promptly dismissed. Although Beecher returned from his summer vacation in the East and tried to put the pieces back together, it was too late. Many documents, debates, and stories circulated, while the students tried to decide what to do. They were dismayed not only by the racist attitudes of the city, the faculty, and the administration; they were extremely upset by the arrogant misuse of power exhibited by the Lane Board.

Not surprisingly, when John Jay Shipherd arrived in Cincinnati in late 1834 and promptly invited the students to come to Oberlin, the Lane rebels were receptive. Shipherd told them that Oberlin was ready; all it needed was students. The students were flattered but shrewd. They wanted Asa Mahan (a Cincinnati pastor and the only member of the Lane Board of Trustees to side with the students) to be elected president of Oberlin Collegiate Institute, and they wanted John Morgan (the only Lane faculty member who had sided with the students) to be appointed to the Oberlin faculty. Furthermore, the students, Mahan and Morgan declared, could not come until the Oberlin Board of Trustees passed a resolution guaranteeing "that students shall be received into this Institution irrespective of color." Shipherd had no problem with their request.[7]

Unfortunately the earliest settlers of Oberlin were not of one mind about slavery. There had been no agreement on this issue when people were invited to settle in Oberlin. Nevertheless, when Shipherd discovered that many Oberlin residents opposed immediate emancipation and the idea of the school admitting blacks, he was astonished, arguing that such an egalitarian policy was "under

God's blessing."[8] Shipherd was sure that things would work out, and with Mahan he promptly set off to raise money to support the revitalized Oberlin Collegiate Institute. While he was gone the question of race and the school admissions policy were hotly debated.

Mahan and Shipherd raised a lot of money. They convinced wealthy abolitionists in the East that there was a weak revival spirit on the western frontier and that religious heresies were threatening to "undermine the foundations of pure religion." They persuaded the famous revivalist Charles Grandison Finney to come to Oberlin to teach. Finney, exhausted from his itinerant life as a revivalist, found the idea of Oberlin attractive. He supported the student requests that the faculty be given control over the "admission of students" and the "internal management" of the institution. He endorsed the election of Mahan as president and Morgan to the faculty. For the students the issues were bigger than race. At its core, the Lane crisis was a conflict between trustee power and student-faculty power. Shipherd, Mahan, Morgan, and Finney insisted that the Oberlin Collegiate Institute had to give the faculty control over its destiny.[9]

THE OBERLIN COLLEGIATE INSTITUTE

Things moved quickly, but not without moments of suspense. In December 1834 the Oberlin Board of Trustees elected Mahan and Morgan, but tabled the motion to admit blacks. Finally in February they met again. Shipherd and Mahan were still traveling in the East raising money for the school, but Mrs. Shipherd and a group of women prayed in a nearby room. The eight trustees, all men, cast ballots and the outcome was deadlocked, forcing John Keep, the chair of the board, to break the tie. Keep's leadership and vote, as much as the ideological commitments of Shipherd, Mahan, Morgan, Finney, and the Lane students, set the stage for Oberlin to become a new kind of place. Keep was a strong supporter of "new measures" revival thinking, an advocate of female education, committed to total abstinence, and a recent convert to "immediate emancipation." By early 1835 Oberlin had built a national reputation as a hotbed of reformist and progressive education.[10]

Hundreds of students flocked to the newly famous school. Only thirty of the students came directly from Lane. Others came from the Oneida Institute and some from Western Reserve College. To handle all of the people, especially those from Lane, a simple barracks building was built, variously nicknamed Slab Hall, Cincinnati Hall, or Rebel Shanty. The Lane students were not in a majority, but their maturity, their passion for immediate emancipation, and their desire for theological education forced Oberlin to take political and theological issues seriously. Furthermore, the manual labor plan opened education to poor students, allowing them to "work their way through their education."[11]

The Oberlin Collegiate Institute garnered impressive financial support from many well-known northern abolitionists. As a consequence it did not need the support of the more conservative local Western Reserve citizens and churches. Indeed, the fact that its students, faculty, and funds came from all over the country gave Oberlin an independence that was lauded, envied, and condemned.

Some observers believed that Oberlin's obsession with abolition before 1840 was excessive. In 1837 a student who could not go along with immediate emancipation was expelled and promptly authored a book titled *Oberlin Unmasked*. He wrote that Oberlin abolitionists were not satisfied with the standard of abolitionists generally, but sought to "steal slaves from their masters and colonize them in Canada." The school, he railed, was promoting "amalgamation" and openly flouting the law.[12]

EARLY OBERLIN PASSIONS

In addition to immediate emancipation and interracial education, seven other passions shaped the culture of early Oberlin. It is not possible to rank them, but along with racial equality they nurtured a unique campus culture. Parts of that legacy, albeit in new forms, still are visible in twenty-first-century Oberlin through its abiding commitment to

1. Manual labor, or educational access for people who are not rich

2. Physiological reform, or concern for the health of body and spirit

3. Moral reform, or overcoming patterns of immoral behavior
4. Joint education of the sexes, or coeducation
5. Curricular reform, or providing an education that is practical and useful
6. Nonsectarian revivalism, or religious cooperation
7. The scripture doctrine of Christian perfection, or openness to new religious perspectives

These seven passions, combined with a deep concern for racial equality, made Oberlin, Ohio, a place that was willing to risk. Oberlin students and faculty thought outside the box. They pushed beyond business as usual and encouraged people to dream in new ways. Seven short descriptions of these passions illustrate my point.

Manual Labor

The manual labor economic system was fundamental to early Oberlin because it enabled many poor students from all over the country to get an education. Typically students spent four or more hours a day working on the farm or in the maintenance of the college buildings. It was compulsory, not merely because it paid the bills, but because the leaders of the Oberlin Collegiate Institute believed that a combination of work and study would give students needed outlets for their *animal energies*. Oberlin considered the combination of manual and mental labor crucial to the moral education of the whole person.[13]

Unfortunately, farming in northern Ohio swamps was not always profitable. The manual labor system might have been successful at Oneida in upstate New York, it might have been good for the students, but it never was able to cover the costs of the Institute. Jobs could not be manufactured unless there was some demand for the products of student labor. Furthermore, critics felt that the hours spent in the fields cut into study time and undercut academic standards.

One graduate looking back admitted that the transition between study and work was not always smooth. Moving from the metaphysical to the physical, "from Greek roots to oak roots, from chopping logic to chopping cord-wood, from logarithms to log-rolling" was only relaxing for a time. Several attempts were made to make it economically profitable. For example, the school planted mulberry trees and tried to grow silkworms, but the trees and the worms did not survive northern Ohio winters. Oberlin held fast to the idea of manual labor longer than most schools, and it did allow some students access to education when other doors remained closed, but it was not sustainable.[14]

Physiological Reform

A second special passion of early Oberlin was its commitment to health reform. Consistent with evangelical enthusiasm about the important relationship between body and soul, Oberlin settlers abstained from the use of strong drink and tobacco. Tea and coffee were also suspect. Very early Oberlin embraced a particular philosophy of health that regulated all community and campus life—Grahamism.

During the cholera epidemic of 1832 the philosophy of Dr. Sylvester Graham became very popular. People flocked to hear Graham lecture about personal hygiene and disease prevention. Graham argued that gluttony was more dangerous than drunkenness and that cleanliness was next to Godliness; "Graham principles" were enthusiastically embraced at Oberlin.

Graham's teachings were simple and not very different from contemporary understandings of health and diet. Clothing should be adequate, but never too warm or too tight. Lacing and corsets were dangerous. Sleep should be for seven hours at night in ventilated rooms, never after meals. Beds should be hard, no popular featherbeds. Regular bathing of the whole body with water year round was important. Meals should be small and consist of foods as near to their natural state as possible. No stimulating drinks, small amounts of meat and fish, plenty of vegetables, fruits and bread made with unbolted wheat. Fats, gravies, sweets, condiments, and spices were unnecessary. Exercise in the open air was crucial.[15]

Most of us think of the Graham cracker as a snack for kids and a sweet treat when combined with marshmallows and chocolate. The Graham cracker, Graham breads, and thick Graham crusts cradling unsweetened apple pies were staples of the early Oberlin diet. Later when whole wheat flour was baked into crackers and broken into small pieces, it was called *Granula*. And much later in 1876, John Kellogg picked up the idea and started marketing a cereal he called *Granola*. Shortly thereafter Kellogg's competitor, Charles Post, processed graham flour another way to produce a cereal he called *grape nuts*. It is astonishing to realize that when we eat our breakfasts we are part of a long theological and physiological history.

During Oberlin's early years most Oberlin faculty and students enthusiastically supported Graham's health-conscious regimen. They believed that there was a close relationship between health and faith. If people injured their health, they diminished their "power of doing good" and therefore sinned against God. People needed to be as concerned about the sacred laws of their constitution as their moral obligations.[16]

Grahamism faded by the mid-1840s, but Oberlin's abstinence from stimulating drink persisted. Oberlin consistently pushed for prohibition, arguing with the apostle Paul that one should not drink or eat anything that might make one's brother or sister stumble. Drinking alcohol, even in moderation, could be a source of temptation to others and undermine the power of the church to spread the gospel.[17]

Moral Reform

In keeping with Oberlin's enthusiasm for clean, healthy living was its involvement in the moral reform movement. *Moral reform* in nineteenth-century literature meant many things. Basically it focused upon all activities that Christian believers considered *immoral*—especially sexual and frivolous pleasures.

Oberlin students were wary of the temptations of the theater, the novel, and the waltz. The theater corrupted people by allowing them to "witness the lewd conduct of impure women."[18] Novels "broke down all barriers of virtue."[19] The newest dance craze, the waltz, condoned such personal familiarities (the hand of the lady on a gentleman's shoulder, while his arm encircled her waist) that it was a wonder that any young lady retained her virtue. Even attending a circus or a racecourse was dangerous.[20]

The Oberlin Female Moral Reform Society began in 1835. Women, more than men, took moral reform seriously in keeping with emerging Victorian ideas of women's role in family and society. Later many Female Moral Reform Societies sought to end prostitution and to rescue young women from the sex trade.[21]

Joint Education of the Sexes

Oberlin was assertive and proud of its admission of blacks to its programs, but its decision to admit women to the regular collegiate arts course happened almost by accident. John Jay Shipherd said from the beginning that the Oberlin Collegiate Institute was committed to the "elevation of the female character."[22] He did not anticipate coeducation, but his commitment supported the idea that women should be able to receive the type of instruction that they needed. Therefore, when women asked permission to take collegiate courses, their request was granted.

By 1835 about a fourth of the students attending the Oberlin Collegiate Institute were women. They were not doing college studies, but the college grew accustomed to their presence. In 1836 the Trustees evaluated the success of the joint education of the sexes, concluding that the mental influence of the sexes upon each other was decidedly happy. Having women and men in classes together corrected "the irregularities, frivolities and follies common to youth." They concluded that the policy resulted in no serious evil and the regular association between the sexes was basic to the very idea of human society.[23]

Gradually the women were ready for the collegiate curriculum and continued their studies alongside male classmates. Finally, in 1841 several Oberlin students became the first women in the English-speaking world to earn a college degree by completing a program of studies identical with that required of men, studying in the same classes for the same degree. In elementary and secondary schools girls and boys received instruction together, but at that time it was considered improper at the college level. Oberlin's joint education of the sexes was an informal experiment, not an aggressive campaign, but it worked.

Many people found it difficult to accept the idea. Male and female instruction together was not considered delicate or proper. Furthermore, if women were supposed to be silent in public, how could they recite in class? Oberlin faculty members were flexible and they did not force the ladies. Although they were convinced that the good manners and social graces produced by the mixing of the sexes was an important benefit, they really did not treat women students equally. During the 1840s they required women graduates to sit mute at commencement while a male classmate read their final papers to the audience. A few radical women students, like Lucy Stone, objected; but most of the women were happy with the arrangement. People generally thought that it was "disagreeable to both sexes to see a woman in a public character."[24]

Curricular Reform

Mixing the sexes was not the only controversial issue at early Oberlin. There were also great debates about the mixing of old and new subject matter in the collegiate curriculum. In 1828 a Yale report *On the Course of Instruction* set forth guidelines for collegiate education on the western frontier. The report upheld the teaching of "dead languages" (Greek and Latin) and defended the traditional liberal arts curriculum.[25]

Professors and clergy in Christian colleges like Oberlin became increasingly uncomfortable with this classical focus of collegiate education. President Mahan argued against dangerous pagan authors and advocated the study of biblical languages. Reading Greek and Latin classics was better adapted to educate heathens, not Christians. The mind, he asserted, might be disciplined by studying the Greek and Latin, but scripture would purify the heart and protect it from corruption. Students ought to acquire "knowledge of the natural sciences, of American law, of history, of men and things." And "colleges should fill their minds with truth, facts, practical and available knowledge."[26]

To this end, the professors at the Oberlin Collegiate Institute promoted a curriculum that was practical and useful, in keeping with a new American spirit in education. Western collegiate education was self-consciously critical of easterners, sure that if the West depended on eastern seminaries or eastern views of education, it was destined to become a "great moral wasteland." Yet because Oberlin faculty wanted their school to be competitive and maintain high academic standards, they continued to require Greek and Latin, making sure that the texts studied were "pure in morals and valuable for sentiments as well as style."²⁷ Philosophical and speculative topics remained central to the curriculum, stressing independent and self-reliant thinking. Oberlin students to this day embody that intellectual legacy.²⁸

Nonsectarian Revivalism

In the 1830s revivals were considered a necessary part of an Oberlin "education." Charles Grandison Finney, the most famous revivalist in the country, arrived in Oberlin in 1834 with a big tent that could seat two to three thousand people for religious meetings. At the top of the center pole was a large blue flag proclaiming in bold letters HOLINESS UNTO THE LORD.²⁹ Finney celebrated the continuous "outpourings of the Spirit" that characterized early Oberlin. Looking back in his later years, he reported that "gales of divine influence swept over us from year to year, producing abundantly the fruits of the Spirit."³⁰

Finney published his *Lectures on Revivals,*³¹ explaining his controversial understanding of revivals. Finney applauded the spontaneous work of the Holy Spirit, but he also insisted that revivals should be intentionally and carefully promoted where natural stimulus was lacking. Like a scout handbook, Finney's lectures spelled out in fine detail a recipe for "how to make a revival." Revivals kept Christians awake and drove sinners to repentance. Revivals channeled student religious energy in constructive ways.

More than anything else, revivalism transformed Oberlin into a center of nonsectarian Christianity. Oberlin professors were all products of schools, congregations, and organizations connected to the 1801 Plan of Union—an agreement between Congregationalists and Presbyterians to streamline their work on the western frontier by minimizing competition. The plan downplayed theological and governance differences, allowing clergy in both denominations to become pastors in either Congregational or Presbyterian congregations. At Oberlin, Plan of Union thinking prevailed, scorning Christian divisions, downplaying denominational loyalties, embracing "New School" theologies, and supporting antislavery politics.³²

In May 1836 Mahan published a sermon on Paul's admonition that "there be no divisions among you" (1 Cor. 1:10). Mahan promoted Christian union and fellowship, maintaining that according to the Scriptures if we require some things from some people we are bound to require the same things of all people. If a person attempts to limit demands on others, she or he is "guilty of being more select than God." The only requirement which Scripture demands for Christian fellowship is "repentance towards God and faith towards the Lord Jesus Christ."[33]

Therefore, Mahan argued, each Christian ought to demand no more and no less. The problem with most Christians, according to Mahan, was that they set up their opinions as Divine will. Naturally, all opinions are not equally true; therefore, honest Christians need to "allow party zeal to bow to universal truth." Instead of dwelling upon creeds, churches should open membership to all people who meet God's requirements. If all Christians adopted the true principles of fellowship and church union, then the discordant elements that hang over the denominations might vanish.[34]

Revivalism at Oberlin was also nonsectarian for very practical reasons. The Oberlin community thought that it was sinful when churches limited the work of revivals by arguing over who would get the new converts and dividing people into camps. Oberlin leaders felt that the Spirit was "grieved" and the "bands of wickedness strengthened" when this happened. In fact, according to Mahan, nothing was ever gained to balance all that evil. Because Mahan believed that there was always a mixture of truth and error in each religious group, he tried to sustain a nonpartisan stance. He was delighted when a critic faulted him by saying that Mahan "would never act his party," and that Oberlin revivalism cultivated religious cooperation and intellectual hospitality.[35]

The Scripture Doctrine of Christian Perfection

Revivalism actually pulled Oberlin in two directions. On the one hand it united Christians of diverse backgrounds and cultivated what today we might call a nonsectarian or ecumenical spirit. At the same time, revivalism created a unique religious environment that became preoccupied with Christian living as well as salvation, and that in turn led to the development of the Oberlin *scripture doctrine of Christian perfection*—a way of thinking that raised great fears of sectarian heresy.[36]

The Oberlin revival of 1836 was a "religious awakening of unusual power." At that revival a recent graduate stood up and asked "what degree of sanctification" the scriptures promised? He wanted to know whether Christ could save them from *all* sin, so that they would be sanctified wholly and "in this present life." Initially this question filled Mahan with surprise and horror. He was concerned that students "would rush to perfectionism," associated with the radical ideas of John Humphrey Noyes at the Oneida Institute, where claims of *perfection* led to promiscuous behavior and notoriously immoral beliefs and acts.[37]

Mahan and Finney struggled with the question, and soon thereafter Mahan reported that he had an answer. Initial salvation or justification by faith alone did not always lead converts to a full Christian life. After careful Bible study, Mahan asserted that the scriptures promised more than justification. He cited many biblical texts to make his point: "The very God of peace sanctify you wholly, and your whole spirit, soul and body be preserved blameless into the coming of our Lord Jesus Christ" (1 Thess. 5:23). "Be ye therefore perfect, even as your Father, which is in heaven is perfect" (Matt. 5:48). Mahan decided that Christians should take these words (and others like them) to heart. Christians can expect perfect, not partial, holiness. After all, Scripture says that Christ's redemption is full and finished.[38]

For many of the students and faculty at Oberlin such knowledge of God's perfecting work in Christ was reassuring. Sinners are saved from their sins by faith in Christ (justification), and a second blessing (also a gift like the first—sanctification) assures Christians that a "higher and more stable form of Christian life is attainable and is the privilege of all Christians."[39]

Mahan and Finney recognized that John Wesley preached a similar message, but they insisted that their thinking about Christian perfection had its origins only in their reading of Scripture. They were Calvinists and could not embrace Wesleyan ideas of free will and gradual sanctification. Furthermore, to keep their thinking from being confused with Oneida *perfectionism*, they insisted that although Scripture promises that one can escape from sin (as a matter of the will), it does not release Christians from ethical restraints and moral law. The *Scripture doctrine of Christian perfection* was totally different from popular antinomian understandings of Christian *perfectionism*.[40]

Perfection in holiness did not give a person perfect wisdom, because only God was all-wise. Yet human holiness might be perfect in kind, while imperfect and finite in degree. Christians disagreed about whether they might, in their present life, "attain to perfection in holiness," and whether it was proper for them to anticipate attaining holiness, but Mahan believed no evil could result from believing what God had promised.[41]

In the 1960s I wrote a 360-page dissertation on Mahan and Oberlin's ideas of Christian perfection, which cannot be revisited here.[42] Suffice it to say, however, that Oberlin thinking was a creative blend of ideas from Scottish philosophy, neo-Calvinism, and Wesleyan theology. It rested on a clear distinction between will and action. It presupposed "New School" Calvinism's confidence in human ability, and it agreed with Wesley's emphasis on grace. The Oberlin *Scripture doctrine of Christian perfection* focused on perfection of the will, not action; on perfection actually attained, not something theoretically attainable; and on perfection as instantaneous, not progressive.

I share a bit of my analysis of the debate over Christian perfection at early Oberlin, because I think it illustrates an important and ongoing dimension of Oberlin as a place where religious or spiritual zeal and intellectual rigor have existed side by side for almost 175 years. Mahan and Finney thought that beliefs were ultimately more important than knowledge or mental discipline, because education alone could never prepare someone to preach the gospel. Yet they refused to lapse into anti-intellectualism and naïve assumptions about morality and the law. The intellectual rigor of Oberlin was never compromised by its religious enthusiasm or conviction.

OBERLIN AND THE FAITH AND ORDER MOVEMENT

As the announcement for this gathering says, the Faith and Order Movement began in the early twentieth century when Christian leaders sought a setting where churches could come together to engage their differences in understanding the Christian faith and in discerning God's intention for the right ordering of Christian churches. In 1957 when the decision was made to hold the first gathering of the Faith and Order Commission in the United States here in Oberlin, Ohio, those who knew the history of Oberlin understood why. Issues of faith and order, and issues of life and work permeated early Oberlin.

I have presented a quick overview of how eight passions shaped and influenced early Oberlin. Those passions are still relevant as we gather here today to celebrate fifty years of "Being Christian Together." Many years ago in the 1830s many streams did indeed come together in this place (Oberlin, Ohio).

1. The zeal of the Lane rebel students for immediate emancipation forced Oberlin into a radical experiment in interracial education.

2. Oberlin's early efforts to finance the school following the manual labor philosophy reflected its desire to make sure that education was accessible for all people.

3. Oberlin's recognition that good health (body and spirit) depended upon wholesome food and exercise made for unconventional food, drink, and campus life.

4. Oberlin's openness to providing educational opportunities for women moved beyond cultural stereotypes to embrace coeducation when most people felt that only same-sex schools were acceptable.

5. Oberlin's concern for cultivating a morally upright society encouraged students not to be distracted by frivolous or questionable activities.

6. Oberlin's conviction that education needed to meet the real needs of people on the frontier produced needed curricular reform.

7. Oberlin's enthusiasm for revivalism led to a gracious openness to religious diversity instead of sectarian competition.

8. Oberlin's commitment to the controversial Scripture doctrine of Christian perfection showed how one school could embrace unconventional thinking to enrich religious faith.

It is fitting that a place with this history hosted the Faith and Order meeting in 1957, and it is fitting that we are gathered here today.

NOTES

1. Robert Samuel Fletcher, *History of Oberlin College* (Oberlin: Oberlin College, 1943), 101–6.
2. Ibid., 117–24.
3. Huntington Lyman, "Lane Seminary Rebels," in *Oberlin Jubilee*, ed. William Gay Ballantine (Oberlin: Goodrich, 1884), 62.
4. *New York Evangelist* 5 (April 5, 1834): 54.
5. Reported many years later in Asa Mahan, *Out of Darkness into Light* (New York and Boston: Willard Tract Repository, 1876), 116.
6. Lane Theological Seminary, Minutes of the Prudential Committee, August 20, 1834. [The Archives of Lane Theological Seminary are located at McCormick Theological Seminary, Chicago, Illinois.]
7. Letter from John J. Shipherd to N. P. Fletcher, December 15, 1834 [Oberlin College Archives].
8. Fletcher, *History*, 170.
9. Letter from H. B. Stanton and G. Whipple to C. G. Finney, January 10, 1835, Finney Manuscripts [Oberlin College Archives], and Fletcher, *History*, 185–86.
10. Minutes of the Board of Trustees, February 10, 1835 [Oberlin College Archives].
11. Fletcher, *History*, 185.
12. Delazon Smith, *Oberlin Unmasked* (Cleveland: S. Underhill and Son, 1837), 59–60 and 65–66.
13. L. F. Anderson, "Manual Labor School Movement," *Educational Review* 46 (November 1913): 369–86.
14. H. L. Hammond, "The First Decade," in *Oberlin Jubilee*, ed. William Gay Ballantine (Oberlin: Goodrich, 1884), 195.
15. *Graham Journal of Health and Longevity* 1 (April 18, 1837): 17.
16. Asa Mahan, "The Intimate Relation between Moral, Mental and Physical Law," *Graham Journal of Health and Longevity* 3 (May 11, 1839): 153–58.

17. Asa Mahan, "Temperance and the Christian Church," a sermon delivered December 23, 1849, Southwark, England (Tract collection 7466.59, Boston Public Library), #10, 33–40.

18. *Advocate of Moral Reform* 4 (January 15, 1838): 10.

19. *Advocate of Moral Reform* 4 (April 1, 1838): 51–52.

20. *Advocate of Moral Reform* 4 (November 15, 1838): 169.

21. Fletcher, *History*, 299.

22. Ibid., 373.

23. Oberlin Collegiate Institute, Minutes of the Board of Trustees, March 9, 1836 [Oberlin College Archives].

24. James H. Fairchild, *Women's Rights and Duties* (Oberlin: James Fitch, 1849), 19.

25. A reprint of the report is found in Richard Hofstadter and Wilson Smith, eds., *American Higher Education: A Documentary History*, 2 vols. (Chicago: University of Chicago Press, 1961), 1:275–91.

26. Asa Mahan, *Ohio Observer* 9 (July 9, 1835): 3.

27. *New York Evangelist* 10 (March 5, 1836): 37.

28. A. B. Rich, "Collegiate and Theological Education in the West," *Congregational Quarterly* 11 (1869): 543–57.

29. Fletcher, *History*, 336.

30. Charles Grandison Finney, *Memoirs of Charles G. Finney* (New York: A. S. Barnes, 1876), 348.

31. Charles Grandison Finney, *Lectures on Revivals* (New York: Leavitt, Lord and Co., 1835).

32. In the Plan of Union of 1801, Presbyterians and Congregationalists, concerned to spread Christianity on the expanding frontier (in what are now the states of Ohio, Michigan, Indiana, Illinois, Wisconsin, Minnesota, and Iowa), agreed to pool their resources to accomplish that task. Theological differences between Presbyterians and Congregationalists were minimal; however, the centralized church government (polity) of the Presbyterians enabled them to organize more efficiently. The plan began to unravel by 1837 and formally ended in the 1850s. The text of the plan is found in Williston Walker, *The Creeds and Platforms of Congregationalism* (Boston: Pilgrim Press, 1960 [1893]), 524–41.

33. Mahan's sermon was published as a small pamphlet. Asa Mahan, *Principles of Christian Union and Church Fellowship* (Elyria, OH: A. Burrell, 1836).

34. Ibid.

35. Asa Mahan, *Oberlin Evangelist* 2 (April 22, 1840): 71, and his *Autobiography* (London: T. Woolmer, 1882), 71–72.

36. Although Methodist writers often wrote about the search for Christian perfection, Asa Mahan's book *Scripture Doctrine of Christian Perfection: With Other Kindred Subjects Illustrated and Confirmed in a Series of Discourses Designed to Throw Light on the Way of Holiness* (Boston: D. S. King, 1839) was an unusual blend of Calvinist and Wesleyan ideas.

37. Ibid., 232, and Mahan, *Autobiography,* 322–24.

38. Mahan, *Scripture Doctrine of Christian Perfection,* 232–33.

39. Finney, *Memoirs,* 340–41.

40. Charles Grandison Finney, *Letters to Professing Christians* (Oberlin: E. J. Goodrich, n.d.), 340–43.

41. Mahan, *Scripture Doctrine of Christian Perfection,* 9–20.

42. "Asa Mahan and Oberlin Perfectionism: 1835–1850" (PhD diss., Duke University, 1969).

Chapter 2

THE ECUMENICAL SIGNIFICANCE OF OBERLIN

Donald W. Dayton

> Following its presentation at Oberlin II, this paper was originally published in the *Journal of Ecumenical Studies* 42, no. 4 (Fall 2007): 511–26, and is copyrighted 2007 by the *Journal of Ecumenical Studies* (*JES*). It is reprinted here with permission from the author and *JES*.

I have represented the American Holiness movement on the National Council of the Churches of Christ in the United States' Faith and Order (F&O) Commission for nearly a quarter of a century, ever since the efforts of Director Jeff Gros in the 1980s to expand the representation of the commission to be more reflective of the texture of American Christianity than the actual membership of the National Council of the Churches of Christ in the USA (NCC). In this position I am something of a low-church Protestant who finds the ways of the ecumenical world somewhat strange and the issues of *Baptism, Eucharist, and Ministry*[1] a little arcane. When I ponder the fact that I do not believe that I was ever denied communion or eucharistic fellowship until I began to attend ecumenical meetings, I begin to wonder about the way we use such words and who qualifies for the label "ecumenical."

I am also leery of some views of sainthood that make such a special calling that could undercut the call to holiness as an expectation of all Christians (because I am inclined, as a layperson, to believe that all Christians are called to be ministers, theologians, and saints). In addition, though I studied in Israel for a year, I am similarly nervous about such labels as the "holy land" (often evoking images of the ancient churches fighting for hegemony over the "holy sites"), having sympathy, as I do, for the Quaker position that all places can become holy if they are dedicated to the service of God. However, if I were to nominate a place and a group of people as candidates for the label "holy," it would likely be the colony and college of Oberlin and the sometimes cantankerous people who served as founders of this school and leaders of the movement called Oberlinism.

I grant that what I have just said may appear to be outrageous to some and rather idiosyncratic to my own experience. I was reared in the Wesleyan Methodist Church, which may be the closest parallel to Oberlin outside this colony. My denominational college (Houghton College, in the "burned over" district—from revival fires—of upstate New York) was modeled after Oberlin and used this institution as a finishing school until the full four-year curriculum was in place. (Our music program was modeled after Oberlin's great conservatory of music, and, in an unusual illustration of serendipitous nomenclature, it was chaired by Charles Finney, our organist, who carried the name of the great evangelist who had dominated early Oberlin and became the second president of the college.)

My PhD contextual (that is, minor) on Oberlin Perfectionism at Chicago was supervised by Martin Marty. (I cheated; when he vetoed the study of my own tradition, I proposed to study the same abolitionist and theological movement in its "reformed" expression.) This study resulted in a series of essays in the predecessor to *Sojourners* magazine that led to my first major book, *Discovering an Evangelical Heritage*,[2] with chapters on the Oberlinism that makes this school the major illustration of the antebellum conjunction of revivalism and social reform. My study of the thought of Asa Mahan, the first president of Oberlin College (and the subject of Barbara Brown Zikmund's dissertation), led me away from a dissertation on the ethics of Karl Barth to what became *The Theological Roots of Pentecostalism*,[3] a study in which figures of the theological faculty of Oberlin are central players. Moreover, Oberlin I in 1957 serves as an appropriate symbol of my ecumenical career over the last quarter of a century. To top all this off, a group of my students, colleagues, and friends chose this week as the occasion to present me with a *Festschrift* in anticipation of my sixty-fifth birthday. You can understand why for me there is a sense in which Oberlin is sacred space.

My purpose here is to urge us to ponder the wider ecumenical significance of Oberlin in four steps. I wish first to offer an analysis of the report of Oberlin I, indicating what I believe to be a major flaw that prevents it from being an adequate guide to the Faith and Order work in the next half-century. I want to suggest, second, that Oberlin's story is a part of all our stories—and that contemplating that fact can help bring us together for the task that lies before us. In the third place, Oberlin pioneered many values associated with the ecumenical movement in our time, and it would be a pity to walk these halls without celebrating these contributions to American Christianity. Finally, I wish to use the later history of Oberlin to open up one of the key ecumenical challenges of our time by reflecting on a tale of two colleges. It is my conviction that Oberlin is something of a sacred space whose spirit can inspire another generation of ecumenical work.

THE WORK OF OBERLIN I

We are gathered first of all to celebrate the meeting at Oberlin in 1957 that in effect planted the work of Faith and Order (F&O) in North America, led to the formation of the F&O Commission of the NCC, and contributed to the founding of such organizations as the North American Academy of Ecumenists (originally founded for professors of ecumenism). Those were heady days for the ecumenical movement. The World Council of Churches (WCC) had been founded almost a decade earlier in Amsterdam in the wake of World War II. The NCC had been founded two years later (1950) in North America. The second WCC Assembly had been held in Evanston, Illinois, three years earlier, and the important Montreal meeting of the WCC's F&O was six years away. These were no doubt the glory days of North American ecumenism.

The choice of Oberlin as the location for the 1957 meeting seems not to have had the level of intention of the decision to return here in 2007. Clues in the literature (I have searched several archives) indicate that the choice of Oberlin was a product of the fact that the dean of the seminary here (in the 1960s the seminary merged into the school of theology at Vanderbilt, where there continues to be a Charles G. Finney Professor of Homiletics) was ascending in the leadership of the WCC's commission and about to become its moderator. This fact presumably led to the invitation to meet here. There is a comment in the report of Oberlin I that the president of the college made a presentation about Oberlin during the meeting, but I have not been able to discover anything of the nature of those comments. Presumably, they were a short introduction to the history and character of Oberlin in something of a public relations mode.

It is clear, however, that the meeting at Oberlin was part of a self-conscious effort to plant (or perhaps transplant from Europe) the work of F&O on the various continents of the world. I mean this image quite literally, because I think that F&O was transplanted to North America without any clear agenda to explore the distinctiveness of the North American situation and to uncover learnings for the rest of the world. It is astonishing to me that the Oberlin report contains no sustained analysis of the North American context. There are several references to a certain distinctive character of the ecclesiastical scene in North America, but there is no theological or historical analysis. There is, however, an extended sociological analysis in an appendix, which finds that American society is distinctive in that it is much more mobile than European society—with the result that there is less loyalty to particular Christian traditions. I consider this a rather trivial conclusion in light of the profound and complex issues that could have been explored.

This is not the place for an extended analysis of the distinctiveness of American Christian culture. We share much continuity with the Old World traditions. Roman Catholicism is the largest denomination in the United States, and due to immigration patterns we have Catholicism of all sorts: French, Spanish, Polish, Irish, Italian, and so on—and more recently various streams of Asian Catholicism (Vietnamese, Filipino, and so forth). We have many forms of Orthodoxy (I am told we have more than forty separate jurisdictions). We have many forms of mainline Protestantism (German, Dutch, Scandinavian, and English, for example). However, all these traditions have had to make major adjustments to the American scene as they left a culture of national churches to find themselves disestablished and forced to take on a denominational structure alongside a bewildering range of Christian traditions in the New World.

In the midst of these continuities are profound differences. The United States became a refuge for dissenting traditions of all sorts, from the very influential Puritan traditions from Holland and Britain to Quakers in Pennsylvania and a number of more radical and communal movements (the Church of the Brethren, the Ephrata Community, and the Moravians and other groups rooted in radical Pietism, for example). Even the mainline traditions took on a new texture as they moved west across the Atlantic. Lutherans, for example, have been tipped in the Pietist direction, because Pietism prospered among the poorer classes that often migrated to the United States to better themselves economically. An American Lutheran often looks more like a Methodist to European Lutherans, not only because of this Pietist orientation but also because of the profound influence of Methodism in setting the religious tone in the United States.

It is not always understood in Geneva that there has been a shift in ecclesiology in the free church direction. Many free churches migrated to the United States to find the space to grow and find their own identity, so that, for example, from Sweden we have not only Lutherans from the state church but also many other sizeable and influential Swedish churches (the Pietists of the Evangelical Covenant Church and the Evangelical Free Church, the Baptists of the Baptist General Conference, and the Pentecostals of the Philadelphia Church, for example). Even the most established American tradition has been the "Congregational" church of New England—from which the Baptists came to found a refuge in Rhode Island. Perhaps most tellingly, it is the populist traditions of Europe, such as the Methodists and the Baptists that, although technically born in continental Europe and England, have found their destiny in the United States, where they have dominated the Protestant scene in a way that seems to elude European ecumenists.

Further complicating the situation has been what we have called in our F&O work the amazing proliferation of the American-born churches. Many of these are now global communions in their own right. These include the variety of black and African American churches, almost always of the populist sort (Baptist, Methodist, and later Pentecostal) that have been better able to treat the slaves and black converts as spiritual equals. There has been a cluster of "restorationist" churches: the mainline and more ecumenically involved Disciples tradition, as well as a variety of more radical variations—each ecumenical in its own way, though often with less involvement in the more formal ecumenical movement. (These splits are often interpreted in the overused conservative/liberal paradigm when they are actually divided by the radicalism of the application of the "restorationist" principle and such questions as whether musical instruments or transcongregational denominational structures are authorized by biblical precedent.) There is a group of eschatologically oriented churches, most notably the Seventh-day Adventist Church, which has been active in the F&O movement on both the NCC and the WCC levels. There is the (largely ignored and off the map of most ecumenists) American Holiness movement, now demographically within the top ten of Christian communions worldwide. Some churches of this movement (most notably the Salvation Army and the Church of God [Anderson, Indiana], which was at Oberlin I and has been represented at F&O since) have been involved in F&O work. There is, of course, the Pentecostal movement that has become in many ways the most important movement in Christianity in the last century. Further, these dynamics have continued ever since, producing a variety of new global churches in the twentieth century, such as the Vineyard and the Calvary Chapel movements, both rooted to some extent in the "Jesus movement" of the 1960s. Also, one should not forget the Metropolitan Community Church, which was formed around the gay issue—and a regular presence (for some an irritant) in ecumenical and F&O discussions in both the NCC and the WCC.

The United States has been such a fertile ground for the formation of new churches that questions of the boundaries of the Christian tradition take on new importance. We now include the Pentecostals, the Seventh-day Adventists, and the Holiness movement in normative Christianity but exclude the Jehovah's Witnesses—and, for the most part, the Mormons—as sects or cults. This last exclusion begs for more exploration in light of the current U.S. presidential election (in which a Mormon is a serious candidate). The NCC has denied membership to the Universal Fellowship of Metropolitan Community Churches but permitted their participation in F&O. When I came on the F&O Commission the issue was the Korean-born Unification Church of the Rev. Sun Myung Moon. What about the black Pentecostal Apostolic Faith movement that has had such a profound influence in our inner cities and has produced national figures (T. D. Jakes and Bishop Art Brazier in Chicago along with his counterparts in other U.S. cities, for example)—or the Pentecostal Assamblea Apostolica that is so influential among Mexican farm workers? Both speak in profoundly Trinitarian language but are driven in their sense of biblical fidelity to go behind the ecumenical creeds to deny the Trinity and assert the oneness of God in a sort of unitarianism of the second person. Is it a concern for Christian orthodoxy that is the reason such movements are excluded, or ignorance, or baser motives rooted in elitism, classism, and racism?

These are some of the ecumenical questions brought to the fore by a careful analysis of the American ecclesiastical scene. They gain poignancy when we move them to the global level. It is often said that the fastest-growing movements in Latin America are four American-born churches: the Pentecostals, the Seventh-day Adventists, the Mormons, and the Jehovah's Witnesses. I rather expect that the Holiness churches would be included in this number if demographers were sufficiently sophisticated to recognize this cluster as a separate movement. Furthermore, because of the extensive missionary activity from North America, Christianity in the rest of the world is often a radicalization of the American configurations. (That is, the American context is, in many ways, a middle term between Europe and the rest of the world.) How we handle such questions may have profound international implications. Surely, it is part of our ecumenical responsibility in the United States to give leadership on such questions—and to use the North American experience to help the world understand why global Christianity has the character that it does.

One result of these facts is that many patterns of thinking assumed in the ecumenical movement or imported from Europe are not adequate, and we at Oberlin II, unlike those at Oberlin I, need to give serious attention to contextualizing our questions to the American scene. One aspect of this issue was revealed in an exchange of memos in the academic culture of Claremont, California—the same academic culture that literally gasped a few years ago when I gave a paper on the oneness (or "Jesus Only") Pentecostal movement among Mexican farm workers. The dean of the Claremont Graduate School circulated a memo indicating that, in light of the changing texture of the American religious landscape, the school needed to think about the appointment of scholars in Islamic, Buddhist, Hindu, and other religious traditions. The president of the Theological School reportedly replied that new academic appointments should reflect the distinctive character of American religion and thus should include Pentecostal, Seventh-day Adventist, Mormon, Evangelical, Holiness, and other such traditions. We probably need to reach to correct both deficiencies, but it is worth pondering why our thoughts are hardly ever drawn in the second direction. We are prevented from seeing the landscape in front of us by lenses that are not adequate for analyzing the American situation.

In Europe, church relations are intertwined with a couple of millennia of political history, and ecumenical events often take on the character of state visits, as I experienced in Moscow when the WCC Central Committee met there. In Europe, the ecumenical questions are often shaped by a political history that speaks of three great blocs that emphasize the divisions between East and West and between Catholic and Protestant. This leads to a framework that privileges three primary players in ecumenical dialogue (Orthodox, Catholic, and Protestant) and a historiographical grid that speaks of the eleventh–twelfth centuries and the sixteenth century as the great church-dividing periods. The application of this grid to the American scene is highly problematic, though it is regularly used, as can be seen in the report on Oberlin I or any discussion of balance in representation on the board of the North American Academy of Ecumenists (NAAE).

I stumbled over these issues a couple of decades ago in the NAAE when I was asked to give a paper on the issue of nontheological factors in church divisions. The NAAE program was generally structured around a topic commented on by representatives of the Orthodox, Catholic, and Protestant traditions—and more recently had added a response usually given by an Evangelical. I agreed to give the response with only one condition: that I do not give papers as an Evangelical and would not speak if so labeled. In the published program, I was listed as an Evangelical; accordingly,

I felt I had to withdraw. I finally agreed to give the paper only if I were allowed to make a twenty-minute presentation before the paper on why I am not an Evangelical and why I prefer to be called by my own name rather than be identified by a label with which I do not identify. In response to some of these issues, we have in the American F&O developed over the last quarter-century a pattern of speaking that emphasizes that the nineteenth century is as church dividing as were the sixteenth and the eleventh through twelfth centuries—even when we have failed to follow through on the implications of this move and relapsed into the inadequate quota systems derived from the European scene.

Even the use of the label "Protestant" as a category to cover the diversity of non-Catholic and non-Orthodox American churches is problematic. This is seen clearly in recent discussions about the Joint Declaration on Justification. The European grid privileges the magisterial traditions of Protestantism and especially Lutheranism. It is sometimes assumed that the rest of Protestantism is well described by the Lutheran position, while John Wesley, for example, found Luther "blasphemous" and might be better described as Catholic in his soteriology. For reasons such as this, some (William McLoughlin, for example) have proposed a category such as "third-force Christianity" to describe such groups as Pentecostalism, Seventh-day Adventism, the Holiness churches, various so-called Evangelical groups, and so forth. The significance of this may be seen in Latin America, where the Joint Declaration fails to speak to the tensions between Roman Catholicism and the so-called Protestantism that is dominated by these third-force churches of the Holiness/Pentecostal variety. I have heard presidents of both the Wesleyan Theological Society and the Society for Pentecostal Studies insist that their traditions are closer to the Council of Trent than to Luther. The European concordat between Lutherans and Catholics does not speak well to either the American or the third-world contexts.

The last generation in F&O has often used the expression "apostolic faith" to recover the unity that lies behind all our traditions and that draws us together as a common Christian movement. The distinctive American contribution to these discussions is not often appreciated. It might be argued that the American churches are dominated by the impulse to recover apostolicity, though often not in the classical patterns of that discussion. The distinctively American churches are often shaped by a radical restorationism that is rooted, at least in part, by the American desire to start over—to usher in a *novus ordo seclorum*, as it says on our one-dollar bills. This rejection of the patterns of the Old World often has profound ecclesiological implications.

The classical discussions of apostolicity have emphasized either the continuity of apostolic succession or the preaching of apostolic doctrine. In many churches in the United States, apostolicity is defined in other ways. In many traditions (especially Anabaptist, Quaker, and the like), the claim to being apostolic involves a behavioral claim—the renunciation of the sword. For Pentecostals the expression "apostolic faith" proclaims the recovery of charismatic gifts, especially the gift of healing—or, in the more radical wings of Pentecostalism, it speaks of a recovery of biblical monotheism and the rejection of later Trinitarian patterns of thought. For others, "apostolicity" means the recovery of a radical congregational ecclesiology, a particular pattern of baptism, or certain patterns of church structure. We have explored these dynamics over the last quarter-century. I remember well Gros's comment after a trip to Europe that Roman Catholic ecumenists were astonished by this work, which had greatly helped them to understand the American experience as a radical search for apostolicity rather than a vague extension of the Protestant principle in always-greater distance from the classical traditions.

The extent to which this restorationism implies what has been called the doctrine of the Constantinian fall of the church is not always appreciated. This idea has always been a staple of the Anabaptist tradition and its critique of the culture of the state-church traditions and their adoption of the sword, but it lies behind many of the broader American church traditions. It is part and parcel of the Baptist position, which usually claims to go back to an apostolic tradition of believers' baptism and involves rejection of the pedobaptism associated with national churches where baptism becomes a form of registration as a citizen. This practice alone falls outside the usual application of the threefold European grid and the basic orientation of BEM, but the extent to which Methodism, the other major form of American Protestantism, presupposes this doctrine is usually not recognized. For Wesley, it was the first three centuries of the church that were normative, and the Ante-Nicene fathers were given pride of place. Moreover, what is true of Baptists and Methodists is perforce even more true of other American restorationist movements (Pentecostalism, for example).

The vast majority of American Protestants presuppose this doctrine of the Constantinian fall of the church, but the issue has yet to be made a centerpiece of ecumenical discussion. I was astonished a few years ago by the response of the NAAE board to my suggestion that we take on this topic while being hosted by Messiah College, an institution of the small Brethren in Christ Church that might be described as Holiness/Anabaptist/Evangelical/Pietist and, of course, pacifist. It seemed to me a particularly propitious union of topic and location. The response of the board (I remember particularly a Canadian Catholic and an American Lutheran) was uniformly "What's that?" We did not program such a discussion, but when we got to Messiah, it was a staple of the conversation, particularly a panel on the peace witness of the church. Board members came back to me recognizing the importance of the discussion, even though they had never heard the term. I am convinced that this issue remains the unrecognized eight-hundred-pound gorilla in the rooms of American F&O dialogue.

I am reluctant to draw out a final implication of this discussion for fear that in the eyes of many it will be too radical and might discredit my contribution as a whole, but I think that I must. It has become increasingly clear to me that American F&O discussions cannot use the starting point assumed in European F&O: the Nicene Creed. This suggestion was first made, I believe, in Lausanne by an Anglican bishop and was given additional impulse by the incorporation of the Orthodox into the WCC. Here I am calling into question one of our own F&O publications in this commission. However, the vast majority of American Protestant churches do not find themselves at home with this creed. They either do not use the creeds at all or prefer the Apostles' Creed in their restorationist search for apostolicity. It is possible that further discussion might find the Nicene Creed a suitable starting point, but the issue needs discussion. The issue may be illustrated by Methodism. When Wesley prepared his Sunday Service for American Methodists, he combined from the *Book of Common Prayer* the morning prayer and the communion services. This left him with two creeds, and he eliminated the Nicene Creed. Was this decision of theological importance? Is it related to Wesley's doctrine of the Constantinian fall of the church? It is not clear how to answer this question, but it does need discussion.

This issue surfaced sharply in one of our consultations several years ago when we were exploring the possibility of ecumenical history. We took the fourth century as a test case, and the consultation was cochaired by an Orthodox and a Mennonite. Another Mennonite in the group protested the assumption of the Nicene Creed as a starting point. He felt that this creed called him to confess the divinity of Christ as a problem of a sort of divine chemistry or a problem of Greek substance metaphysics and suppressed for him the biblical categories of discipleship and Lordship and the interpretation of Christology in the messianic/prophetic traditions of the Bible. Whatever one makes of this claim, it is clear that there is an unexamined issue that needs to be surfaced. I have often used this incident in class to make another point. The objection was raised by a biblicist with a strong doctrine of the Constantinian fall of the church. Conflicts of this sort are often analyzed in terms of the conservative/liberal paradigm. It is often presupposed that the ecumenical movement is a liberal movement and those outside (in the National Association of Evangelicals or the World Evangelical Fellowship) are conservatives. Here the roles were reversed. The mainliners were so enmeshed in Chalcedonian and Nicene theology that they could not even imagine dissent from such, whereas it was the radical biblicist who was questioning the received christological tradition.

This incident makes clear the poverty of the categories of liberal and conservative in ecumenical dialogue. They miss the point and become demonic in maintaining divisions among Christians, which we have worked to overcome for a quarter of a century. We must abandon these terms and the equally misleading categories of evangelical and ecumenical, if we are to make progress in the complex North American context. It is too much to suggest that these problems might have been minimized if I had given more attention to Oberlin as a location of theological and ecumenical significance. With these comments I turn more directly to a consideration of the historical Oberlin.

OBERLIN BELONGS TO ALL OF US

It is hard to imagine a place other than Oberlin that is so distinctively American, while managing to incorporate most of us into its story. I invite your reflection on the ways in which it draws us into a common history and makes a genuine contribution to our ecumenical agenda.

Oberlin's primary identity is, of course, with Congregationalism—as evidenced by the presence of the First Congregational Church here in town. Oberlin was in a sense a New England outpost, as Yankees moved west along the Erie Canal and around Lake Erie into the Western Reserve of the Northwest Territory (the western frontier in the early decades of the nineteenth century). Congregationalism is, of course, the church of the pilgrim fathers, that quintessentially American church that is a major tributary of today's United Church of Christ.

However, Oberlin was founded in the time of a major American experiment in ecumenism: the Plan of Union that attempted to bring together new school (that is, revivalist) Presbyterians and Congregationalists. This is so much the case that one is never sure whether key figures in the early years of Oberlin should be considered Presbyterians or Congregationalists. President Mahan was a Congregationalist who served on the board of Lane Seminary in Cincinnati (which later merged into McCormick Seminary of the Presbyterians, in Chicago) while pastoring a Presbyterian church in that city. He then served the Wesleyan Methodists and the Methodist Protestants (of Wesley Seminary in Washington, DC) as president of Adrian College before retiring to England, where he coedited the journal *Divine Life* with Methodist Asbury Lowry. Evangelist Charles Finney is probably best identified as Presbyterian, though he broke patterns by refusing to attend Princeton (Finneyite churches in New York City constituted the Third Presbytery, with free pews to welcome the poor and the reform movements of the era). When Finney became president of Oberlin, he became identified more with Congregationalism. Jonathan Blanchard was an Oberlinite Presbyterian who wished he could have taught at Oberlin. He left the presidency of Presbyterian Knox College to preside over Wheaton College (founded by the Wesleyan Methodists) and to pastor the college church (originally

Wesleyan but duly aligned with the Congregationalists under Blanchard's ministry). This was a great period of interdenominational cooperation and church union.

Oberlin was known for its controversial theology, Oberlin perfectionism, which developed under the influence of Methodism and was despised by old school Presbyterians at Princeton (Hodge, Warfield, etc.). The century from 1820 to World War I is often called the Methodist Age in American history not only because, by the time of the Civil War, Methodism had become the largest denomination in the United States but also because it had convinced half the rest of the churches to act like Methodists. Finney and Mahan read the work of Methodist founders John Wesley and John Fletcher and began to teach a variation on their doctrine of *entire sanctification*. By the late 1830s Mahan had published (with the Methodists) his *Scripture Doctrine of Christian Perfection*,[4] and Finney was preaching on the theme in his New York City crusades.

Oberlin is perhaps the symbol of the climax of the so-called Arminianization of American theology. I once heard Marty describe Jonathan Edwards as the hinge between Calvinist and Arminian America. This development broke the stranglehold of the Augustinian and Calvinist predestinarian tradition on American Christianity. Many nineteenth-century editions of revivalist works had a profound influence on the development of the Reformed Church in America. It is impossible to understand this denomination and the emergence of such figures as Norman Vincent Peale and Robert Schuller without reference to these currents—however one values the results.

Depending on one's historiographic orientation, one might well argue that Oberlin is the fountainhead of today's Evangelical tradition. If one accepts, as I do, the equation of this tradition with modern revivalism (also the title of William McLoughlin's book on the line from Finney to Billy Graham),[5] then Finney is to Oberlin as Graham is to modern Evangelical icon Wheaton College, founded in imitation of Oberlin. Further, *Decision* magazine would be the modern counterpart to the *Oberlin Evangelist*. Evangelicalism, with its upward social mobility, has drunk deeply at the wells of Princeton, but it has not been able to shake the profound influence of Finney that still crops up in unusual places. The early years of Youth with a Mission, often described as the largest mission agency in the world, show the profound influence of Finney's theology.

Mel Dieter argues in his history of the Holiness movement[6] that this tradition is essentially the confluence of Finneyite revivalism and the camp-meeting and populist wing of Methodism that was attempting to resist the mainstream Methodist rush to become a middle-class church in imitation of Presbyterians and Episcopalians. An early iconic image of Oberlin is a tent used for Finney's protracted meeting, Oberlin commencements, and Anti-Slavery Society meetings; from the central pole flies a banner with the slogan *Holiness to the Lord*. The dependence on Oberlin in the Holiness tradition is personified in A. M. Hills, an Oberlinite (he studied at Oberlin and Yale) Congregationalist pastor and evangelist who wintered in Oberlin before becoming the first theologian of the Church of the Nazarene and president of several of the early Nazarene colleges and universities. One should also note the influence of Finney on the Salvation Army, especially in England. Oberlin is claimed also as an originating force by the Holiness movement and its various churches.

Furthermore, it is not too much to claim that the basic outlines of Pentecostal theology were hammered out at Oberlin. It was my study of the theology of Mahan that drove me to write *The Theological Roots of Pentecostalism*, tracing how Mahan's view of Christian perfection evolved into *The Baptism of the Holy Ghost* (the title of a volume of his chapel addresses at Adrian College).[7] Finney, by the time of his retirement, would address the Oberlin Council of Congregationalism in 1871 on "The Baptism of the Holy Spirit." Modern Pentecostal theology and culture cannot be understood without reference to Finney and Oberlin. One needs only to add glossolalia at the turn of the century to produce the Pentecostal tradition.

At first blush this narrative might seem to leave out the ancient churches of Europe, but one should notice Jay Dolan's book *Catholic Revivalism*,[8] which traces the influence in Catholicism of the revivalist tradition from Finney to the modern charismatic movement. His particular focus is the American Paulist Order, whose "parish missions" sometimes mirrored the shape of revival crusades. Other figures came to the United States, fell under the influence of revivalism, and returned to Europe to found Catholic evangelistic orders. Further, the rise of Holiness themes brought to the fore classical sources that might seem surprising to those outside the tradition. Congregationalist Thomas Upham, professor at Bowdoin College, published a very popular two-volume biography of Madame Guyon and drew attention to Guyon and Fenelon as models of piety.[9] Entire sanctification was perhaps the closest Protestant parallel to the Orthodox doctrine of *theosis*, and the Wesleyan sources for this doctrine were often Eastern: Makarios the Egyptian, Ephraem of Syria, the Cappadocian Fathers of Asia Minor, and so on. I once had the privilege of reading an essay by David Bundy on these connections at a dialogue between Pentecostals and the Orthodox in a Prague meeting—where Kallistos Ware responded in like terms with a study of such figures as Simeon the New Theologian and other figures from the Orthodox side.

In light of these facts, I would call readers to ponder the ecumenical significance of Oberlin in that most of us can find a place in this story and, by doing so, can imagine a history that draws us together rather than pulling us apart.

OBERLIN AS A PIONEER OF ECUMENICAL VALUES

Oberlin is named for Jean-Frédéric Oberlin (1740–1826), a French Protestant pastor in the very small town of Waldbach, southwest of Strasbourg in the Alsace-Lorraine area of France—a place that I have visited many times. (Oberlin is located in Lorain County, named for this region.) This area of France, historically sometimes German and sometimes French, also produced such figures as P. J. Spener, the patriarch of Pietism, and Albert Schweitzer, the twentieth-century scholar, organist, and missionary to Africa. It was in many ways the Appalachia of France, and Pastor Oberlin worked out of a small church whose sanctuary is no larger than an average-sized classroom. He was a pioneer of what might be called holistic ministry. He taught the villagers to build partitions down the middle of their houses and have the people sleep on one side and the animals on the other. He taught trades, especially printing, samples of which are still available in Waldbach. His ministry was so well known that Napoleon is said to have instructed his soldiers to protect it as they swept though. A chain of Christian bookstores in France carries his name. In the United States, a biography celebrating Oberlin's ministry was published early in the nineteenth century,[10] and the name Oberlin was taken for the colony and college of Oberlin.

Oberlin was first a colony founded by figures under the influence of Finney. The Oberlin Covenant maintained private property but verged on communalism, required a simple lifestyle, renounced tobacco and liquor, and discouraged the use of such drugs as coffee and tea. Residents were encouraged to support Christian institutions at home and abroad, especially the emerging Oberlin Institute. The college was really launched when John J. Shipherd started east to raise money for the financially desperate school but felt providentially led southwest to Cincinnati, where he fell into the aftermath of the Lane Rebellion at Lane Seminary. The board and administration of the seminary had cracked down on an emerging abolitionist party of students that was creating controversy with its involvement with the African American community of the city. Over forty students withdrew in protest (the petition of withdrawal is still sometimes displayed at McCormick Seminary in Chicago) to found a "free seminary" with the support of a single faculty member and a key figure of the board, Mahan. In one fell swoop, Shipherd found a student body, a faculty member, and a new president—as well as the financial support of the Tappan brothers, wealthy New York businessmen behind Finney, who were board members of the interlocking directorates of many benevolent agencies of the time (Bible, tract, peace, antislavery societies, and so on).

With such a launching, the slavery cause became the inevitable center of Oberlin's life. The perfectionist edge of Oberlin theology provided a utopian vision to critique the social order. For Finney the social function of religion was to usher in the new—in direct conflict with Princeton Presbyterians, who understood the social function of religion to be conserving the old and preserving the fragile social order from the eruption of chaos rooted in original sin. Among the new things that Oberlin expected was the destruction of the sin of slavery by the means of immediate abolition. Oberlin is sometimes credited with abolitionizing the Northwest Territory. Oberlin students fanned out over Ohio to hold revival meetings in various county seats and then organized antislavery or peace societies in the wake of their revivalist work. This claim has been *cliometrically* confirmed by John Hammond in *The Politics of Benevolence*.[11] He scoured county newspapers for reports of Oberlin revivals and analyzed statistically the shift in voting patterns after such revivals to discover a shift in the abolitionist direction. The title of Nat Brandt's book on Oberlin, *The Town That Started the Civil War*,[12] may not be far from the truth.

It is astonishing how radical Oberlin was on this issue. John Brown of the raid on Harper's Ferry visited Oberlin on several occasions, and the town mourned his execution with the ringing of church bells for an hour. The Oberlin Anti-Slavery Society had two hundred members who vowed to work for the "immediate emancipation of the whole colored race" and provided sixteen of the famous "seventy agents" sent out on the Northwest Territory model to agitate about the slavery issue. Oberlinites usually refused to celebrate the Fourth of July (calling it a cruel mockery), honoring instead the first of August (the day of emancipation in the British West Indies). Oberlin was a station on the Underground Railroad; this activity led to a doctrine of civil disobedience that resulted in the famous Oberlin-Wellington Rescue Case, when Oberlinites defied the fugitive-slave laws by freeing from nearby Wellington a fugitive slave who had been captured while he sought refuge in Oberlin. The college ethics professor and the Oberlin Sunday school superintendent were subsequently imprisoned and brought to trial. The Oberlinites turned this situation into a propaganda campaign for the antislavery cause by publishing a newspaper, *The Rescuer*, from the jail. This event is still celebrated and reenacted at Oberlin.

Some historians (including my black roommate from Columbia, Bob Allen, in *Reluctant Reformers*)[13] have claimed that the abolitionists remained racists, wishing only to rid themselves of complicity in the sin of slavery. However, Oberlin insisted on admitting blacks equally with whites and apparently posed no bar to social intercourse. A student estimated in approximately 1846 that about one in five students in the dining hall was black and that white women were free to eat at tables with black men.[14] Such practices generated fierce opposition to Oberlin, with the result that finances were always problematic. Fundraisers were sent to England, where Oberlinism prospered.

Oberlin was also apparently the first coeducational college. As a result, many women, including some of the early feminists, flocked to the school. In fact, as Alice Rossi demonstrated in the introduction to her anthology *The Feminist Papers*[15] (and she understates the case), many, perhaps most, of the early feminists were under the sway of Finney. At Oberlin the door was half open, and the door was pushed open wider as time went on. One student, Lucy Stone, created controversy by keeping her maiden name in marriage and advocated the wearing of the "bloomer" costume, a more sensible mode of feminine attire than the expected patterns of the time (she graduated in 1847). Not everyone at Oberlin was open to all these new ideas. It was still the policy to have men read in public the graduation essays of women. President Mahan supported the women, especially as his daughter neared graduation, but was unable to carry the faculty. Perhaps most significant for our interest would be Antoinette Brown, generally honored as the first woman to be ordained. Oberlin allowed her to attend the ministerial course informally but would not grant her a theological degree. The college later repented of this position and called her back twice to offer honorary degrees. As a Congregationalist she needed to find only a single congregation willing to ordain her (Olympia Brown was the first to gain the approval of a wider judicatory—in the Unitarian/Universalist tradition); three years later Brown finally found that in a Congregational church in South Butler, New York. Brown was unable to convince a Unitarian/Universalist friend to allow her to preach, so she was forced to turn to Luther Lee, one of the founders of the Wesleyan Methodists. He had earlier defended her then-shocking suggestion that women be allowed to vote in the temperance societies—and it was a congregation of his church that had hosted the 1848 Seneca Falls, New York, meeting that first called for women's suffrage.

One is tempted to go on with other themes. Greater detail is found in the magisterial two-volume history of the early years of Oberlin by Robert Fletcher.[16] Some of the material is repeated in my more accessible *Discovering an Evangelical Heritage*, which contains several chapters on early Oberlin and the figures who dominated its early life; Zikmund has surveyed some of this material above in her comments on the passions of early Oberlin College.[17] I will refer to only a few more themes.

Oberlin was deeply committed to the peace movement of the time. Oberlinites did not debate whether Christians should be committed to peace; they debated the shape of that commitment (the more radical nonresistance, or the more activist struggle for peace). Mahan himself had to take a six-month leave of absence to speak at a European Peace Conference. (It must be admitted that some of these convictions faded as the Civil War appeared on the horizon and the spirit of the "Battle Hymn of the Republic" set the tone). Oberlin had several mission societies that became involved with Native Americans, which resulted in Oberlin's sympathy for this population and a tendency to take their side in struggles over violations of government treaty arrangements. Oberlin was involved in several dimensions of the progressive education of the age (Horace Mann's common schools, the establishment of music and vocational education, nervousness about the use of corporal punishment as an incentive in education, and so on). Oberlin's commitment to health was expressed in a variety of ways—from the health foods of the day (the graham cracker of Sylvester Graham) to the cultivation of manual labor (adopted by Kentucky's Berea College, for example, as a way to provide self-supported college education for impoverished Appalachian students).

One could go on, but this is enough to suggest ways in which Oberlin pioneered values that have found wide acceptance in our churches and culture. Many of these issues recycle themselves in every generation, but perhaps the spirit of Oberlin can again infect us with its ecumenical openness and creativity. I would like to make one final point that needs pondering.

TALE OF TWO COLLEGES

Another distinctive of the American scene is that church differences are not always confessional differences. Otto A. Piper of Princeton commented in his *Christian Ethics*[18] that it is more characteristic of American Christianity to produce great moral crusades (antislavery, temperance/prohibition, civil rights, and so on) than great confessions. Also, H. Richard Niebuhr explored class, race, immigration, and such in his book *The Social Sources of Denominationalism*.[19] The most virulent church divisions of our time are rooted in the so-called (perhaps inappropriately) nontheological factors. American churches have divided over slavery/race, class, the ministry of women, and, in our own time, the gay issue. These issues cut across confessional lines and split churches into parties sometimes called conservative or liberal, leading to huge debates about the social roles of the churches and the place of the social gospel in the churches.

Oberlin speaks to these issues. It was fifty years ago that Nazarene historian Timothy Smith published his now-classic *Revivalism and Social Reform*,[20] a book that shocked American historians and his Harvard advisers by describing the conjunction of antebellum revivalism and the variety of social-reform movements that find paradigmatic expression in the life of early Oberlin. This book was unthinkable in mid-twentieth-century American culture, which was busy at the time setting up the structures that divide us ecumenically—most notably the NCC as the supposedly liberal party and the National Association of Evangelicals as the supposedly conservative party. These structures have become symbolically enshrined in the culture wars of our time and in the categories by which we think about everything.

Oberlin shatters these categories and, by leveling them, opens up the possibility of contemplating a new future for American Christianity. One way of posing these questions is to contemplate a tale of two colleges. Oberlin became the model for several of the so-called evangelical colleges, most notably Wheaton College, which was dominated in the first generation by the spirit of Oberlinism. Over the years since, Oberlin has lost the religious fervor that dominated its early years, and Wheaton has lost the social-reform impulse of its early years. This polarization is in a sense a parable of the divisions that infect American Christianity. Oberlin can give us new categories to think about these divisions. Pondering the life of Oberlin can help raise a model of the possibility of reuniting these impulses in a way that can help us transcend the nontheological debates that are tearing our churches apart.

I invite those gathered to celebrate Oberlin I to contemplate the ecumenical significance of Oberlin in ways that might contribute to Oberlin II as we all seek a vision of Faith and Order that is adequate to inspire another half-century of the search for Christian unity—but this time in a mode sensitive to the American context and its distinctiveness.

NOTES

1. *Baptism, Eucharist, and Ministry*, Faith and Order Paper 111 (Geneva: World Council of Churches, 1982); hereafter, BEM.
2. Donald W. Dayton, *Discovering an Evangelical Heritage* New York: Harper and Row, 1976.
3. Donald W. Dayton, *The Theological Roots of Pentecostalism* (Metuchen, NJ: Scarecrow Press, 1987).
4. Asa Mahan, *Scripture Doctrine of Christian Perfection* (Boston: D. S. King, 1839).
5. William G. McLoughlin, *Modern Revivalism: Charles Grandison Finney to Billy Graham* (New York: Ronald Press Co., 1959).
6. Melvin Easterday Dieter, *The Holiness Revival of the Nineteenth Century*, Studies in Evangelicalism 1 (Metuchen, NJ: Scarecrow Press, 1980; 2nd ed., 1996).
7. Asa Mahan, *The Baptism of the Holy Ghost* (New York: W. C. Palmer, Jr., 1870).
8. Jay P. Dolan, *Catholic Revivalism in the United States, 1830–1900* (Notre Dame, IN: University of Notre Dame Press, 1978).
9. Thomas Cogswell Upham, *Life, Religious Opinions and Experience of Madame de La Mothe Guyon; Together with the Account of the Personal History and Religious Opinions of Fenelon, Archbishop of Cambray* (London: S. Low, 1854).
10. *The Life of John Frederic Oberlin, Pastor of Waldback* (American Sunday School Union, 1830).
11. John E. Hammond, *The Politics of Benevolence: Revival Religion and American Voting Behavior* (Norwood, NJ: Ablex Publishing Corp., 1979).
12. Nat Brandt, *The Town That Started the Civil War* (Syracuse, NY: Syracuse University Press, 1990).

13. Robert L. Allen with Pamela P. Allen, *Reluctant Reformers: Racism and Social Reform Movements in the United States* (Washington, DC: Howard University Press, 1974).

14. Robert Samuel Fletcher, *History of Oberlin College* (Oberlin, OH: Oberlin College, 1943), 524, n. 15.

15. Alice S. Rossi, *The Feminist Papers: From Adams to de Beauvoir* (New York: Columbia University Press, 1973).

16. Fletcher, *History of Oberlin College*.

17. See Barbara Brown Zikmund, chapter 1, "The Legacy of This Place: Oberlin, Ohio," in this volume.

18. Otto A. Piper, *Christian Ethics* (London: Nelson, 1970).

19. H. Richard Niebuhr, *The Source of Denominationalism* (New York: H. Holt and Co., 1929).

20. Timothy L. Smith, *Revivalism and Social Reform in Mid-Nineteenth-Century America* (New York: Abingdon Press, 1957).

Chapter 3

FIFTY YEARS AND RUNNING: OBERLIN '57, BACK AND BEYOND

Jeffrey Gros, FSC

> This paper was originally prepared for an informal introduction to Oberlin I, given on July 19, 2007, and published in *Ecumenical Trends* 36, no. 10 (2007): 11/155–14/158. It appears expanded here with the permission of the author and *Ecumenical Trends*.

In every culture in which the gospel finds itself incarnated, the call to reconciliation takes on a different character and a different set of priorities, as the modern ecumenical movement seeks to inculturate Christ's prayer for the unity of all Christians: "that they may all be one" (John 17:21). Inculturation is as important for the churches and the ecumenical movement in the United States as in any other part of the globe. In the United States, the historic modern ecumenical movement, especially in its conciliar form, has been characterized by a common witness to important social values in the society, growing out of the understanding of the gospel in U.S. culture developed by the historic Protestant churches emerging from the British colonies. Orthodox, Catholic, and other Protestant voices have only gradually been incorporated into this conversation.[1]

In the U.S. conciliar movement, interest in the ecclesiological issues central to Faith and Order has also been slow to emerge as integral to the U.S. ecumenical movement. Therefore, this commemoration of the 1957 North American Conference on Faith and Order is an important marker for the U.S., global, and theological development of the one ecumenical movement. Because of the origin of the National Council of Churches of Christ in the USA (NCC) as a cooperative agency concerned with service and social witness, it has been a constant struggle to keep the ecclesiological research serving the reconciliation of the church at the center of Faith and Order U.S.A.

There is always a tendency on the part of some to look to Faith and Order U.S.A. as a reservoir of theological talent to help legitimate social programs or public witness projects that are current priorities at any particular time in the ecumenical journey. The churches have to be continually reminded that all aspects of their life together in the conciliar movement need to be grounded in the shared biblical faith and that they need to be in dialogue about the conscientious differences in social and personal ethics that continue to divide the churches.

The 2007 Conference at Oberlin was a modest contribution to the commemoration of the 1957 North American Conference on Faith and Order, and an attempt to invite younger scholars into the discussion. It is hoped that someday there may be the resources and ecumenical focus for a second North American Conference on Faith and Order, with the prospect of harvesting the theological work of past decades and charting a course of theological research for the future.[2]

This overview of U.S. Faith and Order history is designed to be a brief and introductory sampling, highlighting especially the link to the one worldwide ecumenical movement and the variety of churches in the United States. The churches can be grateful for the fifty years of service of this U.S. Commission to the unity of Christians worldwide. They can be hopeful for the research efforts of a new generation of specialists doing the hard theological work before us, with the next fifty years—and more—of challenges to come.

In looking at the United States from a global perspective, it will be important to realize that, in the Protestant community, about half the Christians are in churches that relate to the historical ecumenical movement, and about half are Evangelical, Pentecostal, and Holiness churches whose history has placed them at the margins of the ecumenical movement. Because of the worldwide influence of these churches, the religious diversity in the United States, and the tendency of the religious community to be polarized and even politicized, it is a priority for Faith and Order U.S.A. to engage these churches in theological dialogue on the core issues of the Christian faith.

In my view, the primary work of Faith and Order U.S.A. is the reception of the wider ecumenical work.[3] The Commission does produce texts. The influence of Oberlin I—its contribution to Montreal 1963 with its pioneering work on the relationship between Scripture and tradition, the U.S. work on ecclesiology, and the giants present there who influenced three generations of teaching—all are irreversible contributions.

In 1957 Faith and Order was very much a Protestant affair, with even the Orthodox who were members of both World and National Councils needing to write a separate statement. Papanikolaou's paper (part 2) demonstrates that the situation has begun to change.[4] As Cardinal Avery Dulles (part 2) and Msgr. John Radano (part 3) note, the tentative Catholic presence at Oberlin fifty years ago has begun, gradually, to transform the largest worldwide Christian body, and to destabilize[5] and augment[6] the global ecumenical enterprise.[7]

The commission is mandated to "call the churches to full visible unity, in the one Apostolic Faith, in one Eucharistic fellowship, united in worship and witness that the world might believe." This first purpose of the World Council of Churches (WCC) has never been part of the constitution of the U.S. National Council, which was founded as a John D. Rockefeller, corporate-era "cooperative agency."

Former U.S. National Council general secretary Arie Brouwer was wont to say that this council is not the bold ecumenical ship leading the churches toward unity, but a flotilla of dinghies, seldom sailing in a coordinated direction.[8] In fact, the secular corporate language of the 1950 constitution was only replaced by the theological language of a "community of communions" in 1981,[9] a minor but important step toward the reception of the theological ecumenical vision of church unity.[10] This reformulation work was largely done under the influence of the U.S. Faith and Order Commission and its twenty years of ecumenical work, with the leadership of Paul Crow, Jeanne Audrey Powers, and others.[11]

During this author's term as associate general secretary for Faith and Order, 1981–91, the churches restructured their council four times, with little input from those ecumenical partners such as the Lutheran Church–Missouri Synod; Church of God, Anderson, Indiana; Catholic Church, etc., who had entrusted Faith and Order to them in 1957. Three times the commission was dissolved in the restructures, but it never missed a meeting! The council needs a staff and community of ecumenical officers who know the history and theological basis of the ecumenical movement in the 1950 WCC Toronto Statement, and the significance of the ecclesiological discussions.[12] This 1950 text, which has become a classic among ecumenical documents, makes clear what a council is and is not. It affirms the members' unity in Christ and desire for deeper communion, but it also affirms that membership does not imply recognition of one another as churches in the proper sense and does not create some sort of "super church." Churches relate to each other out of their own identity and on their own terms. A council is not a third reality between or above the churches, but is an instrument for the mission of the churches themselves in serving their dialogue and common witness.

For younger theologians, there is much work before the theological community and the churches. While ecumenical scholars leave a rich legacy; as long as the churches are divided there is no dearth of possibilities for service, research, and ecumenical reconciliation.

Twenty-five years ago when U.S. Faith and Order celebrated this anniversary, the commission was the guest of the late John Meyendorff at St. Vladimir's Orthodox Theological Seminary. The late Paul Minear, so active in Oberlin I, spoke. In the Faith and Order file is a picture of the late Letty Russell and William G. Rusch cutting the anniversary cake at Graymoor Ecumenical Institute.

As early as the 1970s Paul Minear noted that the increasing bureaucratization of the churches and the specialization of academic theology made developing ecumenical leadership more challenging.[13] The last thirty years have indeed verified his concerns. Many come into leadership in the churches and even in ecumenical agencies without knowing the decades of relationships among the churches, even their own, and the theology that lies behind them. Many biblical scholars in seminaries, for example, know the Scriptures well, but may not be acquainted with the historic work, among the churches signaled at Oberlin I, on such themes as the relationship of Scripture, tradition, and the histories of the churches.

Yes, Faith and Order and the U.S. churches have come a long way, but there is a long way to go. When a Protestant student can say "when the Catholic Church was over in the sixteenth century," or when a Catholic bishop can say Protestants "do not believe in Christ's real presence in communion," as I have myself witnessed recently, one is taken aback. There is much education needed for the work done to date to become a common heritage. When one reviews church history texts for seminary use—U.S., sixteenth century,[14] Latin American, or general introductions—looking for ones adequate to the fifty years of ecumenical research, one is still at a loss. Yes, there is much work to do.

Of course, not all are called to do this very specific theological research task of Faith and Order for the churches. There is one ecumenical movement, and some are called to social advocacy, some to ecumenical education, some to common evangelical witness, and some to common witness in service to the community. Few are called to build the agreements from which the unity of the church can emerge. Widely published Protestant theologians have dropped out of Faith and Order because mastering Orthodox theology was too much of a stretch. Some Catholics would prefer to talk to Buddhists rather than to Pentecostal fellow Christians. A call to ecumenism does not necessarily mean a vocation to Faith and Order dialogue and research.

It is a complex, specialized, frustrating, and exhilarating task, in service to the church and its Lord. As Reinhold Niebuhr, a leading mid-century Protestant theologian whose own church, the United Church of Christ, was a pioneer in Faith and Order reconciliation, has said, no mission is worth giving one's life to, if it can be realized in one's own lifetime. Surely Faith and Order scholars do not expect to see the full, visible unity of Pentecostal, Orthodox, Protestant, and Catholic churches in their lifetime. But in reprising the post-Oberlin history, I am vividly aware that I could not have imagined the changes since my college graduation in 1959, the year of two popes and the announcement of the Second Vatican Council in my church.

If producing texts of international standing is not the gift or calling of the U.S. commission, how do we speak of Faith and Order U.S.A.'s role in reception? We have noted its role in reception of the theology of the conciliar movement into the U.S. National Council. There are two other dimensions of ecumenical reception which I see as the calling of the U.S. commission:

1. The first is the reception of theological work of other dimensions of the one ecumenical movement: church union, bilateral and World Council results; both by evaluating them and communicating them to U.S. Christians; and by providing U.S. voices into these discussions, voices that might be muted otherwise.

2. The second is the reception and outreach to new voices previously absent from the Christian discussions. Until all Christians are at the table, our work is not complete; and until there is one visibly united church, Christ's prayer will not reach its full realization.

I see these as a (1) convergence, centripetal dimension of Faith and Order work, and a (2) centrifugal, outreach dimension.

In this symbolic overview of five decades, I will just note one or another contribution to each of these vocations. A complete retrospective would include more detailed evaluative, historical papers on how the ecumenical movement since Oberlin has transformed each of the U.S. churches, how it has influenced scholarship on various themes in various disciplines, and how scholars have reformulated their research. In my own classroom, I try to help especially my Methodist, Baptist, Disciples, and Catholic students with such an overview, and have written about Anglican,[15] Lutheran,[16] Reformed,[17] Wesleyan,[18] and Pentecostal[19] developments. However, the present generation of scholars and church leaders need to hear and celebrate the texture of this rich and relatively recent history in all its postmodern particularity!

One has only to trace how the convergences of Oberlin and Montreal have shaped the influential scholarship of Raymond E. Brown,[20] Albert C. Outler,[21] or Jaroslav Pelikan,[22] for example, to see how the American theological landscape remains in the debt of Faith and Order.

THE TURBULENT SIXTIES

Of course, it is the Life and Work heritage of U.S. National Council leadership that is most remembered from this period, with the civil rights[23] and Vietnam War debates being central to the churches' struggle together in the council.

In 1957 the church unity work was relatively new, and marginal for a decade or two, though the careful work on Scripture and tradition and opening of the ecclesiological question for U.S. Protestantism has had irreversible impact on the U.S. churches that relate to the ecumenical movement.[24] In the 1970s I introduced a course on Church and Sacrament, for example, at Memphis Theological Seminary, a Cumberland Presbyterian institution. Upon my return twenty-five years later, there are full-blown electives on both of these themes and an amazing array of ecumenical theological resources unavailable in 1976.

As was symbolized by the leadership of Gilbert Stafford, Church of God, Anderson, Indiana, and Thelma Chambers-Young, Progressive National Baptist Convention, at the 2007 Oberlin conference, the churches represented at Oberlin I were a much wider range than the U.S. National Council membership. The churches of the council have generously stewarded the Faith and Order movement in the United States, for a much larger Christian constituency than its own members.

While convergences on understanding the relationship between Scripture and Tradition and on the importance of ecclesiological dialogue were the major centripetal forces to serve the churches, the major outreach, centrifugal force, was the engagement of the Catholic Church in the wake of the Second Vatican Council.

When I arrived in New York City in 1981 the most widely remembered work of Faith and Order was still the *Living Room Dialogues*, which during the 1960s and early 1970s had brought thousands of Orthodox, Protestants, and Catholics together to discuss issues of faith using resources produced in this commission.[25]

THE TRANSITIONAL SEVENTIES

Many of the discussions that went on in the commissions of World and U.S. National Council on the relationship between Scripture and tradition in the 1950s and 1960s were pursued in the Society for Pentecostal Studies and Wesleyan Theological Society as well. These ecumenical, internal debates made participation of representatives of the Wesleyan and Pentecostal theological traditions in the Faith and Order in the 1980s possible. Within the U.S. commission, outreach in forums around the country contributed to the reception of Faith and Order work. Pioneering ethical contributions on abortion and homosexuality remain important resources.[26]

The principal outreach was the full incorporation of women into the theological leadership of Faith and Order. This U.S. leadership was a catalyst for international changes in the global movement, as the memorial to Letty Russell and the remarks of Dame Mary Tanner reminded members of the Oberlin conference.[27] A good paper on both the integration of women's leadership into the work, and the methodological and content changes in Faith and Order style it occasioned, will be an important contribution to preserving the history of Faith and Order.[28] This was also a moment for attention to Asian and Latin American/U.S. Hispanic voices as well.

During this period the U.S. commission produced an important contribution to World Council ecclesiological work on the shape of the unity we seek as a conciliar communion.[29]

In the U.S. National Council, Faith and Order gave rise first to Christian-Jewish work and then to the Task Force on Christian Muslim Relations, programs that matured through the 1980s and 1990s to become an independent commission in the U.S. National Council, capable of its own theology and dialogue possibilities. Having been so successful in generating this work in the council, Faith and Order will be cautious not to overlap or do the theological work for which a full commission now exists in the council, even as staff will be shared by these two commissions.

The 1970s also marks a moment when the most productive ecumenical work on issues of faith and church order in the United States began to be done in bilateral settings and the Consultation on Church Union. This success caused inevitable tensions between those churches that preferred the multilateral venue of Faith and Order and those that were able to resolve historical differences only by the particularity of bilateral research. This tension provided the impetus for important studies in the 1980s in the commission, on reception and on the complementarity of multilateral and bilateral methodologies and content.[30]

THE PRODUCTIVITY AND OUTREACH OF THE 1980s

The U.S. commission was an important servant of the U.S. churches in their contribution to the WCC *Baptism, Eucharist and Ministry*[31] process and its evaluation and reception in the U.S. community. Study of reception of this text and similar themes in the bilaterals enabled the U.S. churches to see the wholeness of the one ecumenical movement and how convergence in multilateral dialogues served consensus among the churches.[32]

As many of the presentations at Oberlin II documented so well, the apostolic faith study provided an opportunity for both outreach in consultations with the Peace,[33] African American,[34] and Pentecostal churches,[35] and in publications on the ancient pneumatological,[36] historical,[37] and christological[38] issues still dividing Christians—considered now in dialogue with the newer, diverse voices from the U.S. church situation. The fifteen U.S. consultations and twenty-four WCC consultations on the historic core of the Christian faith give a lie to antiecumenical critiques against conciliar ecumenism.[39] The pioneering work on gender and language in the creed was to be a resource for the World Council a decade later when that concern became a pressing global ecumenical issue.[40]

Indeed, one can hold up the volume of work of these two commissions and the bilaterals, documented in the three-volume *Growth in Agreement* series[41] and the *Building Unity/Growing Consensus* series of volumes documenting the U.S. dialogues,[42] in a positive comparison to any witness to the faith published by the theological commissions of the National Association of Evangelicals or the World Evangelical Alliance.

As Donald Dayton[43] and others document, this is the decade of filling out the commission to include the Evangelical, Pentecostal, and Holiness voices, present but marginal in earlier decades of Faith and Order.⁴⁴ The 1970s had also been a time of separatism among many African American scholars, with significant ecumenical bridges like Gayraud Wilmore⁴⁵ welcome exceptions. The 1980s enabled several opportunities for staging African American church voices into World Council discussions. Of course, the leadership of women expanded and deepened.⁴⁶

The pioneering work on ecclesiology and human sexuality occasioned by the study of the application for membership of the Universal Fellowship of Metropolitan Community Churches⁴⁷ remains a resource as the churches continue to face this issue in their own internal quest for unity. This study signaled the early stage of the reception of this question into ecumenical dialogue, and demonstrates some principles of civility, dialogue methodology, and ecclesiology that should be continuing resources for the future, a future that the Anglican Communion demonstrates is already upon us.

THE HARVEST OF THE 1990s

For many, the number of proposals for full communion before the churches for reflection and action during the 1980s was a surprise, especially in the United States. Indeed, the fruits of forty years of bilateral and Faith and Order work were beginning to bear fruit in the lives of the churches themselves.

Reformation issues were also beginning to find resolution, not only within Protestantism but between some of the Reformation churches and the Catholic Church. A "Joint Declaration on the Doctrine of Justification"⁴⁸ was signed between Catholics, Lutherans, and eventually Methodists.⁴⁹ The U.S. commission has contributed and continues to contribute to widening and deepening this discussion and finding ways of helping its reconciling intent to be integrated into the lives of the U.S. Christian community.⁵⁰

The full communion agreements challenged Faith and Order to both deepen common understanding of these developments and expand its implications by studies on full communion, authority in the church, and the authority of the church in the world.⁵¹

As Root points out, common structures of decision making, in a postmodern world, will be continuing challenges even with churches in full communion. The theology behind these agreements has also contributed to the centrifugal moment of reception, by engaging church theologians from traditions who do not have full communion as the goal of their reconciling engagement with other Christians.[52]

During this period and into the new century Faith and Order U.S.A. continues to engage in reaching out to the margins to involve an ever-widening circle of Christians in the quest for unity, attending to the contextual theologies emerging in a variety of places within the United States and around the world, and taking on new issues that threaten to divide the church. Work on racism continues.[53]

The willingness of the U.S. commission to respond to the 1995 invitation to a "patient and fraternal dialogue" on the exercise of the papal ministry by the late John Paul II[54] is a historic and groundbreaking moment in the reception of a new—and very old—issue, into what was once a Protestant and Orthodox movement toward unity.[55] Theologians from churches that would not yet consider formal responses to this invitation from the pope have been able to contribute, through Faith and Order, to this discussion. Other discussions of structures of authority and decision making continue to be a priority, as Root makes clear.[56]

As the World Council peruses its drafting of the "Nature and Mission of the Church"[57] text, U.S. Faith and Order has a unique opportunity to provide a platform for voices from the margin to participate, and to help the churches at the center of the ecumenical movement begin to reflect on the implications of this text for their life together.[58] This work builds on and feeds into the developments on authority *in* the church and the authority *of* the church in the world, two studies under way in U.S. Faith and Order.[59]

So with this somewhat superficial and breathtaking journey through half a century, it is difficult to tell whether we should be most thankful to God for what has been accomplished in this short window of church history, or intimidated by the vocation of reconciliation laid out before us in the decades to come.

CONCLUSION

Those called to serve the unity of the church through theological dialogue, research, and communication in Faith and Order are a small part of the one ecumenical movement. Theological ecumenists are called to collaborate and support the other dimensions and their contributions to the unity of all Christians. Theologians in the Faith and Order U.S.A. have their modest, if significant, contribution to make. However, a caution is in order in this collaboration on two specific suggestions that arose in the conference.

The call for the "blurring of lines" between Faith and Order and Life and Work must be realistic and mutual.[60]

1. The best service Faith and Order can provide to the rest of the U.S. National Council is (a) to help to advise on building an ecumenical constituency from U.S. churches as wide as that in Faith and Order, to supplement NCCCUSA member churches in their common witness; (b) to help identify church-dividing issues to which the Life and Work dimensions of the U.S. National Council need to give their theological and dialogical attention; and (c) to help Life and Work colleagues design theological consultations that will have the ecumenical breadth and theological depth needed to support the common witness of ecumenical life.

2. Care must be taken not to become a general think tank for the member churches of the U.S. National Council, or a place where legitimating theology is formulated for public policy decisions already made elsewhere in the council.

Good papers would be helpful in documenting the reception of the ecumenical movement and its Faith and Order method, goal, and content, in the Life and Work, educational, and social service dimensions of U.S. church life and the U.S. National Council of Churches of Christ.

Papers on the influence of Faith and Order on the churches' seminaries, educational life, and disciplines/canon laws would also help us to evaluate more accurately the road ahead, the successes of the past, and the concrete blocks to this work of the Spirit in the life of the Christian community together. These studies should disclose some achievements and outline some challenges for the U.S. churches, for other sectors of the global ecumenical movement, and for the collaborative agencies that serve ecumenical life.

This has been an exhilarating and refreshing first fifty years of this U.S. commission in the long history of Christianity. We can be grateful to God for generations who pioneered this work, and hopeful for those who will be called to this ministry in the decades to come.

NOTES

1. An informal, undocumented version of this article has appeared in *Ecumenical Trends* 36, no. 10 (November 2007): 11–14; a narrative report has been published as Diane Kessler, "Faith and Order in Oberlin—1957 and 2007," *Ecumenical Review* 59 (2007): 284–92.

2. Jeffrey Gros, "What Are the Factors Necessary for a Conference on Faith and Order in North America?" *Ecumenical Trends* 35, no. 4 (April 2006): 7–9.

3. For a fuller treatment of reception in the ecumenical movement, see William G. Rusch, *Ecumenical Reception: Its Challenge and Opportunity* (Grand Rapids, MI: Eerdmans, 2007). Paul D. Murray, ed., *Exploring a Way for Contemporary Ecumenism* (Oxford: Oxford University Press, 2008).

4. A. Papanikolaou, "Orthodoxy, Postmodernity, and Ecumenism: The Difference That Divine-Human Communion Makes," *Journal of Ecumenical Studies* 42 (Fall 2007): 527–47.

5. Jeffrey Gros, "Reception and Roman Catholicism for the 1990s," *One in Christ* 31, no. 4 (1995): 295–328.

6. Paul Crow, "The Roman Catholic Presence in the Faith and Order Movement," *Bulletin Centro Pro Unione* 62 (Fall 2002): 3–15.

7. Jeffrey Gros, "The Roman Catholic Church and the Contribution to Christian Unity," in *Vatican II: The Continuing Agenda*, ed. Anthony J. Cernera (Fairfield, CT: Sacred Heart University, 1997); "Toward Full Communion: Faith and Order and Catholic Ecumenism," *Theological Studies* 65 (2004): 23–43; "Ecumenism: From Isolation to a Vision of Christian Unity," in *The Catholic*

Church in the Twentieth Century, ed. John Deedy (Collegeville, MN: Liturgical Press, 2000), 131–48.

8. Arie R. Brouwer, "The Real Crises at the National Council of Churches," *Christian Century* 107, no. 20 (June 27–July 4): 631–39.

9. National Council of the Churches of Christ in the USA, *Constitution (*NCCCUSA, 2003). See online *www.ncccusa.org/pdfs/nccconstitution.pdf.*

10. For some of the cultural roots of this difficult development, see Jeffrey Gros, "The Vision of Christian Unity: Some Aspects of Faith and Order in the Context of United States Culture," *Midstream* 30, no. 1 (January 1991): 1–19; "Reception in American Culture: Tendencies and Temptations," in *Twelve Tales Untold: A Study Guide for Ecumenical Reception,* ed. John T. Ford and Darlis J. Swan (Grand Rapids, MI: Eerdmans, 1993).

11. "Future Directions for the National Council of the Churches of Christ in the USA"; Robert W. Neff and Candace C. Weeks, "Next Steps Toward Community: An Inside View"; Robert K. Welsh, "Reorientation or Reorganization: The Challenge to Conciliar Ecumenism," *Journal of Ecumenical Studies* 22, no. 2 (Spring 1985): 205–41.

12. "The Church, The Churches and the World Council," adopted by the WCC Central Committee, Toronto, 9–15 July 1950, *Ecumenical Review* 3 (October 1950): 47ff.

13. See "Ecumenical Theology—Profession or Vocation?" in *United and Uniting* 7, ed. Frederick Trost and Barbara Brown Zikmund (Cleveland: Pilgrim Press, 2005), 573.

14. See, for example, Jeffrey Gros, "Building a Common Heritage: Teaching the Reformation in an Ecumenical Perspective," *Ecumenical Trends* 35, no. 5 (May 2006): 11–15.

15. Jeffrey Gros, "The Chicago-Lambeth Quadrilateral and the U.S.A. Faith and Order Movement," in *Quadrilateral at One Hundred: Essays on the Centenary of the Chicago-Lambeth Quadrilateral,* ed. J. Robert Wright, *Anglican Theological Review Supplementary Series* 10 (March 1988): 195–212.

16. Jeffrey Gros, "The Lutheran-Catholic Pilgrimage towards Visible Unity," *Exchange: Journal of Mission and Ecumenical Research* 29, no. 1 (2000): 23–36; "Lutherans and Catholics in the Origin and Development of the Conciliar Movement," *Lutheran Forum* 25,

no. 2 (May 1991): 14–19; "The Reception in the US Catholic Context," in K. Bloomquist and W. Greive, eds., *The Doctrine of Justification: Its Reception and Meaning Today* (Geneva: Lutheran World Federation, 2003), 25–34.

17. Jeffrey Gros, "Mission and Mystery: Gospel Testimony in Service to the World," in *That the World May Believe,* ed. M. Goheen and M. O'Gara (Lanham, MD : University of America Press, 2006), 155–72; *Journey in Faith: Forty Years of Reformed Catholic Dialogue: 1965–2005,* United States Conference of Catholic Bishops, 2005, www.usccb.org/seia/journey.shtml; "Evangelical and Catholic: The Reformed/Roman Catholic Encounter," *New Mercersburg Review* 14 (Autumn 1993): 18–38; "A Journey of Faith: Reformed and Catholic," *Reformed Review* 52, no. 3 (Spring 1999): 235–53.

18. Jeffrey Gros, "Toward Full Communion: Roman Catholics and Methodists in Dialogue," *Quarterly Review* (Fall 1994): 241–62; "United Methodist Ordained Ministry in Ecumenical Perspective," *Quarterly Review* 24, no. 4 (Winter 2004): 381–98; "The Church in Ecumenical Dialogue: Crucial Choices, Essential Contributions," *Wesleyan Theological Journal* 39, no. 1 (Spring 2004): 35–53.

19. Jeffrey Gros, "An Ecumenical Perspective on Pentecostal Mission," in Murray W. Dempster, Byron D. Klaus, and Douglas Peterson, *Called and Empowered: Pentecostal Perspectives on Global Mission* (Peabody, MA: Hendrickson Publishers, 1989); "Toward a Dialogue of Conversion: The Pentecostal, Evangelical and Conciliar Movements," *Pneuma* 17, no. 2 (Fall 1995): 189ff.; "A Pilgrimage in the Spirit: Pentecostal Testimony in the Faith and Order Movement," *Pneuma* 25, no. 1 (Spring 2003): 29–53.

20. See especially Raymond E. Brown, *The Churches the Apostles Left Behind* (New York/Mahwah, NJ: Paulist Press, 1984); *Peter in the New Testament* (New York/Mahwah, NJ: Paulist Press, 1973); Raymond Brown et al., *Mary in the New Testament* (New York/Mahwah, NJ: Paulist Press, 2001), and with John Meier, *Antioch and Rome* (New York/Mahwah, NJ: Paulist Press, 1983).

21. In addition to his magisterial work in the dialogues, being a key initiator of the Methodist– Catholic work, much of his work on Wesley, on the quadrilateral, and on the catholic roots of Methodism shows an attempt to find in the wider Wesleyan heritage the catholic foundation in the Great Tradition, as articulated

in Montreal. Furthermore, his interpretation of Catholicism and Orthodoxy in the Protestant world began to give a new hermeneutical perspective, especially in the United States. See Albert C. Outler, *History as an Ecumenical Resource: The Protestant Discovery of Tradition, 1952–1963* (Washington, DC: Catholic University of America Press, 1973); Bob Parrot, ed., *The Ecumenical Theologian: Essays by Albert Cook Outler* (Anderson, IN: Bristol House, 2001).

22. Jaroslav Pelikan, *The Christian Tradition: A History of the Development of Doctrine* (Chicago: University of Chicago Press, 1971–84).

23. See, for example, James Findlay, *Church People in the Struggle: The National Council of Churches and the Black Freedom Movement, 1950–1970* (New York: Oxford University Press, 1993).

24. The Department of Faith and Order Studies, National Council of Churches, "The Ecclesiological Significance of Councils of Churches," in *Growing Consensus* (I), ed. Joseph Burgess and Jeffrey Gros (New York/Mahwah, NJ: Paulist Press, 1995), 585–613.

25. William B. Greenspun and William Norgren, eds., *Living Room Dialogues* (New York: Paulist Press, 1965); W. Greenspun and C. Weidel, eds., *Second Living Room Dialogues* (New York: Paulist Press, 1967); James Young, ed., *Third Living Room Dialogues* (New York: Paulist Press, 1970).

26. Faith and Order, NCCUSA, "A Call to Responsible Ecumenical Debate on Controversial Issues: Abortion and Homosexuality," in Jeffrey Gros and Joseph Burgess, eds., *Building Unity* (New York/Mahwah, NJ: Paulist Press, 1989), 451–57.

27. Barbara Brown Zikmund, "Inheriting Letty's Garden," *Ecumenical Trends* 36, no. 8 (September 2007): 8.

28. See, for example, Mary Ann Hinsdale, *Women Shaping Theology* (New York/Mahwah, NJ: Paulist Press, 2006).

29. "Conciliar Fellowship," *Midstream* 21, no. 2 (April 1982): 243–68.

30. Daniel F. Martensen, ed., "The Quest for Christian Consensus: Bilateral Theological Dialogue in the Ecumenical Movement," *Journal of Ecumenical Studies* 23, no. 3 (Summer 1987): passim. John Ford, ed., "A Report of the Bilaterals Study Group of the Faith and Order Commission of the National Council of

Churches," *Midstream* 28, no. 1 (January 1989): 118. Ford and Swan, eds., *Twelve Tales Untold*.

31. *Baptism, Eucharist, Ministry* (Geneva: World Council of Churches, 1982), *www.oikoumene.org/en/resources/documents/ wcc-commissions/faith-and-order-commission/i-unity-the-church- and-its-mission/baptism-eucharist-and-ministry-faith-and-order- paper-no-111-the-lima-text.html; Churches Respond to BEM: Official Responses to the "Baptism, Eucharist and Ministry" Text*, vols. 1–6, ed. Max Thurian (Geneva: World Council of Churches, 1986–88); *Baptism, Eucharist and Ministry: Report 1982–90* (Geneva: World Council of Churches, 1990).

32. Jeffrey Gros, ed., *The Search for Visible Unity* (New York: Pilgrim Press, 1984). "Baptism, Eucharist and Ministry Conference," *Midstream* 25, no. 3 (July 1986): 322–29. Papers for this second conference in *American Baptist Quarterly* 7, no. 1 (March 1988): 38–49. Merle D. Strege, ed., *Baptism and Church: A Believers' Church Vision* (Grand Rapids, MI: Sagamore Books, 1986); David B. Eller, ed., *Servants of the Word: Ministry in the Believers' Church* (Elgin, IN: Brethren Press, 1990); Dale R. Stoffer, ed., *The Lord's Supper: Believers Church Perspectives* (Scottdale, PA: Herald Press, 1997); Jeffrey Gros, "Believers' Church Conference on the Lord's Supper," *Journal of Ecumenical Studies* 31, no. 1/2 (Winter/Spring 1994): 209.

33. Jeffrey Gros, "Expressing the Apostolic Faith: The Peace Churches' Contribution," *Ecumenical Trends* 19, no. 6 (June 1990): 92–94; Marlin Miller and Barbara Nelson Gingrich, eds., *The Church's Peace Witness* (Grand Rapids, MI: Eerdmans, 1994); "The Fragmentation of the Church and Its Unity in Peacemaking: Consultation Report," *One in Christ* 31, no. 4 (1995): 379–85; also in the *Ecumenical Review* 48, no. 1 (January 1996): 122–24; John Rempel and Jeffrey Gros, eds., *The Fragmentation of the Church and Its Unity in Peace Making* (Grand Rapids, MI: Eerdmans, 2001).

34. David T. Shannon and Gayraud Wilmore, ed., *Black Witness to the Apostolic Faith* (Grand Rapids, MI: Eerdmans, 1988).

35. "Confessing the Apostolic Faith from the Perspective of the Pentecostal Churches," *One in Christ* 23, no. 1–2 (1987): 61–156.

36. Theodore Stylianopoulos and Mark Heim, eds., *Spirit of Truth: Ecumenical Perspectives on the Holy Spirit* (Brookline, MA: Holy Cross Orthodox Press, 1986).

37. Timothy J. Wengert and Charles W. Brockwell Jr., eds., *Telling the Churches' Stories: Ecumenical Perspectives on Writing Christian History* (Grand Rapids, MI: Eerdmans, 1995); Jeffrey Gros, "Toward a Reconciliation of Memory: Seeking a Truly Catholic Hermeneutics of History," *Journal of Latino/Hispanic Theology* 7, no. 1 (August 1999): 56–75; S. Mark Heim, ed., *Faith to Creed* (Grand Rapids, MI: Eerdmans, 1991).

38. Paul Fries and Tiran Nersoyan, *Christ in East and West* (Macon, GA: Mercer University Press, 1987).

39. Thaddeus Horgan, ed., *Apostolic Faith in America* (Grand Rapids, MI: Eerdmans, 1988).

40. "Gender and Language in the Creeds," *Union Seminary Quarterly Review* 40, no. 3 (August 1985): passim.

41. Lukas Vischer and Harding Meyer, eds., *Growth in Agreement Reports and Agreed Statements of Ecumenical Conversations on a World Level* (New York: Paulist Press, 1984); William Rusch, Harding Meyer, and Jeffrey Gros, eds., *Growth in Agreement II* (Geneva: World Council of Churches, 2000); Thomas Best, Lorelei Fuchs, and Jeffrey Gros, eds., *Growth in Agreement III* (Geneva/Grand Rapids, MI: World Council of Churches/Eerdmans), 2007.

42. Jeffrey Gros and Joseph Burgess, eds., *Building Unity* (New York: Paulist Press, 1989); Joseph Burgess and Jeffrey Gros, eds., *Growing Consensus* (New York: Paulist Press, 1995); Jeffrey Gros and Lydia Veliko, eds., *Growing Consensus II* (Washington, DC: U.S. Conference of Catholic Bishops, 2004).

43. "The Ecumenical Significance of Oberlin," *Journal of Ecumenical Studies* 42 (Fall 207): 511–26. See also the festschrift that was presented during the Oberlin event: C. T. C. Winn, ed., *From the Margins: A Celebration of the Theological Work of Donald W. Dayton* (Eugene, OR.: Pickwick Publications, 2007).

44. Jeffrey Gros, "Recent Evangelical Engagement in the Ecumenical Movement," *Ecumenical Trends* 19, no. 7 (July 1990); "Evangelical Relations: A Differentiated Catholic Perspective," *Ecumenical Trends* 29, no. 1 (January 2000): 1–9.

45. Thomas F. Best, ed., "An African American Perspective on the Unity of the Church: Harlem Consultation," *Midstream* 28, no. 4 (October 1989): passim.

46. Melanie May, ed., *Women and Church: The Challenge of Ecumenical Solidarity in an Age of Alienation* (Grand Rapids, MI: Eerdmans, 1991).

47. Jeffrey Gros, "The Church, the Churches and the Metropolitan Church," *Ecumenical Review* 36, no. 1 (January 1984): 71–81; "Ecumenical Documents: Report to the Governing Board," *Midstream* 22, nos. 3 and 4 (July–October 1983).

48. Lutheran World Federation and the Catholic Church, "Joint Declaration on the Doctrine of Justification" (Vatican website, Pontifical Council for Promoting Christian Unity, October 31, 1999), *www.vatican.va/roman_curia/pontifical_councils/chrstuni/documents/ rc_pc_chrstuni_doc_31101999_cath-luth-joint-declaration_en.html*.

49. "The World Methodist Council Statement of Association with the Joint Declaration on the Doctrine of Justification" (Vatican website, Pontifical Council for Promoting Christian Unity: Seoul, South Korea, July 23, 2006), *www.vatican.va/roman_curia/pontifical_councils/chrstuni/ meth-council-docs/rc_pc_chrstuni_doc_20060723_text-association_en.html*.

50. William Rusch, ed., *Justification and the Future of the Ecumenical Movement* (Collegeville, MN: Liturgical Press, 2003). For the current studies, see Faith and Order Commission, "2008–2011 Study Groups." NCCCUSA, 2007. *www.ncccusa.org/faithandorder/ sg2008.html*.

51. Faith and Order Commission, "2004–2007 Study Groups." NCCCUSA, 2003. *www.ncccusa.org/faithandorder/sg2004.html*.

52. Jeffrey Gros, "The Requirements and Challenges of Full Communion: A Multilateral Evaluation?" *Journal of Ecumenical Studies* 42, no. 2 (Spring 2007): 217–42.

53. Susan Davies and Paul Teresa Hennessee, SA, *Ending Racism in the Church* (Cleveland: United Church Press, 1998); Jeffrey Gros, "Eradicating Racism: A Central Agenda for the Faith and Order Movement," *Ecumenical Review* 47, no. 1 (January 1995).

54. Ioannes Paulus PP. II, "Ut Unum Sint: On Commitment to Ecumenism" (Vatican website, May 25, 1995), *www.vatican.va*.

55. Faith and Order Commission. "Response to 'Petrine Ministry: A Working Draft.'" NCCCUSA, 2003. *www.ncccusa.org/news/ petrineresponse.html*.

56. Michael Root, "Faith and Order in a Post-modern World: A Response," *Journal of Ecumenical Studies* 42 (2007): 560–70.

57. "The Nature and Mission of the Church—A Stage on the Way to a Common Statement," Faith and Order Paper no. 198, (WCC website, December 15, 2005), *www.oikoumene.org/resources/ documents/wcc-commissions/faith-and-order-commission/i-unity-the-church-and-its-mission/the-nature-and-mission-of-the-church-a-stage-on-the-way-to-a-common-statement.html*.

58. Jeffrey Gros, "Faith on the Frontier: Apostolicity and the American-Born Churches," *One in Christ* 39, no. 2 (April 2004): 28–48; Ted Campbell, Ann Riggs, and Gilbert Stafford, eds., *Ancient Faith and American-Born Churches* (New York/Mahwah, NJ: Paulist Press, 2006).

59. Jeffrey Gros, "Bonds of Communion," *Ecumenical Trends* 28, no. 8 (September 1999): 1–8; *Ecumenical Trends* 31, no. 8 (September 2002): 7–9.

60. For a very important methodological essay on this discussion see John Ford, "Oberlin 2007: The Need for an Expanded Methodology?" *Ecumenical Trends* 36, no. 8 (September 2007): 5–7.

Chapter 4

THE APOSTOLIC FAITH STUDY AND THE HOLY SPIRIT

Cecil M. Robeck Jr.

For more than half a century the World Council of Churches (WCC) has sought a number of ways to move its member churches forward in their mutual recognition of one another. Four projects undertaken over the past three decades stand out. First among them has been the attempt to find a way forward in the mutual recognition of baptism, eucharist, and ministry. Second has been the proposal to work toward some common confession of the apostolic faith. Attention has been focused specifically on the role that the Nicene-Constantinopolitan Creed might play as a common confession of faith. Third, the WCC has hoped that it could then move on to the even more difficult issues of common decision making and acting. Finally, the subject of the unity of the church and the renewal of human community was added to the list. In this paper, I take a look at how the National Council of the Churches of Christ in the USA (NCC) has participated in or contributed to the second of these important studies.

In Lima, Peru, in 1982, the Commission on Faith and Order of the WCC completed its very important study, *Baptism, Eucharist, and Ministry*.[1] The result was a convergence document intended to bring participating denominations and congregations closer to one another through greater understanding and appreciation of the many ways they approach these issues. While baptism and Eucharist, in particular, were originally instituted as sacraments of unity, they have often become sources of division between Christians. In *Baptism, Eucharist, and Ministry*, the churches made significant progress in overcoming misunderstanding and in finding ways beyond the sometimes centuries-old impasse.

But the members of the commission knew that more was necessary if the churches were going to have a long-term, sustainable prospect for visible unity. They would have to see whether the churches themselves would receive the fruit of their labor. As a result, with the publication of *Baptism, Eucharist, and Ministry*, which is now in its thirty-ninth printing, came the invitation for churches to study the document and submit a formal response to the WCC.[2] Thus, as one process ended, another began.

The work on *Baptism, Eucharist, and Ministry* and the request for official responses were not the end of the quest for greater understanding or moves toward visible unity. The commission also recognized that any meaningful efforts toward a genuinely visible expression of Christian unity would require a common recognition of the apostolic faith in one another. Already at the Standing Commission's meeting in January 1981, a study group had been formed on the topic, "Towards the Common Expression of the Apostolic Faith." Later that year, two consultations were held. The first one, "Towards the Common Expression of the Apostolic Faith Today," met in Chambésy, Switzerland, at the end of June 1981, while a second one, "The Ecumenical Importance of the Nicene Creed," convened in October in Odessa, USSR. As a result of this preliminary work, before the Standing Commission on Faith and Order of the WCC completed its work in Lima, the commission authorized a new theological study. It authorized a process that would extend over the next decade and ultimately lead to the publication of *Confessing the One Faith*, in 1991, an explication of the Nicene-Constantinopolitan Creed.[3]

The Commission on Faith and Order of the NCC watched these actions closely. While its life is independent of that of the WCC commission and it has interests that are unique to the American context, members of the Commission on Faith and Order of the National Council of Churches believed that the study on Apostolic faith being conducted by the World Council of Churches would benefit from input derived from the unique testimonies of churches at home for which the American context is home. The United States, after all, has provided not only a unique context; it has produced a unique set of churches. And this context and these churches have had a global impact upon churches everywhere.

Catholic, Orthodox, and Reformation Protestant churches thrive here, though in the United States none of them benefits from being an established church. The United States has also given birth to Orthodox, Anglican, Methodist, Lutheran, and Reformed denominations that have broken or at least individuated from their mother churches in Europe over issues as wide-ranging as state politics, liturgy, language, and internal governance. It has provided space for Puritan, Quaker, and Anabaptist congregations that were frequently persecuted or, at best, tolerated on the fringes of Christianity in Europe, but which have been warmly embraced as vibrant countercultural voices within the American context without fear of persecution.

Before the Civil War, the country generated new denominations as older ones split over the issues of segregation (e.g., African Methodist Episcopal Church) or slavery (e.g., Northern and Southern Baptists, Methodists, and Presbyterians). After the war it also gave birth to new churches that for one reason or another were racially bounded, denominations such as the African Methodist Episcopal Zion Church; the Colored, later Christian Methodist Episcopal Church; the National Baptist Convention; and others within the African American community. And during much of the nineteenth century and the beginning of the twentieth century, it produced a flood of Wesleyan-Holiness (e.g., Wesleyan Church, Church of God [Anderson, IN], Free Methodist Church, Church of the Nazarene) and Pentecostal denominations (e.g., Church of God in Christ, Church of God [Cleveland, TN], Assemblies of God, Pentecostal Assemblies of the World), as well as a hoard of independent congregations.

In addition to producing new denominations and congregations, the American context early on provided space to the Presbyterians and Congregationalists to cooperate, first in the Plan of Union in 1801, and again in 1810 through the American Board of Commissioners for Foreign Missions (ABCFM) founded by Congregationalists. Its existence would ultimately lead to the formation of other mission agencies by other denominations as well as concerned individuals in the United States, to become primary exporters of foreign missionaries around the world. Not only did these missionaries bear witness to the gospel, they also transplanted to other parts of the world American culture, emerging

American denominations, and many of the biases and concerns of these groups, taking division and, at times, a compromised witness with them.

When the Commission on Faith and Order of the NCC decided to undertake a study of the Apostolic Faith, Brother Jeffrey Gros, FSC, was serving as the director of Faith and Order. It was his conviction that because of its unique history and purpose, the Commission on Faith and Order might be able to assemble a table of conversation partners at which a broader range of Christian churches in the United States than those that were members of the NCC could participate. He set about to do just that. Gros worked tirelessly to recruit and include voices in Faith and Order that had not traditionally been heard in earlier ecumenical discussions. He supported the study of the apostolic faith within the Commission's regular meeting schedule, and he encouraged consultations that studied the subject from a variety of vantage points.[4] In the end, the Commission's work led to a series of publications that document its work.[5]

Intersecting with the work done specifically on the apostolic faith as it was expressed in the Nicene-Constantinopolitan Creed right from the beginning was work that was undertaken on the Holy Spirit. It involved previously unheard Pentecostal voices.[6] At first glance, the reasons for this intersection may not be readily apparent. Upon closer examination, however, it becomes less of a mystery. The earliest name that the modern Pentecostal movement took for itself was the "Apostolic Faith movement." The earliest newspaper published by the Movement from a variety of cities was called *The Apostolic Faith*.[7] The byline from the paper was Jude 3 "Contend for the faith that was once for all entrusted to the saints." In its own way, and through the use of a restorationist historiography, early Pentecostals understood themselves as bearing witness not only to what the apostles believed and taught, but also to what the apostles had done. And they believed that it could be done apart from any theory of apostolic succession and apart from the confession of any historic creed. They believed that they had a unique mandate to proclaim the "apostolic faith" as they understood it, that is, to preach and teach what the apostles had preached and taught, and they believed that they were to live "apostolic lives," that is, to live lives marked by personal holiness and as vehicles for God to move with the same kinds of signs and wonders that had been performed through the earliest apostles.[8]

In the earliest publication of Faith and Order on the subject of the apostolic faith in the United States, this intersection was acknowledged, in part, because of the obvious dependence of the modern Pentecostal movement on African American religion.[9] In the initial consultation that featured African American perspectives on the apostolic faith, held in December 1984, participants addressed "the unity, holiness, catholicity, and apostolicity of the Church of Jesus Christ," with the self-understanding that African Americans were marginalized within American society, within American churches, and within the church at large. By doing so, they hoped to make a substantive contribution to the "common expression of the faith."[10] By taking this position they also leveled a powerful critique at the ways that many white Christians in North America and in Europe have interpreted the apostolic faith, ways that have allowed them to oppress Christians of color. Participants made clear their suspicion of any attempt to talk about unity that from the beginning did not take seriously the political, economic, and cultural diversity that is represented by all Christians. They lifted up the vision of unity that is understood solely in "spiritual" terms as particularly onerous because it allows proponents to be dismissive of the tangible realities of inequality between races to be explained as though these inequalities were not related to the issue of Christian unity.[11]

The fact that black folk were frequently given second-class status even in the church meant that the operative understandings of the unity of the church that allowed and encouraged this were inherently racist. The fact that certain perspectives on the unity of the church rested upon presuppositions that they identified as being linked to power, prosperity, and a privileged cultural hegemony clearly indicated the same. They made it obvious that the unity of the church must ultimately include black and white Christians as well as others, in particular Latinos, as equal partners with equally valuable contributions to that unity.[12]

As they turned their attention to the holiness of the church, they bore witness to the fact that the holiness of the church rests upon the work of the Holy Spirit in its midst, but they insisted that the holiness of the church must also manifest itself in works of "justice and liberation."[13] Once again, they brought a stinging criticism of those traditional interpretations of "catholicity" that they viewed as being driven by "Western" norms, norms by which many Africans and African Americans had been deprived of full participation in the life of the church. They repudiated these norms as being heavily influenced by the sins of racism, sexism, and classism that discourage fellowship with many "African Independent church[es] or Black Holiness and Pentecostal denominations, among others in various parts of the world."[14] By building walls between older Christian denominations and these newer expressions of Christianity, they argued, the older denominations were guilty of denying "the catholicity of the Body of Christ."[15]

When it came to the issue of apostolicity, they argued that it does not necessarily rest upon a doctrine of succession of learned clergy, because they were convinced that that which was "apostolic" had been passed down to them even by their "unlearned and ignorant" slave ancestors, who by their deeds even more than by their creeds had demonstrated that they had "fully received and acted upon the faith of the apostles."[16] In fact, each of the traditional marks of the church, they contended, demanded more than a simple confession of faith in words. They demanded actions that were consonant with those words, actions that many Christians had failed to embody.

Participants in the "Black Witness to the Apostolic Faith" consultation noted a number of contributions that Africans and African Americans could make to the larger discussion of the apostolic faith. Among those contributions was the value of its witness or testimony from the "margins" of the church, from those who had been oppressed. And why not, for Jesus had himself been the "Oppressed One of God."[17] Participants pointed to the strong affinities that they shared with many Christians from the developing world, and they offered their own observations on life at the margins as providing a lens on these larger constituencies that had also been oppressed through some interpretations of the apostolic faith. They also noted the substantial contribution that African Americans had made to the birth, life, and worship of Pentecostal churches that had largely gone unacknowledged in the past, and they criticized those white Pentecostals who denied the role played by African Americans in their origins.

Coming on the heels of this important consultation was a second one held at Fuller Theological Seminary in October 1986. It was remarkable for a number of reasons, not the least of which was the fact that Evangelicals and the NCC have not always been on the best of terms with one another. This three-day consultation was intended to focus upon the subject of "Confessing the Apostolic Faith from the Perspective of the Pentecostal Churches," and right from the start the nature of the "apostolic faith" confessed by the Pentecostal churches was questioned by some representatives of Faith and Order.[18]

The questions that were raised came, in part, because many Pentecostals view themselves as noncreedal. As a result, their belief systems are not always clearly articulated, leading to questions from those who come from creedal churches. At the same time, it quickly became apparent that any conversation with Pentecostals soon leads to two observations. First, most of the basic statements affirmed in the creed are shared by Pentecostals and other Christians alike. Second, Pentecostals are wary of creeds because sometimes those who "confess" them do not seem to understand what it is that they confess. The confession of a creed, like the recitation of certain prayers, often appears to Pentecostals to be a rote activity without any real meaning. Echoing to some extent a point made in the African American consultation, it was pointed out that for Pentecostals, "Theology, in its written form, has been less important than the evidence of the Spirit in life, worship, and the gifts."[19]

Clearly this consultation did not settle any major issues regarding the nature of the apostolic faith, in part because a number of underlying issues needed to be addressed before turning to the apostolic faith proper. The consultation was an important beginning, however, for discussions between members of the NCC and some of the Pentecostal churches in the United States. These discussions have been fostered in at least two ways by the commission on Faith and Order since that time. First, the consultation pointed out the need for ongoing Pentecostal participation on the commission itself. Since 1984, the commission has continued to include a number of Pentecostal voices. Second, this consultation led to an annual dialogue between Pentecostals and the NCC that lasted for the better part of a decade. The invitation to begin such a dialogue came from Claire Randall, who had served as the general secretary of the NCC from 1974 through 1984.[20] That invitation and the ensuing discussion resulted in a recommendation from the consultation that further consultations be held between Pentecostals and the Commission on Faith and Order.[21]

During the same years in which the work of these two consultations was published, the Commission on Faith and Order began its own internal work on the subject of "Apostolic Faith in America." It did so by forming two groups that would work together between 1984 and 1987. One of them would work specifically on questions of the American context while the other would study the dimensions of what constituted the "apostolic faith" in America. The result of their work was subsequently published under the title *Apostolic Faith in America*.[22]

Geoffrey Wainwright wrote the foreword to this volume. He outlined four contributions that the churches of the United States had made. First, he described them as a "sampler" of all previous attempts at organizing and expressing Christian faith. Second, he argued that any vision of unity that they might yet demonstrate would likely not be limited to those so far envisioned within the European context. Third, he noted that American Christians were a pragmatic people, thereby ensuring that their focus on the "apostolic faith" would not "remain at the level of words to the exclusion of deeds."[23] Fourth, he pointed to the particularly participatory nature of Christianity in the United States with its unique emphasis upon the local congregation. In the end, he called for local involvement in the apostolic faith process that the Commission on Faith and Order was undertaking, but he urged the churches of the United States to see themselves as standing within a global conversation on the subject in order to counter any temptation to become either isolationist or triumphalist.[24]

Like Wainwright, Thaddeus Horgan pointed to the significance of what he called the "lived fidelity" to the gospel that stood behind so much of the division and the missionary effort sponsored by the various Christian churches in the United States.[25] He lifted up the unique context of North America, in which most churches had broken with the European context or had emerged within the American context, leading to no living memory or no vital sense of a historical link with a European past. Even the tensions that exist between the Catholic Church in the United States and the Catholic Church in Rome had arisen due to the unique context of the United States.[26] Similarly, the missionary enterprise, first from North America to Latin America and the Caribbean and later to Europe itself, had come as a result of breaks between American churches and European ones, with direct implications for the notion of apostolicity.

The complexity of the American context, including over three hundred Christian denominations, many of which have a distinctive American history, was set forth in several papers. Attention was called to the immigrant character and a resulting pluralistic character of the nation that includes many of its churches old and new. When placed alongside the facts that no denomination in the United States is established; that immigration plays a continuing role in its churches; that some churches have shaped the American ethos and culture while others have been more profoundly shaped by America's ethos and culture; and still others have provided countercultural critiques of America's ethos and culture; that recent decades have seen the rise of unique forms of civil religion; that there has been a blurring of denominational lines alongside the softening of commitments to institutional religion and the quest for individualistic spirituality; and that there have been rising levels of materialism in the ranks of some churches that have touched their theology, the complexity of the American situation became much clearer.[27]

During this study, the notion of what constitutes the "apostolic faith" was dominated by discussions on the nature of apostolicity itself. Many of the historic churches in the United States, Catholic, Orthodox, and Protestant, reiterated the claim that the apostolic faith is tied directly to the notion of apostolic succession. Apostolic succession was, in turn, viewed primarily as being "fidelity to the apostolic proclamation and mission" that stands in continuity with the first apostles and is assured by this succession.[28] While these churches criticize the Reformation cry of *sola scriptura* as being inadequate to cover the truth claimed by tradition, James Jorgenson observed that virtually all Christians confess what he called the "nucleus" of the apostolic faith: "belief in the Triune God, the incarnation of the Son of God, his death and resurrection, and our salvation through faith in Him."[29]

A review of various documents inspired by the World Council of Churches led George Vandervelde to observe that in these documents the notion of apostolicity lay as a "dynamic reality" at the heart of the church and that it provides the identity of the many Christian churches which exist in "pluriformity." Yet in the end, he explained, the "fundamental criterion (*norma normans*)" of apostolicity resides in contemporary reflections of the apostolic faith to stand in agreement with the testimony of the apostles to God's revelation in Jesus Christ as recorded in the Scriptures.[30]

Donald W. Dayton developed a threefold typology of ways that the idea of apostolicity gets lived out in American churches. What he called the *tradition*-based model typical of the "Ancient" churches emphasizes the "continuity of ministry, sacraments, and perhaps teaching with [that of] the apostles," each of which plays a role in the equally important doctrine of ecclesiology. The second group, what he described as churches that embraced a *teaching*-based model, includes churches that also emphasize continuity with the apostles, but instead of appealing to the notion of apostolic succession to safeguard their apostolicity, they find the safeguard to apostolicity in specific doctrines and confessional formulations, what they would describe as the "truth" of the gospel. These churches he identified among certain Lutheran and Reformed groups of the magisterial Reformation. He also identified a third group of American churches as being primarily *praxis*-based, that is, Methodist, Anabaptist, and Restorationist, including Pentecostal, churches that attempt to root their ethics and practice in the apostolic practice.[31]

Two other members of Faith and Order developed other typologies. Quaker Dean Friday wrote on what he called "Orthochristianity," while distinguishing between denominations typified by such things as "Orthopraxis on Christ's Model" (Anabaptists/Mennonites), "Covenanting Together to Walk in God's Way" (Baptists), "Orthopresence and Orthotaxis" (Quakers), "Orthopeira—Orthoexperience" (Methodists), and "Orthopraxis and 'Open Membership'" (Church of God, Anderson, IN). At the same time, Clyde Steckel, of the United Church of Christ, contributed thoughts on the African Methodist Episcopal Zion Church, the Assemblies of God, the Episcopal Church, and the United Church of Christ that were focused on the "Christological accents" that they brought to bear on the subject.[32]

In the end, the commission noted that while there was considerable diversity in how the various denominations within the American context expressed the apostolic faith, all of them shared at least four major components. First, they shared a common confession that "Jesus Christ is God and Savior." Second, they trusted in the "guidance and inspiration of the Holy Spirit." Third, they affirmed the "authoritative witness of the Scriptures." Fourth, all Christian confessional bodies that were subjects of this study were communal. They understood the church as "the Body of Christ, God's sacramental blessing in the world, a community of prayer, preaching, healing, and teaching."[33]

In spite of all the diversity that emerged both in the denominations that were part of this study and the factors contributing to the complex context that makes up the United States of America, participants in this study recommended that all churches embrace or at least study further the Nicene Creed as an ancient and "still regulative summary of the apostolic witness."[34] Furthermore, they recommended the development of a commentary on the creed that took seriously the gains of the sixteenth-century Reformation in the field of soteriology as well as the insights of holiness, sanctification, justice, and liberation. And finally, they recommended that while a number of typologies had been studied, they believed that there were yet more, the study of which could strengthen the unity of American denominations and bring them closer to a time of common confession regarding their "apostolic unity in ancient and contemporary expressions."[35]

While work had begun on the "Apostolic Faith in America Study," a related strand of Faith and Order's work was picked up in another consultation. This one, convened on the campus of Holy Cross Seminary in Brookline, MA, in October 1985 was focused on the Holy Spirit. Mark Heim set the stage with the observation that this discussion was part of the broader "contemporary search of the churches for unity in the trinitarian apostolic faith."[36] At the same time, the Klingenthal Memorandum, having much to do with the difficult insertion of the "*filioque* clause" into the Nicene-Constantinopolitan Creed, had only recently (1979) been completed. As a result of the work on that document, with the aid of the Orthodox and Catholics alike, with Holiness and Pentecostal voices only recently come to the Faith and Order table, and the insights of feminists and those calling for greater understanding of the role of the Holy Spirit in the world, it seemed time to look at the Holy Spirit in recent discussions of the apostolic faith. It was the explicit intention of consultation organizers that participants address "issues in the creed which divide East and West on the subject of the Spirit."[37]

Several of the papers, therefore, focused intentionally on the creed. Others gave insight into the ways the Holy Spirit was understood within specific traditions, notably, Lutheran, Presbyterian, Methodist, Holiness, Church of the Brethren, and Pentecostal. In the end, those responsible for listening to the various papers and resulting exchanges noted three major areas of concern: (1) the issue of the *filioque*, (2) the naming of God, and (3) "the dynamic polarity between apostolic doctrine (creed) and apostolic life (experience)."[38]

Issues surrounding the use of *filioque*—that is, the term inserted into the Nicene Creed intended to indicate procession of the Holy Spirit from both the Father and the Son—took substantial energy in the consultation as contributors of the Catholic and Orthodox positions made their cases. The Catholic position viewed the addition of the "*filioque* clause" as a protection against the threat of Arian subordinationism, while the Orthodox argued that the term *perichoresis*, referring to a mutual indwelling between the members of the Trinity, was sufficient to guarantee equal glorification and worship of all members of the Trinity. For the Orthodox, the addition of *filioque* to the creed undermined their understanding of the monarchy of God.

At the time of this consultation, the feminist movement was at its peak in the United States. As a result, part of the discussion of the Trinity revolved around how the church should speak about God—that is, were there other ways than traditional patriarchal ways that could be used to address God? Arguments were given for analogical and antianalogical ways of naming God. The point was made that the doctrine of the *imago Dei* is of necessity analogical because of the creator/creature relationship, but that "gender categories constitute only one kind of language regarding the *imago Dei*."[39] While it was noted that the *imago Dei* is the *imago Trinitatis*, it was also observed that language regarding God need not be sexual. Discussions around the naming of God as representing such things as "persons," "activities," "functions," and "relationships" ultimately made little headway. In the end, it was noted that "all theological language is provisional and a mere human attempt to grasp the mystery. While formed and informed by tradition, theological language is also shaped by context." In the end, participants agreed that the discernment of which names had been inspired by the Holy Spirit and which ones had not stood at the core of the debate.[40]

In a sense, the third issue debated in this consultation, the relationship between "Creed and Experience," was a discussion between the ancient churches and many of the newer ones, especially of the Pentecostal and Charismatic variety. While most participants were somewhat uncomfortable with too much attention being given to the notion of experience, they did affirm the legitimacy of both personal and ecclesial experience as they spoke about experiencing the Spirit. Participants from the ancient churches were helped when they learned that while many noncreedal churches view their experience of the Holy Spirit as more important than what they understand as the sectarian and formalistic character of creedal confessions, these noncreedal churches have often developed their own theological culture and statements of faith that affirm much historic creedal content, and in the end, their intention is to "affirm . . . shared faith in the Spirit."[41] By noting this important point, the discussion seemed to take up some of the concerns of the earlier consultations on the "Black Witness to the Apostolic Faith" and "Confessing the Apostolic Faith from the Perspective of the Pentecostal Churches."

Noting that many Holiness Christians, Pentecostals, and one can also add here African American Christians have come from among marginal and disadvantaged people, participants queried whether the older churches, often composed of people from very different classes of people, had been fair in their "theological and ecumenical" assessment to the experiential claims of the newer churches.[42] From the perspective of the newer churches, faith and experience are viewed as necessarily interrelated. The point was made that the emergence of charismatic renewal in many churches had "added to the quality of that church's spiritual experience," while the renewal had challenged the nature of the church's spiritual formation.[43] This challenge was left for the churches to consider.

The question of the role of the *filioque* clause also came up as impatience was expressed over the continuing debate. Gerald Sheppard, at that time a minister of the Church of God in Christ, observed that the entire debate surrounding the inclusion or exclusion of the *filioque* clause reminded him of a fight between a set of separated parents. It didn't trouble him which way the Eastern and Western churches finally resolved the issue, for Pentecostal churches had only made "passing notice" of the issue.[44] The problem was that in the dispute between the ancient churches over a seemingly philosophical issue, the concerns of the younger churches (e.g., Is there anything experiential at stake in this debate?), the offspring of these older churches, were being ignored. They had not been part of this debate between their parents, but they felt that they were being pushed to choose sides and it wasn't very comfortable to be placed in that position. As a result, participants urged the Catholics and the Orthodox to do their utmost to end this millennium-long dispute.

In the end, participants in the consultation encouraged wider reception of the Klingenthal Memorandum and asserted that the churches of the East and West hold much more in common with one another regarding their Trinitarian faith than what divides them. The consultation also encouraged as an "interim" solution to the *filioque* question, the liturgical use of the Creed as it appeared prior to the addition of the *filioque* clause.[45]

The challenges that Pentecostal and Charismatic congregations posed in the meeting were not ignored. The danger of demonizing another's tradition through the use of caricature was lifted up as was the counterpart of idealizing one's own. Members of the older churches encouraged Pentecostals to expand their understanding of experience and to share with the older churches something of their wisdom of the discernment process by which experience is normed. In the end, the consultation acknowledged the importance of these churches for any future theological or ecumenical discussion to be complete.[46]

In 1988 the Commission on Faith and Order saw the publication of a small but very helpful study guide to the Nicene-

Constantinopolitan creed.[47] In some ways it was a direct, initial response to a request that had been issued by the World Council of Churches for help in preparing people in local congregations to understand the creed. This volume was designed to be studied, preferably by an ecumenical collection of Christians at the local level, in one- or two-hour segments over several weeks. It contained a copy of the creed, a short preface that outlined its use and purpose, and five chapters, including the introduction that set forth four main reasons that various churches use the creed: profession of faith, witness, worship, and safeguarding sound belief.

The introduction was followed by a historical and theological chapter that outlined how the creed came into existence, followed by three chapters laid out in the same Trinitarian schema employed in the creed itself. At the end of each of these chapters, several questions can be used for discussion purposes. The volume concluded with an afterword that provides a brief overview of the vision of Faith and Order for the unity of the church, and three pages of resources for those who might desire to undertake further personal study on the topic. While it provided a useful tool for local congregations and study groups, it seems to have had little effect on any subsequent work of the Commission on Faith and Order.

At the same time that copies of *Confessing One Faith* were distributed to members of the commission, a new program of studies was authorized that continued the work on the apostolic faith through two additional studies. "Toward the Common Expression of the Apostolic Faith Study: History Study" found expression in two ways. One was an October 1989 consultation on the fourth century titled "Faith to Creed," convened in Waltham, MA. The papers presented there were subsequently published in a volume with that same title.[48] The other came as a result of a working group whose work resulted in a book later published under the title *Telling the Churches' Stories: Ecumenical Perspectives on Writing Christian History*.[49]

The focus on the fourth century envisioned by consultation organizers explicitly brought participants into contact with the Nicene Creed. This consultation was important for several reasons. The work of the World Council of Churches, now shadowed in its own unique way by the work of the NCC, seemed to suggest that if a common expression of faith that all churches could confess were to be found, it would most readily reside in the Nicene Creed. More importantly, given the experience of the churches within the American context, it was clear that the ancient churches as well as some of the Reformation churches now at home on American soil were very interested in pursuing this line of reasoning as more or less normative for the whole church.

Other churches in the American context were not so enthusiastic about the prospect. In particular, some of them (e.g., certain Baptists, Anabaptists, Mennonites, and Pentecostals) embrace what is sometimes labeled a "Constantinian" or "post-Constantinian fall" of the church. They believe that the churches of both East and West went into spiritual decline about the time that "Christendom" or the alliance of church with state became a reality. As a result, they have been generally suspicious of the value of creeds, and for some of them, of this creed in particular. Rather than seeing creeds as instruments that facilitated unity, some of these churches had viewed creeds and in some cases even experienced creeds as instruments of separation, persecution, and exclusion.[50]

The question of historical perceptions regarding the reading of a spiritual decline that followed the recognition of the church by Constantine, whether this alleged decline lay at the feet of the church or at the feet of the Roman *imperium,* quickly became a matter of debate. In spite of the sometimes spirited discussion on this subject, the issue was left unresolved.[51] It seems to have been the most divisive issue faced by the consultation, and it clearly points to the need for further work to be done on the healing of historical memories and understanding history ecumenically.

While most of the participants in this discussion clearly favored the use of the Nicene Creed as a common expression of the apostolic faith, voices from a number of younger churches, most dating from the Reformation period or shortly thereafter, were also heard. In addition to the questions of church and state, others were raised by these younger churches regarding the ethical dimensions of the creed.[52]

As a result of these discussions, participants pointed out two facts that are not always acknowledged. First, when judging the Nicene Creed, it is important to place it in its fourth-century context. The creed should be allowed to speak from the rich and complex context of that time, and it should not be judged on the basis of a later context. Second, present-day questions and issues that have arisen within specific traditions that came into existence later should not be read back into the fourth century. These questions may illuminate certain realities from later experience, but they may unfairly judge the intentions of the framers of the creed in the fourth century, and hence the value of the creed for later generations.[53]

Finally, participants in the consultation concluded that there were a number of issues left undone in their work. They lamented the fact that for whatever reason, there were no Pentecostal or historic African American voices in the consultation. Clearly, their absence impoverished the discussion to some extent, though some important insights that would have had a bearing on the subject of this particular consultation within these two traditions are available in the earlier studies of the apostolic faith project conducted by the Commission on Faith and Order from at least 1984.

An equally important omission from this discussion was any discussion of the status that the creed has come to hold within many churches as "unique and authoritative." What was the process by which that came to be? What role did discernment play in this process? A related study might reflect on the normative character of the creed as it is used within the various traditions that appeal to it. What participants did note was the fact that the Nicene-Constantinopolitan Creed succeeded in bringing them together around issues of primary importance to their Christian faith and walk, as well as to the recognition that they all hold much in common with one another when it comes to the question of the apostolic faith.

Finally, "Toward the Common Expression of the Apostolic Faith Today" also found its expression in an ongoing working group of the commission beginning in 1988. The publication of the papers produced for discussion in these sessions was slow in coming.[54] The working group was explicit about its work standing in continuity with earlier studies in the apostolic faith study process, most notably with the *Apostolic Faith in America* and the *Black Witness to the Apostolic Faith* projects. What brought many of this group together was a question. Throughout the apostolic faith study process, many of them had become close friends who accepted one another as being fully Christian and as "valued and valid members of the Body of Christ."[55] At the same time they also recognized that the denominations in which some of them held membership refused to recognize the value and validity of other denominations in which some of them held membership. "How could this be?" they asked. Would it be possible for the discerning process that went on between individuals to be applied in a similar way between churches? Would this be a way to contribute to the visible unity of the church?

In a sense, this project attempted to build on the two interests of Faith and Order from the early 1980s extending into the first half of the 1990s, namely, the apostolic faith and Holy Spirit studies. As they approached the different means by which their respective denominations tended to define the apostolic faith or assess whether the apostolic faith claimed by their denomination was to be found in the claims of other denominations, the working group kept arriving at dead ends. What they realized, however, was that all of the denominations represented in the working group recognized the action of the Holy Spirit in the faith and worship of their denominations. The question was, "How could it be recognized in the others?" Could the exploration of the presence and work of the Holy Spirit in their respective denominations provide a way forward? Not only might this prove to be a valuable tool in the quest for visible Christian unity, but the group also came to believe that its work on the Third Person of the Trinity might contribute something substantial to the lacuna left by the already substantive discussions on theology (God) and on Christology that tended to dominate so many other ecumenical agendas.[56]

The process by which this working group went about conducting its inquiry included a number of papers that were repeatedly critiqued and revised as they were studied from the viewpoint of the various denominations and traditions represented in the group. In the end, the editors affirmed, "We have come to recognize more fully that essential to apostolic faith and our common confession of and witness to it is a fuller and deeper life in the Spirit."[57]

With Scripture as its starting point, the working group studied the person and work of the Holy Spirit before moving on to various ecclesiological questions. Thaddeus Horgan, who died quite suddenly midway into this study, wrote the paper that gave much shape to the work that followed. The charism of the discernment of spirits and the more generalized understanding of processes associated with the exercise of discernment both within and outside the church were then explored, laying groundwork for others. The work of the Spirit was discussed as it is manifested in worship and liturgy; the proclamation of the gospel, the formation and forms of the church, and the Spirit in the ministry, as well as the mission and service of the church, all became part of this project.

A number of points became apparent as the working group went about its tasks. First, Scripture was clearly the starting point, the standard or norm by which all of the traditions entered into the discussion. Second, the role of the Holy Spirit in guiding the churches became equally apparent. Third, the discerning process received considerable attention throughout these studies, both as a discrete study and as part of other studies. Thus, it was necessary for the group to work toward a common understanding of the meaning and practice of discernment within the whole Christian tradition. Fourth, the working group made repeated reference to earlier studies on the apostolic faith, and lifted up the potential contribution of Pentecostals and the black witness to the apostolic faith in particular.[58] Finally, while the work of this group was launched by the larger discussion on the nature of the apostolic faith, its primary contribution seems to have been on the presence and work of the Holy Spirit throughout the Christian community that underlies the Apostolic Faith, for in the end, no one is able to confess that "Jesus is Lord except by the Spirit" (1 Cor. 12:1).

CONCLUSIONS

As we celebrate the fiftieth anniversary of Faith and Order in the United States it is only appropriate to ask what the various studies of the apostolic faith have accomplished in the larger discussion regarding the visible unity of the church. It is safe to say that one note needs to be made before that question is answered. It is to acknowledge the enormous role that was played by the director of Faith and Order at that time, Brother Jeffrey Gros, FSC. Jeff spent countless hours recruiting, training, empowering, and overseeing scores of newer and younger ecumenists in as broad a configuration of the ecumenical table as he could spread at the time. His contribution to the apostolic faith studies was huge, and it needs to be acknowledged as such. That being said, it is also important to acknowledge the number of publications that came into being as a result of various studies along these lines. I do not know of another study or set of studies from Faith and Order that has produced as many books and articles as did these studies on the apostolic faith.

The question of what these studies accomplished is probably as complex as the American context in which they were conducted. The broadening of the ecumenical table in Faith and Order came, in large part, with the decision to pursue studies on the apostolic faith. New to the table were representatives of both Holiness (with the exception of the Church of God [Anderson, IN] which had been represented in Faith and Order for some years) and Pentecostal traditions that had not previously engaged in ecumenical discussion. By focusing on the nature of a common confession, even the Nicene-Constantinopolitan Creed, it brought a range of churches into conversation with one another over mutual doctrinal concerns. At the same time, it provided opportunity for open discussion on where various parties differed on the issue of the apostolic faith.

The focus on the Apostolic Faith also made it possible for a new set of discussions within the NCC. It was within the American context that the Pentecostal movement had arguably made its most significant appearance. At the same time, this study made possible a new discussion on the third article of the creed, that having to do with the Holy Spirit, to be undertaken with partners who felt at home talking about the Holy Spirit. The consultation, "Pentecostals and the Apostolic Faith," held at Fuller Theological Seminary in 1986 was a watershed of sorts. It was the first time that Faith and Order had been hosted by an Evangelical organization, and it was the first time that Faith and Order had an in-depth conversation with a variety of Pentecostals. In the end, it made possible the series of "Pentecostal–National Council of Churches Conversations" that ran from 1988 through 1997.[59]

In all the discussions on the apostolic faith, and in a number of the discussions that focused either on the Pentecostal contributions or on the Holy Spirit, considerable emphasis was placed upon the Nicene-Constantinopolitan Creed. This may have been necessary, and for many it was even desirable. After all, if everyone could confess a common creed, and this creed seemed to be the desirable one, then perhaps the churches could be thought of as coming closer to accepting one another fully. The pressure from some who simply assumed that this creed should be normative was intense. True, people were mostly always gracious. But in many ways, even though resistance to the ways the creed had traditionally been interpreted (e.g., African American churches), or resistance to the ways that creeds had been used to silence dissidents in times past (e.g., Anabaptists), or resistance to the limitations that some traditions saw in the use of creeds at all (e.g., Holiness and Pentecostals) were expressed and even noted, in the end they seem to have been ignored. Most discussions of the apostolic faith seem still to be focused on a common confession of faith, notably the Nicene-Constantinopolitan Creed.

In the end, it may be that this position can and should be the position that all churches will embrace, but it should not be undertaken at the expense of any churches. Until everyone involved in the discussion agrees that the questions, criticisms, and fears have been genuinely acknowledged and addressed, the pressure to accept a common creed will continue to be experienced as an imposition by force that values some churches over others. For the sake of the unity of the whole church, Faith and Order cannot afford to allow this to happen. Still, we may rightfully look back on the decade between 1985 and 1995 during which most of these studies in Faith and Order took place in the United States as one of the richest decades in the past half century of its work.

NOTES

1. *Baptism, Eucharist, and Ministry,* Faith and Order Paper no. 111 (Geneva: World Council of Churches, 1982).
2. Ibid., x.
3. *Confessing the One Faith: An Ecumenical Explication of the Apostolic Faith as It Is Confessed in the Nicene-Constantinopolitan Creed (381),* Faith and Order Paper no. 153 (Geneva: WCC

Publications, 1991), 139. The Commission on Faith and Order of the National Council of Churches (NCC) had already produced a booklet titled *Confessing One Faith: The Origins, Meaning and Use of the Nicene Creed: Grounds for Common Witness* (Cincinnati: Forward Movement Publications, 1988), 68, for use in ecumenical small groups.

4. Several consultations related to the apostolic faith study were sponsored by the Commission on Faith and Order of the NCC, in addition to the ones that are mentioned in the body of this paper. For a list of them, see S. Mark Heim, "The Holy Spirit Consultation: An Introduction," in *Spirit of Truth: Ecumenical Perspectives on the Holy Spirit*, Faith & Order/USA, ed. Theodore Stylianopoulos and S. Mark Heim (Brookline, MA: Holy Cross Orthodox Press, 1986), 2.

5. David T. Shannon and Gayraud S. Wilmore, eds., *Black Witness to the Apostolic Faith*, Faith & Order/USA (Grand Rapids, MI: Eerdmans, 1985); Thaddeus D. Horgan, *Apostolic Faith in America,* Faith & Order/USA (Grand Rapids, MI: Eerdmans Publishing Company, 1988); S. Mark Heim, ed., *Faith to Creed: Ecumenical Perspectives on the Affirmation of the Apostolic Faith in the Fourth Century, Papers of the Faith to Creed Consultation Commission on Faith and Order NCCCUSA, October 25–27, 1989— Waltham, Massachusetts*, Faith & Order/USA (Grand Rapids, MI: Eerdmans, 1991), 206.

6. Sylianopoulos and Heim, *Spirit of Truth*; *Pneuma: The Journal of the Society for Pentecostal Studies* 9, no. 1 (1987), published a number of the papers that were given at the October 22–24, 1986, consultation on Pentecostals and the apostolic faith at Fuller Theological Seminary in Pasadena, California. This issue of *Pneuma* was subsequently published under the title *Confessing the Apostolic Faith: Pentecostal Churches and the Ecumenical Movement* (Pasadena, CA: Society for Pentecostal Studies, 1987). The articles in these volumes were also published in *One in Christ* 23 (1987), and William R. Barr and Rena M. Yocom, eds., *The Church in the Movement of the Spirit* (Grand Rapids, MI: Eerdmans, 1994).

7. *The Apostolic Faith* was initially published by Charles F. Parham, who played a significant role in the early years of the Pentecostal movement. He published a newspaper from Melrose, Kansas, and then Houston, Texas, and finally from Baxter Springs,

Kansas, where he established his own denomination and named it "The Apostolic Faith." When the famous Azusa Street Mission distanced itself from any relationship with Charles Parham and was incorporated in California under the leadership of William J. Seymour, it did so as the Apostolic Faith Mission. Beginning in September 1906, it published a newspaper called *The Apostolic Faith* through the summer of 1909. In 1908 Florence Crawford broke with Azusa Street and established a new denomination in Portland, Oregon, once again naming it the Apostolic Faith Mission of Portland, OR. She attracted the primary editor of Seymour's paper to join her in Portland, and from 1909 they published *The Apostolic Faith* from that city.

8. On this, see Cecil M. Robeck Jr., "The Holy Spirit and the Unity of the Church: The Challenge of Pentecostal, Charismatic, and Independent Movements," in *The Holy Spirit, the Church and Christian Unity: Proceedings of the Consultation Held at the Monastery of Bose, Italy (14–20 October 2002)*, *BETL* 181, ed. D. Donnelly, A. Denaux, and J. Famerée (Leuven, Belgium: Leuven University Press, 2005), 353–81.

9. Gayraud Wilmore and David Shannon, "Introduction," in Shannon and Wilmore, *Black Witness to the Apostolic Faith*, iv. On the relationship between African American religion and the emergence of Pentecostalism see Cecil M. Robeck Jr., *The Azusa Street Mission and Revival: The Birth of the Global Pentecostal Movement* (Nashville: Thomas Nelson, 2006).

10. "Toward a Common Expression of Faith: A Black North American Perspective," in Shannon and Wilmore, *Black Witness to the Apostolic Faith*, 64.

11. Ibid., 65.

12. Ibid., 6.

13. Ibid., 67.

14. Ibid., 68.

15. Ibid.

16. Ibid., 69.

17. Ibid., 64.

18. Most of the papers from this conference were published in *Pneuma: The Journal of the Society for Pentecostal Studies* 9, no. 1 (1987). They were also published as a separate volume for the National Council of Churches under the title *Confessing the*

Apostolic Faith. Many of the papers were also published in *One in Christ* 23 (1987). On this particular point, see Jeffrey Gros, FSC, "Confessing the Apostolic Faith from the Perspective of the Pentecostal Churches, *Pneuma: The Journal of the Society for Pentecostal Studies* 9, no. 1 (1987): 8–10.

19. Gros, "Confessing the Apostolic Faith from the Perspective of the Pentecostal Churches," 8.

20. Claire Randall, "The Importance of the Pentecostal and Holiness Churches in the Ecumenical Movement," *Pneuma: The Journal of the Society for Pentecostal Studies* 9, no. 1 (1987): 50.

21. Thaddeus Horgan, "Consultation Summary: A Conciliar Perspective," *Pneuma: The Journal of the Society for Pentecostal Studies* 9, no. 1 (1987): 102. This dialogue began in October 1988 (St. Louis, MO), and continued in November 1989 (Fresno, CA), October 1990 (Louisville, KY), November 1991 (Lakeland, FL), October 1995 (Hartford, CT), March 1996 (Pasadena, CA), and March 1997 (Oakland, CA). While it had been the intention of the dialogue partners to publish a volume of their papers and findings in the Faith & Order/USA series, the decision was made by the new director of Faith and Order at the Oakland meeting not to pursue the dialogue or this publication any further.

22. Thaddeus D. Horgan, ed., *Apostolic Faith in America* (Grand Rapids, MI: Eerdmans, 1988), 68.

23. Geoffrey Wainwright, "Foreword," in Horgan, *Apostolic Faith in America*, viii.

24. Ibid., ix.

25. Thaddeus Daniel Horgan, "Introduction: Confessing the Apostolic Faith," in Horgan, *Apostolic Faith in America*, xi.

26. One need only think of the work of James Cardinal Gibbons of Baltimore, MD, who argued for an indigenous expression of Roman Catholicism in the United States and the counter concern for what Pope Leo IX called "Americanism" in his 1899 encyclical *Testum benevolentia*, to understand the substantive differences that seemed to separate American Catholics from European Catholics.

27. See Thaddeus Horgan, SA, and Thomas Hoyt Jr., "Characteristics of the American Context," in Horgan, *Apostolic Faith in America*, 7–13, and Donald W. Dayton, "Reflections on Apostolicity in the North American Context," in Horgan, *Apostolic Faith in America*, 28–29.

28. James Jorgenson, "Apostolicity in the Roman Catholic, Eastern Orthodox, Lutheran, and Reformed Traditions," in Horgan, *Apostolic Faith in America*, 16.

29. Ibid., 18.

30. George Vandervelde, "The Meaning of 'Apostolic Faith' in World Council of Churches' Documents," in Horgan, *Apostolic Faith in America*, 25.

31. Dayton, "Reflections on Apostolicity in the North American Context," 31–33.

32. Dean Friday, "Apostolicity and Orthochristianity," in Horgan, *Apostolic Faith in America*, 34–52, and Clyde Steckel, "The Apostolic Faith in the African Methodist Episcopal Zion Church, Assemblies of God, the Episcopal Church, and the United Church of Christ," in Horgan, *Apostolic Faith in America*, 53–58.

33. "Dimensions of Apostolicity," in Horgan, ed., *Apostolic Faith in America*, 60–63.

34. Ibid., 67.

35. Ibid., 68.

36. Heim, "The Holy Spirit Consultation: An Introduction," in Stylianopoulos and Heim, *Spirit of Truth: Ecumenical Perspectives on the Holy Spirit*, 1.

37. Lloyd G. Patterson, "The Spirit, The Creed, and Christian Unity," in Stylianopoulos and Heim, *Spirit of Truth*, 5.

38. Heim, "The Holy Spirit Consultation: A Summary Statement," in Stylianopoulos and Heim, *Spirit of Truth,* 188.

39. Ibid., 191.

40. Ibid., 192.

41. Ibid., 193.

42. Ibid.

43. Ibid.

44. Gerald T. Sheppard, "The Nicene Creed, Filioque, and Pentecostal Movements in the United States," in Stylianopoulos and Heim, *Spirit of Truth: Ecumenical Perspectives on the Holy Spirit*, 179.

45. "The Holy Spirit Consultation: A Summary Statement," in Stylianopoulos and Heim, *Spirit of Truth: Ecumenical Perspectives on the Holy Spirit*, 195.

46. Ibid., 197.

47. *Confessing One Faith*, 68.

48. Heim, *Faith to Creed,* 206.

49. Timothy J. Wengert and Charles W. Brockwell Jr., *Telling the Churches' Stories: Ecumenical Perspectives on Writing Christian History* (Grand Rapids, MI: Eerdmans, 1995), 134. This volume will not be discussed in this paper because it ultimately focused less on the apostolic faith discussion and more on issues that originally stemmed from that discussion regarding whether it is possible to write Christian history from an ecumenical perspective.

50. Heim, "Introduction," in Heim, *Faith to Creed,* xvii.

51. "Faith to Creed Consultation: Summary Statement," in ibid., 200–201.

52. Ibid., 201.

53. Ibid., 200–202.

54. Barr and Yocom, *The Church in the Movement of the Spirit,* 136.

55. Clyde J. Steckel and Robert E. Hood, "Preface," in ibid., x. In the introduction to this volume, the editors raised a similar question. "Why is it that Christians often find it much easier to see and affirm the Spirit at work in the lives of individual persons than in the denominations and traditions to which these persons belong and in which they have been nurtured and shaped? See Barr and Yocom, "Introduction," in ibid., 2.

56. Steckel and Hood, "Preface," in ibid., x.

57. Barr and Yocom, "Introduction," in ibid., 5.

58. Ibid., 2, n. 2; Cecil M. Robeck Jr., "Discerning the Spirit in the Life of the Church," in ibid., 29–49; George Vandervelde and William R. Barr, "The Spirit in the Proclamation of the Church," in ibid., 82, n. 5; and Tom Hoyt Jr. and Clyde Steckel, "The Spirit in the Mission and Service of the Church," in ibid., 123–36.

59. The background and goals of these conversations were spelled under "Other Projects" in *Program of Studies 1988–1991 of the Commission on Faith & Order* (New York: Commission on Faith & Order/NCCCUSA, n.d.), 15–16.

Chapter 5

EVALUATING FAITH AND ORDER'S PUBLISHING RECORD: THE *PERICHORESIS* OF TEXTS AND CONTEXTS

Joseph A. Loya, OSA

The initial words here are devoted to a few notes about my church affiliation and the title of my presentation. I am a Byzantine Catholic, a member of a church *sui iuris* of Metropolitan rank that worships in accordance with the Byzantine Rite as one of twenty-two autonomous churches in communion with the Bishop of Rome.[1] I appreciate being afforded the opportunity to contribute to this event in this particular way. I also appreciate the honesty and forthrightness of the conference organizers in informing me that I was not the one they originally imagined to be rendering this service. Fr. Paul Meyendorff was first offered the invitation, but, unfortunately, he was not able to accept. There is great reason for one to pause before consenting to compose, stand, and deliver in the stead of such a distinguished Orthodox ecumenist and scholar. I proceeded to agree in light of a cherished fact of personal history. In 1980 Fr. John Meyendorff agreed to serve as mentor for my PhD in Christian history while at Fordham University. So it is that this presentation is offered, if not by Fr. John's worthy blood son, then at least by one of his (eternally grateful!) academic adoptees.

Oliver Crisp of the University of Bristol elucidates the term *perichoresis* in the history of theology as a kind of theological "black box" employed to condition proper reflection upon, first, the relation of the two natures of Christ and, second, the ontology of the Holy Trinity.[2] Gregory Nazianzen used the term as an aid in the attempt to express the mystery of the hypostatic union.[3] Subsequently, the term appears in John of Damascus's treatment of John 14:10: "Do you not believe that I am in the Father and the Father is in me?"[4] In the Eastern Christian theological tradition the term is associated with the deification process in which the redeemed are drawn into the circulation of divine love and participation in the coinherence of the Divine Persons.[5] *Perichoresis* is employed in this paper to convey the interrelation between published volumes of the Faith and Order Commission of the National Council of Churches of Christ USA on one hand, and post-Oberlin social and ecumenical history to date on the other. One may think here of this summer's cultural exhibition, "Celluloid Skyline: New York and the Movies," set up in the old main waiting room of Grand Central Station. An intended effect of the assembled displays is to demonstrate the manner in which filmmakers' "texts" and the real city itself "feed each other in a never-ending circle."[6] A secondary intent of this presentation is to demonstrate the degree to which Faith and Order publications have served to transmit and amplify the ecumenical voices of the Roman Catholic Church and the churches of the Eastern Christian tradition. The texts subjected to contextualization here are selected mainly, though not exclusively, from the "Resources" list for this conference.

1960s–1970s

Melanie May, in her published 1992 retrospective on this period, referred to the "stormy decade of the 1960s" as a "period in which increasing theological pluralism threatened the ecumenical synthesis of the earlier era."[7] The authors of *Introduction to Ecumenism* write:

> During the 1960s and 1970s the World Council's Faith and Order Commission faced the great task of integrating the variety of Orthodox voices from Eastern Europe, the Roman Catholic members after that Church joined in 1968, the emerging Third World voices with their particular theological concerns, and the increased number of women's voices.... It is during this period that greater attention was given to the contextual method, especially through

such WCC studies as *The Unity of the Church and the Renewal of Human Community* and *The Community of Women and Men in the Church*. Of particular importance were the studies on patristics, authority, and church order. As a result of these studies, and taking account of the rich resources of the bilateral dialogues of this period, the World Council was able to put before the churches a vision of a united church as a Conciliar Fellowship (Koinonia) that is grounded in an understanding of Acts 15 and of the early ecumenical councils.[8]

Forward striding in the areas of human rights and extended inclusion of minorities are also to be noted.[9]

Taking a step back to take in a wider cultural perspective, it is during this period that Clifford Geertz (1926–2006) began establishing himself as the single most influential and controversial cultural anthropologist in the United States, a distinction he would enjoy through three subsequent decades. As one of the world's most significant proponents of cultural, moral, and scientific pluralism,[10] Geertz believed with Max Weber that humans are creatures suspended in webs of significance of their own spinning: "I take culture to be those webs, and the analysis of it to be therefore not an experimental science in search of law but an interpretative one in search of meaning."[11] This aesthetic understanding of culture gained currency across various disciplines, including sociology, political science, history, and literary studies. He sought to find meaning in small-scale observations of simple human interaction—what he called "local knowledge," a title of one of his seventeen books.[12]

The Living Room Dialogues series was a joint effort of the Faith and Order Commission and the Apostolate of Good Will of the Confraternity of Christian Doctrine that began in the late 1960s and continued through the early 1970s. The series was recognized as a new and imaginative initiative that conditioned fruitful grassroots Catholic, Orthodox, and Protestant encounters.[13]

In the initial volume of the series, *Living Room Dialogues: A Guide for Lay Discussion, Catholic-Orthodox-Protestant,*[14] Michael J. Taylor, SJ, pressed the point that the Gospels lead all Christians to a common response with Peter to Jesus' query, "Who do men say that I am?"[15]

John Meyendorff, in his contribution titled "The Liturgy and Orthodoxy," highlighted the traditional Trinitarian character of the Liturgy's canon that reaches its culmination point in the solemn invocation of the Spirit (Epiclesis): the lack of this feature is considered by the Orthodox to be a grave liturgical defect. Meyendorff also pointed out that the Christian East, in adopting Catholic terms to describe sacramental realities to Protestants, did so without adopting the Aristotelian philosophical underpinnings of those terms.[16]

The second volume of 1967, from the same publishers and without Orthodox input, focused in significant part on youth and the future. John J. Kirvan, CSP, registered his observation that the new generation does not easily accept faith life as a heritage, as part of family tradition, or as some kind of manifest destiny. Certain, too, is that while faith is coming to be seen as a personal response, young Catholics need to know that faith's core of truth, while true in all times and places, is at the same time uniquely experienced and differently expressed.[17]

The post–Vatican II National Faith and Order Colloquia, which included Orthodox and Catholic participation, were marked by sharp debate on the question of whether Christians should place emphasis on bringing persons outside the community of faith into the church or on the stimulation of such persons to serve God in their existing situations. This in turn gave rise to further polarity over whether priority should be placed on the task of bringing about personal conversion to Christ as the starting point of all subsequent activity, or give emphasis to the inseparability of personal conversion and obedience in relation to contemporary social issues. Practical realities such as how church agencies would allocate funds depended on clarification of this theological issue.[18] Hence it was decided to devote the 1968 and 1969 Colloquia to an investigation of "Salvation and Man's Life." The materials of the 1968 colloquium were published in a dedicated issue of *Mid-Stream*.[19]

The essentially Protestant concerns that moved colloquia concern from evangelism to soteriology created an opening for the Orthodox participant George S. Bebis of the Greek Orthodox Archdiocese of North and South America to describe the bases of "economic" or "philanthropic" theology. He defines *salvation* as the effect of Christ's triumph over nature, sin, and death, through his incarnation, death, and resurrection. This enables full participation of creatures in the eternal divine glory of the Creator, known as "theosis." The letters of St. Paul and the commentary of the celebrated Byzantine theologian of the fourteenth century, Nicholas Cabasilas, are employed to underscore the idea that salvation "embraces the totality of human experience and the cosmic development of man's behavior."[20] Social involvement is to be seen as "askesis," the "exercise and practical application of Christian love, made for the sake of our perfection."[21] Social involvement itself neither saves nor offers real hope: service to the world should be understood as a "means which can develop our spiritual commitment to Christ and nothing else."[22]

Robert L. Faricy, SJ, concluded his reflection on the individual, societal, and cosmic dimensions of salvation by describing the task of the church as being much broader than conversion, for "the work of the Church is transformation ... of persons, society and the world."[23] The reestablishment of thirteenth-century European Christendom is not to be the object of Christian effort. Rather, the Christian task is "to build up the world in every way in the direction of the final fulfillment when God will intervene, the world will be transformed, Christ will definitively weld the world to himself and hand over the kingdom to the Father, and God will be all in all."[24]

Bernard Cooke's paper called attention to how Christians were only beginning to recover from the anti-Christian "rugged individualism" that marked much so much of the thinking and activity of the past few centuries. He pressed the point that soteriology and Christian anthropology are significantly identical. This fact points to the extent to which "our theological study of salvation must draw from the insights of the behavioral and social sciences which together formulate so much of our contemporary anthropology."[25] This direction should be followed without, of course, allowing "one or other type of human thought—be it psychology, biology, or logic—to become ultimately normative for us in our theological endeavor."[26]

John Cobb's position paper on the meaning of salvation was published in this same edition, as was a response to it authored by students in a Catholic University seminar course. Cobb's paper provided the unnamed students with an opportunity to reflect on the consequential expression "subsist in" in Vatican II's *Lumen Gentium* (Constitution on the Church): "the Church of Jesus Christ subsists ('exists in') the Roman Church, i.e., that the 'quality' of being-Church-of-Christ can be attributed to the Roman Church. What is not said is that only the Roman church can be called the Church of Christ. The Church of Christ exists in the Roman Church but transcends it."[27]

1980s–1990s

The late 1970s begins the time from which Vincent J. Miller began drawing upon resources for his work *Consuming Religion*, a theological consideration of culture as seen through the optic of consumer desire. A few of his main points are here summarized:[28]

- The issue between culture and Christianity is not a matter of opposition. It is not that there is a conflict of goals of desire (for example, the love of God vs. the love of things); rather, issues arise from the "focus and texture of desire." Desire is, surprisingly, not really attachment to things, but about the joys of the desiring itself. Unlike Augustine, we do not experience restlessness, *inquies*, as an anxious discomfort, as a spur to change the way life is lived. The ultimate goal of the spiritual quest for union with God, where all desire and anticipation cease in their absolute fulfillment, seems less than compelling.

- The moments of choice are the fundamental instances of self-actualization. People no longer hunger for salvation or an era of justice, but for "the feeling, the momentary illusion, of personal well being, health, and psychic security"—to quote from Christopher Lasch's 1978 work, *The Culture of Narcissism*. Consumer culture is experienced by most as liberation from the constraints of closed cultures, small communities, and tightly scripted class, gender, and social roles. Each individual is free to pursue his or her own religious synthesis, whether ingenious and inspired, or banal and conforming while global capitalism goes about its business unopposed.

♦ Unlike those of the boomer generation who stressed over the existential conflicts with institutions and organized religion with an all-or-nothing hermeneutic, more recent generations formed by the offerings of the corporate culture industries have little angst about picking and choosing from a tradition's offerings. They are, for that reason, not likely to confront religious authorities or even attempt to engage them.

♦ When we relate to culture and religious traditions as commodities, they lose their power to inform the concrete practice of life. The instrumentalized and commodified self is expressed in a shift of emphases from character to "personality." In the commodification of culture, beliefs and commitments are easily reduced to "a decorative function of providing private meaning." Low commitment to particular institutions and communities can be understood as driven by the seriousness of their searching, leaving communities challenged by questions about their reason for being, their missions, and their methods of accomplishing it.

Within the ecumenical realm, and I speak here as a Catholic ecumenist, the "Baptism, Eucharist and Ministry" convergence statement (1982) was experienced as a Second Great Awakening of ecumenical vitality. *The Search for Visible Unity: Baptism, Eucharist, Ministry*[29] provided for comparison a summary of the reception processes within the churches as reported and discussed by participants in the 1983 Hyde Park (Chicago) Conference on BEM. Included in the summary were descriptions of reactions and responses within the Roman Catholic Church, the Armenian Church of America, the Greek Archdiocese (even though not actually present at the meeting), and the Orthodox Church in America.[30]

An essay by Edward Kilmartin (Roman Catholic) outlined the theology of reception through the ages, concluding with the suggestion—the hope—that churches in the practice of the faith (more than mere assent to crystallized dogmatic formulations) may "be prepared to affirm together the same faith while respecting the diversity of traditions, after the model of the Council of Florence."[31]

Fr. Thomas Hopko, writing for the Orthodox Church in America, raised "questions which are most pertinent to the U.S. environment and opens challenges to the worldwide experience of Orthodoxy from the U.S. context."[32] With reference to specific content, Fr. Hopko judged the Lima statement as a "remarkably successful" consensus statement, to be respected for the inclusive scope of the body of theologians who produced it and lauded as an effective means by which "faith and order, doctrine and worship, are kept at the heart of ecclesiastical life and ecumenical activity."[33]

Under the section, "Questions for the Churches," Hopko voiced concern among the Orthodox that "most Protestant churches, and perhaps even the Roman Catholic Church, are no longer capable of acting authoritatively as churches because they have lost the sense of 'collegiality' within their membership, what the Slavs call 'sobornost'. . . and have no hierarchical structure capable of acting decisively in the name of all believers of the given community."[34]

Under "Specific Issues of Concern," he registered Orthodox commitment to the distinction, relationship, and manner of administering Baptism, Chrismation, and Eucharist. Discomfort was registered over language issues (e.g., "believers' baptism" vs. "nonbelievers' baptism"). A number of cautionary notes were registered regarding Roman Catholic and Reformed responses to BEM having to do with what can be called "Western" language, categories, and problematics.[35] In the concluding "Judgment on the Orthodox" section, Hopko inquires, "Are the Orthodox willing to tolerate in others, for the sake of Christian unity, the same sorts of deficiencies and deviations which they are obviously willing to tolerate in many of their own members? And, if not, why not?"[36]

Francine Cardman's (Roman Catholic) contribution, "BEM and the Community of Men and Women," highlighted BEM's own preface note of its publication within a "kairos" moment in the ecumenical movement. She then affirmed the following: "This is a time of choice that has as much to do with the sort of community that is seeking unity as it does with the sort of unity that is sought. In particular, it has to do with participation of and attentiveness to women—and, thereby, to the possibility of a community of women and men—in the process of reception of BEM."[37]

In the fourth and concluding point of her "Reflections for the Future" section, Cardman suggested that it may be time to refocus ecumenical discussion about the ordination of women. Rather than the Roman Catholic and Orthodox churches continuing to regard the ordination of women by many Protestant churches as further evidence for their lurking suspicions about the legitimacy or reality of Protestant orders and sacraments, might it now be time for these churches—and those Anglican bodies that do not ordain women—to consider stepping toward unity with Reformation churches by ordaining women to sacramental ministry and priesthood? "It is just possible," she contends, "that out of our efforts to hear and respond faithfully and freely to the questions raised by women's ordination the churches will come to know the nature and extent of both unity and diversity."[38]

Kevin W. Irwin, in *Religious Studies Review*, commended the excellence of Kilmartin's study, Hopko's particularly well-argued composition, and Cardman's able assessments in contributing to a recommended work for anyone who apprehends the gravity of the Lima text.[39]

The volume *Apostolic Faith in America*[40] is a response to the 1982 worldwide Faith and Order movement's call to the churches to the goal of visible unity in one faith and one eucharistic fellowship in Christ in order that the world may believe. In their piece titled "Contexualization," Horgan and Thomas Hoyt Jr. noted that "Orthodox Christians from Eastern-Europe and the Eastern Mediterranean are the new Christian immigrants" in the American religious scene.[41] James Jorgenson (Orthodox Church in America), in his treatment of the concept of "Apostolicity," emphasized what the Catholic and Orthodox churches hold in common—for example, apostolic succession, or the orderly transmission and continuity of apostolic teaching, ministry, and the sacraments that is signified, guaranteed, and effected through ordination of bishops through the centuries. In both the Latin and Eastern traditions, at the ordination of bishops, the imposition of hands is preceded by an examination and statement of faith by the ordinand. Points of divergence include different readings of the form of the Petrine ministry pertaining to universal jurisdiction and infallibility, the development of doctrine, and fundamental ecclesiological convictions.[42]

Donald S. Armentrout's *Journal of Ecumenical Studies* review touts this work—along with Faith and Order's published volume *Black Witness to the Apostolic Faith*[43]—as valuable aids in understanding more fully what it means to confess and live apostolic faith in the North American context.[44] William R. Barr concurs in his review in *Mid-Stream*. After locating both books within the "larger picture" of WCC and National Faith and Order study efforts, and the churches' responses to them, he asserted that nevertheless these volumes can stand on their own as significant and helpful resources.[45]

The 1960s witnessed, in Europe, very productive bilateral dialogues between the Oriental Orthodox churches and the Eastern Orthodox churches. Likewise, the phrase "very productive" could be used to describe the outcome of similar dialogues between the Roman Catholic and Oriental Orthodox theologians that transpired through the decade that followed. Indeed, the historically and theologically significant churches of the Syrian, Egyptian (Coptic), Ethiopian, Indian, and Armenian Orthodox traditions each possess a proven record of ecumenical engagement. The work *Christ in East and West*[46] is the product of a 1985 Consultation constituted by members of the National Faith and Order Commission and representatives of the Armenian, Ethiopian, and Syrian Orthodox churches. Jeffrey Gros's "Introduction" stated that this volume is directed toward deeper understanding of the centrality of Jesus Christ in the quest for Christian unity (ecumenism), and assisting Christians who confess his true humanity and true divinity to understand and transcend controversies that have kept their churches separated for over fifteen hundred years.[47] A number of areas of convergence were identified and a recommendation was made to pursue issues relating to questions of Christology and authority in the churches in the context of the WCC's Apostolic Faith Today study.

Klaus Klostermaier, in his review in the *Journal of Ecumenical Studies*, predicted "classic" status for this work. He suggested its principle of openness to the possibility that an articulation of what on first hearing seems to be a contradiction, but may actually be an acceptable expression of a commonly held truth, could be applied fruitfully in interreligious dialogue as well.[48]

The elements that constituted the background of the consultation that produced *Spirit of Truth: Ecumenical Perspectives on the Holy Spirit*[49] were manifold: the WCC's Faith and Order major study, "Towards the Common Expression of the Apostolic Faith Today," initiated at the World Council Assembly at Nairobi in 1975; the labors of individual scholars and bilateral dialogues; the WCC's 1979 "Klingenthal Memorandum" that sought to articulate possible formulations expressing relationships within the Trinity that would obviate the use of the *filioque* clause. The introduction of this book explicitly recognizes the significance of the roles played by Orthodox and Roman Catholic communions.[50]

The Orthodox paper by Stylianopoulos affirmed that *filioque* marks not a decisive difference in dogma but an important difference in the interpretation of dogma due to the differing Cappadocian and Augustinian approaches to the mystery of the Trinity.[51] Francine Cardman asserted her conviction that the Holy Spirit is in this day offering a chance for the church to turn from patriarchal modes of being and to become instead a new community of men and women to live in the presence of the inclusive reign of God.[52]

George D. Gregory's review of this work commends it as a source of valuable insights into the divergence of theological thought and a foretelling of the difficult journey before us in the quest for unity. He recommended its reception as a substantial beginning of extensive debate and as an indicator of direction for the pursuit of ecumenical investigation into the subject of the Holy Spirit.[53]

It is my personal evaluation that the content of this volume constitutes the most significant bridge between the Klingenthal document and the 2003 work of the official U.S. Orthodox-Catholic dialogue in this area of study.

Faith to Creed: Ecumenical Perspectives on the Affirmation of the Apostolic Faith in the Fourth Century[54] was the title of a 1989 consultation organized by the history subsection of the Apostolic Faith study group. The material generated by this event intended to contribute to what can be called "ecumenical history." Convergence of views is generated by the recognition of the value of historical perspectives formed in their different theological contexts. Members of the history subsection assumed not only that varied theological views needed to be tested against history, but that different theological orientations might illuminate aspects of the historical record itself.[55]

The initial articles of this volume came from the Orthodox and Catholic traditions (i.e., those traditions that affirm the Nicene Creed as an integral part of their authoritative and liturgical structure), and the latter articles came from Protestant scholars. The notion that Roman Catholic and Orthodox scholars own the Patristic period, and Protestants the Reformation, is exposed as an unwarranted assumption.[56]

Kelly McCarthy Spoerl wrote a substantial review in the inaugural issue of the North American Patristic Society's *Journal of Early Christian Studies*. She credits this "informative and stimulating" work as "well worth reading for patristic scholars, for they make us aware that our researches, which may sometimes seem hopelessly arcane and devoid of practical value even to ourselves, can influence significantly the experience of Christians in our own times and in the future."[57] Eugene Heideman wrote in *Reform Review* that Faith and Order in the USA "is to be congratulated" for making this book available.[58]

Patricia Allwin DeLeeuw's review of this volume in *Journal of Ecumenical Studies* credits it as being an ample demonstration of the way "the creed and the fourth-century church that produced it are viewed by scholars and believers through the prisms of different ecclesial contexts."[59] Peter C. Phan went on record to praise this work as exemplifying "'ecumenical history' at its best."[60] A writer for the *Christian Century* was somewhat less enthusiastic: "Admittedly, [the themes of this book] are not fashionable at the moment: this production of a book about Cappadocians, the Nicene Creed, Kainotic history, Basil of Caesarea, etc., must have been a labor of love for Eerdmans."[61]

The early 1990s was the period in which the phrase "ecumenical winter" appeared in the titles of articles commenting on the state of the ecumenical (non)movement. Former WCC general secretary Emilio Castro did well in reminding that the season is not a time of death but of life and work in anticipation of better days, and while it is winter in some parts of the world, spring blossoms and summer reigns in other regions.[62]

One such spring blossom, *Women and Church: The Challenge of Ecumenical Solidarity in an Age of Alienation*,[63] containing Catholic contributions, was hailed by Carolyn Craft in *Cross Currents* as a call for "a new, genuinely caring ecumenism with women's full participation and empowerment."[64]

Twelve Tales Untold: A Study Guide for Ecumenical Reception[65] met the need of synthesizing dialogue reports with information about local-level ecumenical work, as well as the need to make connections among the dialogue reports themselves.[66] These needs are met through the utilization of a case-study format that also serves as an effective means of encouraging the reception process whereby the results of ecumenical dialogue become part of the life and faith of the churches.[67] The particular case that involved a Catholic-Orthodox marriage presents itself as the opportunity for reflection and discussion about the treatment of mixed marriages, the administration of sacraments, and the recognition of non-Orthodox sacraments within the Greek Orthodox Church.

John C. Cooper, in his review, writes: "Acceptance, cooperation, and forward movement come from local situations where men and women on the firing lines in small towns and urban areas know that they need each other. This book points out this vital factor... Reading over these case studies, one is struck by the difficulties of faithfully accommodating almost two millennia of theology and parish practice to the new realities of contemporary ecumenism—and of the present-day weaknesses in growth and finances that so many communions are experiencing."[68]

Douglas Foster's review commends the book's versatile format that lends itself to being effectively used in both informal nonacademic and formal scholarly settings.[69]

The year 1995 saw the publication of *Telling the Churches' Stories: Ecumenical Perspectives on Writing Christian History*[70]—a "ground breaking" endeavor, in John Ford's published estimation.[71] George H. Shriver, in his review in *Church History*, after noting that "nonecumenical church history is an absolute contradiction in terms," asserts that this volume "certainly gives a useful model as to how church history should be done in an ecumenical mood of 'detached attachment,' to use a C. C. Morrison phrase."[72]

The Fifth World Conference on Faith and Order at Santiago de Compostela in 1993 noted that churches, as part of a global community marked by religious pluralism, possess varied responses to this situation in ways that condition divisions among, and within, the churches. In contrast to past ages, contemporary Christians are frequently tested by interreligious encounters. *Grounds for Understanding: Ecumenical Resources for Responses to Religious Pluralism*[73] is the product of a 1994 consultation devoted to exploring the various groundings of such engagement.

Michael Oleksa's theological reflection on interfaith dialogue in this volume stressed, from the Orthodox perspective and therefore with deep sacramental and liturgical sensitivity, the cosmic scope of God's power as manifested in all of nature and history. All of nature and human aspirations are to realize and anticipate their place in the final consummation that has its source in the triune God that is made known in Christ.[74]

Mary Ann Donovan, from the Roman Catholic perspective, probed the implications of recent Catholic theology that stresses that both proclamation and dialogue are the proper modes of Christian presence to others, with dialogue—which is to convey an offer of salvation to all persons—being the preferred mode in interreligious encounter.[75]

The delegates of the Eighth Assembly of the World Council of Churches in Harare (December 1998) decided to inaugurate the new millennium with a "Decade to Overcome Violence," having "The Churches Seeking Reconciliation and Peace" as its theme. *The Fragmentation of the Church and Its Unity in Peacemaking*[76] is a substantial building upon the efforts published under the title, *The Church's Peace Witness*.[77] Of that earlier work, D. Stephen Long, writing in *Pro Ecclesia*, thought that although the essays it comprised did not form a tight, coherent thematic unity as whole, they are well worth reading as a salutary reminder of the unfinished business that needed to be attended after the end of the Cold War.[78] A reviewer writing for the *Journal of Church and State* regretted a lost opportunity to treat the Christian dialectic of transformation of and retreat from the world and its goals.[79] To be fair, the book did conclude with the statement: "Further questions about a possible change in paradigm of churchly and scholarly understandings of peace and the significance of such a change for traditionally church-dividing positions merit further examination, clarification, and response."[80]

Returning to the content of The *Fragmentation of the Church and Its Unity in Peacemaking*, John Erickson, although casting the Orthodox peace witness in relief against the crusading and just war traditions of the West, commented most favorably on a Catholic bishops' Pastoral Letter ("The Challenge of Peace," 1983). It explicitly and clearly called for recognition of the necessity to balance the demands of peace with the demands of justice. In his personal judgment, Erickson suggested that Orthodox have historically tended to insist more on justice than on peace on the level of international relations as well as in matters of domestic concern.[81]

James F. Puglisi, SA, early in his chapter titled "Catholic Commitments to Peace, Unity and Dialogue," noted how within the spiritual traditions of both East and West an "anthropology of peace" has been elaborated. The traditions share to a significant extent an eschatological understanding of the reality of the reign of God breaking into our world, anticipating that new world of God's peace. It is at this very point that the church and its unity enter into discussion.[82] Further in his article, Puglisi recommends continued courage, energy, and the spirit of peace in meeting obstacles along the ecumenical way, so that what has already been accomplished by Catholic dialogue with Oriental Orthodox and other Orthodox churches may not be lost.[83]

David F. D'Amico's review in *Missiology* commented favorably on this work as the product of a small, committed group of scholars working in an academic setting; as such, it stands as a favorable complement to traditional types of resources such as declarations of assemblies and church encyclicals.[84]

Rose Marie Berger, in her review in *Sojourners*, noted that there are basically three kinds of power: domination, collaboration, and "satyagraha" (truth force, or spiritual power). She asserted that whereas many books touch lightly upon the spiritual influences in human rights campaigns, this book "digs in deep." Gospel peacemaking is carried to the heart of the identity of the Christian church. With the rise of late-twentieth-century "holy wars," these essays are credited with imparting insight into Christian dialogue on how commitment to faith generates spiritual power that motivates mass movements for peace.[85]

Bridget Burke Ravizza's review in *Horizons* judges that the theological and historical depth of the essays, together with their overall clarity and accessibility, make the text a valuable resource for vital questions on war and peace for the undergraduate or graduate classroom, especially in the midst of a "war on terror, which has no end in sight."[86]

2000–2007

"Globalization" holds pride of place as a prime principal subject in contemporary social commentary. The term is variously interpreted: a morality play on a world scale, a conceptual tar baby attaching every perceived "big picture" ill (fast-food imperialism, American cultural hegemony, outsourcing, global warming, etc.); a relatively benign descriptor of late capitalism, a positive expression of human aspiration to transcend local limitations and injustices with ever widening notions of community.[87]

Ingrid Volkmer, writing at the very end of 1999 for the MIT Communications Forum, posits that global processes in which knowledge, values, ethics, aesthetics, and lifestyles are exchanged make for an autonomous "third culture" possessing a generative frame of unity within which diversity can take place. Such a "global world culture is shaped by—communication."[88]

This development has not proceeded without its unexpected perplexities. David Brooks in 2005 writes:

> Not long ago, people said that globalization and the revolution in communications technology would bring us all together. But the opposite is true. People are taking advantage of freedom and technology to create new groups and cultural zones. Old national identities and behavior patterns are proving surprisingly durable. People are moving into self-segregating communities with people like themselves, and building invisible and sometimes visible barriers to keep strangers out.... Forty-million Americans move every year, and they generally move in with people like themselves, so as the late James Chapin used to say, every place becomes more like itself. Crunchy places like Boulder attract crunchy types and become crunchier. Conservative places like suburban Georgia attract conservatives and become more so. Not long ago, many

people worked on farms or in factories, so they had similar lifestyles. But now the economy rewards specialization, so workplaces and lifestyles diverge. The military and civilian cultures diverge. In the political world, Democrats and Republicans seem to live on different planets.[89]

Ancient Faith and American-Born Churches: Dialogues between Christian Traditions[90] can be read as an admirable corrective of the assumption that speed, efficiency, and sheer amount of communication are sufficient to commit unity. The work of the 1996–99 quadrennium of the Ecclesiology Study Group of the Faith and Order Commission USA was aimed at increasing the communicative success of the more preliminary steps towards mutuality among churches in the United States, so that more developed stages of recognition would ensue in the years to come. The preface of this work holds up the 1996 mutual and formal recognition between Pope John Paul II and Catholicos Karekin I of "the deep spiritual communion" that already unites the two and the bishops, clergy, and lay faithful of their churches.[91]

This book is the product of dialogues that intentionally paired representatives of churches that are deeply invested the World and National Councils of Churches with those who represent communions that do not, ordinarily, involve themselves with these ecumenical bodies. Within a previous 1985 series of *Journal of Ecumenical Studies* articles dedicated to the future directions of the NCC, Robert K. Welsh suggested more unexpected and unusual dialogue pairings in order to provide a "new element of making the community of communions a reality, while strengthening the overall network in linkages between the churches not in documents but in persons."[92] *Ancient Faith and American-Born Churches* can be seen as the fruition of that suggestion.

John Erickson, in his contribution titled "The Hermeneutics of Reconciliation: Perspectives from the Orthodox Liturgical Experience,"[93] cataloged the qualities of worship: vehicle for mission and evangelization; formative factor of Christian identity and self-understanding; fundamental point of reference in matters of faith, church order, and ethics; test for integrity, authenticity, and solidarity. He concludes with a question that Orthodox Christians need to ask not only of their own worship but also that of other

Christians, namely, "Is the same Spirit [who accomplishes the aforementioned qualities] in fact at work, ever forming anew, in each new cultural context, the same one body of Christ?[94] Although Erikson's interlocutor spoke from the Wesleyan/Holiness tradition, he did respond to his respondent by making reference to the fact that Orthodox theologians have often times criticized Western Christianity, and particularly Roman Catholicism, for its neglect of pneumotology.[95]

John Ford recounted Irenaeus of Lyon's major line of teaching on apostolicity: the apostles placed the total riches of truth in a deposit ("depositorium"), from which anyone who wishes may draw and drink. Accordingly, one should avoid the Gnostics, but love with greatest affection the things of the church and to learn the tradition of truth (*Adversus Haereses* 3.4.1.).[96]

Laura E. Everett, in her review in the *Ecumenical Review*, was very taken with the tripartite resonance–dissonance–"nonsonance" structure of the reported dialogues: "The innovation and major gift of this text is indeed the format.... [it] may be the sort of simplicity needed to wade through the often murky waters of theological exchange." Everett also speculated that the format could have wide application, especially in light of its usefulness in ecumenical dialogues where participants speak in a number of different languages. Also, "Another gift of this text is the creative matching of dialogue partners, which I take to be a sort of fantasy bracket of strange and wonderful match-ups.... I hope that the next step for this format is to add another variable of multiple national locations within a common ecclesial family such as the Episcopal Church USA and Anglican Church of Nigeria on teaching authority in the Church, or Presbyterian Church USA and Presbyterian Church of Korea on eschatology and mission."[97]

GENERAL APPRAISAL

By the close of the 1980s, Roman Catholic participation in local ecumenical agencies was judged to have broadened these councils ecclesiologically while bringing new priorities to the ecumenical table such as the centrality of worship and a eucharistic understanding of the goal of unity.[98] To examine Faith and Order's published record is to gain insight into the matter and form of such beneficial Catholic contributions. Similarly, the record reveals the essence and energy of Orthodox contributions that served to overcome distorted perceptions of Orthodoxy, challenge Reformation and Counter-Reformation perspectives, and transcend false dichotomies such as between nature and supernature and the sacred and secular. These benefactions were offered with a considerable degree of critical self-insight.[99]

Gilbert Stafford, in his "Introduction" in *Ancient Faith and American-Born Churches*, pronounced that quality ecumenical conversation serves to heighten understanding of the variegated texture of church life in the divine economy.[100] An august participant in the BEM deliberations reported the frustration of free-church and Reformed theologians: "[We] felt we were always tugging at cassocks to get heard. . . . I do wonder sometimes whether our Orthodox friends, particularly those who are resident in Eastern Europe and the Soviet Union and Greece, have any real understanding of what Protestantism is . . . and what we mean in the West by the critical method."[101] An attentive reading of Orthodox contributions to the written record leaves one convinced that this could not be readily said of Orthodox in the American context of recent history.

Bishop Kallistos Ware wrote in 1963 that "Roman Catholics do not usually realize how deep a sense of misgiving and apprehension many devout Orthodox—educated as well as simple—still feel when they think of the Church of Rome."[102] Admittedly, such unease among some Orthodox still exists, especially in Eastern Europe in light of the post-Soviet "troubles" that continue to test patience, willingness to trust, and respect for international directives to honor freedom of conscience. At the same time, the special ministry to model interchurch relations for the improvement of the ecumenical climate in other parts of the world[103] remains in effect for Catholics and Orthodox here in the Americas. Faith and Order's body of published works shows how Catholic and Orthodox together have provided new frameworks for congenial yet substantial discussions on the meaning of the relationship of Scripture and tradition, salvation, and the nature of unity as the full practical consequence of imaging life in the Holy Trinity. Not reviewed here is much more material in the published volumes attesting to like-mindedness regarding elements of devotional life relating to the significance of Mary and the communion of saints. Not to be overlooked is a shared sacramental imagination that Miller poses as a specific and rich religious resource that possesses a power to counter naked commodification that is endemic to consumer culture.[104]

Ecumenical Patriarch Dimitrios I wrote of the instances of interchange between the ancient sees of Rome and Constantinople as being "so many stones in the construction of the edifice of reconciliation and union in Christ of our Churches."[105] Rather than an edifice, let us think of a roadway. With regard to Catholic and Orthodox contributions to deliberations published by Faith and Order, I see them as living path stones constituting the way to unity. I think of the Eastern and Western traditions as the right and left boundaries of that way. Eastern Catholicism is the roadbed between the boundaries in that it contemplates and serves the theology and liturgies of the East, but exists in the mind of the Orthodox as the most unfortunate issue of a Roman Church propelled, not by the Council of Florence, but by the Council of Trent.[106]

Can the two parallel boundary lines and what is between them ever culminate in a point of unity that seems entirely intelligible, correct, and desirable? The answer is, yes, of course—in elementary two-dimensional perspective where the boundary lines are drawn to meet at a unifying point on the horizon line. Certainly such a unity will be the mark of a world that is fully transformed in the added dimension of the fully revealed reign of God to come. May the kingdom's horizon and its point of unity approach ever more quickly and envelope us all.

NOTES

1. The ecclesial life of Eastern Catholic Churches is governed in accordance with the *Code of Canons of the Eastern Churches,* which obtained force of law in 1991. According to this code, the Eastern Catholics fall into four categories: Patriarchal, Major Archepiscopal, Metropolitan *sui iuris,* and "other *sui iuris.*" For more on the Eastern Catholic Churches, see Ronald G. Roberson,

The Eastern Christian Churches: A Brief Survey (Rome: Orientale Christiana, Fifth Revised Edition, 1995), 119–64.

2. Oliver Crisp, *Divinity and Humanity: The Incarnation Reconsidered* [excerpt online] (Cambridge University Press, 2007), 1; available from *http://assets.cambridge.org/9780521873529/ excerpt/9780521873529_excerpt.pdf*.

3. Ibid.

4. G. W. H. Lamp, "Christian Theology in the Patristic Period," in *A History of Christian Doctrine*, ed. Huber Cunliffe-Jones and Benjamin Drewery (Philadelphia: Fortress Press, 1984), 120.

5. See John Meyendorff, *Byzantine Theology: Historical Trends and Doctrinal Themes* (New York: Fordham University Press, 1974), 163–65.

6. "Starring New York, City of Grit and Glamour," *New York Times*, May 25, 2007, Sec. E. 1.

7. Melanie May, "Faith and Order in the USA: A Future Glance," *Mid-Stream* 31 (October 1992): 296.

8. Jeffrey Gros, Eamon McManus, and Ann Riggs, *Introduction to Ecumenism* (Mahwah, NJ: Paulist Press, 1998), 145–46.

9. See Jeffrey Gros, "The Vision of Christian Unity: Some Aspects of Faith and Order in the Context of United States Culture," *Mid-Stream* 30, no. 1 (January 1991): 16.

10. Richard A. Shweder, review of Geertz's *Available Light: Anthropological Reflections on Philosophical Topics* (This review first appeared in *Science*, November 24, 2000); *www.quantonics.com/ Review_of_Available_Light_by_Richard_Shweder.html*.

11. Clifford Geertz, "The Interpretation of Cultures," in *The Interpretation of Cultures: Selected Essays* (New York: Basic Books, 1973), 5; from *www.indiana.edu/~wanthro/theory_pages/Geertz.htm*.

12. Matt Schudel, "Clifford Geertz: Altered Foundation of Anthropology," *Washington Post*, November 2, 2006, Sect. B.

13. Paul A. Crow Jr., "North America," in *A History of the Ecumenical Movement,* vol. 3, *1968–2000*, ed. John Briggs, Amba Oduyoye, and Georges Tsetsis (Geneva: World Council of Churches, 2004), 625.

14. William B. Greenspun, CSP, and William B. Norgren, eds., *Living Room Dialogues: A Guide for Lay Discussion, Catholic-Orthodox-Protestant* (Glen Rock, NJ: Paulist Press and the National Council of Churches of Christ in the USA, 1965).

15. Ibid., 93.
16. Ibid., 99.
17. William B. Greenspun, CSP, and Cynthia C. Wedel, eds., *Second Living Room Dialogues: A Guide for Lay Discussion, Catholic-Orthodox-Protestant* (Glen Rock, NJ: Paulist Press and the National Council of Churches of Christ in the USA, 1967), 96.
18. Richard N. Johnson, "Introduction," *Mid-Stream* 9, no. 4 (Spring 1970): ix.
19. *Mid-Stream* 9, no. 4 (Spring 1970).
20. George S. Bebis, in "A Selection of Statements on Salvation," *Mid-Stream* 9, no. 4 (Spring 1970): 35.
21. Ibid., 36.
22. Ibid., 37.
23. Robert L. Faricy, SJ, "Individual, Societal, and Cosmic Aspects of Salvation," *Mid-Stream* 9, no. 4 (Spring 1970): 50.
24. Ibid.
25. Bernard Cooke, SJ, "Salvation of the Individual," *Mid-Stream* 9, no. 4 (Spring 1970): 57.
26. Ibid., 58.
27. Students of the Catholic University of America School of Theology, "A Response to Professor Cobb's 'The Meaning of Salvation,'" *Mid-Stream* 9, no. 4 (Spring 1970): 216.
28. Vincent J. Miller, *Consuming Religion: Christian Faith and Practice in a Consumer Culture* (New York: Continuum, 2004). See 7–13, 85–96, 127–29, 189–96, 212–28.
29. Jeffrey Gros, ed., *The Search for Visible Unity: Baptism, Eucharist, Ministry* (New York: Pilgrim Press, 1984).
30. Rastko Trbuhovich, "Summary of U.S. Churches' BEM Reception Processes," in Gros, *The Search for Visible Unity,* 22–33.
31. Edward J. Kilmartin, "Reception in History: An Ecclesiological Phenomenon and Its Significance," in Gros, *The Search for Visible Unity,* 54.
32. Jeffrey Gros, "Baptism, Eucharist, and Ministry: Introduction," in Gros, *The Search for Visible Unity: Baptism, Eucharist, Ministry*, 4.
33. Thomas Hopko, "The Lima Statement and the Orthodox," in Gros, *The Search for Visible Unity: Baptism, Eucharist, Ministry*, 55.
34. Ibid., 56.

35. Ibid., 57–63.
36. Ibid., 63.
37. Francine Cardman, "BEM and the Community of Men and Women," in Gros, *The Search for Visible Unity: Baptism, Eucharist, Ministry*, 82–83.
38. Ibid., 94.
39. Kevin W. Irwin, book review of *The Search for Visible Unity: Baptism, Eucharist, Ministry*, in *Religious Studies Review* 12, no. 2 (April 1986): 138.
40. Thaddeus Horgan, SA, ed., *Apostolic Faith in America* (Grand Rapids, MI: Eerdmans, 1988).
41. Thaddeus Horgan and Thomas Hoyt Jr., "Contextualization," in Horgan, *Apostolic Faith in America,* 14.
42. James Jorgenson, "Apostolicity in the Roman Catholic, Eastern Orthodox, Lutheran, and Reformed Traditions," in Horgan, *Apostolic Faith in America,* 16–18.
43. David T. Shannon and Gayraud S. Wilmore, eds., *Black Witness to the Apostolic Faith* (Grand Rapids, MI: Eerdmans and Faith and Order Commission, U.S.A., 1988).
44. Donald S. Armentrout, review of *Apostolic Faith in America*, in *Journal of Ecumenical Studies* 26, no. 2 (Spring 1989): 382.
45. William R. Barr, book review of *Apostolic Faith in America*, in *Mid-Stream* 19, no. 2 (April 1990): 192–93.
46. Paul Fries and Tiran Nersoyan, eds., *Christ in East and West* (Macon, GA.: Mercer University Press, 1987).
47. Ibid., ix.
48. Klaus Klostermaier, book review of *Christ in East and West*, in *Journal of Ecumenical Studies* 25, no. 2 (Spring 1988): 309–10.
49. S. Mark Heim and Theodore Stylianopoulos, eds., *Spirit of Truth: Ecumenical Perspectives on the Holy Spirit* (Brookline, MA: Holy Cross Orthodox Press, 1986).
50. Ibid., 4.
51. Theodore Stylianopoulos, "The Filioque: Dogma, Theologoumenon or Error?" in Heim and Stylianopoulos, *Spirit of Truth,* 58.
52. Francine Cardman, "The Holy Spirit and the Apostolic Faith: A Roman Catholic Response," in Heim and Stylianopoulos, *Spirit of Truth,* 80.

53. George D. Gregory, book review of *Spirit of Truth: Ecumenical Perspectives on the Holy Spirit*, in *Journal of Ecumenical Studies* 27, no. 1 (Winter 1990): 134–35.

54. S. Mark Heim, ed., *Faith to Creed: Ecumenical Perspectives on the Affirmation of the Apostolic Faith in the Fourth Century* (Grand Rapids, MI: Eerdmans, 1991).

55. Ibid., xvii–xviii.

56. Ibid., xvii.

57. Kelly McCarthy Spoerl, book review of *Faith to Creed: Ecumenical Perspectives on the Affirmation of the Apostolic Faith in the Fourth Century*, in *Journal of Early Christian Studies* 1, no. 1 (1993): 100–102.

58. Eugene Heideman, book review of *Faith to Creed: Ecumenical Perspectives on the Affirmation of the Apostolic Faith in the Fourth Century*, in *Reformed Review* 45, no. 3 (Spring 1992): 239.

59. Patricia Allwin DeLeeuw, book review of *Faith to Creed: Ecumenical Perspectives on the Affirmation of the Apostolic Faith in the Fourth Century*, in *Journal of Ecumenical Studies* 29, nos. 3–4 (Summer–Fall 1992): 476.

60. Peter C. Phan, book review of *Faith to Creed: Ecumenical Perspectives on the Affirmation of the Apostolic Faith in the Fourth Century*, in *Religious Studies Review* 18, no. 2 (July 1992): 219.

61. *Christian Century* 13 (November 1991): 1073.

62. Todor Sabev, *The Orthodox Churches in the World Council of Churches: Towards the Future* (Geneva: World Council of Churches, 1996), 20.

63. Melanie May, ed., *Women and Church: The Challenge of Ecumenical Solidarity in an Age of Alienation* (Grand Rapids, MI: Eerdmans, 1991).

64. Carolyn M. Craft, in "Feminism, Humanity and Remembrance," *Cross Currents* 42, no. 4 (Winter 1992): 557.

65. John T. Ford and Darlis J. Swan, eds., *Twelve Tales Untold: A Study Guide for Ecumenical Reception* (Grand Rapids, MI: Eerdmans, 1993).

66. Michaeal Rogness, "Introduction," in Ford and Swan, *Twelve Tales Untold,* 1.

67. Darlis Swan, "Use of Educational Materials," in Ford and Swan, *Twelve Tales Untold,* 4.

68. John C. Cooper, book review of *Twelve Tales Untold: A Study Guide for Ecumenical Reception*, in *Journal of Ecumenical Studies* 31, nos. 3–4 (Summer–Fall 1994): 358.

69. Douglas A. Foster, book review of *Twelve Tales Untold: A Study Guide for Ecumenical Reception*, in *Religious Studies Review* 21, no. 2 (April 1995): 120.

70. Timothy J. Wengert and Charles W. Brockwell Jr., eds., *Telling the Churches' Stories: Ecumenical Perspectives on Writing Christian History* (Grand Rapids, MI: Eerdmans, 1995).

71. John T. Ford, book review of *Telling the Churches' Stories: Ecumenical Perspectives on Writing Christian History*, in *Religious Studies Review* 22, no. 4 (October 1996): 339.

72. George H. Shriver, book review of *Telling the Churches' Stories: Ecumenical Perspectives on Writing Christian History*, in *Church History* 65, no. 4 (December 1996): 788–89.

73. S. Mark Heim, ed., *Grounds for Understanding: Ecumenical Resources for Responses to Religious Pluralism* (Grand Rapids, MI: Eerdmans, 1998).

74. Michael Oleksa, "All Things New: An Orthodox Theological Reflection on Interfaith Dialogue," in Heim, *Grounds for Understanding*, 122–38.

75. Mary Ann Donovan, "Catholics and Interfaith Relations: A Place for Speakers, Listeners, and Intuition," in Heim, *Grounds for Understanding*, 24–25.

76. Jeffrey Gros and John D. Rempel, eds., *The Fragmentation of the Church and Its Unity in Peacemaking* (Grand Rapids, MI: Eerdmans, 2001).

77. Marlin Miller and Barbara Nelson Gingerich, eds., *The Church's Peace Witness* (Grand Rapids, MI: Eerdmans, 1994).

78. D. Stephen Long, book review of *The Church's Peace Witness*, in *Pro Ecclesia* 5, no. 1 (Winter 1996): 240.

79. Stephen J. Casey, Book Review of *The Church's Peace Witness*, in *Journal of Church and State* 38 (Winter 1996): 196.

80. Lauree Hersch Meyer and Jeffrey Gros, "Introduction," in Gros and Rempel, *The Fragmentation of the Church and Its Unity in Peacemaking*, 5.

81. John H. Erickson, "An Orthodox Peace Witness?" in Gros and Rempel, *The Fragmentation of the Church and Its Unity in Peacemaking*, 56.

82. James F. Puglisi, "Catholic Commitments to Peace, Unity, and Dialogue," in Gros and Rempel, *The Fragmentation of the Church and Its Unity in Peacemaking*, 66–89.

83. Ibid., 97.

84. David F. D'Amico, review of *The Fragmentation of the Church and Its Unity in Peacemaking,* in *Missiology* 30, no. 4 (2002): 542.

85. Rose Marie Berger, "A Toast to Freedom," *Sojourners* 31, no. 4 (July–August 2002): 53–54.

86. Bridget Burke Ravizza, book review of *The Fragmentation of the Church and Its Unity in Peacemaking,* in *Horizons* 30, no. 2 (Fall): 369–70.

87. William Grimes, "The Rise of Globalization, A Story of Human Desires," a review of *Bound Together*, by Nayan Chanda. *New York Times*, May 30, 2007, Sec. E-6.

88. Ingrid Volkmer, "International Communication Theory in Transition: Parameters of the New Global Public Sphere," MIT Communications Forum, *http://web.mit.edu/comm-forum/papers/volkmer.html* (posted December 1999).

89. David Brooks, "All Cultures Are Not Equal," *New York Times*, August 10, 2005, Sec. A-23.

90. Ted A. Campbell, Ann K. Riggs, and Gilbert W. Stafford, eds., *Ancient Faith and American-Born Churches* (New York and Mahwah, NJ: Paulist Press, 2006).

91. Ann K. Riggs, "Preface," in ibid., xii.

92. Robert K. Welsh, "Reorientation or Reorganization: The Challenge to Conciliar Ecumenism," *Journal of Ecumenical Studies* 22, no. 2 (Spring 1985): 237.

93. John H. Erickson, "The Hermeneutics of Reconciliation: Perspectives from the Orthodox Liturgical Experience," in Campbell et al., *Ancient Faith and American-Born Churches*, 53–59.

94. Ibid., 57.

95. Gilbert W. Stafford, "The Holiness Perspective on Reconciling Love in Worship," in Campbell et al., *Ancient Faith and American-Born Churches*, 67.

96. John T. Ford, CSC, "Irenaeus on Apostolicity," in Campbell et al., *Ancient Faith and American-Born Churches*, 89–90.

97. Laura E. Everett, book review of *Ancient Faith and American-Born Churches,* in *Ecumenical Review* 58, nos. 3–4 (July–October 2006): 403–5.

98. Paul A. Crow Jr., in *A History of the Ecumenical Movement*, vol. 3, ed. John Briggs, Mercy Amba Oduyoye, and Georges Tsetsis (Geneva: World Council of Churches, 2004), 616.

99. For summations of what the Orthodox have given and received from involvement in the ecumenical movement, consult the following: Thomas E. Fitzgerald, *The Ecumenical Movement: An Introductory History* (Westport, CT: Praeger Publishers, 2004), 155–62; Todor Sabev, *The Orthodox Churches in the World Council of Churches: Towards the Future* (Geneva: World Council of Churches, 1996), 11–12.

100. Gilbert Stafford, "Introduction," in Campbell et al., *Ancient Faith and American-Born Churches*, 10–12.

101. Robert W. Bertram, "Chicago Theologians on BEM," in Gros, *The Search for Visible Unity*, 67.

102. Vladimir Kharlamov, "Vatican II on Ecumenism and the Eastern Orthodox Church," *Journal of Ecumenical Studies* 8, nos. 2–3 (Spring–Summer 2001): 183. Kharlamov reports that this statement was edited out of a subsequent edition of Bishop Kallistos's *Orthodox Church*.

103. John Borelli, "A Critical Moment in Orthodox and Catholic Relations," *Ecumenism* 27, no. 107 (September 1992): 34.

104. Vincent J. Miller, *Consuming Religion: Christian Faith and Practice in a Consumer Culture* (New York: Continuum, 2004), 188–89.

105. Thomas Stransky, "Introduction," in *Ecumenical Documents III. Towards the Healing of Schism: The Sees of Rome and Constantinople. Public Statements and Correspondence between the Holy See and the Ecumenical Patriarchate 1958–1984,* ed. E. J. Stormon, SJ (New York/Mahwah, NJ: Paulist Press, 1987), 13–14.

106. Robert M. Haddad, "A Response to Rev. David M. Petras' 'The Ecumenical Status of the Eastern Catholic Churches,'" *Greek Orthodox Theological Review* 37, nos. 1–4 (1992): 384.

Chapter 6

FAITH AND ORDER IN OBERLIN: 1957 AND 2007

Diane C. Kessler

> This paper was written as a reflection immediately following the author's participation in the Oberlin II conference. It was originally published in the *Ecumenical Review* 59, no. 2–3, April/July (2007): 284–92, and is reprinted here with permission from the author and the *Ecumenical Review*.

In July 2007 on the fiftieth anniversary of the first North American Conference on Faith and Order, about three hundred people met on the campus of Oberlin College to reflect "On Being Christian Together: The Faith and Order Experience in the United States." A series of ten pink, green, blue, and gray banners linked together by a red line adorned the stage of the hall where plenary sessions were held. The red line seemed to move steadily downward, prompting quizzical looks and morbid humor about the symbolism. On the third day of the conference, the banners were rearranged, an effect suggesting erratic development. This evoked some good-natured laughter. It also probably is an accurate assessment of the ecumenical quest.

Anniversaries are occasions that invite stock-taking: "Where have we been? Where are we now? Where are we going? Why does it matter?" The goals of Oberlin II were to honor the intentions of the original meeting, to place them in context, to explore developments in five decades of Faith and Order, and to assess current challenges.

So what has happened to Faith and Order in North America in fifty years? To prepare for the event and consider these questions,

I reread the Official Report of the [1957] North American Conference.[1] What follows are some reflections on the fiftieth anniversary meeting in light of its predecessor.

The theme of the '57 Conference was "The Nature of the Unity We Seek." The meeting was initiated by members of the Faith and Order Commission of the World Council of Churches (WCC). It was hosted at Oberlin College, which then also had a graduate school of theology, because the president of Oberlin was active in the Faith and Order movement. The WCC appealed to the National Council of Churches of Christ in the USA (NCC) and the Canadian Council of Churches to create "a permanent program of Faith and Order Study" (p. 5). The WCC gave the rationale that "churches located within one great continental area, in the midst of one more or less homogeneous culture, have special responsibilities toward one another in their quest for unity." The mandate was outlined as follows: "to proclaim the essential oneness of the Church of Christ and to keep prominently before ... the churches the obligation to manifest that unity and its urgency for the work of evangelism ... to study questions of faith, order, and worship with the relevant social, political, racial and other factors in their bearing on the unity of the Church" and "to study matters in the present relationships of the churches to one another which cause difficulties and need theological clarification" (p. 35). Martin Marty, a speaker at Oberlin II, offered some historical perspective on the situation in 1957:

> Europeans didn't think the US would have anything to say about faith and order. They had an image of Americans as a practical people. It is hard to picture now how remote Christians were from each other in the 19th century. History helps. It shows how far we have come. We are becoming Christians together.[2]

The 2007 gathering, initiated by NCC's Faith and Order Commission, gave visible witness that the primary mandate of the '57 meeting is being met. Despite cutbacks in funds and staff in the National Council of Churches and its member-communions, persistent institutional introversion by the churches, and tepid interest in tough theological issues by most Christians, participants were able to proclaim, "We're still here, and these issues still matter."

FAITH AND ORDER IN OBERLIN: 1957 AND 2007

In both cases many attendees came not as individuals but as designated representatives of their churches. The 1957 meeting involved 274 "churchmen"—representatives of thirty-eight Christian bodies, plus consultants and accredited observers. The 2007 session included eighty churches and traditions, and involved approximately 300 people. Some sent official delegations. Others came as individuals with or without the blessing of their churches. Both meetings made an effort to achieve diversity as it was perceived in their context, picking up on a continuing theme of the ecumenical movement from the WCC Assembly in New Delhi—"all in each place." Some expressions of this diversity, however, have changed—reflecting development among the churches in the ecumenical movement. Oberlin II planners especially sought to invite new generations of Christians to understand, appreciate, and appropriate this work. They also wanted to encourage people in traditions at the periphery of the ecumenical movement to move to its center. Twelve women were delegates in '57, whereas in 2007 women were present in significant numbers. African Americans, though still a minority, also were more visible and vocal in 2007. The Church of God Anderson (also present at Oberlin I) and National Baptist Convention, two predominantly African American Evangelical denominations, were represented. Self-identified "Evangelicals" had leadership roles. And a conscious effort was made by the planners to seek out younger theologians. These initiatives echoed the intentions of the '57 meeting, which involved the then-thriving Interseminary Movement and the U.S. Student Christian Council.

One noticeable difference, however, was the degree to which preparatory study was part of Oberlin I, but not of the '07 event. Oberlin I involved sixteen regional agencies in two-year programs of study that fed into the conference with working papers. These studies often were initiated by state and local councils of churches through the Association of Council Secretaries. In '57, 350 groups had used a pamphlet called "Ecumenical Conversations" to draw attention to the issues that would be addressed in the meeting. To the degree that state and local councils of churches in the United States now are enfeebled, nonexistent, or have become interfaith bodies, this also negatively impacts the "means of interconnectivity in relationships between the global and local" appropriately valued by the ecumenical movement. Although several state and local council of churches executives were present—a sign of their recognition of the significance of Faith and Order concerns among their member-churches—too little time and too few staff prevented any significant preparatory activity. The one exception to this was an effort to stimulate an Oikoumene Film Festival, the products of which were shown on Friday and Saturday evenings. One colleague observed that the changed situation actually heightens the need for periodic national Faith and Order gatherings as a stimulus to continued study and discussion of relevant issues, a means of supporting and affirming regional and local Faith and Order discussions, and a vehicle to promote networking among them.

Although Orthodox and Roman Catholic leaders were prominent presenters at Oberlin II, many spokespersons were Protestant or Anglican. Thus, the public presentations unwittingly had a Protestant perspective that would not always have been shared by the Orthodox and Roman Catholics. This has been an ongoing challenge in councils of churches, whose members often reflect the plethora of divisions among Protestant denominations. (Reportedly thirty-three thousand distinct denominations have surfaced around the globe since the Reformation.) In '57, in part because of this tilt in perspective, the Eastern Orthodox felt compelled to make a separate statement from the main message concerning their position "that unity has been historically embodied and is realized today in the Orthodox Church." Nevertheless, they were present at and involved in Oberlin I, and continue to be committed to institutional expressions of the ecumenical movement, and have assumed significant leadership roles. One important sign of this was the presence of Archbishop Viken Aykazian, representing the Diocese of the Armenian Church of America (Eastern) and the NCC (its new president as of November 2007), who brought greetings to open the '07 event.

Both Oriental and Eastern Orthodox churches were represented at the 2007 meeting. Peter Bouteneff, a professor at St. Vladimir's Seminary and former member of the WCC Faith and Order staff, sought to provide an interpretive window into Orthodox involvement. He explained that the "Orthodox have been on the defensive through most of the ecumenical movement. Many symptoms, included in the Orthodox statement at Oberlin I, raised concerns about basic ecclesiological presuppositions. Those concerns led to the Toronto Statement." He continued with this candid comment: "We seek mutual understanding and patience. The Orthodox often express their concerns in a clumsy and arrogant way, but the issues have an inherent logic."[3]

The presence of official representatives both from the Pontifical Council for Promoting Christian Unity (PCPCU) and the Secretariat for Ecumenical and Interreligious Affairs of the U.S. Conference of Catholic Bishops marked a significant development since the '57 meeting. In 1957, participants had raised questions about the relationship of other churches to the Church of Rome. Just a few years later, the Second Vatican Council paved the way for the Roman Catholic Church's active engagement in the ecumenical movement. In retrospect, reflecting on this rapid change in the course of just a few years was a good reminder that the quest for Christian unity sometimes progresses in unpredictable lunges. The best way for the faithful to be prepared is by steady slogging. So the adjusted banners with a jagged red line were an appropriate symbol.

Cardinal Avery Dulles[4] was one of the featured presenters. He raised questions about the "limitations of the [dialogical] method," saying that "the method of convergence has nearly exhausted its potential.... Critics fear a political correctness replaces theological candor and rigor of earlier decades." Instead, he said that "to surmount remaining barriers, we may need an ecumenism of mutual enrichment by means of testimony." In a sign of the maturity of Roman Catholic participation in the ecumenical movement, Dulles's observations subsequently were diplomatically challenged by other Catholic representatives, who said that genuine ecumenical dialogue is a common search for the truth of the gospel.

A handful of '07 participants had attended the previous event as consultants, stewards, or staff. They welcomed the opportunity to pass the mantle to future generations. Cecil M. "Mel" Robeck Jr. received a standing ovation after his address. When he began his involvement with Faith and Order in 1983 ("My church told me, if the Lord speaks to you, *do* it!"), it was with the approval of the leader of his denomination. Yet this "didn't come easily as a member of Assemblies of God." The approval initially given subsequently was withdrawn when a new religious leader arrived and the denomination voted that the "Assemblies of God disapproves of any church or minister to participate in the ecumenical movement because of the lowest common denominator theology, giving up evangelism for social justice." Despite this opprobrium, Robeck grew increasingly involved in Faith and Order—a renegade action only affirmed two years ago. "Don't forget the past," he said, "because a price was paid to get you here."

Robeck also offered some insights into the mind-set of Pentecostals. Traditional Faith and Order assumptions challenge Pentecostals, he said, because the latter are noncreedal. They concur with most statements in the creeds, but are wary of people who recite them by rote yet do not internalize their meaning. For Pentecostals, Robeck said, written theology is less important than gifts of the Spirit.

His story was echoed in conversations between newcomers and other ecumenical veterans—for example, Paul A. Crow Jr. (Christian Church, Disciples of Christ), Jeffrey Gros (Roman Catholic), Lewis Mudge (Presbyterian Church [U.S.A.]), John A. Radano (Roman Catholic), Mary Tanner (Church of England), and Barbara Brown Zikmund (United Church of Christ). It was a reminder of the importance that individuals play in the progress their churches make toward Christian unity, and of the patience, persistence, commitment, and spiritual rootedness demanded of them.

Brother Jeff Gros,[5] former director of NCC Faith and Order, emphasized the relational nature of the movement. He said that although the primary work of Faith and Order is through texts, the process brings people into conversation who previously had not communicated with each other.

In 1957, Albert Outler said, "Thus far our only real consensus centers on the importance and relevance of our problem rather than in any massive substantive conclusions." Since then, some conclusions have been reached. Rev. Msgr. John A. Radano, a representative from the Pontifical Council for Promoting Christian Unity (PCPCU), identified a number of significant accomplishments between the two meetings.[6] 1965: The Common Declaration of Pope Paul VI and Ecumenical Patriarch Athenagoros I, asking followers to erase from memory the mutual sentences of excommunication issued in 1054, and to pursue dialogue toward full communion in faith and sacramental life; 1973: Joint christological declarations among leaders of Oriental Orthodox Churches resolving christological controversies; 1982: publication of *Baptism, Eucharist and Ministry* by the Faith and Order Commission of the World Council of Churches, which became a reference point for several subsequent agreements; 1999: the Joint Declaration on Doctrine of Justification signed by the Lutheran World Federation and the Catholic Church, resolving a major controversy of the Reformation, affirmed by the World Methodist Council in 2006. A continuing challenge vexing ecumenists in all the churches, however, is how to maximize the impact of these achievements in local settings—the importance of reception. To the degree that councils of churches in every setting—local, state, national, and regional—include Faith and Order as a significant aspect of their ecumenical ministry, they are assisting the churches in this process of reception.

That these agreements have not led to greater rapprochement and full communion among churches points to another dimension of the '57 conference—the nondoctrinal factors that contribute to divisions among communions. In 1957 Walter Muelder (then dean of Boston University School of Theology) gave a paper titled "Institutionalism in Relation to Unity and Disunity"—the result of a commission on institutionalism that addressed the perversions to which religious institutions are prey. The aims of the commission were as follows:

1. The self-criticism of churches by which they may see their own structures sociologically as well as theologically.

2. The relations both positive and negative of the churches to each other in the ecumenical conversation.

3. The pattern of church relations that is finding expression in the WCC as an institution.

Muelder defined institutionalism as follows: "When the churches divest their institutions from their true purposes or use them as ends in themselves, they manifest what may be called *institutionalism*" (p. 94). He listed a daunting number of nondoctrinal factors affecting ecumenical negotiations: "language, nationalism, race, class, power, establishment, polity, denominational size, geographical location and the like" (p. 91).

In a sobering litany as fresh today as it was when Dean Muelder spoke fifty years ago, he observed:

> Though bureaucracy makes for rational efficiency and institutional security, it also tends to develop certain dysfunctions, such as: blindness to needed change; trained incapacity to sense new needs; inflexibility in applying skills and resources to changing conditions; occupational psychoses whereby personnel develop special preferences, antipathies, discriminations and emphases not adapted to social reality as a whole; fixation on goals and objectives however obsolescent; excessive conformity to prescribed patterns which have become routine; transference of sentiments and motivations from the aims of the organization to the particular details of behavior required by rules and rubrics, and transforming means into ends so that instrumental values become terminal values. These dysfunctions are no respecters of denominational polities and apply to boards and agencies as well as to fundamental church structure. (p. 97)

It is time for a fresh look at these continuing challenges—an opportunity not fully recognized by Oberlin II, but in need of candid conversation by the movement.

A panel on "Faith and Order in the Context of Religious Plurality"[7] highlighted a significant difference from 1957—namely, a heightened awareness of other faiths. Lewis Mudge[8] said, "Sometimes it's providential that not all of our plans have succeeded. We don't want to be locked into ecclesial forms not open to the Holy Spirit. If you find yourselves stuck, try enlarging your categories." He recommended that Faith and Order work with denominational interfaith relations offices on particular programs and issues. John Borelli[9] urged that we keep interreligious dialogue *religious* by reading Scripture together and developing a hermeneutic of nonviolence. He said that Christians need to be engaged both in ecumenical and interfaith relations, and we need to do both well. David Wagschal pointed out that, of necessity, the Orthodox always have been active in interfaith relations. He noted that in the Middle East this long has been a critical element because the Byzantines grew up alongside Islam, and bad memories have left wounds that are quite deep. Nevertheless, he suggested that the Orthodox now may be developing a growing sense of call to engage in Christian/Muslim dialogue. He said that the Eastern Church has a distinct dialogical approach—unsystematic, rhetorical, textual, distinct in tone and method—which might allow for different points of contact with people of other faiths.

Churches in the ecumenical movement demonstrate a heightened awareness of the challenges and opportunities that dialogue with people of other faiths poses for Christians. All too often, however, these conversations are occurring on a bilateral basis—one church/denomination in conversation with Jews, Muslims, or other traditions. This approach strains the capacities of dialogue partners. It also gives a distorted picture of Christians by failing to show the diversity and divisions among Christian churches. All Christians together should engage their interfaith dialogue partners, so the partners can see Christianity in its fullness and complexity. Christian churches also need to continue discussing the basis on which Christians should engage in interfaith dialogue. Some churches have a more fully developed understanding of interreligious relations than others; confusion abounds among clergy and laity; not all churches agree on the basis; and this is an area for fruitful dialogue as theories continue to develop. Councils of churches, in particular, provide a venue to counter this tendency, if their members will avail themselves of the ecumenical opportunities they provide for interfaith relations.

Speakers also identified neuralgic challenges within and among churches today: varied understandings of the nature and mission of the church and its ministry; differing perspectives about theological anthropology and its implications for issues of human sexuality; disparate understandings of the nature of authority; and the importance of healing memories as necessary for reconciliation among churches and in the world. These challenges are being addressed in a context that in some ways differs significantly from fifty years ago. American churches have endured the pedophilia scandal, an increased secular culture, and front-page debates about human sexuality. It is heartening to note that the Faith and Order movement has been and will continue to address these issues through the World Council of Churches and the National Council of Churches mindful of a changing context.

At times, participants spoke in encompassing terms about the Faith and Order mandate, making some of the veterans nervous.

In one of the rare opportunities for comments and questions from the floor, Michael Root (ELCA) reminded the group that "everybody can not do everything all of the time. The goal of the ecumenical movement is full communion. If Faith and Order becomes too inclusive in its agenda, it could have the unintended side effect of losing focus within the ecumenical agenda." This was a useful precautionary comment. At the same time, some of the old silo separation between Faith and Order and Life and Work seemed less potent than it had been.

This cautionary note occurred during the final plenary session. When one is in the midst of a meeting, it is difficult to get an overview of its significance, and participants are tempted to continue widening the circles of significance into oblivion. I confess that when I was there, it sometimes was hard to comprehend how all the information fit together. Yet in retrospect, the anniversary succeeded in sharing information about the past, present, and future of Faith and Order as a crucial component of the ecumenical movement. Through prodigious efforts by the planners, the meeting succeeded in drawing new generations into the Faith and Order orbit. Thanks to new modes of technology with which those generations are especially comfortable, I expect that some of the relationships developed there will continue to grow and benefit the quest for Christian unity and human community.

Many veterans talked about the importance of human relationships in healing divisions and strengthening unity among churches. Mary Tanner said it well:

> Ecumenical experiences enable us to identify with others so you never again see things in the same way. If the divided churches are to meet and draw together, they can only meet through persons, through imperfect persons such as we are. When we are *renewed* into unity, then credibly we can minister in the midst of the world's brokenness.

In hindsight, that series of pink, green, blue, and gray banners could be an appropriate image of the unity for which we pray and long—full, visible, diverse without division. In the mid-term, the lines may continue to be erratic, with successes here, setbacks there. The vision of the unity we seek may be clearer to some than when the question was asked in 1957, but not all would assent to the work that has been done, and churches are reluctant to respond to the vision that has been unfolding. Yet the reconciling nature of the God we know through Jesus Christ in the Holy Spirit makes claims on Christians and our churches to which we must respond. As the planners said in their introductory brochure, "We are convinced that when Jesus prayed before his death that we all should be one (John 17:21), he meant all of us." Amen!

NOTES

1. *The Nature of the Unity We Seek*, ed. Paul S. Minear (St. Louis: Bethany Press, 1958). Page numbers cited throughout this article are from the Minear text, unless otherwise noted.

2. These remarks were made by Martin Marty in his "Anniversary Lecture" delivered at Oberlin II on July 19, 2007.

3. Peter Bouteneff made these remarks on July 22, 2007.

4. See chapter 10, "The Search for Unity since 1957: A Catholic Perspective," in this volume for Cardinal Avery Dulles's presentation.

5. See chapter 3, "Fifty Years and Running: Oberlin '57, Back and Beyond," in this volume for Brother Jeffrey Gros's presentation.

6. John A. Radano, chapter 13, "The Future of Our Journey: Issues Facing Ecumenism," in this volume.

7. This panel took place on July 21, 2007.

8. See chapter 18, "Christian Unity and the Abrahamic Faiths," in this volume for the paper presented by Lewis Mudge.

9. See chapter 17, "How the Work of Christian Unity Relates to Interreligious Relations and Dialogue: When Good News Sounds Bad," in this volume for John Borelli's paper.

PART II
THE PRESENT MOMENT

VISIONS OF CHRISTIAN UNITY
AND THE POSTMODERN CONTEXT

PART II

Chapter 7

ORTHODOXY, POSTMODERNITY, AND ECUMENISM: THE DIFFERENCE THAT DIVINE-HUMAN COMMUNION MAKES

Aristotle Papanikolaou

> Following its presentation at Oberlin II, this paper was originally published in the *Journal of Ecumenical Studies* 42, no. 4 (Fall 2007): 527–46, and is copyrighted (2007) by the *Journal of Ecumenical Studies* (*JES*). It is reprinted here with permission from the author and *JES*.

When I was a student at the University of Chicago, I attended David Tracy's course titled "Postmodernity." During a break, he said to me, and I'm paraphrasing, "You know, Aristotle, the Orthodox have a certain advantage—they did not go through the well-known chain of events within the West, meaning the Reformation, Counter-Reformation, Enlightenment, Romanticism, Modernity, Postmodernity—and because of this, those within the tradition have the advantage of knowing what it is like to think like a tradition." As with many, many things that Tracy said during my time at Chicago, it took me a while to fully understand what he was saying. However, with but a simple phrase, as he has done so often in his career, Tracy provided an important hermeneutical key for understanding Orthodoxy's place within the cultural situation that is now called postmodernity.

In this essay I will expand on what I think Tracy means by "thinking as a tradition," in a way that clarifies an Orthodox

Christian response to the postmodern situation. I will begin by offering a brief and select summary of contemporary Orthodox theology that will illustrate a remarkable consensus around the centrality of the principle of the realism of divine-human communion for theology. Orthodoxy is, in essence, a tradition of thinking on the realism of divine-human communion manifested in the person of Jesus Christ. It is this particular core of the tradition that will shape Orthodoxy's response to central questions of a present situation, even beyond postmodernity, and that constitutes the single most important contribution that Orthodoxy can bring to ecumenical dialogue.

THE POSTCOLONIAL CONTEXT

In addition to ending the long reign of the Byzantine Empire, the fall of Constantinople in 1453 silenced a long and vibrant intellectual tradition in the Orthodox Christian East, whose last notable theologian was Gregory Palamas (1296–1359). It would take nearly four hundred years before a revival would occur in Russia, which is discernible in part with the establishment of the intellectual academies of the Russian Orthodox Church in various cities throughout Russia.

I speak of contemporary Orthodox theology in terms of "revival" because it is often forgotten that much of the Orthodox Christian world after the thirteenth century was colonized either by the Mongols, the Ottoman Turks, or the Communists. Contemporary Orthodox theology is a postcolonial attempt to shed the "effective history" of oppression so as to reconstitute Orthodoxy as an intellectual tradition that draws on its past in order to confront contemporary questions. The usual caricatures of Orthodoxy are clear manifestations of this forgetfulness: the mystical smells-and-bells form of Christianity; a hopelessly male-dominated, androcentric, and hierarchical vestige of a Christendom that is much vilified in theology today; a community that refuses to encounter the modern world in its stubborn adherence to ancient doctrinal formulations. A striking example of this forgetfulness is Friedrich Schleiermacher's description of the Eastern Church as "torpid," within which "the combination of knowledge about religion with a really scientific organization is almost entirely destroyed. But just because of this purely negative character there was the less to be said here about that Church, since it cannot be determined whether it will again step back more into connexion with the world's intellectual intercourse, and so have the strength to elicit and develop within itself an antithesis analogous to the Western one."[1]

The accusation that Orthodoxy never confronted modernity is most perplexing, because the obvious question is: How could Orthodox Christians engage modern currents of thought when the Ottoman Turks would not let them? It is true that the Ottomans did not occupy Russia, but the common opinion that Russian modernization was always a step behind the rest of Europe never takes into account the postcolonial effect of the nearly two-hundred-year Mongol occupation of Russia. Most of the Orthodox world was under Ottoman Turkish oppression for over four hundred years, up to the first decade of the twentieth century. The Ecumenical Patriarchate in Constantinople to this day still suffers from violations of its religious freedom by the Turkish government. The forgetfulness of this fact by most of the Christian world is exacerbated by the audacity of some scholars to describe the Ottoman Empire as tolerant.[2] "Tolerance" is not a word my grandmother would have used; even though she was only nine years old when the Ottomans finally left her village, she had vivid memories of their abuse. The fact that most Orthodox theology in Russia in the early nineteenth century and in Greece in the twentieth century up to the 1960s was primarily imitative of Protestant and Catholic dogmatic manuals can only make sense if one sees those contexts through postcolonial eyes. Soon after liberation, most Orthodox countries had to suffer through the tyranny of Communism for most of the twentieth century. As is known by anyone who has suffered oppression—because of race, gender, color, or domestic abuse—the oppressor's shadow lingers long after liberation, and much time is needed to recover any sense of authentic identity. Orthodox theology, as I will show, does not easily fit into the traditional Western divisions of history into the premodern, modern, and postmodern, since it is a postcolonial attempt to recover a tradition that was decimated through oppression and to discern how to retrieve that tradition in the face of contemporary questions.

In this postcolonial situation, Orthodox Christianity stands in an unusual middle position: It is often identified with the Christendom-like, male-dominated form of Christianity that most Christian theology today argues is irrelevant and possibly dangerous; yet, like many of the liberation theologies today, a close reading of contemporary Orthodox theology reveals a similar complaint against traditional Western forms of theology, primarily the intellectualization of theology. Like so much of the liberation theology today, contemporary Orthodox theology emphasizes the role of "experience," especially the experience of union with God. There is a remarkable affinity between contemporary Orthodox theology and Latino and Latin American theologies on the relational notion of the person and the link among presence, symbol, and sacrament. This affinity is especially evident if one compares Robert Goizueta's *Caminemos con Jésus*[3] and John Zizioulas's *Communion and Otherness*.[4] The place of Orthodox Christianity in the postmodern world is not quite as evident as might be expected. One thing is certain: Contemporary Orthodox theology can be rightly understood only if one takes into account the postcolonial situation of Orthodox Christianity.

CONTEMPORARY ORTHODOX THEOLOGY: A TRADITION OF THINKING ON DIVINE-HUMAN COMMUNION

After the fall of the Ottoman Empire, theological faculties were established in traditional Orthodox cities throughout Eastern Europe. A movement to return to more authentic forms of the Orthodox spiritual and theological traditions began in the late eighteenth century with the Slavonic translation of the *Philokalia* compiled by Nikodemus of the Holy Mountain (1749–1809), which was followed by a series of Russian translations of Eastern patristic texts. The revival of the Orthodox intellectual tradition, however, is also indebted to individual thinkers who were not affiliated with the emerging theological institutions of higher learning in traditional Orthodox countries and who, in fact, were reacting to the theology emerging from these institutions. Although the theological academies throughout the Orthodox world did play an indispensable role in the revival of the Orthodox intellectual tradition, especially in their creative appropriation of the *Philokalia* and in producing translations of patristic texts, they were established on the models of German universities, and much of the theological work produced by these theological schools' faculties was considered primarily imitative of the Protestant and Catholic scholastic manuals.[5]

Early-nineteenth-century Russia saw the emergence of an intellectual tradition that was simultaneously rooted in the Orthodox theological and liturgical tradition and also seeking to engage the modern philosophical currents streaming into Russia, especially German idealism. From this particular trajectory emerged what is referred to as the Russian school.[6] The most well-known and influential intellectual from the Russian school is Vladimir Sergeevich Soloviev (1853–1900), considered to be the father of Russian sophiology. Two ideas were central to Soloviev's thought: the humanity of God (*bogochelovechestvo*) and Sophia. The fact that both concepts remained central to Russian religious philosophy allows Rowan Williams to claim, echoing Whitehead's remark on Plato, that "all subsequent Russian metaphysics is a series of footnotes to Soloviev."[7] The concept of the humanity of God is related to the Orthodox dogmatic principle of the divine-human union in Christ. Soloviev, however, was far from a dogmatician. His philosophy attempts to express this Orthodox principle of the divine-human union in Christ in the categories of German idealism, particularly the philosophy of Friedrich Wilhelm Joseph von Schelling (1775–1854). Although he appropriates the thought of Schelling, Soloviev's philosophy is a unique synthesis of the Orthodox affirmation of divine-human communion and German idealism that attempts to critique the inadequacies of modern philosophies. The humanity of God forms the basis for Soloviev's attempt to conceptualize a God who is both transcendent and immanent to creation. For Soloviev, affirming the humanity of God means that creation is intrinsic, not extrinsic, to the life of God. God relates to creation from all eternity, and creation exists in the life of God insofar as God's life is the reconciliation of all opposites: the material and the spiritual, freedom and necessity, finite and infinite. Creation is a movement of recovery of that original unity that is manifested in the God-man—Christ. Soloviev expresses this particular understanding of the God-world relation with the concept of Sophia and thereby gives birth to the sophiological tradition of the Russian school. God is Sophia, which means that God eternally relates to creation, and creation itself—created Sophia—is a movement of reconciliation toward divine Sophia.

As a result of the particular understanding of God's relation to the world that is implied in Soloviev's sophiology, he had a higher estimation of secular knowledge than the more extreme Orthodox Slavophiles of his time. However, Soloviev was critical of the determinism and meaninglessness of the materialism of modern atheism. His sophiology was a *via media* between extreme ideas and currents of thought prevalent throughout nineteenth-century Russia: rationalism and materialism, freedom and necessity, modern atheism and Orthodox Slavophile nationalism. The identification of the humanity of God with Sophia allowed Soloviev to affirm that all of created reality reflects the divine Sophia and is the movement of created Sophia toward the unity of all in God, which is divine Sophia.

Although the thought of the Russian school bears the stamp of Soloviev's sophiology up until the revolution of 1917, it would be Sergei Nikolaeivich Bulgakov (1871–1944) who would advance the most sophisticated theological development of Soloviev's thought. Bulgakov was more conversant than Soloviev with the Eastern patristic tradition, and his sophiology is expressed explicitly in the idiom of the traditional theological dogmas and categories of the Orthodox tradition. Bulgakov was a convert from Marxism to Orthodoxy and was eventually ordained in 1918. After being exiled from Russia, he became the cofounder and first dean of St. Sergius Orthodox Theological Institute in Paris in 1925. Bulgakov was active in the ecumenical movement and was one of the most prominent spokespersons of Orthodoxy to the Western world.

The most developed form of Bulgakov's sophiology appears in his dogmatic trilogy, *On Divine Humanity*.[8] Bulgakov follows Soloviev in identifying the humanity of God with Sophia and affirms the core meaning of Soloviev's sophiology—God is always the God for "me," that is, for creation. God's being is not dependent on creation, nor is God exhausted in God's relation to creation; God's being, however, is such that God *is* the God who creates and redeems creation. Bulgakov would affirm the distinction between the world that God relates to from all eternity and the created world, but it is impossible for humans to think of God as not eternally relating to the world.

Unlike Soloviev, Bulgakov's sophiology is more explicitly Trinitarian and appropriates the traditional Trinitarian language. Sophia is identified with the *ousia*, but as such *ousia* comes to mean much more than that which the persons of the Trinity possess in common. God in God's being exists as the creator and redeemer of the world. *Hypostasis* does not simply indicate that which is particular in the three persons of the Trinity. The divine Sophia does not exist monistically but as Trinity. For Bulgakov the relations among the persons of the Trinity are best understood in terms of *kenosis*, as a movement of self-giving and self-receiving that has the capacity to overflow and reflect itself in the creation of the world. This kenotic movement is the source of and is reflected in the world, especially in the incarnation and crucifixion of Christ. Anticipating later liberation theology, Bulgakov argued that the crucifixion of Christ reveals the *kenosis* of each of the persons of the Trinity, which includes the co-suffering of the Father with the Son. Always participating in the divine Sophia, the world as created Sophia is moving toward the unity of all in God's life, which is given in and made possible by the *kenosis* of the Son and completed by the Holy Spirit.

The mark of German idealism, particularly the philosophy of Schelling, is evident on Bulgakov's theology, but equally as evident is his embeddedness within the Orthodox patristic and dogmatic tradition. Like Soloviev, Bulgakov's own understanding of the God-world relation allows him to have a more positive estimation of nontheological disciplines. Moreover, Bulgakov identified problems within the patristic tradition, which the resources of German idealism could assist in resolving. The Fathers did not have the last word for Bulgakov, and, as they used the philosophical categories of their time, so must theology today make use of modern philosophy to continue to extract the implications of the divine-human communion in Christ.

Sophiology did not survive in any influential form past Bulgakov. Its demise is partly due to the explicit refutation of sophiology by Orthodox thinkers in the Russian diaspora, whose own understanding of Orthodox theology would come to be known as the neopatristic school. Although this school has roots in the translations of the Eastern patristic texts in Russia, it is most associated with Georges Florovsky (1893–1979) and Vladimir Nikolaeivich Lossky (1903–58). Both Florovsky and Lossky were part of the "Sophia Affair" in 1935—the accusation of Bulgakov's theology as heretical by both the Moscow Patriarchate and what would become known as the Synod of the Russian Orthodox Church Abroad. During the time of the Sophia Affair, Florovsky was professor of patristics at St. Sergius and would later serve as dean of St. Vladimir's Orthodox Theological Seminary in Crestwood, NY (founded in 1938). Florovsky framed the debate with Russian sophiology in terms of the relation between theology and philosophy. For Florovsky, theology had to be rooted in the language and categories of the Eastern patristic texts. He coined the phrase "neopatristic synthesis," but such a synthesis must retain the Hellenistic contours of patristic thought. Florovsky argued that any attempt to de-Hellenize the language of the Fathers would only distort their theology and divide the church.

Lossky was also a part of the Russian émigré community in Paris, but he was never affiliated with St. Sergius.[9] For Lossky, much as for Bulgakov, the divine-human union of Christ is the starting point for theological thinking about God. Insofar as this union is one between two opposites, between what is God and what is not God, it is beyond the grasp of human reason, whose capacity for understanding is restricted to created reality. Whereas human reason functions on the basis of the law of noncontradiction, the incarnation demands that theology be antinomic—the affirmation of the nonopposition of opposites. Theology's function is to give expression to the divine-human communion in Christ, which reveals the antinomic God—the God who is radically immanent in Christ and whose very immanence reveals God's radical transcendence. Its purpose is not to attempt to resolve the antinomy through reason but to stretch language so as to speak of the divine-human communion in Christ in such a way that guides one toward true knowledge of God, which is mystical union with God beyond reason. Theology is apophatic, by which Lossky meant two things: that language is inadequate to represent the God beyond all representation, and that true knowledge of God consists in experience of God rather than in propositions rooted in human logic.

The affirmation of the God who is beyond being yet radically immanent to creation is the basis for the essence/energies distinction. The (hyper)essence of God refers to God's transcendence, whereas the energies refer to God's immanence and are the means for communion with God. True knowledge of God consists in participation in the energies of God, which are uncreated. The crystallization of the essence/energies distinction can be traced back to Palamas. Lossky, together with Florovsky and John Meyendorff (1926–92), presented the essence/energies distinction as uniquely characteristic of and central to Orthodox theology. Its centrality is affirmed by virtually every twentieth-century Orthodox theologian, including the most famous outside of Russia and Greece, the Romanian Dumitru Staniloae (1903–93), and it is the reason that Orthodox theology today is often referred to as neo-Palamite. The distinction was also used in polemics against neoscholastic understandings of created grace. For Lossky, the truth of the essence/energies distinction lies in its antinomic character: It expresses the transcendent and immanent God without attempting to resolve the antinomy.

In addition to the essence/energies distinction, there is an additional antinomy that is foundational for theology: God as Trinity. For Lossky, the revelation of God as Trinity is a "primordial fact" given in the incarnation. The goal of theology is not to explain how God is Trinity but to deconceptualize philosophical categories in order to express the antinomy. The patristic categories of *ousia* and *hypostasis* are given in the tradition in order to express what is common and incommunicable in God as Trinity. The Trinitarian categories, however, also provide the foundation for an understanding of personhood that is defined as irreducible uniqueness to and freedom from nature. Salvation as the event of mystical union through participation in the divine energies means a realization of true personhood in which the human person is irreducible to the common human nature; thus, the person is unique but also free in transcendence from the limitations of human nature to experience what is other than creation—the God beyond being. For Lossky, this mystical experience of God occurs though union with the deified nature of Christ and through the power of the Holy Spirit. Lossky was also a vehement opponent of the *filioque*, which he interpreted as the natural result of the rationalization of the doctrine of the Trinity.

At this point, I stop my cursory history of contemporary Orthodox theology to address one relevant question: Did Orthodox theology respond to modernity? It should be clear to all that the Russian school is, in fact, an Orthodox response to modernity. A wider reading in Russian philosophy and theology during the nineteenth and early twentieth centuries would reveal two things: the stamp of Soloviev, and an engagement with the same questions that were central to modern philosophical and theological currents of thought.[10] There is also one discernible feature evident in this response to modernity, particularly in the thought of Soloviev and Bulgakov: the response is rooted in the traditional Orthodox principle of divine-human communion. It is the case that the Russian school was drawn more to the German idealism of Schelling, but I would argue that such an attraction stems from the fact that there was a greater affinity between the conceptualization of the union of the God-world relation in German idealism and the Orthodox principle of divine-human communion than between the latter and the neo-Kantian emphasis on the divide between God and the world. The sophiology of the Russian school was never a wholesale appropriation of German idealism; aspects of the thought of Schelling, in particular, were appropriated, while the whole of his thought was critiqued on the christological principle of divine-human communion. Even the appropriation of a modern philosophical idiom was justified on the basis of the principle of divine-human communion, the logic being that, since God's presence pervades all of creation, then even so-called secular knowledge is able to reflect the truth about God.

The debate between the Russian and the neopatristic schools is often cast in terms of contrasting attitudes toward tradition.[11] The Russian school is portrayed as rooted in, yet going beyond, tradition as it attempts to bring Orthodoxy into an engagement with the modern world through a creative reconstruction of traditional dogmatic formulas; the neopatristic school is described as wedded to classical dogmatic language and resistant to reinterpretations. This particular way of looking at the debate can be misleading if the narrative does not also include the fact that the Russian school and the neopatristic school agree on one essential point: the principle of divine-human communion. I would argue that the core of the debate is not about the role of tradition within theology but, rather, about the implications of the principle of divine-human communion for conceptualizing the God-world relation.

For Lossky—who contributed a pamphlet to the Sophia Affair, *The Debate on Sophia* (*Spor o Sofii*), which he produced for the Brotherhood of St. Photius and which rejected Bulgakov's attempt to unite certain aspects of German idealism to dogmatic theology—the debate with sophiology was not primarily about the relation between theology and philosophy; rather, it was about conceptualizing the transcendent and immanent God. Both Bulgakov and Lossky agreed that divine-human communion is not simply the goal of the Christian life but the very presupposition, the first principle, in all theological thought. The essence/energies distinction, central to Lossky's thought, especially in his critique against neoscholasticism, also constituted Lossky's response to Bulgakov's sophiology. The attributes of God, such as Sophia, are identified with God's energies, and not with God's essence, since the latter is beyond all being and, thus, unknowable. Lossky also argued that the logic of apophaticism, of affirming the incomprehensibility of God's essence, requires a strict division between *theologia*, or knowing God in Godself, and *oikonomia*, knowing God as God relates salvifically to the world. To think of God as eternally relating to the world, as Bulgakov did, is to transgress this apophatic boundary and to negate the otherness between the world and God that is the very basis for a divine-human communion based on love and freedom. Lossky's fear was that any attempt to justify the principle of divine-human communion philosophically, which is what he saw in neoscholasticism and Russian sophiology, ultimately forgets that the only justification is the actual experience of union with God.

Bulgakov would not have disagreed with Lossky that the highest form of knowledge of God is *theosis*; however, for Bulgakov, the God who creates so as to bring the created into communion with Godself was the God who is eternally free to create in such a way and, as such, is eternally relating to creation. For Bulgakov, one could not think God without thinking creation and vice versa. This leads to a much less suspicious and more positive appraisal of the role in theology for philosophy and all the nontheological disciplines. Philosophy has its own integrity and reveals truths about being human. Theology does not appropriate those truths to validate the principle of divine-human communion, but it cannot ignore those truths in its never-ending attempt to interpret the realism of divine communion in Jesus Christ.

Despite Bulgakov's and Lossky's differences on the interpretation of the principle of divine-human communion, it is important to see that they were in full agreement that any response to modernity must be rooted in the Orthodox principle of divine-human communion. This consensus makes the labels of "modern" for Bulgakov and "traditionalist" for Lossky inaccurate; both would claim that the traditional Orthodox affirmation of divine-human communion in Christ is nonnegotiable and is the basis upon which to assess and to critique modern intellectual currents. Bulgakov and Lossky would have essentially agreed that nothing in modern thought could compel Orthodox theology to abandon its central claim: God has created the world for communion with God, which is effected in the person of Jesus Christ. The disagreement is over the implications of this claim for the particular questions and challenges faced by the Christian tradition in the modern period.

To continue with the brief history of contemporary Orthodox theology, the work of Lossky and Florovsky had a significant influence on a group of young theologians in Greece in the 1960s, most notably Nikos Nissiotis (1925–86), Christos Yannaras (b. 1935), and John Zizioulas (b. 1931). Elements of Lossky's theology, such as apophaticism, the essence/energies distinction, and the theology of personhood, are evident in Yannaras's major work, *Person and Eros* (1970).[12] The most influential of these theologians is Zizioulas, who synthesized the eucharistic theology of Nicolas Afanasiev (1893–1966) and Alexander Schmemann (1921–83) with the theology of personhood of Lossky via Yannaras. Zizioulas was a student of Florovsky when the latter was a professor of Harvard; he also taught dogmatics at the Holy Cross Greek Orthodox School of Theology in Brookline, Massachusetts (founded in 1938), before taking a permanent position at the University of Glasgow.

Zizioulas, like Bulgakov and Lossky, would affirm the principle of divine-human communion as the starting point of all theology, but, unlike Lossky's emphasis on the ascetical, mystical ascent to God, Zizioulas would argue that the experience of God is communal in the event of the Eucharist.[13] According to Zizioulas, early Christians experienced the Eucharist as the constitution of the community as the eschatological body of Christ by the Holy Spirit. This experience of Christ in the Eucharist is the basis for the patristic affirmation of the divinity of Christ and the Spirit and, hence, of the affirmation of God as Trinity. Zizioulas's emphasis of the experience of God in the *hypostasis*, or person, of Christ has several implications. First, it is a noticeable break with the virtual consensus in Orthodox theology on the use of the essence/energies distinction for expressing Orthodox understandings of salvation as the experience of the divine life. Second, it is the foundation for what Zizioulas calls an "ontological revolution," insofar as it reveals God's life as that which itself is constituted in freedom and not necessity. If the Eucharist is the experience of God, and, if such an experience is for created reality the freedom from the tragic necessity of death inherent to created existence, then God exists as this freedom from necessity, even the necessity of God's nature, since God gives what God *is*. The freedom of God from the necessity of God's nature is the meaning of the patristic assertion of the monarchy of the Father—the Father "causes" the Son and the Spirit and in so doing constitutes God's life as Trinity through a movement of freedom and love. With the doctrine of the Trinity, for the first time otherness, relation, uniqueness, freedom, and communion become ontologically ultimate. This understanding of divine-human communion in the life of the Trinity through the *hypostasis* of Christ also grounds Zizioulas's theology of personhood. Person is an *ecstatic* being—free from the limitations of created nature—and a *hypostatic* being—unique and irreducible to nature. This freedom and irreducibility are only possible in relation to God the Father through Christ by the Holy Spirit because only in eternal relations of love is one constituted as a unique and free being, that is, a person. Zizioulas has maintained the building blocks of Lossky's theology of person, but with an emphasis on relationality and in a decidedly nonapophatic approach. Zizioulas's theology of personhood is the organizing principle for this theology, and it is evident in his theology of ministry, in his ecclesiology, and in his theology of the environment.

In order to understand the place of Orthodox Christianity in the postmodern world, there are at least three aspects from the thought of the post-1960s generation of Greek theologians that are relevant: first, the continuity with the neopatristic school and the virtual absence of any trace of the Russian school; second, the general audience for this generation of theologians, which is primarily other Christian theologians and traditions; third, the appearance of postmodern concepts and themes, such as difference, otherness, particularity, and desire, without any substantial engagement with some of the icons of postmodern thought, such as Foucault, Derrida, and Kristeva. What emerges in this post-1960s generation is an Orthodox theology with striking affinities with postmodern thought that developed, however, primarily in conversation with other Christian theologies and not with postmodern classics, and which extends the tradition of consensus on the Orthodox principle of divine-human communion—in continuity primarily with the neopatristic school, while self-consciously rejecting the Russian school.[14]

ORTHODOX RESPONSES TO POSTMODERNITY

Two contemporary Orthodox theologians have directly addressed the question of the relation between Orthodoxy and postmodernism: Yannaras and David Bentley Hart. Yannaras belongs to the post-1960s generation of Greek theologians who were influenced by the neopatristic thought of Florovsky and Lossky. He was instrumental in spearheading the critique of the imitative theological style of the pre-1960s generation of Greek theologians. The influence of Lossky is especially evident in Yannaras's emphasis on the centrality of apophaticism in theological discourse. In 1967 Yannaras wrote a book that was recently translated into English under the title *On the Absence and Unknowability of God: Heidegger and the Areopagite*.[15] In this book, Yannaras attempts to argue for a revival of Dionysian apophaticism via Heidegger's critique of the Western philosophical and theological tradition as "ontotheological." A similar move that received much attention was made by Jean-Luc Marion in *God without Being*, first published in French in 1982. Since the publication of *God without Being*, Marion and Derrida have engaged in a debate about the nature of apophaticism, ontotheology, and postmodernity, which is indicative of the clear affinities between apophatic and postmodern understandings of the nature of language.[16] It is clear, however, fifteen years before Marion, that Yannaras argued for the priority of apophaticism in theological discourse based on Heidegger's judgment of traditional philosophical and theological discourses as ontotheological.[17] In some sense, Yannaras was ahead of his time, and his emphasis on apophaticism in theology can be interpreted as a kind of postmodern theology before the explosion of postmodern thought.

Yannaras more directly engages postmodern thought in a book first published in Greece in 1993 and recently translated under the title *Postmodern Metaphysics*.[18] Yannaras argues that one can detect in "post-Newtonian physics" recourse to an apophatic language in an attempt to describe what exceeds language. Post-Newtonian physics also hints at an ontology whose constitutive features are relationality, personal otherness, and existence understood dynamically as a mode (*tropos*) rather than as substance (*ousia*). Though Yannaras is quick to argue that "a metaphysical interpretation and understanding cannot be a result of the scientific study of the world,"[19] "the language of contemporary physics ... liberates and 'validates' other modes of cognitive access to the cosmic fact."[20] An example of another mode of cognitive access for Yannaras is the personal encounter with a work of art, which yields a knowledge of "personal otherness" that is simultaneously "an experience of *relation*."[21]

This engagement with "post-Newtonian" physics has one central point in common with Yannaras's earlier work on Heidegger: both make possible an ontology that is implied in the Eastern Christian affirmation of divine-human communion and is expressed in its most succinct form in the doctrine of the Trinity. For Yannaras, postmodern critiques of modern rationalism and of bourgeois individualism resonate with aspects of Eastern Christian thought, particularly its emphasis on knowledge as experience and on relational notions of personhood. Such postmodern buzzwords as otherness, difference, particularity, relationality, and desire are all central to a relational ontology that is inscribed in the Christian doctrine of the Trinity. Yannaras is not saying that postmodern thought validates Eastern Christian thought; rather, there is a tone of vindication in Yannaras's work in his critical appropriation of postmodern thought. It is modern philosophical and theological intellectual currents that Yannaras sees as inimical to Eastern Christian thought. Postmodern thought has revived ideas, themes, and concepts that were always central to Eastern Orthodox Christianity but marginalized by modern philosophy and theology. Yannaras would clearly argue, however, that postmodern notions of otherness, difference, particularity, relationality, and desire work only within a Trinitarian ontology.

Hart's more direct engagement with postmodern thought in *The Beauty of the Infinite*[22] is similar to Yannaras's but more explicit in its critique of postmodern understandings of difference. Like Yannaras, Hart affirms the postmodern critique of modern rationalism. Lest there be any doubt, he states that "the West at long last awakes from the nightmare of philosophy, even the last ghosts of Enlightenment reason having been chased away, to discover and rejoice in the irreducibly aesthetic character and ultimate foundationlessness of 'truth.'"[23] Hart analyzes the thought of many of the postmodern icons, including Nietzsche, Heidegger, Deleuze, Derrida, and Foucault, only to conclude that "the discourses we tend to recognize as critically postmodern, however little else they may share, all come sooner or later to depend upon one or another account of the 'unrepresentable.'"[24] These accounts of the unrepresentable, far from being an overcoming of metaphysics, are themselves, according to Hart, a metaphysics of immanence that prioritizes all that traditional metaphysics excluded as the ontological—change, becoming, and absence, that is, difference. Insofar as postmodern notions of the unrepresentable reject any notion of transcendence, difference—the condition for the possibility of which is the original difference of the unrepresentable—is possible only through negation and, hence, through violence. Ironically, postmodern thought essentializes difference as violence and in the end offers nothing more than the choice of being "saved from violence by violence, or else by withdrawal (which is death)."[25] Postmodern thought is

> a mystical faith in the reality of the veil, an immanent metaphysics. And the only moral effort permitted by such a faith takes the

form of paradox and tragedy. However one phrases the matter, this much is certain: insofar as the "postmodern" is the completion of the deconstruction of metaphysics, it usually depends upon one immense and irreducible metaphysical assumption: that the unrepresentable *is*; more to the point, that the unrepresentable (call it *différance*, chaos, being, alterity, the infinite . . .) is somehow truer than the representable (which necessarily dissembles it), more original, and qualitatively *other*: that is, it does not differ from the representable by virtue of a greater fullness and unity of those transcendental moments that constitute the world of appearance, but by virtue of its absolute difference, its dialectical or negative indeterminacy, its no-thingness.[26]

Hart adds:

If the world takes shape against the veil of the unrepresentable, is indeed given or confirmed in its finitude by this impenetrable negation, then the discrimination of peace from violence is at most a necessary fiction, and occasionally a critical impossibility; as all equally *is*, and power alone sustains the game of the world, violence is already present in all "truth," though all truthlessness too—sadly or joyously—is violence.[27]

Postmodern thought, according to Hart, contains the seed for the subversion of its account of difference. This seed is in its critique of rationality and its affirmation of the rhetorical and aesthetic, or the rhetorical as aesthetic. It is not a critique of Christianity, as Nietzsche thought, to affirm the priority of the aesthetic, because beauty, Hart argues, is at the heart of the Christian understanding of God revealed in Jesus Christ. The proper Christian response to postmodern accounts of difference is simply the claim that the Christian understanding of difference is more persuasive because it is more beautiful. Christian difference is not about violence but about peace. The difference that is inscribed in finite being is not the result of a more original unrepresentable difference but of the Trinitarian difference, of the unity-in-difference of the Father, Son, and Holy Spirit. The plenitude of God's Trinitarian being is the precondition for constituting creation as gift. The ontological divide between God and the created other is the precondition for distance to result in real difference that is an event of communion that bridges the divide. Difference as divine-human communion does not totalize the other, but lets the other simply be other. Difference that hardens into distance is a result of violence; the distance that is transformed into real difference is an event of peace realized by the prior gift of God's love for the created other. As Hart puts it,

> [T]he Trinity's perfect act of difference also opens the possibility of the "ontico-ontological difference," as the space of the gift of analogous being, imparted to contingent beings who, then, receive this gift as the movement of an ontic deferral.... The distance between God and creation is not alienation, nor the Platonic *chorismos* or scale of being, but the original ontological act of distance by which every ontic interval subsists, given to be crossed but not overcome, at once God's utter transcendence and utter proximity.[28]

In the end, for Hart, it comes down to a choice between two competing narratives of difference that cannot be adjudicated. For Hart, Christians must stand confident in the persuasiveness and beauty of their narrative of the divine-human communion effected in the person of Jesus Christ. In the battle between the "New Nietzsche" and the Christian narrative of divine-human communion, "[t]he most potent reply a Christian can make to Nietzsche's critique is to accuse him of a defect of sensibility—of bad taste. And this, in fact, is the last observation that should be made at this point: Nietzsche had atrocious taste."[29]

In the brief history of contemporary Orthodox theology that I have offered, one can trace a line of influence from Soloviev to the post-1960s generation of Greek theologians. The neopatristic theologians did reject the Russian sophiologists, but even this rejection forms part of a singular history. Hart's work does not fit easily into this trajectory—he is neither a neopatristic theologian nor retrieving Russian sophiology. In fact, both Lossky and Yannaras may gasp at Hart's affirmation of Thomistic notions of analogy, which they judge as antithetical to Dionysian apophaticism. Hart, however, stands within this trajectory in one very important way: the ground of his theology, its very presupposition, is the realism of divine-human communion. In essence Hart is arguing, much like Yannaras and Zizioulas, that postmodern concerns with difference, otherness, particularity, relationality, and desire are only secured through an affirmation of the principle of divine-human communion. In the centrality of the principle of divine-human communion, Hart's response to postmodernity mirrors that of Bulgakov's and Lossky's response to modernity.

ORTHODOXY, POSTMODERNISM, AND ECUMENISM

In what is now a classic essay in its own right, Tracy discussed three different responses to the present situation: the (late) modern, the antimodern, and the postmodern. Toward the end of the essay, Tracy concluded that, though Christian theology can agree and retrieve elements of each of these trajectories, it does not easily fit into any of them. As he wrote, "Nowhere in all this conflict of interpretations among moderns, anti-moderns, and post-moderns does a full Christian theological naming of the present as interruptive eschatological time before the living God occur."[30] In my brief history of contemporary Orthodox theology, I have tried to show how Orthodox thought does not easily fit into either the modern or postmodern trajectories, nor is it easily categorized as a fossilized form of the premodern. Orthodox theologians have consistently responded to both modern and postmodern theological and philosophical currents united around a shared consensus on the fundamental principle of the realism of divine-human communion. Nothing within modern or postmodern thought has convinced Orthodox Christians to surrender what is at the heart of their tradition—that God has created the world so as to effect a communion between God and the world. No matter how one interprets the central questions in the postmodern situation, whether they are on epistemology, subjectivity, or pluralism, the Orthodox response will continue to be shaped by the fundamental presupposition of the realism of divine-human communion. No Orthodox theologians, their differences notwithstanding, would dispute the centrality of this principle; this consensus over the past two centuries, which I would argue extends back to the patristic period, illustrates what Tracy meant by "thinking as a tradition."

Yannaras's and Hart's attack on modernity as fundamentally a mistake may lead one to categorize their theologies as antimodern. The antimodern camp, associated with such theologians and philosophers as Stanley Hauerwas and Alasdair MacIntyre, often speaks about the incommensurability between Christian and modern philosophical discourses. This position often results in the wholesale rejection of modern thought. Hart and Yannaras share elements of this antimodern trajectory, rejecting in particular the modern attack on premodern forms of knowing, modern rationalism, and the excesses of modern individualism; whether they fit neatly into the antimodern camp is ambiguous.

The ambiguous relation between Orthodoxy and modernity is further evinced in Orthodox rhetoric on democracy. This issue of Orthodoxy and democracy is especially acute since the fall of communism, where the Orthodox churches in traditional Orthodox countries have been forced to face questions for the first time but without the necessary intellectual resources, which were decimated during the course of both Ottoman and communist occupation. In traditional Orthodox countries, one will find Orthodox church leaders issuing prodemocracy language while simultaneously spewing invectives against the excessive individualism of the West. One will also find Orthodox Church leaders lending support to what appear to be antidemocratic initiatives, such as restrictions on religious freedom, mandatory religious education in Orthodox Christianity (even for minorities within the country), or resistance to the construction of mosques. The situation in Eastern Europe in particular is one where Orthodox churches are trying to figure out how to exist politically without an emperor. Orthodox Christians have a unique history insofar as they lay claim to a proud imperial heritage in the Byzantine Empire, which provided the space for the development of their rich traditions, but they are only now emerging from a half-millennium's worth of oppression. Orthodox Christians have been the colonizers and the colonized and often return to their imperial past to confront their postcolonial situation. I have argued elsewhere that the experience of the imperial past cannot adequately provide the resources to address contemporary questions.[31] The modern and postmodern situations are presenting questions to the Orthodox churches that they have never before faced in their history; one cannot seek specific answers in the past to questions that were never posed in that past.

The Orthodox response to the present situation is complicated by the lack of any institutional infrastructure that would allow the Orthodox churches to deliberate in a meaningful way on contemporary challenges and questions. This lack of infrastructure is a vestige of their imperial past; since the disappearance of the emperors, both pro- and anti-Orthodox, the Orthodox churches have yet to develop a transnational, pan-Orthodox authority that would facilitate meaningful deliberation on the present situation as a global church.[32] When I talk about a transnational authority, I am not necessarily alluding to a popelike figure; such an authority could take many forms. Nor is it the case that the presence of such an authority would violate the Orthodox principle of conciliarity. Recent events, however, illustrate how impotent conciliarity can be without a transnational authority. As one example, a few years ago the Ecumenical Patriarchate and the Church of Greece had a dispute over the election of the next presiding bishop of Thessalonika. In a move reminiscent of the Byzantine past, the dispute was resolved only after the intervention of the minister of education and religious affairs of Greece, who brokered the solution that was not really a resolution.

I mention these institutional problems within Orthodoxy only to highlight the lingering effects of its imperial past—Byzantine, Bulgarian, Serbian, Russian, Ottoman, and communist. The lack of any global, institutionalized infrastructure on the part of the Orthodox Church has resulted in the absence of any meaningful deliberation on the contemporary challenges and questions confronting the Orthodox churches. One of those questions in the post-communist Eastern European situation is Orthodoxy's stance toward liberal, Western forms of democracy. It is only in the past sixty years that Orthodoxy has had to confront the question of what it means to be a church in a democratic, secularized space. There were very vibrant and substantive debates on transitions to democracy in Russia in the early part of the twentieth century, but these were tragically cut short by the Bolshevik Revolution. The lack of a transnational authority to facilitate a meaningful deliberation on this new situation has resulted in confused, contradictory, antimodern, and anti-Western statements from Orthodox Church leaders.

Even in the midst of this global institutional fragmentation, there is a remarkable, discernible unity within the Orthodox Church that is especially visible in its eucharistic celebration. The Eucharist has the power to dispel "all the cares of this world"[33] and focus one's attention on what is real in this world. This unity in the Eucharist reflects the consensus that exists among contemporary Orthodox theologians on the principle of divine-human communion, since the Eucharist itself is the event of such a communion. It is this shared faith in the realism of divine-human communion that must somehow shape the Orthodox response to the present situation. Returning to the issue of Orthodoxy and democracy, there are some, such as the Armenian Orthodox theologian and ethicist Vigen Guroian, who would argue that Orthodoxy should never endorse any political arrangement, since such an endorsement would betray its prophetic principle. I have argued, however, that the logic of the Orthodox understanding of divine-human communion realized in the Eucharist leads to the judgment of support for a democratic and secularized space over the prevailing options.[34] Support of democracy and secularization does not mean an endorsement of excessive individualism or ideological secularism. To those who question how Orthodoxy can support any form of thought in which God is not the object of intentionality, I would respond by referencing the prophetic and ironic caution throughout history that God's presence is often most manifest in spaces that appear in a superficial way to be godless.

I have discussed Orthodoxy's relation to democracy at length to illustrate the simple point that Orthodoxy's stance to modernity is not and should not be a wholesale rejection. I agree with Tracy when he argues that although Christian theology does not easily fit into the three common namings of the present situation, it can recognize elements that are retrievable in each of these namings. The hermeneutical key for the Orthodox is the principle of divine-human communion, which, I would argue, allows Orthodox thought to recognize the genuine accomplishments of the modern period. The "truths" of modern intellectual currents were recognized by the Russian sophiologists, and perhaps the recent translations in English of Russian sophiology, especially Bulgakov's work, might reinfuse Orthodox theology with this particular sophiological spirit that for too long has remained dormant. Orthodox theology can learn from the sophiologists that many modern human advancements are not necessarily incommensurable with Orthodoxy simply because they emerged, in part, from an attack on religion but are, perhaps ironically, entailed within the logic of divine-human communion.

It is this very principle of divine-human communion that must also shape the Orthodox response to postmodern questions on epistemology, subjectivity, and pluralism. I have already spoken of the affinity between postmodern thought and contemporary Orthodox theological understandings of difference, otherness, particularity, relationality, and desire. It has been the singular achievement of contemporary theologians such as Lossky, Yannaras, Zizioulas, and Hart to unpack the existential implications of the doctrine of the Trinity. Zizioulas, in particular, has shown that the Christian understanding of God as Trinity is much more than a simple affirmation that God is simultaneously one and three. For Zizioulas, Christians know that God is Trinity because of the experience of divine-human communion in the Eucharist, which is not simply a partaking of the body of Christ but is the event of the resurrected body of Christ. The Christian affirmation of the divinity of Christ, crystallized in the fourth century, is at the heart of the doctrine of the Trinity. In the person of Jesus, God has become history; in the life of Jesus, one witnesses, as Williams has so elegantly put it, "a humanity soaked through with divine life."[35] It is this original Trinitarian difference, not a difference whose primary presence is only an absence, that is the condition for the possibility of a difference that is created for communion.[36] That of God who becomes history, the Son of the Father, realizes and makes possible an eternal communion with God the Father that is effected only by that Trinitarian difference that is faceless yet ever present and filling all things—the Holy Spirit. Personhood, for Zizioulas, *is* difference as particularity, but such a difference, if it is to be one of communion and not negations, is constituted in relations of love and freedom.

Given that there is a great deal of affinity between Eastern Christian notions of apophaticism and the doctrine of the Trinity and postmodern notions of language and difference, the temptation would be great to use postmodern thought as a means for validating Christian thought. I think, however, that Hart is correct in asserting that Christians need to be more self-confident about the fact that their account of difference is simply more beautiful and, hence, more persuasive than the many postmodern variations. Karl Rahner, in his theology of the Trinity, argued that the Christian doctrine of the Trinity is the affirmation that God can become history without ceasing to be the immutable, triune God and that this very possibility *is* God's very being as the self-differentiated triune God. Responding to those who might claim that this sounds Hegelian, Rahner wrote, "This we can and must affirm, without being Hegelians. And it would be a pity if Hegel had to teach Christians such things."[37] Echoing Rahner, I would say that it would be a pity if Derrida had to teach Christians about difference.

For Tracy, a Christian naming of the present "as interruptive eschatological time before the living God" is one that is dialectically mystical and political. The general perception in the Christian world is that the Orthodox tradition is a great resource for the mystical side of this dialectic. There is, however, a rich tradition of attention to the "political" in Orthodoxy, particularly in the rhetoric against poverty embodied in the sermons of John Chrysostom or the living examples of the Holy Fools of Russia. It is also evident in the writings of the Russian sophiologists, who, because of their more generous appraisal of the "secular," based on their conceptualization of divine-human communion, were much more engaged with the cultural and "political" spheres. Two women of the Russian diaspora whose work reflects the Russian sophiological tradition continued this engagement with the political: Mother Maria Skobtsova[38] with her work on social justice, and Elizabeth Behr-Sigel[39] with her work on gender and the role of women within the church.

It is fair, however, to assert that this "political" trajectory within the Eastern Christian tradition is not the one most visibly represented today in the Orthodox churches. This judgment often does not take into account the effect of the Ottoman and communist oppressions on the Orthodox churches; in the United States, it does not take into account the fact that only now the Orthodox communities are moving beyond issues relating to preservation of national and ethnic identities.[40] It is becoming more evident that the new generation of church leaders, clerical and lay, in the Orthodox churches in the United States are shaping their communities to engage in social concerns. It is correct, however, to claim that one of the greatest challenges for the Orthodox Church is the recovery of this "political" trajectory within the tradition. Participation in ecumenical organizations such as the National Council of the Churches of Christ in the USA is an opportunity not only to be reminded of this particular heritage in the Orthodox traditions but also to be challenged to bring this heritage into conversation with the present situation. In particular, the Orthodox tradition can learn from Latin American liberation theologians that the problem of poverty is not simply about the individual sins of pride and greed but that it involves systemic sin; the Orthodox can learn from black and feminist liberation theologies that the "political" must be expanded to include issues of race and gender. Ecumenical gatherings presuppose conversation, which presupposes listening, which presupposes risk of a realized experience of recognition that leads to such statements as "I never thought of that" or "That seems right." To recognize that a particular prohibition or practice within a tradition needs change is not to surrender to an incommensurable language game; instead, it is a form of prophetic self-critique that allows a community to examine whether it is being faithful to its own central principles.

For the Orthodox churches, the principle of divine-human communion is absolutely nonnegotiable, in modernity, postmodernity, and beyond postmodernity; it is also the most substantial contribution that it can bring to any ecumenical gathering—to remind the world constantly, almost incessantly, that God has created the world for real communion with God, which is effected in Christ and by the Holy Spirit. Orthodoxy can also draw on its rich tradition to assert the priority of the mystical—the mystical and the political are not dialectically related to each other, as Tracy argued, but any authentic gain in the political is the realization of the mystical. The mystical cannot be reduced to the individual ascent to or manifestation of God, because any experience of the love of God must be embodied and manifested in particular relations. If sin is, in fact, systemic, then structural change that allows for the affirmation of each human being as a unique and irreplaceable child of God simultaneously manifests a greater participation of the world in the event of divine-human communion. To identify such structural change with divine-human communion is not naively to identify the realm of God with earthly structures; rather, it affirms the Orthodox understanding of the world as sacramental, as imbued with the presence of God that is latent in the world and desiring to burst forth. The world is already participating in God's life, and the challenge for humans is to create the kinds of relationships, both political and ecclesial, that would maximize the degree of participation of the world in God. To be Christian is to recognize and accept the paradoxical state of being that strives to realize God's realm on earth while always knowing that it is yet to come. The particular challenge for the Orthodox Church is to find a way in which the very heart of its tradition, the realism of divine-human communion in the person of Jesus Christ, is able to permeate and shape its institutional structures so as to enable responses to "political" questions that are faithful to all that is entailed in this principle of divine-human communion. Such faithfulness means working to create a world in which particularity, otherness, difference, relationality, and freedom are the norm and reflect the glory of God, which is the presence of God's love that is always striving to show itself.

NOTES

1. H. R. MacKintosh and J. S. Stewart, eds., *The Christian Faith* (Edinburgh: T&T Clark, 1989), 101–2.

2. "The millet system of the Ottomans suggests another version of the imperial regime of toleration, one that was more fully developed and longer lasting" (Michael Walzer, *On Toleration* [New Haven, CT: Yale University Press, 1997], 17).

3. Roberto S. Goizueta, *Caminemos con Jesús: Toward a Hispanic/Latino Theology of Accompaniment* (Maryknoll, NY: Orbis Books, 1995).

4. John Zizioulas, *Communion and Otherness: Further Studies in Personhood and the Church* (London and New York: T&T Clark, 2006).

5. See Christos Yannaras, *Orthodoxy and the West*, trans. Peter Chamberas and Norman Russell (Brookline, MA: Holy

Cross Orthodox Press, 2006 [orig.: *Orthodoxia kaj Dysi sti neoteri Ellada* (Athens: Domos, 1992)]).

6. The best account of the Russian school is Paul Valliere's *Modern Russian Theology: Bukharev, Soloviev, Bulgakov—Orthodox Theology in a New Key* (Grand Rapids, MI: Eerdmans, 2000).

7. Rowan Williams, *The Theology of Vladimir Nikolaievich Lossky: An Exposition and Critique* (PhD diss., Oxford University, 1975), 209.

8. All three volumes have been translated by Boris Jakim and published by William B. Eerdmans Publishing Co., Grand Rapids, MI: *The Lamb of God* (forthcoming), *The Comforter* (2004), and *The Bride of the Lamb* (2002, with T&T Clark, Edinburgh).

9. For an overview of Lossky's theology, see my *Being with God: Trinity, Apophaticism, and Divine-Human Communion* (Notre Dame, IN: University of Notre Dame Press, 2006).

10. See V. V. Zenkovsky's *A History of Russian Philosophy*, 2 vols., trans. George L. Kline (London: Routledge & Kegan Paul; New York: Columbia University Press, 1953).

11. See Valliere, *Modern Russian Theology*, especially 373–403.

12. Christos Yannaras, *Person and Eros*, 4th ed., trans. Norman Russell (Brookline, MA: Holy Cross Orthodox Press, 2006 [orig.: *To Prosopon kai o Eros* (Athens: Domos, 1970)]).

13. For an overview of Zizioulas's theology, see Papanikolaou, *Being with God*.

14. Much of the preceding section will also appear in my "Orthodox Theology," in Erwin Fahlbusch, Jan Milič Lochman, John Mbiti, Jaroslav Pelikan, Lukas Vischer, eds.; Geoffrey W. Bromiley, English-language ed.; David B. Barnett, statistical ed., *Encyclopedia of Christianity*, vol. 5 (Grand Rapids, MI: Eerdmans; Leiden: Brill, 2007), 414–18. I am grateful to the publishers for permission to use material from that entry for this essay.

15. Christos Yannaras, *On the Absence and Unknowability of God: Heidegger and the Areopagite*, trans. Haralambos Ventis (London and New York: Continuum International Publishing Group, 2005); see my review of this book in *Modern Theology* 23 (April 2007): 301–4.

16. For an account of this debate, see Arthur Bradley, "God *sans* Being: Derrida, Marion, and 'A Paradoxical Writing of the

Word *Without,'" Literature and Theology* 14 (September 2000): 299–312.

17. This argument has been acknowledged, as far as I know, only in Thomas A. Carlson, *Indiscretion: Finitude and the Naming of God* (Chicago: University of Chicago Press, 1999), 5.

18. Christos Yannaras, *Postmodern Metaphysics*, trans. Norman Russell (Brookline, MA: Holy Cross Orthodox Press, 2004 [orig.: *Meta-neôterikê meta-physikê* (Athens, 1993)]).

19. Ibid., 112.

20. Ibid., 115.

21. Ibid., 112–13, emphasis in original.

22. David Bentley Hart, *The Beauty of the Infinite; The Aesthetics of Christian Truth* (Grand Rapids, MI: Eerdmans, 2003).

23. Ibid., 5.

24. Ibid., 44.

25. Ibid., 89.

26. Ibid., 52.

27. Ibid., 91.

28. Ibid., 193–94.

29. Ibid., 125.

30. David Tracy, *On Naming the Present: Reflections on God, Hermeneutics, and Church* (Maryknoll, NY: Orbis Books; London: SCM Press, 1994), 18.

31. See my "Byzantium, Orthodoxy, and Democracy," *Journal of the American Academy of Religion* 71 (March 2003): 75–98.

32. On the absence of a transnational authority in Orthodoxy and its effects on the Orthodox experience in the United States, see my "The One Becomes the Many: Orthodox Christianity and American Pluralism," in Elizabeth H. Prodromou, ed., *Orthodox Christianity in American Public Life: The Challenges and Opportunities of Religious Pluralism in the Twenty-First Century* (Notre Dame, IN: University of Notre Dame Press, forthcoming).

33. From the Cherubic Hymn sung during the Liturgy of St. John Chrysostom.

34. See Aristotle Papanikolaou, "Byzantium, Orthodoxy, and Democracy."

35. Rowan Williams, *The Dwelling of the Light: Praying with Icons of Christ* (Grand Rapids, MI: Eerdmans, 2004), xvi.

36. For Zizioulas's recent reflections on difference and communion, see Paul McPartlan, ed., *Communion and Otherness: Further Studies in Personhood and the Church* (Edinburgh: T&T Clark, 2006).

37. Karl Rahner, "On the Theology of the Incarnation," in his *Theological Investigations*, vol. 4, *More Recent Writings*, trans. Kevin Smyth (London: Darton, Longman & Todd; Baltimore, MD: Helicon Press, 1966 [orig.: *Schriften zur Theologie, IV* (Einsiedeln: Benziger, 1966)]), 113–14, n. 3.

38. See *Mother Maria Skobtsova: Essential Writings*, trans. Richard Pevear and Larissa Volokhonsky (Maryknoll, NY: Orbis Books, 2003). For a biography, see Michael Plekon, *Living Icons: Persons of Faith in the Eastern Church* (Notre Dame, IN: University of Notre Dame Press, 2002), 59–80.

39. See Elizabeth Behr-Sigel, *The Ministry of Women in the Church* (Redondo Beach, CA: Oakwood Publications, 1991).

40. See the essays in Prodromou, *Orthodox Christianity in American Public Life*.

Chapter 8

THE BIBLE ON POSTMODERN SUR*f*ACES

Jione Havea

> Following its presentation at Oberlin II, this paper was revised and published under the title "Is There a Home for the Bible in the Postmodern World?" in the *Journal of Ecumenical Studies* 42, no. 4 (Fall 2007): 547–59, and is copyrighted (2007) by the *Journal of Ecumenical Studies* (*JES*). The original paper as delivered at Oberlin II is printed here with permission from the author and *JES*.

What place do ancient texts have in situations that are radically different from, in terms of both structure and drive, the worlds in which they were formed, revised, transmitted and authorized? Can "premodern texts" (which were questioned in the "modern era") be at-home in the "postmodern world"? Can ancient scriptures still [be made to] speak in the postmodern world? In other words, would the postmodern world accommodate the Bible? How may the Bible serve as "home" in the postmodern world?

POSTMODERNITY, eSCAPEGOATED

"Postmodernity" is the new beast at whose feet many people lay the blame for whatever ideas and behaviors make them nervous. It has been shoved into places usually reserved for the mischievous (woman) temptress that must be domesticated, the wild (queer) orientations that must be tamed, and the reckless (satanic) tendencies to confuse values and violate boundaries that must be ruled. Many defy postmodernity because they feel that it does not exhibit and sustain *faith* or have respect for *order*. They do not feel at home in the postmodern world because it is unsteady, fragmentary and fragmenting, hostile to the principles of Faith and Order, which presuppose certainty, harmony and fixity.[1]

Postmodernity, the specter behind "postmodernism" (see distinction below), is a scapegoat for whatever exposes and agitates people's insecurities. Some of my colleagues and friends accuse me as being postmodern whenever, for instance, I challenge religious or cultural traditions. Previously, in their eyes, I was just silly. But now I am postmodern (for the same reasons). They, however, do not realize that being critical and difficult does not necessarily make one postmodern. I might still be silly, but that does not mean that I am therefore postmodern. I argue, on the other hand, that the onslaughts of the Western Enlightenment Era (or "modernity") and its scientific modes of thinking are much more contentious against cultures and traditions, and matters of Faith and Order, which do not always stand on the kind of positivist evidences and reasoning that modern minds prefer, than postmodernity.

This chapter does not address the [dis]connections between modernity and postmodernity (cf. Docherty,[2] Hassan,[3] Jameson,[4] Norris,[5] Waugh[6]), but rather joins the chorus of voices that seeks to demystify postmodernity (cf. Smith,[7] Rollins[8]) and to ponder how we may still appreciate the Bible (differently) in our postmodern world.[9] The chapter circles around the Bible primarily because it is one of the points of intersection for any Christians, a site of contact that signifies Christian unity. I circle around the Bible also because it contains multiple voices and it is open to a diversity of responses, so it is a lighthouse that points to the harbor of diversity in unity and unity in diversity.

This article aims to show and tell, in form and content, that postmodernity is not as spooky as people fear it to be. It will hopefully help relax the dis-ease with the place of other teachings and doctrines in the work of Faith and Order at various spheres of the Christian life.

POSTMODERNITY, UNSPOOKED

Postmodernity is like a rip current that pulls swimmers away from shallow shores. A rip current forms when waves break unevenly, usually with the ends breaking first then the waves fold inward then gush back out to sea at the middle creating a ripping pull that is much stronger than the power of the waves that came from the deep. The rip current is scary for swimmers who try to swim against it, for it is like swimming upstream against the strong whitewaters of a narrow but deep river, and it can be deadly (those swimmers can drown). But it can also be "deadly" according to the way indigenous Australians use the word vis-à-vis referring to something that is pleasurable, fun, cool, awesome, and so forth. The best way to enjoy the rip current is to ride it out to sea, feel for a place where one can swim away from the pull of the current (by swimming outward to the left or to the right of the rip), then circle around the current and back to shore. As the sea gets deeper, the rip current weakens and one can easily swim away and around it.

Comparing postmodernity to a rip current allows me, at the risk of oversimplification, to imagine two pulls in postmodernity, one scary and the other can be fun. There are more than two pulls, of course, but these two suffice for this article. I am referring to, first, the destabilizing effect of postmodernity, the pull that rips and carries one away from the safety of the shallow shore, and second, the playful aspect of postmodernity, the pull that one can ride into the deep where it sinks, thus releasing one to swim away. The rip of postmodernity whirls one into, at once, pain and pleasure, danger and enjoyment, fear and tranquility, disempowerment and freedom, and so forth, the kind of experience that Julia Kristeva calls *jouissánce*.[10] Together, they are "deadly." I linger to address the two pulls in turn.

I turn first to the scary pull. Postmodernity haunts people who imagine that it shakes the foundations of order and disturbs structures of meaning and faith.[11] This perception often dismays the unsteady and misguides the skeptic. I hold on the other hand that postmodernity does not smash belief systems or raze structures and havens of meaning. It does not, to use an image with which Pacific Islanders are familiar, pull the mats from under us. Rather, postmodernity shows that the mats on which we sit were woven with many strands and they are already frayed. The strands are supposed to hold each other into place, but every time that the mats are rolled out and people sit or walk on them, the furry surfaces of the strands are flattened and smoothened out so that the strands can slip out of place and thus the mats continually unravel. Along this line, postmodernity calls attention to the fraying composition of our mats, but it does not pull the strands apart or push us away from our mats. Postmodernity exposes the flux as well as the woven- and constructed-ness of our mats (our "security blankets"), the places where we sit and stand, and challenges us to come to terms with the wavering stability of our placements. Put simply, postmodernity reminds us that we occupy both real and ideological spaces that continually unravel (crumple and disintegrate) and thus, so to speak, we need to find meanings in the fray.

The first framed image I ever owned[12] was a postcard that shows a globe open at the bottom, with all sorts of things falling out at the bottom to form a trash heap below. The image is Michel Granger's *la grande décharge* ("the great dump," 1977). This image matched how I, a struggling Third World student at that time, saw the world: the world was unraveling, falling apart, in pieces. This was one of the reasons why postmodernity made sense to me, simply, because it also saw how "the world" was unraveling, falling apart, fraying.

Postmodernity is not preaching something new. In the Judeo-Christian biblical tradition, for instance, realizing that the world is falling apart goes back to the two creation stories. In the first story, after each day's creative activities, God sees, and the narrator announces, that the things called into existence that day were "good" (Gen. 1:4, 10, 12, 18, 21, 25). Then on day six, God judged that everything called into existence was "very good" (Gen. 1:31) before resting up on day seven. The world was intact and in a "good" state. Everything was according to plan, and the creating God was satisfied; so God could now have a rest.

The second (garden) story, on the other hand, starts with God noticing two *lacks* in the creation: God had not sent rain and there was no man to till the soil (Gen. 2:5). The world was not as good as God saw it in the first story. And in trying to make up for these lacks, especially the second one (the man created to till the soil needs a helper, suggesting that he was not properly endowed for the task for which he was created), the world began to unravel. In trying to plug up what was lacking, more lacks were exposed, and it feels as if, as in the postcard, the world was open at the bottom and its contents are falling off. According to this perspective, the garden story was not about the loss of paradise or the fall of humanity but about how the creative acts of God also unraveled the creation. The world was falling apart even before the talking serpent revealed the truth about the forbidden fruits, that they will enable one to know "good and bad" (which is a divine characteristic; cf. Gen. 2:15–17; 3:1–5).

The world falls apart in a different sense at the beginning of the *Bhagavad Gītā*. This Hindu text contains a conversation just before the battle at Krukshetra between Prince Arjuna and his charioteer and guide, Krishna (a divine being, *Bhagavan*). The battle lines have been drawn, the conch shells of war blown, vibrating in the sky and on the earth, and the parties are ready to fight. At that moment, Arjuna asked Krishna to draw his chariot between the armies so that he can see who is fighting whom. What he saw melted his courage: "There Arjuna could see, within the midst of the armies of both parties, his fathers, grandfathers, teachers, maternal uncles, brothers, sons, grandsons, friends, and also his fathers-in-law and well-wishers" (1:26). He can not gather the spirit needed to fight his friends, relatives, and teachers: "I do not see how any good can come from killing my own kinsmen in this battle, nor can I, my dear Krishna, desire any subsequent victory, kingdom, or happiness" (3:1). At that very moment, on the spot, Arjuna's world[view] falls apart. He becomes confused about his duty (2:7), and the rest of the conversation contains Krishna's instructions about *dharma* (duty and harmony).

Both of these religious texts predated postmodernism and Granger's *la grande décharge*. But they coincide in the awareness that "the world" is not as constant, secure and meaningful as we often assume (hope) it to be. The Bible and the *Gītā* say more about the world, and other things, but the awareness of the flux and brokenness of the world is one of their points of intersection with postmodernism. Such awareness echoes the elusive concept of *Shunyata* (emptiness or zero-ness) in Mahayana Buddhism, which suggests that everything is in flux, constantly becoming and collapsing, and void of essential substance or self, because everything is interdependent. This Buddhist perspective also predated postmodernism.

I divert to distinguish postmodernity from postmodernism. I stated above that the Bible and the *Gītā* predated postmodernism, but I imagine also that the kind of energy characteristic of postmodernity, which pulls postmodernism, ticked in the pulse of ancient societies also.[13] Postmodernism is the *ism* that lays claim to the spirit of postmodernity, an *ism* that can be located in time as the cultures that superseded modernism (around the 1960s, according to Fredric Jameson,[14] and the mid-1970s, according to Steven Connor.[15] The spirit of postmodernity here echoes what Lyotard refers to as the "postmodern condition," which he characterizes as incredulity toward totalizing metanarratives or grand narratives, which assume some form of transcendent and universal truth.[16] Postmodernism gives expression to postmodernity, but postmodernity is not limited to postmodernism. Can postmodernity be limited to a place and time, or to anything at all? This seems impossible given that the pull of postmodernity, evident in postmodern theories, has "the desire to project and to produce that which cannot be pinned down or mastered by representation or conceptual thought, the desire which has been identified by Jean-François Lyotard as the pull towards the sublime."[17]

Since, as I imagine, the pull of postmodernity was present in ancient texts and in religious cultures, so it is not totally new or irreligious, then there is no reason to fear it. Postmodernity is present almost everywhere. Lift a text or a tradition, whether ancient or recent, and turn over a story or a memory, and one finds the ripping pull of postmodernity in play. To fight the ripping pull of postmodernity might pull one under. One would be better off by riding it out before circling around and relocating oneself, possibly at another place. This is the second pull of postmodernity that I wish to briefly address, the opportunity to be playful that postmodernity creates.

By reiterating the volatility of "the world," postmodernity raises the anchors of the powers-that-be, setting those adrift and opening up a space for the rafts of marginalized, exploited, and displaced subjects. The de-centering arm of postmodernity also raises a flag for the politics of difference and otherness. The second pull of postmodernity is liberating, and I will briefly turn to three of its codependent ripples—story, identity, and diaspora—and how they may impact the way we read the Bible in the postmodern world.

Story

In kindling incredulity toward metanarratives, maintaining that not one narrative controls over all other narratives, Lyotard opens a portal for people to look for and listen to local narratives. In other words, incredulity toward grand narratives is an invitation for alternative and multiple stories, including stories from *la grande décharge*.

Unfortunately, (esp. Western) churches dread the postmodern challenge as if it seeks to reject Christian narratives and so, in response, we give up, withdraw from, the storytelling functions. The challenge and the response do not coincide: the challenge is against the *power of stories,* and the response is to neglect the *joy of telling.*

When did Christian narratives become metanarratives?[18] In whose eyes? and for whom? Are we exaggerating the place of Christian narratives in a world where Christianity is not the dominant religion? Even though governments with strong military powers and rigorous warfare tactics are from Christian

Identity

In promoting heterogeneity, which seeks to embrace subjects who have traditionally been marginalized, especially with respect to race, gender, and class, the postmodern critique of identity is liberating. This *turn to the Other* has taken root and bore many fruits in many lands and circles.

The decentering of dominant mastering subjects needs to go together with the sensitizing and empowering of displaced and outcast subjects. But it does not always happen this way.

Sometimes, the decentering process takes place in order to install another master from within the same circles of sovereignty, and the new master extends the empire of his forefathers. The boundaries of control are not broken, and the cultures of domination grow.

And sometimes, decentered subjects can't shed the scales of the master cultures, both the language and the models of domination; thus they become shadows and puppets of their masters. With respect to race, for instance, those

Diaspora

Awareness of limits, margins, and acts of marginalization draws attention to space and placement. Where one is, one's contexts, help condition who one is, how one thinks and operates.[20] Things are interesting for the postmodern subject because s/he spreads over several places (a hybrid) at once. Recently, many governments legalized dual citizenship, as if one can occupy and have "home" in two countries at the same time (a possibility for the haves and wealthy).

We need to reconsider what "home" (and citizenship) means in our postmodern age. Home is no longer just about land and space.

As people spread throughout the world, away from their homelands, and as technology brings people from distant lands closer together, home is no longer the place where one lives. A Fijian might have grown up in Seattle and now lives at Rhode Island, partner to an Italian from across the border with Canada, but "home" for her is somewhere on the shores of Fiji. Home is not where she countries, Christianity is not the grand religion.

And why do we imagine that Christian narratives are the only narratives that postmodernity challenges?

Given that we are Christians, we see our narratives as grand. They are grand for us, and we are many; but they are not grand for everyone, and they are more.

Postmodernity creates a space where Christian narratives can be in conversation with narratives that are grand for other people, both people from other faiths and people from outside the dominant Christian cultures. Postmodernity welcomes such conversations which, illustrated in my musings above, is one way to engage in the storytelling function.

Once we calm down from stressing over the postmodern incredulity to metanarratives, and come to terms with our illusion concerning Christian narratives, we should consider reclaiming the storytelling function. If we don't, we leave storytelling in the hands of the media (which feeds viewers' hunger for information) and the subjects are often said (by members of racially oppressed communities) to be "whiter than white people" and, with respect to gender, they are "manlier than man," and so forth.

The postmodern critique of identity is not just about paying lip service to our heterogeneous makeup, but it calls for resistance against homogenizing tendencies (e.g., essentialism) and for the reconstruction of identities (of both the Other and the decentered master-subjects). It affirms the agency of the Other and embraces our fraying mass consciousness and woven mass cultures.

The postmodern reconstructed identity has a crosscultural face, a face that belongs across ethnic and cultural (e.g., gender, age, sexual orientation, and so forth) divides. The reconstructed postmodern identity is multiple and varied;[19] e.g., there are multiple Pacific Island identities, and there are variations within each island group.

The postmodern reconstruction of identity can help us see, ., how the "people of is, but where she draws her identity. Home is more than space; it is also about the harbors of one's security and identity.

I make a simple point here but others might misunderstand, so I reiterate—a Fijian living in the United States is not in diaspora (to say that she *lives in diaspora* is to keep her in perpetual displacement), rather, her *home is in diaspora*. Likewise, a European in India, or an African American returning to Ghana, will long for home, which will not be at where they are. The location of identity, their home, is not at where they are; they are strangers where they live.

What is (or makes something) home for a postmodern subject? What in a place, memory, event, and so forth, makes those homely for a postmodern subject? In light of the foregoing, whatever it is must be elusive. *Home is elusive*. At the same time, *home is illusive* (in the Freudian sense), that which is not present but for which one longs and thirsts.

Context conditions identity, and so does home (in the form of gazes of moviemakers (who aim to dazzle and entertain).

Reclaiming storytelling is one way of refusing to let go of our narratives. To continue to tell them is to not let them slip out of sight. They will now and then slide out of place, but we can reweave them back into our mats, at different places than before.

With regard to the Bible, it contains many strands that await retelling, and weaving with other narratives.

the land" is varied and multiple. From Genesis on, "people of the land" refers to groups of non-Israelites (Canaanites, Hittites, Hivites, and so forth). But when we get to Ezra, "people of the land" also refers to Jews left at home, not taken in the exile.

The critique and reconstruction of identity open up our narratives for (mass) varied conscious retelling and crosscultural interweaving.

family, food, customs, clothes, memory, story, tradition, and so forth). Context is present; home is transcendent, across "the river," at the yonder. One of the ways of making this elusive home present is through recalling memories and telling stories.

Alas, I am back to storytelling and the quest for a home for the Bible in the postmodern world. The Bible is home for Christians; it is a home that is in diaspora. (Those who imagine that they can master the Bible bear the cuts and scars of essentialism.)

The foregoing imagines postmodernity to be bestowing opportunities upon us to reclaim our storytelling roles, to affirm differences and variations when we reconstruct identities, and to account for the ways in which context and home (which is in diaspora) condition who we are. Postmodernity oozes with liberating and reconstructive energies, more so than threatening waves of destruction.

POSTMODERNITY REFRAMED, BIBLE REPOSITIONED

Turn Michel Granger's *la grande décharge* over and the world fills up, as if to say that turning the world as we know it upside down is an opportunity to reconstruct it. My software allows me to rotate *la grande décharge* over, in order to illustrate what I have in mind, and in so doing I see that the reconstructed world is filling up with rejected junk. That is an appropriate image for this article, for it embodies the hope for the return of the repressed (Freud, Lacan), the abject (Kristeva), and the sublime (Lyotard). We may end up reconstructing the world with rejected materials, and with repressed subjects, but this does not mean that we will end up with the same world. Since we will reorganize (differently) the previously "dumped" materials, we will therefore end up with a different world. A reordered world, even with the same material, is a different world.

I unpacked my understanding of postmodernity around the Bible and the task of reading the Bible,[21] which are, figuratively speaking, strands woven into the Christian mat. Though I limit myself to the Bible and the task of reading, others may extend the opportunities that postmodernity bestows to other strands, such as the various understandings of (Trinitarian) God and humanity, of tradition and order, of rituals and sacraments, or of how those may intersect, and so forth.

I focus on the Bible also because it successfully weathered the ripping currents of postmodernity. The Bible contains multiple stories, none of which we should read as a metanarrative. We should on the other hand read the stories in creative tension, like the way the persons of the Trinity relate to one another. This is a healthy challenge against the tendency on the one hand to see the Bible as a metanarrative, and on the other hand to use one biblical narrative (e.g., John's understanding of Jesus) to control the meanings of all other (biblical and nonbiblical) narratives. There can't be a biblical center, or a canon within the canon. As the three persons of the Trinity are diverse yet united, different but the same, so are the biblical narratives. All of the biblical narratives should therefore get an opportunity (under the direction and leniency of readers) to talk with and listen to each other, as well as to interact with narratives from beyond the covers of the Bible, in written and oral forms, ancient and more recent. At the urgings of postmodernism, we can no longer keep the Bible separate from the sea of stories that flow through public channels. And we in churches should not sit back and leave the task of telling [our] stories to Pixar, Disney, Paramount, and others.

THE BIBLE ON POSTMODERN SUR*f*ACES

Storytelling is subjective, and it forms subjects. It is an opportunity for many to become subjects, both the ones who tell and the ones who listen, for the latter in time would tell more people, so storytelling constructs identity (of both the tellers and the listeners) and empowers the rippling of the circles of storytelling. Among the indigenous people of Australia, for instance, to participate in storytelling is a chance to share the traditions that form their identities (which has to do with from where they come and to where they are heading) and to swim in their sea of stories. The challenge for indigenous Australians is not about finding a story to tell, but about feeling that one has received permission to tell a story. Permission here is not about sanction, as if some people are prohibited from participating in storytelling events. Rather, this permission has to do with feeling (especially when one is away from home) that the story one wants to tell belongs in the circle of stories in the place from where one comes. The currents of postmodernity can be formative in this regard, for in resisting metanarratives and homogeneity the storytelling circle should be permissive for many, including indigenous peoples.

Storytelling is an opportunity to cross boundaries, for to really tell a story one must enter the world of the story. One sits in a current setting and tries to manifest a story from another time and place. Without crossing into the storyworld, one merely tells a story for the sake of sharing information and entertaining an audience.[22] To really tell a story one must enter the storyworld and assume the identity re-membered in the story.

And upon entering the storyworld one realizes that the story invites weaving with other stories. The task of manifesting a story will draw the teller and the listener toward other memories and stories. So a double movement, a double *crossing*, takes place in storytelling: (1) the storyteller crosses into the world of the story, and (2) the story invites the storyteller and the listener to cross into the world of other stories.

Given that the Hebrew Bible–Old Testament privileges the Judean story and the Israelite identity, we from outside those cultures do not need to adopt those. We may choose to do so, and that is our choice. But we must remember that we are adopting a story that our ancestors did not construct, a story that contributed to the enslavement and massacre of our ancestors. We are making the home (story) of another as our home (story). We must therefore be responsible for the story (home) of another people and for our foreignness to their story, their home. Some of us, on the other hand, may privilege stories from outside the Bible, and we too should bear the postmodern incredulity toward metanarratives in mind. Privileging nonbiblical stories is not sacrilegious, for in doing so we participate in a biblical (canonical) process, insofar as the stories in the Bible were not biblical (canonical) from their beginnings. The Judean biblical story contains elements from outside the experiences and cultures of their ancestors,[23] so the privileging of stories and ideas from outside the covers of the Bible is something done in the Bible itself. These are further evidences of the spirit of postmodernity that operates in the Bible.

In positioning the Bible on the currents of postmodernity, we encourage the Bible to cross its literary and cultural boundaries, and to engage other narratives. Postmodernity gifts readers and storytellers with the opportunity to weave biblical narratives with other narratives. In other words, in positioning the Bible on the currents of postmodernity we return it to its "home," and we remind ourselves that the Bible is not a (or, our) mat, but a strand in our mat (woven with multiple stories).

BIBLE RESUR*f*ACED, AT HOME

I suggested above that the Bible is home for many Christians, but we Christians do not share the same understanding of what a home is and what transforms something into a "home" or appreciate our homes in the same way. The home to which I am referring here is the one in diaspora (see above).[24] This home is whatever anchors one's sense of security and identity. It might be a place that has become home because of a custom and/or a memory, and/or a story, and/or a song, and/or a teaching, and so forth. Without the latter, that place is just a space, a site, rather than a home. A space is home because it is loaded. Home is loaded. A space is home also because it is welcoming. It does not imprison, but draws one to its limits, giving one security and the opportunity to feel that one belongs.

Saying that home is in diaspora is a paradox; "home" gives the impression of comfort and security, certainty and availability, but locating it in diaspora suggests that this home is also removed and transcendent. This home is comforting and not present, so one cannot own and control it, as if it is divine.

This is the kind of home to which the Hebrew Bible leads readers, especially those who read it as a story that extends from Genesis to 2 Chronicles (rather than from Genesis to Malachi as in the Christian Old Testament). The Hebrew Bible presents readers with a story that interweaves many stories, starting with creation events and a garden episode and ending with curses and expulsion, followed with a story of sibling rivalry, murder, and the marking of the murderer for endless wandering. The story picks up with the proliferation of human iniquity and the floods of God's punishment, from which God saves one family with many animals in an ark. The deluge and the constructed ark seem to invite humans to build a high tower (in case God breaks the covenant sealed with a rainbow), and God responds to this construction by coming to confuse languages and to disperse the people further. Expulsion from home and dispersion of humans are two of the strands that hold these stories together. There are other strands, of course, but I privilege these two in this retelling.

Abram and his sons, and their sons and grandsons,[25] servants and daughters, wives and handmaids, with many animals, move back and forth between the land that God promised them, a land that already belonged to other "people of the land," and other lands (one of which was Egypt). The land of promise was not always fertile and abundant, and the story of the patriarchs circles around famine and departure from their home (a space that became home because God promised it, but the same space was home for others before Abram laid claim to it).

From Egypt Moses led the populous Israel back to the land of the Canaanites, and the Israelites had to fight, kill (and some of their people were killed), and grab both land and wealth, thereby fulfilling God's promise. The majority of the people who left Egypt died on the way, in the lands of other peoples (that is to say that Israel did not exodus through an empty wilderness), under the eyes and arms of their God. Descendants of the people who came out of Egypt, upon their arrival, divided the land of the Canaanites among themselves, some choosing to accept their portion across the Jordan but others preferring to stay in Transjordan, and consequently they dispersed throughout the land. Dispersion continues, even in the land that God promised. In this land, Israel falls into and out of favor with its God, who graciously and patiently sent judges to deliver the chosen people.

After the kingship was established, ongoing internal and international tensions and unrest caused further dispersions of the people. The house of David overtakes the throne of Saul, and two generations later the empire divides into northern and southern kingdoms, with centers in Samaria and Jerusalem. Israel (in the north) turns away from the house of David (in Jerusalem, to the south), and the unity of the descendants of Abraham falls apart. Foreign nations later arrive to take control over them, Assyria taking over in the north and Babylonia in the south. Dispersion thus continues, with some people running back to Egypt, and neighbors standing aloof while foreign invaders tear down the walls of the capital cities.

My retelling is selective, and it follows a plot that leads into exile, where the people long and lament for "home" with songs, questions, and stories. This umbrella story ends in 2 Chronicles with the people in exile, poised to return home. It is a story of dispersion, of longing for a home that is not at the place where people are. There are places in the story where readers get the impression that the people have returned from exile and started to rebuild their homes, but the overall flow of the narrative is from creation to exile, with "home" not fully owned or captured.

The Christian Scriptures in their received form also point toward departure for a home that is beyond reach, as if it is in diaspora. The New Testament starts with four versions of the Jesus event, ending with the resurrected Christ ascending to a home that is yonder, leaving the followers with the expectation of his return. The second coming, however, does not happen right away, but delays even up to the end of the New Testament in Revelation, which looks toward the consummation of time and the ultimate end of suffering. Reading the Bible as a whole brings to mind the story of Odysseus who, in Homer's *Odyssey,* arrived back at Ithaca after journeying for ten years since the end of the Trojan War and he had to compete for his wife Penelope. He won his wife back, and found out that she was faithful during the long time he was away, but then he had to face a test Penelope designed to find out if he is really her husband. Odysseus's homecoming was a return to a place that was no longer home to him. The story ends with Odysseus setting off again, as if he is destined not to be at home. For him, too, home is not at where he is; home is in diaspora.

How different are the foregoing stories from those of refugees who have come within the borders of your country? They live among you, but "home" for them is not where they are, and that is no fault of yours. You might be most hospitable, but there is something about belonging that is mysterious.

There are four strands in the foregoing that we should interweave in order that they can hold each other in place. First is the affirmation that the Bible is home for Christians. Second is the awareness that the Bible contains stories about peoples whose homes are in diaspora. Third is the recognition that we cannot lay claim to, as if we can own and thus control, that which is in diaspora, beyond our reach. And fourth is the realization that the Bible is one strand in the mat of our faith and our perception of order. The Bible is loaded and divine, and is open for interweaving with other narratives, other strands, other homes. It is through interweaving (which serves as a metaphor for storytelling) that we can bring the Bible closer to where we are, so that the Bible can surface among us, as a home that is at hand.

This article circles around the Bible and the *jouissánce* in the task of reading the Bible in a postmodern world, waving a flag for storytelling as a way of assuring that our narratives do not slip out of sight. In response to the postmodern celebration of otherness, difference, and heterogeneity, storytelling encourages the interweaving of our narratives with those of other peoples. In this regard, storytelling can be a tool for upholding unity in faithful diversity. Moreover, storytelling is a helpful way of making present that which is not within reach, the home that is in diaspora.[26]

In response to the postmodern challenge, therefore, I argue that we do not really need metanarratives. What we need are storytellers. We need storytellers because we are addicted to stories, because we need stories to live. We need storytellers to survive, and storytellers will now and then give the Bible homes, here and there.

NOTES

1. See James K. Smith, *Who's Afraid of Postmodernism? Taking Derrida, Lyotard, and Foucault to Church* (Grand Rapids, MI: Baker Academic, 2006), 15–30.

2. Thomas Docherty, ed., *Postmodernism: A Reader* (New York: Columbia University Press, 1993).

3. Ihab Hassan, *The Postmodern Turn: Essays in Postmodern Theory and Culture* (Columbus: Ohio State University Press, 1987).

4. Fredric Jameson, *Postmodernism, or, The Cultural Logic of Late Capitalism* (Durham, NC: Duke University Press, 1991).

5. Christopher Norris, *The Truth about Postmodernism* (Oxford: Blackwell, 1993).

6. Patricia Waugh, *Postmodernism: A Reader* (London: Edward Arnold, 1992).

7. Smith, *Who's Afraid of Postmodernism?*

8. Pete Rollins, *How [Not] to Speak of God* (Orleans, MA: Paraclete, 2006).

9. Cf. A. K. M. Adam, *Faithful Interpretation: Reading the Bible in a Postmodern World* (Minneapolis: Fortress, 2006).

10. Cf. Anita Monro, *Resurrecting Erotic Transgression: Subjecting Ambiguity in Theology* (London: Equinox, 2006), 15, 109ff.

11. Cf. Crystal L. Downing, *How Postmodernism Serves (My) Faith: Questioning Truth in Language, Philosophy and Art* (Downers Grove, IL: IVP Academic, 2006), 16–18.

12. Displaying a framed photograph or image was not common in my home island when I was growing up, where people (old and young) were more interested in telling stories and sharing memories than in showing dead moments. To have a picture or image framed was a privilege associated with Westerners.

13. I must confess: I see postmodernity in the pulse of ancient texts and religious cultures *also* because I resist the divide between premodern, modern, and postmodern, which gives the implication that the premodern (including the natives of the South Seas, my ancestors) were simple and unsophisticated.

14. Jameson, *Postmodernism*.

15. Steven Connor, *Postmodernist Culture: An Introduction to Theories of the Contemporary*, 2nd ed. (Oxford: Blackwell, 1997), 5–6.

16. Cf. Jean-François Lyotard, *The Postmodern Condition: A Report on Knowledge,* trans. Geoff Bennington and Brian Massumi (Minneapolis: University of Minnesota Press, 1997 [1984]), xxiv–xxv.

17. Connor, *Postmodernist Culture,* 17.

18. Cf. Adam, *Faithful Interpretation,* 9, 62.

19. Cf. Stephen E. Fowl, "The Importance of a Multivoiced Literal Sense of Scripture: The Example of Thomas Aquinas," in A. K. M. Adam, Stephen E. Fowl, Kevin J. Vanhoozer, and Francis Watson, *Reading Scripture with the Church: Toward a Hermeneutic for Theological Interpretation* (Grand Rapids, MI: Baker Academic, 2006), 35–50.

20. Cf. David Tuesday Adamo, *Biblical Interpretation in African Perspective* (New York: University Press of America, 2006). See also Daniel Patte et al., eds., *Global Bible Commentary* (Nashville: Abingdon, 2004).

21. A. K. M. Adam, ed., *Handbook of Postmodern Biblical Interpretation* (St. Louis: Chalice, 2000).

22. Storytelling among Pacific Islanders and indigenous Australians is not about sharing information but about locating our roots and naming our identity, who we [think we] are, in an exercise that exposes our interconnected webs of relations. Storytelling is not just another opportunity to entertain an audience, but a process of constructing our sense of belonging, through rituals and ceremonies; storytelling is a process that forms our hopes for where we are going. Storytelling engages the past with the present, and merges time and space.

23. Frank Moore Cross, *Canaanite Myth and Hebrew Epic: Essays in the History of the Religion of Israel* (Cambridge, MA: Harvard University Press, 1973).

24. I must confess one other thing: As a migrant worker, it appears paradoxical that I imagine that I am not in diaspora, but rather, for me, my home is in diaspora. I am not in diaspora because I am in a place of comfort. But my home is in diaspora because it is not where I am.

25. Except for Benjamin, all of Jacob's children were born outside of the land that God promised to the patriarchs; their places of birth were outside Canaan, thus problematizing claims to belong to the land of the Canaanites.

26. Since storytelling is not free of biases, there is always a threat that a storyteller will harmonize and sanitize the story by removing multiple and alternative meanings. The readings I present herein illustrate how storytelling can resuscitate multiple meanings, thus affirming that diversity of meanings can coexist in the same text.

Chapter 9

FAITH AND ORDER IN A POSTMODERN WORLD: A RESPONSE [TO HAVEA AND PAPANIKOLAOU]

Michael Root

> Following its presentation at Oberlin II, this paper was originally published in the *Journal of Ecumenical Studies* 42, no. 4 (Fall 2007): 560–70, and is reprinted here with permission from the author and *JES*.

PROLOGUE: A SNAPSHOT OF THE POSTMODERN SITUATION

I am responding to a paper by a Methodist theologian from Tonga, who now teaches in Australia, and an American Orthodox theologian teaching at a Catholic university in New York City. I am myself a Lutheran, born, raised, and resident in the South of the United States, but have also lived ten years in France and am of French-Canadian, Irish, Puerto Rican, Cuban, Scots-Irish, Dutch ancestry. One of my great-grandfathers was the president of the Burman Baptist Seminary, now the Myanmar Institute of Christian Theology, in Insein, Myanmar. One grandfather was the principal of a high school in Bayamón, Puerto Rico. A cousin of one grandmother was a Roman Catholic priest in the diocese of Springfield, Massachusetts.

Heterogeneity in a nutshell.

THE THEME: FAITH AND ORDER IN THE POSTMODERN WORLD

Every aspect of the phrase gives one pause.

First, "Faith and Order." The Faith and Order movement came into existence early in the twentieth century to address the differences over Faith and Order that divide the church. These divisions and the disputes are not new. The problem that sets the Faith and Order agenda predated modernity and will, short of a new outpouring of the Spirit, be around when postmodernity is a footnote in history textbooks. Is a discussion of postmodernity a distraction from the real work of Faith and Order?

Second, "the postmodern world." "Postmodern" is a notoriously slippery concept. What makes the postmodern world *post*modern? One can focus on simple definitions, such Lyotard's well-known "incredulity toward metanarratives," but will that do if one is seeking an analysis that will guide fruitful discussion and action? The devil is in the details.[1]

And is postmodernity actually postmodern? Has it left modernity behind, or is it just another moment in the dialectical evolution of modernity? The end of modernity has been declared repeatedly, at least since the Romantics at the beginning of the nineteenth century. Modernity has buried generations of its undertakers. And "postmodernity" is not all that new; the term was apparently first used in 1917.[2] Does the very term "postmodernity" skew an accurate cultural analysis by emphasizing discontinuity with modernity?

Even the preposition "in" needs to be considered. At least since Schleiermacher, theologians have pursued methods of correlation, in which some sort of philosophical anthropology or cultural analysis have formed a hermeneutical framework for the interpretation of the faith. From Schleiermacher, to Ritschl, to Bultmann and Tillich, and into at least the early work of David Tracy, the anthropology or cultural analysis changes, but the larger structure remains constant. If, like me, one shares Karl Barth's judgment that this approach to theology was a wrong turn, then one wants to know just how the "in" is going to operate. Are we going to pursue another variation of a failed model?

FAITH AND ORDER IN A POSTMODERN WORLD: A RESPONSE

Yet when one pauses, one sees the need for the topic. Yes, division over matters of Faith and Order predate the modern and postmodern worlds, but modernity and the division of the church, especially the division of the Western church that resulted from the Reformation, are thoroughly intertwined. On the one hand, the division of the church was an important causal factor in the development of modernity in the seventeenth and eighteenth centuries. The individualism, the secularity, the search for rational foundations that typify modernity were shaped and partially caused by the disappearance of a single, inclusive, authoritative church. Would Descartes have sought certainty in the way he did without the quite literal war of competing certainties that ravaged Europe in the wake of the Reformation?[3] On the other hand, the present denominational order of friendly or at least polite competition has been shaped by modernity and, at least in North America, by the modern consumer-oriented market. At this conference, the division of the church may be looked upon as problematic, but for many in and beyond our churches, the division of Protestant, Catholic, and Orthodox is no more problematic than the division of Coke and Pepsi. One might have one's own strong preferences (my father saw drinking Pepsi as close to a moral failing), but *de gustibus non disputandum*.

Second, however postmodernity and its relation to modernity are defined, there have been cultural, intellectual, political, and economic changes in the last decades that can be grouped together as a move into at least a new form of modernity. Few here today believe that the world is following a script, a metanarrative, of a universal movement toward the utopia of Karl Marx or of an inevitable and universal development toward Western liberal democracy and its allied economic order. The certainties of modernity are now dubious, at best.

And thus, the "in" of our theme is unavoidable. Postmodernism and perhaps postmodernity itself challenge the central concepts of Faith and Order ecumenism—unity and truth. If Faith and Order is about anything, it is about the pursuit of unity in truth and truth in unity. But how does the unity we seek relate to the postmodern celebration of the play of diversity and plurality? What is the truth that will reconcile us if truth itself is at best an illusion we can live without or, at worst, an ideological curtain that conceals the will to power?

The questions raised by postmodernity go beyond such conceptual challenges. The ecumenical movement itself is a child of modernity, and the metanarratives of the modern world have shaped its outlook. When one reads the works of such a founder of the ecumenical movement as Nathan Söderblom, one gets the distinct impression that unity will come when all the churches reach a mature and modern attitude to doctrine and division, which ends up looking much like liberal Protestantism.[4] Postmodernity should force us to ask, in what sense has ecumenism and Faith and Order been shaped and misshaped by the assumptions of the modern world? How do we now disentangle Faith and Order from those aspects of modernity that are being and should be left behind?

All of these questions cannot be discussed in what, after all, is only a response. In this presentation, I will try to touch upon these larger questions as I respond to the papers by professors Papanikolaou and Havea.[5]

THE PRESENTATIONS

What can we learn about Faith and Order in a postmodern world from the presentations by professors Havea and Papanikolaou? Their similarities and their differences are both revealing. They point toward similar, but also different, paths.

Particularity

Both presentations manifest one of the predominant traits of postmodern discourse: the appearance of previously absent or repressed particularities. Papanikolaou traces the repression of Orthodox theology and its encounter with modernity under the rule of Islam and communism and the development of new trends in Orthodox thought over the last 150 years. Havea speaks out of the experience of a home in diaspora, of an experience rooted beyond the North Atlantic world that was the center of the early ecumenical movement. Neither refers to that list of Germanic theological names that I have already, in good academic fashion, trotted out in the first pages of my response. Neither evinces a sense of urgency to relate their reflections to the traditions that were so dominant in American theology as recently as the 1970s.

Particularity does not mean individualism (although here already differences will begin to appear between the two presentations). Papanikolaou begins his presentation with a comment about "what it is like to think like a tradition."

> When I was a student at the University of Chicago, I attended David Tracy's course titled "Postmodernity." During a break, he said to me, and I'm paraphrasing, "You know, Aristotle, the Orthodox have a certain advantage—they did not go through the well-known chain of events within the West, meaning the Reformation, Counter-Reformation, Enlightenment, Romanticism, Modernity, Postmodernity—and because of this, those within the tradition have the advantage of knowing what it is like to think like a tradition." As with many, many things that Tracy said during my time at Chicago, it took me a while to fully understand what he was saying. However, with but a simple phrase, as he has done so often in his career, Tracy provided an important hermeneutical key for understanding Orthodoxy's place within the cultural situation that is now called postmodernity).[6]

His presentation is both a description and a development of a specific tradition of theological and ecclesial reflection. The break with modernity here is significant. In his manifesto of modernity, *What Is Enlightenment?* Kant found the key to enlightenment in the courage to think without tutelage, to throw off tradition.[7] Much modern, especially Protestant, theology has accepted that ideal and valued creativity, innovation, as an unqualified good. The individual virtuoso theologian who thinks outside the box has been lionized. Papanikolaou's presentation takes up a different, in many ways more difficult, challenge: creative reflection inside the box, thinking within a tradition, handing on the tradition, moving it forward, in continuity with the discourse of the community. One aspect of the postmodern situation is a renewed willingness to think within a tradition.

But the situation is complex. Havea displays a contrasting aspect, particularly in his discussion of identity. The opening anecdote in Papanikolaou's presentation notes an advantage of the Orthodox theologian, a still-living tradition of thinking within a tradition. For the Orthodox, this tradition is almost two thousand years old, rich, and diverse. It provides a home for thought. For many of the rest of us, our theological homes require, to use a term taken up by some postmodern thinkers, *bricolage*, cobbling together what we can from various sources as they come to hand.[8] Tradition and community are more fragile, more obviously a creation, less internally integrated. The identity of community, tradition, and the self that lives within these is de-centered. Thought is less inside the box, for there is far less of a box to think within.[9] Community is more fluid. If Papanikolaou is thinking from within a particularity, Havea is weaving together diverse particularities into a never finished, always fraying mat.

The differing particularities and differing attitudes toward particularity manifest in the two presentations present an intensified form of an old challenge for Faith and Order, and a new challenge. Faith and Order has always faced the question of how diverse forms of theological discourse can be mutually understandable. Simple misunderstanding has always been a part of church division. But as repressed or previously absent particularities assert themselves, that challenge becomes greater. Just as an expanded European Union must now find interpreters who can translate Finnish into Portuguese, we need persons attuned to a widening range of forms of theological reflection. And my sense is that the goal of a common discourse arising out of this diversity is not what is sought. The goal shifts. How can these diverse forms of language be preserved in their particularity while living together in communion? Herein lies the deeper challenge of postmodernity for the project of Faith and Order.

The Bible and Differing Approaches to Postmodernity

Both Havea and Papanikolaou, however, point to one means for facing this challenge: the shared discourse of Scripture. Havea is explicit in this appeal; the Bible appears to have "weathered the currents of postmodernity." It provides examples of storytelling. It provides examples of storytelling. His reading of the Bible bears similarities to premodern interpretative practices in its focus on narrative and its freedom[10] (although I will note some important differences below). He seems unconcerned with the historical questions and the pursuit of a fixed meaning that have typified much modern biblical study. The Bible is read not as a source of historical information or of religious, moral, or theological concepts, but as a home in which to live. I am reminded of George Lindbeck's understanding of the Bible as forming a world that the Christian inhabits.[11]

Papanikolaou does not explicitly appeal to the Bible in the same way, but the Bible narrative is implicitly central. Explicitly central is "the realism of divine communion in Jesus Christ" , the "narrative of the divine-human communion effected in the person of Jesus Christ." This narrative is, of course, the biblical narrative, the narrative of the Gospels, and, with the Gospels at its center, the narrative of the entire Bible, as organized and read by the Christian tradition. This divine communion in and through Christ, narrated in Scripture, is the "absolutely nonnegotiable" in the Orthodox encounter with modernity and postmodernity.

Again, differences appear in the use of the Bible in the two presentations, and they point to larger differences in how one approaches postmodernity. While Papanikolaou seems no more interested than Havea in historical-critical results, he does move quickly to speak of the principle of divine-human communion. I would want to press him on just what "principle" means here and how principle relates to narrative. Does the event of Jesus Christ merely illustrate a logically independent principle of divine-human communion or does it constitute that principle, even though that principle then has a cosmic application? How does the biblical narrative shape Christian experience, in particular the experience of the Eucharist through which, according to Zizioulas, "Christians know that God is Trinity" 203–4)?

These are not just academic questions with no relevance to ecumenical discussions. How does the Bible shape our work in Faith and Order? I believe a focus on narrative as framing Christian thought and practice is more ecumenically fruitful than an emphasis on doctrinal schemes. As Havea puts it, the Bible is "a site of contact that signifies Christian unity," and, I would add, a uniquely privileged site of contact. When we can agree on language and practices in relation to Scripture and worship, then we can be more open to diversity in our more precise conceptual languages. (That Catholics and Orthodox share various practices in relation to the Blessed Virgin Mary makes their divergence on Mariological doctrine more ecumenically bearable than the Catholic-Protestant divergence, which is not bridged by shared practice.)

As noted, Papanikolaou's approach to postmodernity is neither simple acceptance nor simple rejection. The postmodern critique of modernity and its emphases on difference and the Other not only provide openings for Christian reflection, but opportunities for Christians to learn. Nevertheless, he approaches reflection on the postmodern situation on the basis of the "principle of divine-human communion which must shape the Orthodox response to postmodern questions on epistemology, subjectivity, and pluralism." The specificity of Christian tradition and its reading of Scripture remain the framing elements.

Here Havea presents an alternative. Havea wishes to swim with the rip tide and see where it takes him. Papanikolaou's reading of the Bible, with its focus on divine-human communion in Christ, adheres to the overarching narrative structure of creation-Israel-Christ-Pentecost-consummation that shapes the canon and has provided the scaffolding for most Christian theology over two millennia. Havea is leery of any metanarrative, which seems to imply for him a resistance to any "biblical center" that will organize the Bible into a single whole, such as the "overarching narrative" I referred to above. What is desired is an open conversation, in which "all the biblical narratives should therefore get an opportunity (under the direction and leniency of readers) to talk with and listen to each other." He goes on, however, to describe two "umbrella stor[ies]," readings of the narrative arch of Scripture, one on the basis of the structuring of the canon of the Tanakh, the Hebrew Scriptures, ending in 2 Chronicles, and the other on the basis of the Christian Bible, ending in Revelation. Each ends, he notes, with a "departure for a home that is beyond reach," the land of Israel in one case; the eschatological kingdom of God in the other.

I agree with Havea's rejection of a "canon in the canon" and his critique of privileging one book of the Bible as the controlling factor in the interpretation of all others (his example is John, My own Lutheran tradition has been guilty of privileging Paul in ways that have impoverished our theology and life. But can we read

Scripture as the sort of home Havea desires without some sort of umbrella story, some organization that structures the conversation among them? "Incredulity toward metanarratives" goes too far when we ignore the way later texts of the Bible (and this includes all the texts of the New Testament) themselves imply readings of earlier texts according to some sort of organization, usually a narrative organization. Think of the larger narrative implications of the prologue of John, or of Stephen's sermon in Acts 7, or of Paul's agonized wrestling with the election of Israel and its place in God's saving intent in Romans 9–11, or of the discussion in Hebrews of the temple and of Jesus as the true and final sacrifice, or of the consummation of all things in the New Jerusalem at the end of Revelation. Overarching structures, umbrella stories—yes, metanarratives—are implicit in the biblical text. Havea rightly reminds us that these metanarratives are themselves diverse. The text does not dictate any single way of organizing its stories into one umbrella story. But I see no way of reading the canon as a whole, especially as it has been ordered by the church with a significant degree of unanimity, without reading it as telling a story whose axis is creation–Israel–Christ–church–eschaton. The variations that can be spun around that axis are perhaps limitless. Gregory of Nyssa, John Calvin, and Gustavo Gutiérrez tell different stories, but they are recognizably variations on the same umbrella story, especially in the central role ascribed to Jesus Christ.

Again, I believe the issue I am raising is of significance for Faith and Order. If Faith and Order is a conversation, and not a collection of voices speaking past one another, then we need some sense that we are speaking about the same thing and some criteria, however informal, for distinguishing true insight from distracting mirages. The common (for the most part) Bible, ordered in a generally agreed fashion, implying a relatively stable narrative scaffolding has been a necessary background for Faith and Order; ecumenical discussion without such a background would be, I believe, condemned to frustration.

As noted, Havea does not speak out of a single particularity, but wishes to weave particularities together. One of the promises of the "ecumenical gift exchange" is that we all will deepen our faith and theology as we receive from one another. We will also learn the deep ways our own traditions have been deformed by the dynamics of division, the ways we have shaped our traditions to make it clear that we are not the other, the one-sidedness we have embraced to affirm our distinctiveness from other Christians.[12] I worry about an approach to ecumenism so rooted in a single tradition as that of Papanikolaou. Division may be less deeply written into the Orthodox tradition than it is in most Western traditions, but in the description of twentieth-century Orthodox theology that Papanikolaou lays out, a strong contrast with Western Christianity appears to be part of the goal, particularly for the émigré theologians, and not an unintended side-effect. We must be ready to reconsider how our particularities have adapted to and now undergird division. Herein lies the deep problem of an "ecumenism of profile," where the assertion of a communal identity shaped by division becomes a precondition of discussion.[13]

Havea raises a question from the other end of the spectrum. How wide do we cast the net in this gift exchange and what criteria shape our reception? He notes that, while the Tanakh/Old Testament privileges the story of Judea and Israelite identity, "Those of us from outside those cultures do not necessarily need to adopt those. We may choose to do so, but that is our choice." Along these lines, he encourages interweaving biblical and other narratives without comprehensively privileging the biblical stories. The question becomes inescapable (at least for me): are there, to use Papanikolaou's term, nonnegotiables, fundamental Christian commitments, that we take into an engagement with postmodernity? Are there "givens" from which the Christian starts and which Christian reflection is to respect? For example, I believe God's election of Israel (and thus the privileging of the story of Israel) is such a given. How to interpret that election is one of the oldest problems of Christian theology, and I am not sure the New Testament offers a unified answer to that question. Nevertheless, I do not believe Christians can choose whether the story of the election of Israel is or is not part of the backbone of the narratives that shape who we are. The attitude of the Gentile Christian (which includes most of us at this conference) to the narrative of Israel must be complex. I need not become Jewish to follow Christ. But the privileging of the story recounted in the Old Testament is, as far as I can see, a given, a given because of God's action of calling Israel out from among the nations in preparation for the incarnation.

Involved here is a concept unpopular in both modernity and postmodernity, but I believe central for Faith and Order, especially in ecumenically unpromising times: the concept of obedience.[14] A truth that I believe everyone here can agree with, without qualification, is that God is God and we are not. We are called to be disciples, followers along a path the basic shape of which is not of our choosing. We do not choose Jesus (John 15:16); the Logos is uniquely incarnate in Jesus by a sovereign decision of God. We gratefully acknowledge that decision as the key to the destiny of the world and follow in obedience. Obedience is not blind; it requires interpretation and discernment, and these always involve an element of creativity. Unfortunately, one reason the churches are divided is that we do not agree on just what are the divine givens, the reception of which is an act of obedience. But we do agree on the central givens: the gift of salvation in Christ, the gift of the Holy Spirit, the gift of the Word.

Obedience of this sort is doubly important for Faith and Order. Amid our disagreements about matters of Faith and Order, there is the shared commitment that the Christian faith over which we struggle is of supreme importance because within it, clothed in human garments, is the supreme divine gift. Without that sense of shared commitment obediently to receive what God has given, I do not see how Faith and Order proceeds. In addition, I do not believe that I could go on doing ecumenical work without the belief that ecumenism is part of what obedience demands. Faith and Order is a form of obedience to Jesus' call to love the sister and brother in Christ, an effort to "maintain the unity of the Spirit in the bond of peace" (Eph. 4:3). For that reason, our commitment to ecumenism must be, as John Paul II put it, "irrevocable."[15] Our ecumenical efforts may bear fruit, despite their inadequacies, or may prove irrelevant to the intentions of the Holy Spirit for the church. The central ecumenical orientation, however, is not toward success, but toward faithful obedience. Postmodernity changes the context of that obedience and perhaps changes the precise focus of our efforts, but the underlying dynamic of Faith and Order remains unchanged.

FAITH AND ORDER, UNITY AND TRUTH

Let me briefly add some comments that are less a response to the presentations than reflections of my own on two particular challenges for Faith and Order in the postmodern world, though I will continue to refer to the presentations.

Unity, Diversity, and Heterogeneity

As almost all commentators on postmodernity note, one of its salient characteristics is the affirmation of plurality, even of "radical plurality" or heterogeneity.[16] Plurality and unity have been a theme of Christian reflection on the church at least since Paul's discussion of the diversity of gifts in 1 Corinthians 12. There Paul does not see plurality and unity as a zero-sum game, but as mutually reinforcing. Plurality serves unity; it does not destroy it.

But how are we to understand "the unity we seek" in relation to the mind-boggling and increasing diversity of Christianity in contemporary North America, not to mention the wide world? The models of unity dominant in the first decades of the ecumenical movement, up through perhaps the early 1970s, were all too modern. They seem to have involved either "organic unity" (which ended up looking much like a Protestant church merger) or mere conciliar cooperation.[17] Interestingly, work in preparation for the 1957 Oberlin conference already found a rejection of both "one visible church organization" and of "spiritual oneness without interest in organizational cooperation."[18] Church unity efforts have struggled over the last fifty years to find a model of unity that seems both theologically adequate and sociologically effective, as the history of the Consultation on Church Union graphically demonstrates. The most popular present approach, in which denominations remain completely autonomous while living in full communion with one another, is in my estimation proving itself inadequate.[19] Note the way the Episcopal Church and the Evangelical Lutheran Church in America (ELCA), allegedly in full communion, are being torn by debates on sexuality in almost complete isolation from one another. But what is the alternative? In a postmodern world increasingly suspicious of centralized institutions, the form of communion remains elusive.

I think we simply must confess that we cannot give a precise picture of the unity we seek. It will not be homogeneity. To extend Havea's image, it will be a common home, but with separate rooms. After all, Jesus said, "In my Father's house are many mansions" (John 14:2). We can say that unity means a common life, a shared existence in Christ and the Spirit. I believe that such a common life means a common way of stating the faith, a shared mission to the world, an ability to make decisions together on matters that affect us all, a shared ministry, and, most centrally, a shared household table, the table of the Eucharist. What we cannot produce today is a detailed blueprint of that common house.

We will have to muddle ahead. We will undoubtedly make missteps, but to err is human.

What is needed is an openness to experimentation, a bit of *bricolage*, even a bit of playfulness.

Truth and Jesus

We can live with this lack of clear vision, I believe, because we are confident that Jesus is Lord. Jesus did not tell Peter, "on this rock you *must* build my church," but rather, "on this rock I *will* build my church" (Matt. 16:18).[20] The unity willed by the Spirit will come, in its time.

This confidence presupposes a firm conviction about the truth of the gospel.

Postmodernity has raised challenges to any meaningful notion of truth.[21] Theologians need to engage those challenges.[22] Faith and Order requires a firm sense of truth, but also must be sensitive to the social dynamics of truth, the way claims of truth relate to the assertion of power. Faith and Order is about the reconciliation of churches and not primarily about the reconciliation of concepts and thus must attend to these social dynamics. How to address this dynamic is a task for decades, not just for one conference. Papanikolaou points to one conceptual resource in this process, David Bentley Hart's emphasis on truth embodied in persuasive beauty rather than in coercive argument. "For Hart, Christians must stand confident in the persuasiveness and beauty of their narrative of the divine-human communion effected in the person of Jesus Christ." We should be confident that as that story is retold in new ways by new storytellers, the beauty of its truth will continue to shine.

Those of us engaged in the work of Faith and Order should have a similar confidence. The rich and diverse beauty of the common home we seek must be our decisive ecumenical tool. The pull of attraction is always more effective (and more evangelical) than the push of obligation (however much the push of obligation is also a necessary ecumenical moment). Karl Barth once said that theology should be a happy science;[23] ecumenism also should be a happy endeavor, for we know, however off the mark we may be in our detailed efforts, what we are about is the truth which is Jesus (John 14:6).

CONCLUSION

Havea and Papanikolaou are alike correct: postmodernity is not something we should fear, but an aspect of our contemporary world we must engage. I still believe that the primary work of Faith and Order concerns a matter internal to the church—its unity in truth and the divisions that hinder the full realization of that unity in truth. Our Lord, however, did not pray that we be taken out of this world (John 17:15). We live within it and it lives within us. But, echoing Havea, I would add that we have a home in this world only as in diaspora, "for here we have no lasting city, but we seek the city which is to come" (Heb. 13:14). And that city is the New Jerusalem of Christ, who is the same, yesterday, today, and forever (Heb. 13:8).

NOTES

1. For a survey of the variant meanings of "postmodern" from a theological perspective, see Paul Lakeland, *Postmodernity: Christian Identity in a Fragmented Age* (Minneapolis: Fortress Press, 1997).

2. The term was used by Rudolf Pannwitz; see discussion in Walter Kasper, "Die Kirche angesichts der Herausforderungen

der Postmoderne," in *Theologie und Kirche,* vol. 2 (Mainz: Mathias-Grünwald-Verlag, 1999), 249–50.

3. See Jeffrey Stout, *The Flight from Authority: Religion, Morality, and the Quest for Autonomy* (Notre Dame, IN: University of Notre Dame Press, 1981), 37–76.

4. See, for example, his programmatic work for the first Life and Work Conference, Nathan Söderblom, *Christian Fellowship, or The United Life and Work of Christendom* (New York: Fleming H. Revell, 1923).

5. The literature that explicitly deals with Faith and Order ecumenism and postmodernity is not large. By far the most important, although it addresses a "postliberal age" rather than a "postmodern world," is still George A. Lindbeck, *The Nature of Doctrine: Religion and Theology in a Postliberal Age* (Philadelphia: Westminster Press, 1984). (See 135, n. 1, for his reasons for using the term "postliberal" rather than "postmodern.") Also useful is Ilse N. Bulhof, "The Postmodern Challenge of the Ecumenical Movement: New Concepts and New Goals," in *Ecumenism and Hermeneutics: Findings of the VIIIth Consultation of the Societas Oecumenica Association of the Ecumenical Institutes in Europe, Driebergen 25–31 August, 1994,* ed. Anton Houtepen (Utrecht: Interuniversitair Instituut voor Missiologie en Oecumenica, 1995), 31–50, and various essays in Giuseppe Ruggieri and Miklós Tornka, eds., *The Church in Fragments: Towards What Kind of Unity?* Concilium (Maryknoll, NY: Orbis Books, 1997). I believe the most profound theological response to postmodernity is that discussed by Professor Papanikolaou in his treatment of David Bentley Hart, *The Beauty of the Infinite: The Aesthetics of Christian Truth* (Grand Rapids, MI: Eerdmans, 2003).

6. All references to these two presentations refer to chapter 7 of this volume, "Orthodoxy, Postmodernity, and Ecumenism: The Difference That Divine-Human Communion Makes," by Aristotle Papanikolaou, and chapter 8, "The Bible on Postmodern Surfaces," by Jione Havea).

7. Immanuel Kant, "What Is Enlightenment?" in *Foundations of the Metaphysics of Morals and What Is Enlightenment?* trans. Louis White Beck (Indianapolis: Bobbs-Merrill, 1959), 85.

8. On this sense of *bricolage,* see Jeffrey Stout, *Ethics after Babel: The Languages of Morals and Their Discontents* (Boston:

Beacon Press, 1988), 74–77. When I lived in France, stores with various forms of "bricolage" in their names sold do-it-yourself home improvement supplies. I did my best not to go into these.

9. See discussion of the contingency of selfhood and of community in Richard Rorty, *Contingency, Irony, and Solidarity* (Cambridge: Cambridge University Press, 1989), 23–69.

10. "Through most of Christian history, the Bible has been construed as a typologically unified narrative centered on Jesus Christ, in which all parts from Genesis to Revelation interact with all other parts. This interaction allows free play to imaginative intertextual and intratextual interpretations which are often not dissimilar to those of contemporary deconstructionists" (George A. Lindbeck, "The Church's Mission in a Postmodern Culture," in *Postmodern Theology: Christian Faith in a Pluralist World*, ed. Frederic B. Burnham [New York: Harper & Row, 1989], 41).

11. George A. Lindbeck, *The Nature of Doctrine: Religion and Theology in a Postliberal Age* (Philadelphia: Westminster Press, 1984), 113–24.

12. See here, on "contrastive identifiers," Ephraim Radner, *The End of the Church: A Pneumatology of Christian Division in the West* (Grand Rapids, MI: Eerdmans, 1998), 321. Along with Lindbeck, Radner represents I believe the most profound ecumenical theology of the last twenty-five years.

13. An *"ecumenism* of profile" has been proposed by German Protestant church leaders, but picked up by Walter Kasper in commenting on the recent *Responsa* by the Congregation for the Doctrine of the Faith; Walter Kasper, "Cardinal Kasper on An Invitation to Dialogue" 252 (2007), *www.oecumene.radiovaticana.org/en1/Articolo.asp?c=144460*.

14. "The problem in the mainline Protestant churches is that we no longer can imagine what it would mean to obey" (Stanley Hauerwas, *Sanctify Them in the Truth: Holiness Exemplified* [Nashville: Abingdon Press, 1988], 166). This problem affects more, I believe, than just mainline Protestants.

15. John Paul II, *Ut unum sint: On Commitment to Ecumenism* (Vatican City: Libreria Editrice Vaticana, 1995), para. 3.

16. On "radical plurality," see Ilse N. Bulhof, "The Postmodern Challenge of the Ecumenical Movement: New Concepts and New Goals," in *Ecumenism and Hermeneutics: Findings of the*

VIIIth Consultation of the Societas Oecumenica Association of the Ecumenical Institutes in Europe, Driebergen 25–31 August, 1994, ed. Anton Houtepen (Utrecht: Interuniversitair Instituut voor Missiologie en Oecumenica, 1995), 31–50.

17. On models of unity, see Harding Meyer, *That All May Be One: Perceptions and Models of Ecumenicity,* trans. William G. Rusch (Grand Rapids, MI: Eerdmans, 1999), 79–101.

18. Walter G. Muelder, "Institutionalism in Relation to Unity and Diversity," in *The Nature of the Unity We Seek: Official Report of the North American Conference on Faith and Order, September 3–10, 1957, Oberlin, Ohio,* ed. Paul S. Minear (St. Louis: Bethany Press, 1958), 92–93.

19. On this model and the tests it faces, see Michael Root, "A Striking Convergence in American Ecumenism," *Origins* 26 (1996): 60–64. On the limits of "unity in reconciled diversity," see Root, "Once More on the Unity We Seek: Testing Ecumenical Models," in *The Unity We Have and the Unity We Seek: Ecumenical Prospects for the Third Millennium* (London: T&T Clark, 2003), 167–77.

20. At the ELCA Churchwide Assembly in 1997, which rejected the Episcopal-Lutheran Concordat by a narrow margin, many of us were consoled by a sermon by Fred Meuser that emphasized this point.

21. Particularly powerful is still Richard Rorty, *Consequences of Pragmatism: Essays 1972–1980* (Minneapolis: University of Minnesota Press, 1982), xiii–xlvii.

22. The more analytic forms of this challenge are addressed with skill and, I believe, success in Bruce D. Marshall, *Trinity and Truth*, Cambridge Studies in Christian Doctrine (Cambridge: Cambridge University Press, 1999).

23. Karl Barth, *Evangelical Theology: An Introduction,* trans. Grover Foley (Grand Rapids, MI: Eerdmans, 1983), 144.

Chapter 10

THE SEARCH FOR UNITY SINCE 1957: A CATHOLIC PERSPECTIVE

Avery Cardinal Dulles, SJ

> Following its presentation at Oberlin II, this paper was published under the title "Saving Ecumenism from Itself" in *First Things,* no. 178 (December 2007): 23–27, and is printed here with permission.

REFLECTIONS ON OBERLIN 1957

The Oberlin conference on "The Nature of the Unity We Seek," which met fifty years ago this coming September, marks an important stage in the ecumenical movement. For the first time the churches in North America in large numbers committed themselves to the quest for Christian unity. The composition of the conference was very diverse; it included delegates from several Orthodox churches, the Protestant Episcopal Church, Lutheran, Reformed, Methodists, Baptists, Disciples of Christ, Adventists, and others. The delegates heard thoughtful addresses by a brilliant array of theologians from North America, Europe, and Asia, including a sermon by the secretary general of the World Council of Churches, Willem A. Visser't Hooft. After some days of discussion the delegates came up with a "Message to the Churches" recommending steps toward a greater visible manifestation of the unity of the church.[1]

Although I had to leave the United States in June 1957 for a three-year sojourn in Europe, I can recall the interest that the scheduled Oberlin Conference aroused in the Catholic Church even before I left. My own professor and mentor in ecumenism, Father Gustave Weigel, SJ, took part in the conference as one of the two Catholic observers. The other was my good friend, the Paulist editor of the *Catholic World*, John B. Sheerin.[2]

The judgment of H. P. Van Dusen to the effect that the Oberlin conference "cast virtually no light on the theme which the gathering was summoned to examine"[3] is theologically defensible. But in my estimation the conference achieved all that could reasonably have been expected of it. Large multilateral conferences of this type, gathering for the first time, cannot be expected to come up with profound new consensus statements. The delegates were effectively exposed to the complexities of the problem in the areas of faith, liturgy, and the Christian life. They became conscious of the length of the road ahead but at the same time eager to bring their respective churches, with God's help, as far as they could along that road. The ecumenical movement, which had been going on for a generation in Europe, was formally launched in the United States.

Oberlin stands near the beginning of a half century of thriving ecumenical activity. The impetus toward unity was strengthened, four years later, by the General Assembly of the World Council of Churches at New Delhi and then, in 1963, by the Fourth World Conference on Faith and Order at Montreal. The full and official entry of the Catholic Church into the ecumenical movement came with the Second Vatican Council (1962–65).

ECUMENISM AS A CATHOLIC CONCERN

Catholic ecumenists, like their Orthodox colleagues, were conscious that their participation in the ecumenical movement was in some ways problematic because of the claims of their own church to possess all the means of salvation entrusted by the Lord to his church. The Central Committee of the World Council of Churches in its Toronto statement of 1950 indicated that such claims to exclusivity were not an obstacle to membership in the World Council of Churches, provided that the churches in question were at least able to recognize "vestiges" or elements of the true Church in communities other than their own.[4]

Without concealing or minimizing the specific claims of the Catholic Church, the Second Vatican Council found ways of showing how that Church could and should pursue ecumenism. Four important insights, all expressed by Vatican II, undergirded the commitment of Catholics to this new apostolate.

First of all, the scandal of Christian division posed difficulties for the Catholic Church's own missionary work. It was a stumbling block that impeded what the council called "the most holy cause of proclaiming the gospel to every creature" (*UR,* 1).[5] Non-Christians often reacted to missionary efforts with the feeling that before asking them to be converted, the missionaries ought to agree among themselves about what Christianity is. Why should the past quarrels among European or American Christians, some asked, be visited upon young churches from other parts of the world? Did it make any sense for an African, for example, to join the Swedish Lutheran church or to become a Southern Baptist?

In the second place, the Catholic Church recognized that the divisions among Christians impoverished her catholicity. She lacked the natural and cultural endowments that other Christians could have contributed if they were united with her. Catholicity required that all the riches of the nations should be gathered into the one Church and harvested for the glory of God (*LG,* 13).

Third, the fullness of Christianity in Catholicism did not imply that all other churches were devoid of truth and grace. For all their mutual differences, they shared considerable commonalities in faith, worship, and ministerial order. The council taught, in fact, that non-Catholic churches and communions were "by no means deprived of significance and importance for the mystery of salvation" because the Holy Spirit could use them as instruments of grace (*UR,* 3). Vatican II, therefore, represents a sharp turn away from the purely negative evaluation of non-Catholic Christianity that was characteristic of the previous three centuries.

Fourth, the Catholic Church, insofar as she was made up of human members and administered by them, was always in need of purification and reform (*LG,* 8; *UR,* 6). Through ecumenical contacts, other Christian communities could help her to correct what was amiss, to supply what was lacking, and to update what was obsolete.

Regarding the ecclesial status of non-Catholic Christians, Pope Pius XII had taught as late as 1943 that they could not be true members of the church because the Body of Christ was identical with the Roman Catholic Church.[6] Such Christians could not belong to the body except by virtue of some implicit desire, which would give them a relationship that fell short of true incorporation. From a different point of view Vatican II taught that every valid baptism incorporates the recipient into the crucified and glorified Christ, and that all baptized Christians were to some extent in communion with the Catholic Church (*UR*, 22). Their status, therefore, was quite different from that of non-Christians, although even these could be related by desire or orientation to the People of God (*LG*, 15–16).

Relying on the new ecclesiology of communion, Catholic ecumenists now perceived their task as a movement from lesser to greater degrees of communion. All who believed in Christ and were baptized in his name already possessed a certain imperfect communion, which could be recognized, celebrated, and deepened. The ecumenical movement aspired to the full restoration of the impaired communion among separated churches and communities. Paul VI felt authorized to declare that even now the communion between the Catholic and Orthodox churches was almost complete.[7]

Following the example set by Pope John XXIII, the next few popes cultivated cordial relationships with prominent leaders of other churches. Paul VI enjoyed relations of deep affection and respect with Patriarch Athenagoras I of Constantinople and Archbishop Michael Ramsey of Canterbury. Pope John Paul II continued this tradition and in his encyclical of 1995, *Ut Unum Sint*, reaffirmed the Catholic Church's commitment to ecumenism as a permanent priority. Benedict XVI in his inaugural homily as pope on April 24, 2005, renewed this commitment. His meetings with Patriarch Bartholomew of Constantinople and with Archbishop Rowan Williams of Canterbury have been major landmarks in his pontificate.

BILATERAL DIALOGUES SINCE 1960

The principal instrument of ecumenism over the past half century has been a series of theological conversations between separated churches. Proceeding on the basis of what they held in common, the partners tried to show that their shared patrimony contained the seeds of much closer agreement than had yet been recognized. Rereading their confessional documents in light of Scripture and early creeds as shared authorities, they produced remarkable convergence statements on traditionally divisive subjects such as justification, Mariology, Scripture and tradition, the Eucharist, and the ordained ministry. The achievements of the Anglican-Roman Catholic International Commission (ARCIC), the Groupe des Dombes, and the World Commission on Faith and Order in its Lima paper on Baptism, Eucharist, and Ministry deserve our admiration. I personally stand by the ecumenical statements that I have signed, including those of the Lutheran-Catholic Dialogue and Evangelicals and Catholics Together.

Valuable though it was, the convergence method was not without limitations. Each new round of dialogue raised expectations for the future. The next dialogue, at the price of failure, was under pressure to come up with new agreements. The process would at some point reach a stage at which it had delivered about as much as it could. It would eventually run up against hard-core differences that resisted elimination by this method of convergence.

When the dialogues attempted to go beyond convergence and achieve full reconciliation on divisive issues, they sometimes overreached themselves. Although not all would agree, I personally judged that the much-vaunted Lutheran-Catholic Joint Declaration on Justification by Faith, signed in 1999, exaggerated the agreements.[8] After stating quite correctly that the Lutheran and Catholic dialogues of previous decades had come to a basic consensus on the doctrine of justification by grace through faith, the Joint Declaration goes on to assert, more dubiously, that the remaining disagreements could now be written off as "differences of language, theological elaboration, and emphasis," and therefore as not warranting condemnation from either side. It even described these differences as "acceptable" (§40). In my judgment some of the unresolved differences are more correctly classified as matters of doctrine. Is the justified person always and inevitably a sinner, worthy of condemnation in the sight of God? Are human beings able, with the help of grace, to dispose themselves to receive sanctifying grace? Can they merit an increase of grace and heavenly glory with the help of the grace they already have? Do sinners, after receiving forgiveness, still have an obligation to make satisfaction for their misdeeds? On questions such as these, Lutherans and Catholics seem to give incompatible answers. Nothing in the Joint Declaration persuades me that such differences are mere matters of theological speculation or linguistic formulation. The picture painted by the Joint Declaration is therefore somewhat overoptimistic.

The bilateral conversations have been particularly useful for churches with a firm and ample doctrinal tradition, such as the Orthodox, the Lutheran, the Anglican, and the Catholic. They have dispelled past prejudices, identified real but unsuspected agreements, and enabled the parties to say more together than they previously deemed possible. But to the extent that churches rely on different normative sources or different exegetical methods, the dialogues, while still useful up to a point, have been less fruitful.

Many of the twentieth-century dialogues have opted to take Scripture, interpreted by historical-critical method, as their primary norm. This method has worked reasonably well for mainline Protestant Churches and for the Catholic Church since Vatican II. But many Christians do not rely on the critical approach to Scripture as normative. Catholics themselves, without rejecting historical-critical method, profess many doctrines that enjoy very little support from Scripture, interpreted in this manner. They draw on allegorical or spiritual exegesis, authenticated by the sense of the faithful and long-standing theological tradition. As a consequence, certain Catholic doctrines, such as papal primacy, the Immaculate Conception, the Assumption, and Purgatory, have been banished to the sidelines. Unable to cope with doctrines such as these, the dialogues have treated them as an ecumenical embarrassment.

RECONFESSIONALIZATION

For the reasons just explained, dialogues conducted according to the dominant methodology of the past century have tended to be reductive. Many doctrinally conservative Christians, strongly wedded to their own beliefs, have abstained from ecumenical involvements for fear of doctrinal compromise. Since the 1980s, some of the churches heavily committed to ecumenical dialogue have shown anxiety about maintaining their own identity. Some observers speak of a reconfessionalization in the ecumenical landscape.[9]

The negative criticisms of the Joint Declaration from both the Protestant and the Catholic sides (including my own reservations mentioned above) are illustrative of this new tendency. Without wanting a return to the polemics of the past, some critics fear that a vague spirit of civility is being allowed to replace the theological candor and rigor of earlier centuries. This reaction against immoderate irenicism may be found in some recent official teaching of the Catholic Church. A new concern for orthodoxy, as Walter Kasper has noted,[10] lies behind the "Letter on Some Aspects of the Church Considered as *Communio*" issued by the Congregation for the Doctrine of the Faith (CDF) in 1992. The same is true of the Declaration *Dominus Iesus* issued by the same congregation in 2000 and of the "Note on the Expression 'Sister Churches,'" issued by the CDF at the same time. *Dominus Iesus*, in particular, goes further in the direction of Catholic exclusivity than Vatican II, as it has generally been understood. Reacting against ecclesial relativism, it vigorously denied that the church exists today in a fragmented form, in which no one body could claim identity with the Church of Christ. This declaration contains no suggestion that the Body of Christ is broader than the Catholic Church or that one may be incorporated in the former without being a member of the latter. Instead it asserts that in holding that the Church of Christ "subsists" in the Roman Catholic communion, the council intended to say that the Church of Christ, his Body and Bride, is identical with the Catholic Church, outside of which there are only elements or fragments of the true church (*DI*, 16–17).

The teaching of *Dominus Iesus* is repeated in substance in the "Responses to Some Questions Regarding Certain Aspects of the Doctrine of the Church" made public by the CDF on July 10, 2007. One minor difference is that where *Dominus Iesus* had asserted that the Church of Christ is "present and operative" in all churches that have preserved the apostolic succession and a valid Eucharist, the "Responses" state that same may be true of ecclesial communities that have not preserved these structural elements.[11]

Some would regard the recent trend toward reconfessionalization as a defeat for ecumenism. This judgment would be true if it meant a retreat of the confessions into their own shell and a refusal to encounter others. But reconfessionalization need not mean what Cardinal Kasper calls "an apprehensive, self-absorbed, defensive attitude."[12] It may be an opening to a new kind of dialogue, in which the partners are eager to express their own distinctive heritage so that they may be able to share it with others.

DIALOGUE AS AN EXCHANGE OF GIFTS

Pope John Paul II consistently opposed styles of ecumenism that seemed to aim at settling for a least common denominator. In an address to the Roman Curia, on June 28, 1980, he laid down the principle that "the unity of Christians cannot be sought in a compromise between the various theological positions, but only in a common meeting in the most ample and mature fullness of Christian truth."[13] In his encyclical *Ut Unum Sint* he proposed a better alternative. After stating that "the unity willed by God can be attained only by the adherence of all to the content of revealed truth in its entirety" (*UUS*, 18), he went on to say that dialogue is not merely an exchange of ideas but also, in some way, an exchange of gifts (*UUS*, 28). Later in the same encyclical he wrote: Communion is made fruitful by the exchange of gifts between the churches insofar as they complement each other (*UUS*, 57). In these words he called for a new chapter in the history of ecumenism.

For some years now, I have felt that the method of convergence, which seeks to harmonize the doctrines of each ecclesial tradition on the basis of shared sources and methods, has nearly exhausted its potential. It has served well in the past, and may still be useful, especially among groups that have hitherto been rather isolated from the conversation. But to surmount the remaining barriers we may need a different method, one that invites a deeper conversion on the part of the churches themselves. I have therefore been urging an ecumenism of mutual enrichment by means of testimony.[14] This proposal corresponds closely, I believe, with John Paul II's idea of seeking the fullness of truth by means of an "exchange of gifts."

There are not many examples of the kind of ecumenical encounter I am envisaging, but one comes to my mind. In January 2006 the theology department at Durham University hosted at Ushaw College, a neighboring Catholic seminary, an international conference of Catholics in conversation with Orthodox, Anglicans, and Methodists. Conducting an experiment in what the conference called "receptive ecumenism," the speakers were asked to discuss what they could find in their own traditions that might be acceptable to the Catholic Church without detriment to its identity. The Catholic participants, including Cardinal Kasper, were asked to evaluate the suggestions and judge their practical feasibility. The discussion, I am told, was informal and did not lead to any set of agreed conclusions.[15]

Unlike some recent models of dialogue, ecumenism of this style leaves the participants free to draw on their own normative sources and does not constrain them to bracket or minimize what is specific to themselves. Far from being ashamed of their own distinctive doctrines and practices, each partner should feel privileged to be able to contribute something positive that the others still lack.

This does not mean, of course, that the churches should be uncritical of themselves or others. Where they express, or hear others expressing, singular beliefs, they should carefully examine the grounds for such views. But that is a very different thing from abdicating or suppressing their special convictions as a matter of principle.

With this mentality we Catholics would want to hear from the churches of the Reformation the reasons that they have for speaking as they do of Christ alone, Scripture alone, grace alone, and faith alone while Catholics tend to speak of Christ and the church, Scripture and tradition, grace and cooperation, faith and works. We would want to learn from them how to make better use of the laity as sharers in the priesthood of the whole People of God. We would want to hear from Evangelicals about their experience of conversion and from Pentecostals about perceiving the free action of the Holy Spirit in their lives. The Orthodox would have much to tell us about the liturgical piety, holy tradition, sacred images, and synodical styles of polity. We would not want any of these distinctive endowments of other ecclesial families to be muted or shunted aside for the sake of having shared premises or an agreed method.

Conversely, we Catholics would not hesitate to go into the dialogue with the full panoply of our beliefs, sustained by our own methods of certifying the truth of revelation. We are not ashamed of our reliance on tradition, the liturgy, and the sense of the faithful, and of our confidence in the judgment of the magisterium.

One of the doctrines most distinctive to the Catholic Church is surely the primacy of the pope as the successor of Peter—a primacy that the First Vatican Council set forth in clear, uncompromising language. Because we Catholics cherish this doctrine, we should not be content to keep it to ourselves. The successor of Peter, we believe, is intended by Christ to be the visible head of all Christians. Without accepting his ministry, Christians will never attain the kind of universal concord that God wills the church to have as a sign and sacrament of unity. They will inevitably fall into conflict with one another regarding doctrine, discipline, and ways of worship. No church can simply institute for itself an office that has authority to pronounce finally on disputed doctrines. If it exists at all, this office must have been instituted by Christ and must enjoy the assistance of the Holy Spirit. We Catholics believe that the Petrine office is a precious gift that the Lord has given us not only for our own consolation but as something to be held in trust for the entire *oikoumene*.

John Paul II in *Ut Unum Sint* expressed a desire to work with leaders and theologians of other churches in seeking ways for the Petrine office to be exercised in ways that could be beneficial to them as well as to Catholics (*UUS*, 95–96). These other churches and communities will have to consider the ways in which they could receive the primatial ministry of the Bishop of Rome. A dialogue on this subject is already under way. For some communities, perhaps, the papacy will be the final piece by which to complete the jigsaw puzzle of Christian unity.

Each party will engage in ecumenical dialogue with its own presuppositions and convictions. As a Roman Catholic I would make use of the methods by which my church derives its distinctive doctrines. I would also expect that any reunion to which Catholics can be a party would have to include as part of the settlement the Catholic dogmas, perhaps reinterpreted in ways that we do not now foresee. Other churches and ecclesial communities will have their own expectations. But all must be open to possible conversion. We must rely on the Holy Spirit to lead us, as Vatican II recommended "without obstructing the ways of divine Providence and without prejudging the future inspiration of the Holy Spirit" (*UR*, 24).

How then can Christian unity be envisaged? That is the question asked at Oberlin and repeated today. The first condition, I believe, is that the various Christian communities be ready to speak and listen to one another. Some will perhaps receive the grace to accept what they hear credibly attested as an insight from other communities. The witnesses and their hearers need not insist on rigorous proof, because very little of our faith can be demonstrated by deductive methods. Testimony operates by a different logic. We speak of what has been graciously manifested to us and what we have found to be of value for our relationship with God. If others accept what we proclaim, it is because our words evoke an echo in them and carry the hallmark of truth.

The process of growth through mutual attestation will probably never reach its final consummation within historical time, but it can bring palpable results. It can lead the churches to emerge progressively from their present isolation into something more like a harmonious chorus. Enriched by the gifts of others, they can hope to raise their voices together in a single hymn to the glory of the triune God. The result to be sought is unity in diversity.

I come, then, to my last point. True progress in ecumenism requires obedience to the Holy Spirit. Vatican II rightly identified spiritual ecumenism as the soul of the ecumenical movement (*UR*, 8). It defined spiritual ecumenism as a change of heart and holiness of life, together with public and private prayer for the unity of Christians. We must pray to God to overcome our deafness and open our ears to what the Spirit is saying to the churches, including our own. No mutual rapprochement can be of any value unless it is also a closer approach to Christ the Lord of the Church. We must ask for the grace to say only what the Spirit bids us say, and to hear all that he is telling us through the other. Then we may hope that by accommodating what other communities are trying to tell us, we may be enriched with new and precious gifts. By accepting the full riches of Christ we lose nothing except our errors and defects. What we gain is the greatest gift of all: a deeper share in the truth of Christ, who said of himself, "I am the truth."

NOTES

1. Paul S. Minear, ed., *The Nature of the Unity We Seek: Official Report of the North American Conference on Faith and Order, September 3–10, 1957, Oberlin, Ohio* (St. Louis: Bethany Press, 1958). The "Message to the Churches" appears on pages 28–30.

2. For a reaction of one of the Catholic observers, see John B. Sheerin, CSP, "The Sin and Agony of Disunity," *Catholic World* 186 (November 1957): 81–85.

3. Henry P. Van Dusen, "The Significance of Conciliar Ecumenicity," *Ecumenical Review* 12 (April 1960): 310–18, at 313, quoted by Bernard Leeming, "Ecumenical Conclusions: The Methods," *Heythrop Journal* 1 (October 1960): 285–99, at 293.

4. "The Church, the Churches and the World Council of Churches," a statement received by the Central Committee at Toronto in 1950; text in Lukas Vischer, *A Documentary History of the Faith and Order Movement 1927–1963* (St. Louis: Bethany Press, 1963), 167–82.

5. The parenthetical references to Vatican II documents refer to the Dogmatic Constitution on the Church, *Lumen gentium* (*LG*), and the Decree on Ecumenism, *Unitatis redintegratio* (*UR*).

6. Pius XII, Encyclical *Mystici Corporis Christi*, June 29, 1943.

7. Paul VI, Letter to Patriarch Athenagoras of Constantinople, in E. J. Stormon, ed., *Towards the Healing of Schism,* Public Statements and Correspondence between the Holy See and the Ecumenical Patriarchate, 1958–84 (New York: Paulist Press, 1987), 232.

8. Lutheran/Catholic Dialogue, Joint Declaration on the Doctrine of Justification, *Origins* 28 (July 16, 1998): 120–27.

9. Cardinal Johannes Willebrands in his address to the Seventh Assembly of the Lutheran World Federation (LWF) at Budapest in the summer of 1984 gave a description and assessment of what he perceived as a move toward reconfessionalization in the churches. See the Official Proceedings of In Christ—Hope for the World, LWF Report No. 19–20, ed. Carl H. Mau (Geneva: Lutheran World Federation, 1984), 128–35.

10. Walter Cardinal Kasper, "The Current Ecumenical Transition," *Origins* 36 (December 7, 2006): 407–14.

11. Congregation for the Doctrine of the Faith, "Responses to Some Questions Regarding Certain Aspects of the Doctrine of the Church," officially dated June 29, 2007. See Response to Question 2, on the meaning of "subsist."

12. "The Current Ecumenical Transition," 409.

13. John Paul II, Address to the Roman Curia §17; *Origins* 10 (August 10, 1980): 166–74, at 171.

14. See, for instance, Avery Dulles, "Method in Ecumenical Theology," chapter 12 of *The Craft of Theology*, 2nd ed. (New York: Crossroad, 1995): 179–95.

15. On this conference see the article of Ladislas Orsy, a participant, "A Time to Ponder," *America* 196 (February 5, 2007): 14–19; also Elena Curti and Michael Hirst, "Amid the Cold, Signs of a Thaw," *Tablet* (London) 260 (January 21, 2006): 12–13.

Chapter 11

ISSUES FACING ECUMENISM: A PERSPECTIVE FROM THE WORLD COUNCIL OF CHURCHES

Sarah Heaner Lancaster

It is appropriate that as the National Council of Churches looks back in celebration of the beginning of its Faith and Order work that it also look ahead to the challenges and possibilities it faces in the future. I have been invited to help you imagine that future by highlighting issues that appear from the perspective of the World Council of Churches Faith and Order Commission. I will organize these issues in two categories: first, issues facing ecumenism because of its own success, and second, issues facing ecumenism because of the changed situation in which this work is now done.

THE CHALLENGES POSED BY SUCCESS

One way of seeing the impact of the ecumenical movement is to look at the number of dialogues taking place and the number of agreements that are being reached. In December, the third volume of *Growth in Agreement* will be made available in the United States through Eerdmans.[1] At more than six hundred pages, this volume contains forty-three different statements, most of which have resulted from international bilateral dialogues. As impressive as this volume is, it is not the complete record of all the dialogues or official statements that are taking place around the world, such as statements documenting church union negotiations or local full communion agreements.[2] Even in a time that some people have called "the winter of ecumenism," much important work is going on.

The very existence of so much dialogue and agreement, though, raises important questions. Because Councils of Churches can operate on international, national, and even regional levels, and because dialogues can take place at the level of world communions and also distinct church bodies within those communions, questions arise as to how decisions made at one level affect decisions made at another level.[3] To take an example from my own tradition, Methodists and Lutherans are making significant progress on different levels. First, the bilateral dialogue between the United Methodist Church and the Evangelical Lutheran Church in America has already reached an Interim Eucharistic Agreement, and it is moving forward with a proposal for full communion between these two church bodies. Second, the World Methodist Council agreed in 2006 in Seoul, Korea, to join the Lutheran World Federation and the Roman Catholic Church in the Joint Declaration on the Doctrine of Justification. In both cases, Lutherans and Methodists were talking with each other, but the agreements were arrived at independently of each other.

One way of looking at this situation is that arriving at agreements through different means reinforces the strength of the conclusions that each of them have reached, if you will, the kind of confirmation that science achieves through replication of experiments. But another way of looking at it raises the question of communication and accountability across levels of dialogue that are taking place. What would have happened, for instance, to our local agreement on full communion if the World Methodist Council had not been able to agree with the Lutherans on justification? What would have happened to the WMC agreement on the Joint Declaration if the UMC and the ELCA has determined in its negotiations that we simply could not agree on the doctrine of justification?

Issues like these have not escaped the attention of the Faith and Order Commission of the WCC. In March 2008 Faith and Order will host a forum (the ninth of its kind) on bilateral dialogues, and it will include discussion of several issues, two of which directly address the way that the multiplicity of dialogues affects the larger ecumenical movement. The first of these is the issue of transitivity. That is, "If A and B agree, and if B and C agree, do A and C necessarily agree?" To return to my own tradition, the United Methodist Church is in dialogue not only with the ELCA but also with the Episcopal Church. The ELCA is already in full communion with the Episcopal Church, so if the UMC succeeds in approving full communion with the ELCA, should that in any way determine the outcome of our dialogue with the Episcopal Church? Or conversely, if the UMC reaches an agreement with the ELCA and then fails to do so with the Episcopal Church, would that threaten or damage our agreement with the Lutherans?

A second issue has been named "extensibility," that is, "How far can the results of one dialogue be extended to other confessions?" The Lutheran and Catholic agreement on justification was a major achievement, and immediately interested ecumenists began to wonder what effect that would have on other traditions. Methodists moved rather quickly to become a part of the discussion and did succeed in joining the agreement. Anglican and Reformed communions, each for different reasons, have not joined the agreement. What are the consequences for agreement between specific traditions beyond those traditions? How far can an agreement be opened to other confessions? What complications arise when other traditions respond in different ways?

The multiplicity of dialogues raises an even more basic question than these, and that is the question of the meaning of "unity" itself. In his 2007 director's report, Tom Best said, "The term 'unity' is claimed by a widening circle of churches, recognition agreements, partnerships, to the extent that its specific meaning becomes less and less clear. What precisely is the goal of unity for which we are striving? What degree of structural integration is necessary for unity to be visible, and real?"[4] Cooperation, partnership, mutual accountability, *koinonia*, communion, and union are all expressions of unity to some degree. Different agreements seek to achieve different representations of unity, ranging from spiritual to structural. Even the adjectives that modify the word "unity" can raise questions about what it means. For some time, the phrase "visible unity" was the accepted phrase. Recently, though, in the twenty-fifth anniversary edition of *Baptism, Eucharist, Ministry,* the term "real unity" appears in the introduction. This shift in terminology has prompted some discussion about whether visible unity and real unity indicate slightly different goals. In the sentences I quote above, Tom Best handles this problem by using both terms.

One of the earliest terms in the ecumenical movement was "organic union," used first in 1937 at the Second World Conference on Faith and Order in Edinburgh.[5] This phrase suggested the kind of unity that an organism has, where diverse members function together for the health of the whole body. While diversity has its place in this image, it is held together in a structural whole. Some churches have in fact achieved structural unity, and others continue to work toward it. The Faith and Order Commission conducts consultations for united and uniting churches, that is, those churches which have achieved or which seek to express their mutual accountability in a common ecclesial structure. These churches keep alive a vision for unity as more than mutual recognition, but even here, there are some important questions that need to be addressed. Tom Best notes that these churches continue to struggle with how much agreement in theology and practice is necessary for union, how a new entity should be organized, how united structure best serves mission rather than survival, and to what extent the component parts retain their own distinctive identity and connection to world communions.[6]

Achieved unity on different levels is not the only way to demonstrate success in ecumenism. Another form of success is the clarity about what really divides us that has been uncovered through dialogue, and this, too, shows us challenges to be faced in the future. Sustained dialogue about sacrament and ministry has exposed that we have very different understandings of the way in which Jesus Christ makes us and enables us to be church. The work for unity often stumbles on this very point. Matters such as the extent to which the church can be thought of as sinful, whether the church itself should be considered sacrament, the relationship of individual congregations to the church universal, and what truly links the church today to the apostles are all matters upon which there is significant disagreement that has so far hindered advances toward mutual recognition of sacrament and ministry. The Faith and Order Commission of the WCC has been studying these questions of ecclesiology for decades now, and its most recent statement is currently being circulated among the member churches for response. Deep, identity-shaping convictions are at stake, and the way forward is not at all clear at this point.

One of the reasons that ecumenists often give for their work is that a united church will bear better witness to the world than a divided church can. I certainly agree with that motivation, but sometimes I wonder whether a better witness is needed even for those of us who are already Christian. After all, we are the ones who are most likely to see each other turn away from each other's tables. Without this visible expression to one another that we are indeed part of the same body, it is easy for Christians to harbor suspicions of one another and to think the worst rather than the best of another's motives, beliefs, practices, and so on. For that reason, unity beyond cooperation will always have to be our goal until it is finally achieved.

CHALLENGES THAT COME FROM A CHANGED SITUATION

While in the grand sweep of history the ecumenical movement is very young, it is old enough to have witnessed changes in the world and to have undergone changes itself. In most cases, old divisive questions—such as the ones I mentioned with regard to ecclesiology—have not yet been settled, but even as we continue to work on them, new questions arise that redirect attention and that could be potentially divisive themselves.

One of the most potentially divisive new questions has to do with the different responses that the churches make regarding issues concerning homosexual persons. Decisions about ordination, marriage, and even membership of homosexual persons threaten to split communions and to hinder the overcoming of division between communions. Although this issue gains attention right now, it is not the only one that could pose this kind of threat. Indeed, in the past, churches have divided over slavery, women's ordination, war, and more. To understand better how churches can come to different decisions about issues that are seen to be ethical as well as theological, the Faith and Order Commission of the WCC is beginning a study that will use case studies to display decision-making processes used by churches. For instance, the study will ask questions such as the following: what kind of information is taken to be relevant to an issue, how is Scripture employed, how does tradition guide the church? This study, together with a second study on how the different churches appeal to sources of authority within their traditions, will help to clarify why we have the differences that we have.

Another aspect of our changed situation is a shift in theological interest. The dominant voices and exciting directions for theology are not the same now as they were in 1948 when the WCC was organized (or in 1957 when the NCC began its work in Faith and Order). Postmodernism, postcolonialism, and liberation theologies have called attention to issues that were simply not on the table for a previous generation of scholars. Traditionally divisive questions do not always hold interest for present-day theologians, partly because those questions have not seemed to get any closer to resolution and partly because they seem misguided in the first place. As particularity supersedes universality, even the idea of bringing diverse communities into common agreement may seem an ideal from the past that has little or no currency today. Furthermore, doctrinal questions may seem very far removed from the lived experience of people, especially the oppressed. In this climate, ecumenism can easily become an enterprise that is more and more isolated from mainstream theological work. The Faith and Order Commission of the WCC is trying to pay attention to these theological currents. Some of its recent publications have contributed reflections on peace and conflict; on understanding human worth with regard to disability, genetic technology, and other current questions; and on diverse hermeneutical understandings.[7]

The landscape of churches that call themselves Christian has not remained the same, either. Churches with vital ministries are not necessarily connected to traditional denominations any longer. While more recent forms of Christian community (such as nondenominational congregations or the emerging church) are growing, mainline churches are facing decline in membership. This situation has led to two almost opposite reactions. First, in the United States, some congregations within a specific tradition hide their association with it. They may call themselves "community churches" or drop any identifying marks from their names, websites, and so forth. Second, some denominations are becoming more "confessional" as they pay closer attention than they have to their own traditions, both in terms of scholarship and resources for laypeople, in order to shape a distinctive identity in the ecclesial marketplace.

The former reaction—hiding association with a tradition—seems to be rooted in the idea that it is possible to be a generic Christian, and in that sense it creates the kind of "false universal" that current theology warns against. Because it erases the identity of other traditions as well as one's own, it is not a good ground for ecumenism. Understanding and embracing one's theological and ecclesial history is not a bad thing because the better a church understands who it is, the better able it is to present its views clearly in dialogue with others. But the other tendency—to cling to one's own tradition to try to survive in a competitive market—does not serve ecumenism well either. It may not make churches into enemies producing anathemas (as in a former time), but it certainly can make them rivals. Ecumenists have a particularly important role to help their traditions navigate a way between both these survival techniques so that the church as a whole may find a way to thrive.

The context of interfaith relations must be mentioned, even though the NCC is very much aware of it already, having sponsored a panel on the issue at this very conference. I will note here only briefly a few things that have been discussed on this topic at the World Council level. First, the way that Christians relate to other faiths has the potential for being another church dividing issue, or for hindering the overcoming of divisions that already exist. Behind any approach to people of other faiths lie assumptions and convictions about how the church preserves and manifests in the world the truth of God's revelation in Jesus Christ. Differences on these points already lie behind issues we discuss among ourselves and affect our relations with each other. It is not so much that the question of interfaith relations adds a new problem as that it presents in a new form, and therefore heightens, problems that we already have.

Second, interfaith relations are different around the world. It is one thing in this country to think about how Christians relate to other faiths in the context of our Constitution and a history of religious freedom and another to think about those relations in a country where Christianity is a minority religion and its activities may be severely restricted because of laws that guarantee the dominance of another religion. Since so many of our churches in the United States are tied to other churches around the world, it is well for us to be mindful of the different situations that they may face even as we search for a workable understanding in our own contexts.

Finally, the World Council has been producing resources for interreligious relations and dialogue for several years, and those resources can be helpful on the national level as well.[8] They include materials focused on specific relationships (for instance, between Christians and Jews) as well as more general topics (such as how people of different faiths may pray together). The WCC promotes interfaith work in other ways. Just this month, the Ecumenical Institute at Bossey is hosting a gathering of Christians, Jews, and Muslims from different parts of the world for a seminar called "Building an Interfaith Community." The seminar includes devotion and meditation, studying sacred Scriptures, and conversation about how to address the pressing questions that we all face. Last year, the WCC began working with the Vatican to sponsor the production of a code of conduct for conversion. This project plans to include, not only a variety of Christian participants, but also participants from other religious traditions.

FINAL REMARKS

One of the major insights in the academy today is the awareness of social location. A person needs to be understood in terms of the particular location in which she or he lives, not simply according to general theories. We become unique individuals through the intersection of interests in the different communities in which we participate. But another major insight in the academy is the awareness of globalization. This word can mean different things, but it at least indicates a connection that reaches beyond one's regionalism and makes one have to pay attention to others who are not right next door. I have thought about the pull of these two forces on ecumenism as I have considered the different perspectives that one might have from a National Council or World Council point of view.

Churches, too, have a social location. Members of the same communion look different in different parts of the world (and even sometimes in different parts of the same country). And yet churches also have connections that go well beyond the specific regions in which their identities are shaped. Many North American Churches are related to churches around the world through associations and federations and councils. But even more fundamentally, we are united in some way through Jesus Christ. Negotiating these two realities is complex, but it seems to me that we are challenged to try to make sure that our work—on the national and world levels—is always mindful of what the other is doing because each will somehow affect the other.

Negotiating changes through time is also complex. Those who began the work of Faith and Order in the mid-twentieth century knew that it would be lengthy and difficult and that they would depend on subsequent generations to see it through to fruition. I wonder if they knew how much unity would become a moving target as new divisive issues would emerge. Ecumenism is developing a dual focus, still paying attention to past questions but having to deal with new questions at the same time. It cannot ignore either, although the attempt to do both will surely tax our resources. National ecumenism must face this situation as well as world ecumenism, and we may need to think about how our work can be mutually supportive so that we can each be more effective, not with the idea that there will be one answer to any problem but with the idea that we have a shared interest in promoting dialogue on the issues of our time.

As I think about the many decades of work in Faith and Order, I am struck by how much has been accomplished and how much is yet to be done. There is no simplifying the complicated layers of intersecting issues that we face already, and more are likely to be added in the future. Still, we are making progress, at least in understanding each other. Will growing understanding lead to unity? That may depend on what kind of "unity" we decide we are looking for. As we have seen, that is a question that presses itself on our work with considerable force. While the answer is not obvious, it will no doubt have to take account, not only of diverse denominational viewpoints, but also of the push and pull of our local and global situations that affect every tradition.

NOTES

1. *Growth in Agreement III: International Dialogue Texts and Agreed Statements, 1998–2005*, Faith and Order Paper 204, ed. Jeffrey Gros, FSC; Thomas F. Best; and Lorelei F. Fuchs, SA (Grand Rapids, MI: Eerdmans, 2007).

2. Thomas F. Best and Union Correspondents, *Survey of Church Union Negotiations 2003–2006*, Faith and Order Paper 203 (Geneva: World Council of Churches, 2006). Reprinted from the *Ecumenical Review* 58 (July/October 2006).

3. To provide a personal example of the problem, I have been appointed by my denomination to a bilateral dialogue between the ELCA and the UMC, to the World Methodist Council, and to the Faith and Order Standing Commission of the World Council of Churches. My experience has been that my position on each of these groups is held together primarily in my own person rather than through formal connections that would exist even if three different people occupied these positions. The staff members of the General Commission on Christian Unity and Interreligious Concerns certainly provide oversight to all the ecumenical work of the UMC and staff involvement in formal dialogues is crucial for that reason. Still, the connection among all the different participants in all the different components of the ecumenical work of the UMC, does not seem to include direct communication of information or strategic consultation.

4. Thomas F. Best, Director's Report, Faith and Order Standing Commission, June 12–18, 2007, Crans-Montana, Switzerland.

5. Best, *Survey of Church Union Negotiations 2003–2006*, 2.

6. Best, "Appendix 1, United and Uniting Churches—An Overview," in ibid., 69.

7. *Participating in God's Mission of Reconciliation: A Resource for Churches in Situations of Conflict,* Faith and Order Paper 201; *Nurturing Peace: Theological Reflections on Overcoming Violence; Christian Perspectives on Theological Anthropology: A Faith and Order Study Document*, Faith and Order Paper 199; *A Treasure in Earthen Vessels: An Instrument for an Ecumenical Reflection on Hermeneutics*, Faith and Order Paper 182.

8. A list of these resources can be found on the WCC's website (Inter-Religious Relations) at *http://publications.oikoumene.org/index.php?2076&backPID=2076&alp=A&aalp=A&catId=14*.

Chapter 12

EVANGELICALS, ECUMENISM, AND EMERGING QUESTIONS: REFLECTIONS ON COMPLEXITY IN LIGHT OF OBERLIN II

R. M. Keelan Downton

> Following its presentation at Oberlin II, this paper was originally published in *Ecumenical Trends* 37, no. 6 (2008): 13/93–15/95. It is reprinted here with permission from the author and *Ecumenical Trends*.

The second Faith and Order conference at Oberlin explored the present reality of ecumenism and articulated challenges it will face in the twenty-first century. While laments of the onset of an "ecumenical winter" were notably absent, a clear consensus became apparent that the present trajectory is one of increasing complexity rather than the reverse. The location at a school that historically pioneered in educating black and white, female and male persons as an integrated student body provided the occasion for asking why the assembled participants did not more adequately represent the diversity of the church in America. The participation of seminarians and graduate students (aided by the funding provided for them to be present) made it possible to express continuity between those who paid significant spiritual, emotional, and professional costs for their ecumenical efforts and those who benefit from their struggle. Attention to both these matters produced a consultation on "ecumenism from the margins" that took place at Morehouse College in April and a proposal to establish a regular conference for graduate students and seminarians that would regularize such generational exchanges within the broader ecumenical scene. Furthermore, the presence of evangelical voices at Oberlin II highlighted four critical distinctions that provide the primary framework for this paper.

CAFETERIA VS. MATRIX

In ecumenical discourse, the phrase "cafeteria spirituality" is akin to the historical use of "enthusiasm" as a term of derision designed to signify the proverbial slippery slope destined to carry one to a fiery end. It seems to arise out of fear that aspects of one's tradition might be used in ways that do harm by removing important boundaries that depend on other aspects of the tradition or polluting the tradition by well-meaning but erroneous attributions. Though these fears are based in realistic possibilities (and actualities!) within a pluralist society, uncritical use of the cafeteria metaphor raises serious questions about the nature of the ecumenical gift-exchange that parallel the contemporary controversy concerning music copyright. The idea that *emerging church communities conceive of their promiscuous borrowing from a wide variety of traditions like DJ's sampling tracks created in disconnected contexts*[1] locates their discourse somewhat closer to Jione Havea's mat of interwoven narratives[2] than the Orthodox understanding of tradition articulated by Aristotle Papanikolaou.[3] As Havea contrasts a monolithic, static reading of Scripture with an ongoing process of reweaving the already-woven biblical stories, so the conception of tradition embedded within the *cafeteria* metaphor might be contrasted with the mathematical metaphor of a *matrix*. Whereas the cafeteria metaphor seems to imply the selection and removal of discrete elements from their respective locations and reincorporation into a meal on one's (personal) tray, a matrix suggests that the elements of tradition are not *removed* from the tradition itself but rather dealt with in terms of complex and sometimes changing *intersections* with elements in other traditions. The role of the individual is not to select and consume but simply navigate this complexity—to find some way to live *well* amid intersecting systems. Once the church is perceived in this way, it is difficult to imagine an escape from the aporia of the apparent inability to locate oneself in a single tradition without recourse to criteria that form the basis of such a tradition. To rely on such criteria is not simply question-begging but also a reversion to precisely the individual-subjectivist approach one is attempting to avoid by virtue of choosing a criterion (or several) that will carry more weight *for oneself* than the multiple possible criteria that carry weight for others. What seems from *outside* to be perusing various stations of the great ideological cafeteria appears from *within* to be adapting whatever tools are on hand to navigate the "flux" of contemporary existence.

REPRESENTATIVE VS. EXEMPLAR[4]

A second distinction is brought to light by consideration of Michael Root's response to Havea and Papanikolaou. It was a significant moment for an ecumenist of his stature to declare, "The models of unity dominant in the first decades of the ecumenical movement, up through perhaps the early 1970s, were all-too-modern.... The most popular present approach, in which denominations remain completely autonomous while living in full communion with one another, is in my estimation proving itself inadequate."[5] Though Root addresses the *goal* of ecumenism, he does not consider the extent to which there is something fundamentally modern about the *process* of ecumenism. Twentieth-century ecumenism was profoundly influenced by the forms of international organization available during its formative stages. The fact that the initial proposal of the Ecumenical Patriarchate of Constantinople explicitly drew from the idea of a League of Nations in the 1920 proposal for a "league of churches" (repeated perhaps independently by J. H. Oldham in 1921) suggests that the similarities between the United Nations and the World Council of Churches are not incidental but related to the notion of representation foundational to parliamentary democracy. At the present stage of history, ecumenism appears to be predicated on the capacity of a Christian body to provide a *representative*—a framework apparently compatible with, but certainly not identical to, the historic exercise of *episkope*.[6] For those whose identity as Christians is expressed in ways distinct from their institutional embodiments, however, the idea of representation seems both foreign and culturally conditioned. Far from being peripheral to theological concerns, this understanding is a direct extension of an understanding of mission that interprets apostolicity with an emphasis on being *sent* and a broad conception of how an individual's sense of calling might be confirmed by discerning community.[7] Attention to God's use of prophetic individuals both in the Bible and at critical moments in the church's history, in a way that may appear initially as "self-sending" but is affirmed later as the work of God, promotes tendencies toward experimentation within an understanding that ecclesiology is essentially malleable. The result is that persons who participate in such communities can engage in ecumenism as *exemplars* of this approach to mission but never as *representatives* since the term connotes a link to structures of authority that, while not quite logical impossibilities, are vastly improbable. If ecumenism is conducted by those who are merely exemplars of a tradition, there is little guarantee that the results of a dialogue will produce transformation beyond individuals engaged in dialogue. On the other hand, the problems many churches face concerning reception illustrate that the representational model is not necessarily immune to similar charges.

PROBLEM VS. REALITY

The third distinction shifts focus from the church as an object with properties of invisible and visible unity to the perceptions of subjects who view unity as a *reality to be experienced* and *problem to be solved*. What are theologians and educators to make of the fact that the starting point in many classrooms is not convincing students that Catholics and Orthodox believers are not going to hell (much less Presbyterians, Lutherans, or Baptists), but that they have differences significant enough to worth bothering about? Encountering such students is a nagging reminder that a significant level of education is required to understand many of the nuances that dictate appropriate ecumenical protocol. The strange result is that a vast chasm separates those who approach Christian unity "as a little child" (or even as boisterous adolescents) from those who identify unity as their vocation. On the one hand, entering into a relationship with limited or inaccurate understanding of the other party's expectations is a recipe for sorrow, but on the other hand, without significant capacity to perceive the other's response to the gospel *as a response to the gospel*, there can be no movement toward unity. Can the strangeness of a situation where unity is experienced as a *problem* for theologians but a *reality* for everyday Christians who move fluidly between divided traditions be dismissed simply as ignorance? This seems to be another example of what Sarah Heaner Lancaster described as "the challenges posed by success" that amplifies the ambivalence of significant numbers of churches dropping denominational labels in favor of a generic "community church" label while other churches display a renewed emphasis on their theological tradition to distinguish themselves in "the ecclesial marketplace."[8]

RECEPTION VS. FORMATION

Such concerns are closely linked to the fourth and final distinction: *reception* vs. *formation*. In 1957 Oberlin I recorded that the mobility of the U.S. population resulted in situations where 30–50 percent of local membership came from different denominations. The study report preceded Lancaster's ambivalence by fifty years, speculating that it might be a "powerful force for unity" on one hand and asserting that "denominational loyalties . . . are valuable resources which should be conserved"[9] on the other. If this was a product of population mobility in 1957, one can hardly imagine the situation after fifty years of development in transportation and communication technologies. After the churches at Oberlin I called for cooperative action in "leadership recruitment and training," "church planning," and "ecumenical study," no one should be surprised when a new generation views problems that animated prior generations so vigorously as matters of lesser importance superseded by the enduring quality of relations between churches. Though Oberlin II found a few occasions to touch on the problem of reception, its relation to the dynamics of formation were eclipsed by other concerns. Exploration of this relation might be furthered by noting that while *reception* occurs within a horizon of (a) the activity of a representative in producing a document, (b) the relevant ecclesial authority, and (c) the communion as a whole, *formation* occurs within a horizon of (p) intergenerational relationships,

(q) personal spiritual development, and (r) cultures of rapid change. Though reception is dependent on formation in the long term, in the short-term reception works to postpone formation in order to preserve continuity through a process (a preemptive ecumenical formation that introduces the products of dialogues directly to the young would inhibit reception by creating a rift between young and old while formation that did not take the products of dialogues into account would preserve division indefinitely).

CONCLUDING POSTSCRIPT ON NARRATIVE THEOLOGY

Though this essay does more to articulate problems than provide solutions, it concludes more hopefully with a few thoughts on the potential contribution of narrative theology's focus on the role of stories in developing a coherent expression of selfhood. One need not be an *exemplar of a Christian formed to conceive of unity as a reality to be experienced within a matrix of traditions* in order to bump up against the issues these distinctions bring to light. There are increasing numbers of individuals across the spectrum of communions whose identity bridges multiple theological traditions. It seems unfortunate that in dialogue settings, each of those individuals is necessarily in the position of saying, "quite apart from how I work this out personally and communally, my tradition teaches thus and thus." While such bridging certainly occurs for persons educated in a plurality of theological traditions, it is even more obvious for children of so-called mixed marriages who have no choice in being formed by two or more traditions. As much as such hybrids challenge the process of ecumenism, they surely express something of the goal of ecumenism—a body in which the diversity of the people of God is integrated. If narrative theology's concern to make sense of *how a differentiated set of beliefs, actions, and experiences are integrated within a single self* can be brought into dialogue with *the healing of memories* and other common-history projects, there may be space for such hybrids to engage a "patient and fraternal dialogue" about how their testimonies might further illumine the journey of the church on its pilgrim way.

NOTES

1. R. M. Keelan Downton, "Ecclesiological Malleability as Ecumenical Horizon" (unpublished paper presented at Oberlin II, July 20, 2007).

2. See Jione Havea, chapter 8, "The Bible on Postmodern Surfaces," in this volume.

3. See Aristotle Papanikolaou, chapter 7, "Orthodoxy, Postmodernity, and Ecumenism," in this volume.

4. In discussion of this distinction, John L. Drury pointed out that just as the category "representative" is limited by the locus of political science, "exemplar" is likewise limited by the locus of social sciences, particularly in terms of incapacity to account for the agency of those playing a *prophetic* role in relation to both the wider ecumenical community and their own traditions. Developing an adequate framework to describe an alternative to "representation" clearly requires further work.

5. Michael Root, chapter 9, "Faith and Order in a Postmodern World: A Response [to Havea and Papanikolaou]," in this volume.

6. Some tensions between parliamentary and conciliar methods of decision-making are addressed by the *Final Report of the Special Commission on Orthodox Participation in the WCC* (World Council of Churches, May 2002), *www.oikoumene.org/fileadmin/files/wccassembly/documents/english/pb-03-specialcommission.pdf*.

7. I have elsewhere asked whether churches that have driven the ecumenical movement in the twentieth century might find greater resonance with Evangelicals, Pentecostals, and others by exploring ecclesiology through Luke 10; Matthew 28; and Acts 1.

8. Sarah Heaner Lancaster, chapter 11, "Issues Facing Ecumenism: A Perspective from the World Council of Churches," in this volume.

9. Paul S. Minear, ed., *The Nature of the Unity We Seek: Official Report of the North American Conference on Faith and Order September 3–10, 1957, Oberlin, Ohio* (St. Louis: Bethany Press, 1958), 253.

PART III
LOOKING FORWARD

ISSUES FACING ECUMENISM
AND INTERFAITH ISSUES

Chapter 13

THE FUTURE OF OUR JOURNEY: ISSUES FACING ECUMENISM

John A. Radano

> Following its presentation at Oberlin II, a revised version of this paper was published under the same title in *Ecumenical Trends* 37, no. 5 (2008): 4/68–10/74. This original version, as delivered at Oberlin II, is printed here with permission of the author and *Ecumenical Trends*.

The 1957 Oberlin Conference on Faith and Order took place at a critical time. The World Council of Churches had been organized in 1948, the third world conference on Faith and Order was held in 1952 in Lund, and the second World Council of Churches Assembly in Evanston only in 1954. The Second Vatican Council was to come just a few years after. In the midst of this, the Oberlin Conference provided American ecumenists, and significant ecumenical leaders from overseas, an important opportunity to reflect on the state of ecumenism at that time. It is good to celebrate its fiftieth anniversary. For this celebration, I have been asked to address "issues facing ecumenism" as our journey continues into the future, and to do so from the perspective of the Pontifical Council for Promoting Christian Unity.

Before addressing some of the issues facing ecumenism, as we continue our journey, a few reflections on the character of the present situation in ecumenism in July 2007 could be in order, to set the context.

THE FUTURE OF OUR JOURNEY: ISSUES FACING ECUMENISM

SOME HISTORICAL PERSPECTIVE

The twentieth century was a century of ecumenism. It is generally acknowledged that the 1910 World Missionary Conference at Edinburgh made a very decisive contribution to the beginning of the modern ecumenical movement. With this ecumenical concern relating to mission, there came almost immediately, thanks to the Episcopal Church, the clear message that, for the cooperation in mission to be truly effective, Faith and Order questions also need to be faced, and doctrinal issues which separate Christians must be resolved. At the same time, the Life and World movement emerged, fostering the cooperation of Christians in facing some of the great issues of the modern world: peace and social and economic development, and so on. This process, of course, led to the creation of the World Council of Churches in 1948, which even today continues to be the preeminent ecumenical instrument fostering deeper relations among its Orthodox, Protestant, and Anglican member churches. With the Second Vatican Council and the full entrance of the Catholic Church into the ecumenical movement, an ecumenical partnership between the WCC and the Catholic Church began almost immediately.

Some Significant Ecumenical Achievements

In a variety of ways, ecumenical progress has been made in the twentieth century. Many bilateral and multilateral dialogues have taken up issues that have divided Christians for centuries. Some great results have been achieved. From my perspective, some of these are as follows:

In 1965. The Common Declaration of Pope Paul VI and Ecumenical Patriarch Athenagoras I asking their Orthodox and Catholic faithful "to erase from the memory and midst of the Church" the sad events of the past which included the mutual sentences of excommunication in 1054, and other events, and then to pursue the dialogue that will lead them to live again the full communion of faith and sacramental life which existed in the first millennium. While not healing the schism of nine hundred years, we have begun to face it in a new way. Orthodox and Catholic churches have begun to recognize each other as "sister churches" again.

From 1973ff. Joint christological declarations between popes and patriarchs of Oriental Orthodox churches (Coptic Orthodox, Syrian Orthodox, Armenian Apostolic churches) in which both have been able to express common faith in Jesus Christ as true God and true man. In the view of the Pontifical Council, these agreements taken together illustrate the virtual resolution of christological controversies resulting from reaction to the Councils of Ephesus (431) and Chalcedon (451), and which led to divisions at that time.

1982. *Baptism, Eucharist, and Ministry* (*BEM*), the Faith and Order convergence text that brought new levels of common understanding on these issues. BEM has helped change relationships between churches in the direction of unity. BEM is representative of the growing consensus on baptism, which makes mutual recognition of baptism possible, at least on the part of most Christians.

1999. *The Joint Declaration on the Doctrine of Justification* (*JDDJ*) signed by the Lutheran World Federation and the Catholic Church, and affirmed also by the World Methodist Council in 2006, expresses agreement on basic truths of the doctrine of justification. In our view this virtually resolves the controversy over justification, which was perhaps the central theological issue at the basis of Martin Luther's conflict with church authorities in the sixteenth century, and led then to mutual condemnations on the issue.

1960s ff. Convergences on ecclesiology found in reports of various bilateral and multilateral (Faith and Order) dialogues. For example, there is a growing consensus that the biblical notion of *koinonia* is a useful concept in explaining the church.

And of course here in the United States, one can count many great contributions to the global ecumenical movement and to ecumenism specifically in this country. The Oberlin Conference on Faith and Order 1957 takes its place as one of the great ecumenical conferences. Its participants included not only American theologians and ecumenists, but a number of other significant figures and leaders from the larger ecumenical movement: WCC General Secretary, Visser't Hooft, to name just one. Oberlin 1957 sparked important developments—for example, bringing a Faith and Order process into the National Council of Churches in the USA, which continues today. The Oberlin Conference was also one of several stimuli to an important ecumenical initiative of international significance just beginning then, but which continues up to our time. That is the effort of the ecumenical community, through statements promulgated by WCC Assemblies, to articulate the nature of the unity we seek. Lesslie Newbigin, in his description of the initial stages of the first statement (New Delhi, 1961), points out that the North American Conference on "the Nature of the Unity We Seek" was one of three major impulses to encouraging that process.[1]

And of course there have been many other ecumenical developments, the Consultation on Church Union/Churches Uniting in Christ (COCU-CUIC; 1960ff.), and today, Christian Churches Together in the USA (2007ff.); bilateral agreements changing relationships among churches such as those between the ELCA and the ECUSA, the ELCA and Reformed Churches, the ELCA with the Moravian Church; and many other developments concerning state and local councils of churches. In short the ecumenical movement has been lively in the United States.

Division Continues

It is good to review this history. But despite all that has happened in many parts of the world since Edinburgh 1910, despite many great achievements, another significant reality faces us, namely, division. There had been great divisions in the fifth century, the eleventh century, and the sixteenth century. But especially during and since the sixteenth century, division has continued to take place. In the midst of the twentieth century, the ecumenical century, division continued to take place even as ecumenical achievements were reached. David Barrett's *World Christian Encyclopaedia* (1982) counted 20,800 distinct Christian denominations around the world. The second edition (2001) counts 33,820 distinct Christian denominations. Many of these are found in some ecumenical relationship such as Councils of Churches, or federations/alliances of confessional families. But even here the degree of unity existing in these bodies is often partial at best. Today division continues to take place among Christian families. In a certain way, the twentieth century was not only the century of ecumenical growth and achievement. Tragically it seems to have also been a century of continuing divisions. Ecumenical growth, and the persistence and growth of divisions, seem to have paralleled one another.

JOHN A. RADANO

ISSUES FACING ECUMENISM: SOME SPECIFIC THEOLOGICAL ISSUES

The current WCC Faith and Order Agenda provides a good starting point for describing some specific and important issues facing ecumenism, as we continue the journey. The recent F&O Standing Commission, June 12–18, 2007, presented three study programs to which it will give considerable attention in this period of Faith and Order life.

First, *ecclesiology*, the nature of the church. The responses to the 1982 Faith and Order convergence text, *BEM*, lifted up ecclesiology as one of the basic areas on which Faith and Order should focus as sequel to *BEM*. Some of the issues *BEM* treated, the responses said, could be deepened with further reflection on the nature of the church.

Faith and Order has followed through on this, publishing two studies: in 1998 the *Nature and Purpose of the Church*, and in 2005 the *Nature and Mission of the Church*. The WCC has sent the latter to the churches for comment and response. The Faith and Order Commission is awaiting responses to it so as to allow further reflection and, eventually, another even more refined text. The Pontifical Council for Promoting Christian Unity is working on a response to *Nature and Mission of the Church*, having asked about ten Catholic theologians to study and comment on it. We have a small commission that will study their commentaries, synthesize them, and develop a coherent Catholic response to be sent to Faith and Order as a contribution to this. We did this for the 1998 volume, *Nature and Purpose of the Church*. It is the hope of the PCPCU that, as the result of this continuing study, Faith and Order will develop a *BEM*-like text on the nature of the church to be sent to the churches for response at the highest level, as was done for *BEM*. It would be great if the text could be developed for the next General Assembly of the World Council of Churches in 2013. And it would be great if it could make something of the same historical impact made by *BEM*.

A hopeful sign in relation to this ecclesiology study is the brief statement on ecclesiology titled "Called to Be the One Church," adopted by the WCC General Assembly, in Porto Alegre in 2006.

This statement can be understood as another in that series of brief statements of WCC General Assemblies concerning the nature of the unity we seek, which were published by the New Delhi Assembly (1961), Nairobi (1975), and Canberra (1991). This Porto Alegre statement focuses perhaps more on the church itself than previous statements. It has been sent to the churches not with the intention of changing it, but, and this is a development, to challenge them by asking them to answer a series of questions relating to their ecumenical relations. But its focus on the church, along with the F&O statement *Nature and Mission of the Church,* reflects a deepening concentration on ecclesiology within the ecumenical movement.

In a number of international bilateral dialogues in which the Catholic Church has engaged, important statements on the church, or significant aspects of the church, have been published. These include dialogues of the Catholic Church with the Orthodox, the Anglican Communion, the Lutheran World Federation, the World Alliance of Reformed Churches, the World Methodist Council, Disciples of Christ, Pentecostals, and the World Evangelical Alliance. To give one example, the report of our second phase of dialogue with the World Alliance of Reformed Churches (1990) claimed convergence between the Reformed notion of the church as *Creatura Verb*, and the Catholic notion of the church as sacrament of grace. The report of the third phase (2006) goes further, saying that a proper understanding of the church requires both of these perspectives.

A particular issue on ecclesiology facing us for the future concerns the relation of the local and universal aspects of the Church. It is interesting to read Dr. Paul Minear's interpretive essay in 1957 introducing the official report of the Oberlin Conference on Faith and Order, which he edited.[2] This issue comes up in 1957. He writes, "If I were to select one feature of the conference which most clearly indicates its dominant thrust into the future, I would describe it thus: the radical telescoping of the distance between the global and local work of the Church." He gives different glimpses into this from the conference.

> I refer to what takes place within the Christian Church through increased participation in "the common life in the Body of Christ." In him God acts to eliminate entirely the distance between the

global and the local. The more *his* ministry to the world is accepted, the more solidarity is realized with every congregation and its work in its home town. The more fully this local ministry embodies the ministry of Christ, the more truly global is its significance.[3]

Again,

> The very fact that the conference was held is evidence that shepherds of the world-wide Church are coming to realize that concern for the Church's Catholicity compels them to manifest this oneness in the church local. Shepherds of local congregations, on the other hand, are coming to realize that they cannot fulfill their vocation at home unless their congregation participates fully in the Church universal.[4]

He writes about the scandal of division: "Local congregations are as deeply involved in this scandal as are the world confessional bodies. And to ignore this scandal is to deny the lordship of the one Lord."[5]

The ecumenical question of local and universal expression of the church, and the proper balance therein, is still a continuing ecumenical challenge today, perhaps a dominant issue to face in the future. And, of course, into this discussion, the Catholic Church will bring the question of a universal personal ministry of unity, which has already been studied both in bilateral dialogue (e.g., Anglican-Catholic "The Gift of Authority"), as well as in multilateral dialogue (F&O "Nature and Mission of the Church") and, we hope, will continue to be studied. John Paul II's call to dialogue on this question (*Ut Unum Sint,* 1995) is still a continuing challenge. Oberlin also recognized the way that differing views of the church have an impact on other issues, such as baptism!

In its report of Division I, Section 3, *Baptism into Christ* recognized that "most of our significant differences (on baptism) appear to be rooted in our differing views of the Church" (p. 198).

A second Faith and Order priority is *Moral Discernment in the Churches*. This theme continues Faith and Order's concern for theological anthropology. An ecumenical study of moral discernment is one of the most important contemporary questions for various reasons, not least of which is the danger that conflict over moral issues can lead to further divisions. In his address to the celebration of the seventy-fifth anniversary of Faith and Order in 2002 in Lausanne, Cardinal Kasper had mentioned this question as important for Faith and Order.

A third F&O priority is *Tradition and Traditions: Sources of Authority for the Church*. F&O is planning to explore, from our different confessions and traditions, how the teachers and witnesses of the early church (the Patristics) are sources of authority for us. This study could shed insight into the question of the relationship of Scripture and tradition; that is also one of the major issues that responses to *BEM* lifted up, an issue which continues to be an ecumenical challenge. This recalls, too, the benefit of studying the ancient heritage of the Church together. In our Pentecostal-Catholic international dialogue, we have just completed a report titled "On Becoming a Christian: Insights from Scripture and Patristic Writings, with Contemporary Reflection." We study together biblical and patristic perspectives on questions of faith, conversion, discipleship, experience, and baptism in the Holy Spirit.

To these three major Faith and Order issues facing us today, I would like to add two more. A fourth issue is *The Healing of Memories*. I am influenced here by our Catholic-Mennonite dialogue, which gave considerable attention to the notion of a healing of memories. We had done this, as well, in our second phase of dialogue with the World Alliance of Reformed Churches. The tragic developments, the conflicts of the sixteenth century, have left lasting scars, bitter memories that still need to be healed today. Theological dialogue can help. Resolving theological issues that have long separated Christians contributes to a healing of memory. But other things that help us to see one another in a new light can contribute as well, such as a spirit of repentance for conflicts we have had with one another in the past, recognizing the degree of apostolic faith we hold in common today despite our divisions, and creating new relationships between us, to be the basis of better memories in the future. Here in the United States, the action of the Presbyterian Church (USA) in 2005 to distance itself from anti-Catholic statements in sixteenth- and seventeenth-century confessions of faith is a good contribution to a healing of memory.

Fifth, the healing of bitter memories over conflicts of the past helps to bring peace between those previously in conflict. This in turn can help them to be peacemakers together. The title of the 2003 report of the Mennonite-Catholic dialogue is "Called Together to Be Peacemakers." In our very unstable political world, the old Life and Work thrust at the beginning of the twentieth century of fostering Christian witness to peace becomes very important again at the beginning of the twenty-first. An immediate opportunity before us is in the proposed 2011 International Ecumenical Peace Conference, the culmination of the WCC's Decade to Overcome Violence. How can we all contribute to this theologically? How can Christians, together, promote peace?

These, then, are some specific "issues facing ecumenism" today. More could be cited from various dialogues now in progress.

ISSUES FACING ECUMENISM: RECEPTION AND THE BEGINNINGS OF A NEW ECUMENICAL ERA

The Twenty-first Century: A New Beginning?

Another larger issue facing ecumenism today concerns reception—the receiving and implementing of the achievements of ecumenism. As I look at those achievements, they suggest to me that, with the beginning of the twenty-first century, we turn a new page also in ecumenical relations. The first Oberlin Conference in 1957 came in the middle of the twentieth century, just after the founding of the World Council of Churches and just before the Second Vatican Council. Good developments had taken place, but great and unforeseen developments lay ahead. Now as we begin the twenty-first century we are in a different situation. We stand on the basis of many achievements, some just mentioned. We need to appreciate and receive what has been achieved and to allow our churches and communities to be shaped by what has been achieved. Have we not, today in fact, in this twenty-first century, made something of a break with our divisive past, even if a very small break? When we look at the achievements mentioned before, all together, has not something new happened? Consider:

- Although the East-West schism is not fully healed we follow a new perspective in East-West relations. One important example is that two great leaders, Ecumenical Patriarch Athenagoras I and Pope Paul VI in 1965 called on their constituencies to put out of mind and the midst of these churches the sad decisive events of 1054, and instead seek, through dialogue, to re-establish full communion.

- We have virtually resolved the christological conflicts following the Councils of Ephesus (431) and Chalcedon (451) through common christological declarations of popes and several Oriental Orthodox patriarchs starting in 1973, speaking together of Christ as true God and true man. Other Christians can agree as well.

- We are virtually free from the Reformation conflict over justification. The theological work has been done to show consensus on justification. Authoritative decisions have made this consensus official for Lutherans and Catholics, and now Methodists. Today instead of the sixteenth-century mutual condemnations on justification, Lutherans and Catholics and Methodists can say "we confess" together seven basic aspects of the doctrine of justification (JDDJ #25, 28). I believe other Christians could join us in doing that as well. Reformation Sunday should now be "Reconciliation Sunday."

- From dialogue reports such as *BEM* and others, most Christians share a consensus on baptism. Mutual recognition of baptism by most Christians is possible today.

- Through bilateral and multilateral dialogues and reports, many Christians share many perspectives on the nature of the church.

- A lot of healing of memory has taken place through dialogues; much more must take place. Compared even with the last decades of the twentieth century, with the beginning of this twenty-first century we can say that relationships between separated Christians are now based on a better theological foundation. One of the issues facing us is that of receiving this, in recognizing this new situation, and seeing ourselves as Christians of the twenty-first century. We are all victims of divisions of the past. But today we have more theological insights to help us be architects of a shared heritage.

Again, I do not say all issues have been resolved. Our ecumenical work needs to continue. I am saying that, in my view, what has been achieved creates something of a small break with the Reformation–Counter/Catholic Reformation past that has dominated our thinking from the sixteenth to the twentieth centuries. The twenty-first century offers something of a new situation: a new beginning.

Continuing Divisions: Can We Face Them in a New Way?

Another issue facing ecumenism concerns the fact that—despite the ecumenical progress which has been made—parallel to this ecumenical growth, divisions among Christians have persisted and continue to happen today, and one gets the impression that perhaps this happens with no end in sight. This is one reason for the recent serious discontent of the Orthodox member churches of the World Council of Churches, which led to the Special Commission composed of equal members of Orthodox and other member churches during the last six years. While the numbers of Orthodox member churches in the WCC remain stable, more and more new Protestant churches were gaining membership in the WCC, some of them perhaps the result of splits that had taken place. The Orthodox in the WCC were becoming more and more of a minority.

One of the results was that the Special Commission report recommended changes in rules for membership that increase the minimum size of a church for WCC membership to fifty thousand members instead of twenty-five thousand.

The Oberlin Conference of 1957 took as its theme "The Nature of the Unity We Seek." In this Oberlin Conference of 2007, perhaps we need to ask also about "the reasons of the divisions that persist and continue to happen" and how we can face that. We need to ask, in light of the ecumenical progress of the twentieth century, why dividing is so prominent and seems to happen too easily. I would make three points.

1. First, we need to have a sense of mutual responsibility for the divisions that have taken place over the centuries and which the ecumenical movement has been facing. Vatican II said,

describing divisions over the centuries, "in subsequent centuries more widespread disagreements appeared and quite large Communities became separated from full communion with the Catholic Church—developments for which, at times, men of both sides were to blame" (*UR*, 3).[6]

2. We can all be challenged by the temptation of division. The Catholic Church in the United States a century ago experienced a schism among Polish Catholics, which led to division and the birth of the Polish National Catholic Church. Among the reasons were ethnic conflicts. In 1988 the Catholic Church experienced schism when Archbishop Lefevre's followers broke communion with the Church of Rome. Their reasons included their disagreement with some liturgical changes and with ecumenism. The Orthodox have experienced schism. But it seems that the Protestant world especially experiences divisions.

3. Two images from recent times about handling and facing division might be useful here:

The First Image: "Here I Stand and I Cannot Do Otherwise"

This is a phrase usually attributed to someone in the sixteenth century making an act of conscience, which could lead to a very unwanted division. But this is a phrase used this year, 2007, by the Archbishop of Canterbury, Rowan Williams, in his presidential address to the General Synod of the Church of England. His address, in the midst of the present crisis of the Anglican Communion, came shortly after the February meeting of the Primates of the Anglican Communion. He was concerned with the significant dangers of splitting among provinces of the Anglican Communion, and even possibly of splitting within provinces. And he wanted "to try and identify some . . . factors which, if not addressed, will lead us into more of the same unedifying divisions."[7]

I do not want to go into the delicate internal situation he addressed, but I thought that two points that he made are significant not only for Anglicans in this moment of crisis but are significant for all of us in different ways, at all times. The archbishop referred to the draft covenant being developed for the Anglican Communion which outlines what a wholly consultative approach to deciding contentious matters might look like, with some inevitable consequences spelled out if this is not followed. In contrast he said, "You may feel imperatively called to prophetic action, but must not be surprised if the response is incomprehension, non-acceptance or at least a conviction that time is needed for discernment."[8] Then he said,

> Much has been made of the relative nobility of a "Here I stand" position as compared with the painful brokering and compromising needed for unity sake.... Yet—to speak personally for a moment—the persistence of the Communion as an organically international and intercultural unity whose aim is to glorify Jesus Christ and to work of his Kingdom is for me and others just as much a matter of deep personal and theological conviction as any other principle. About this, I am entirely prepared to say, "Here I stand and I cannot do otherwise." And I believe the Primates have said the same.[9]

He finished by commenting on the implication of what is at stake in Anglican unity by reflecting on his coming trip to Africa to a consultation regarding Anglican strategy, exploring what is needed for better coordination in the development resources of the communion. He commented, "Like it or not, this work will be harder and more poorly resourced if the structures of the Communion are loosened, destroyed or so localized that they cannot work flexibly on the global scene." But he raised, for me, the question of where we must focus today when we speak about prophetic actions.

The Second Image: The "Reformation Reflex"

The World Alliance of Reformed Churches, in preparation for its Twenty-second General Council in 1989 in Seoul, Korea, studied the problem of division among Reformed churches. Its second section report titled *Mission in Unity* made a fine, remarkable analysis of the problem of division among the Reformed churches.[10] The analysis described Reformed theological values and emphases at the Reformation. While these values were and are still important, the study showed that focus on these has also led to a deemphasis of other important values, which in turn has led to divisions.

According to this study, the profound respect for the continuity of the church has been eroded over wide stretches of the Reformed tradition. Thus,

> It is true that if the Church is to remain in the truth it is in need of constant reform. But this truth has repeatedly been misused to justify a breach with the existing Church at a given time. In Reformed circles there is something of a "reformation reflex," i.e. an unconscious urge to repeat today the breach which the Reformers in the 16th century were forced to make against their inclinations. A destructive role is played here by the too facile and often unconsidered use of the dictum *ecclesia reformata semper reformanda*. It becomes too easy to assume that a Church can only lay claim to the truth if it has first disowned the existing Church.[11]

They give further examples showing that the deemphasis of related aspects of what the Reformers emphasized can result in losing some important aspects of the church's tradition, and the de-emphasis on the church itself and, thus, division. For example,

> The Reformers emphasized that Jesus Christ becomes present anew by his living Word and by the power of the Holy Spirit, "Where two or three are gathered together in my name, there am I in your midst." It is through God's self-revelation that the Church becomes a reality. However, the Reformation insight can easily be turned inside out and lead to disdain both for the fellowship of the Church and for the continuity of the tradition through the centuries. The Reformed Churches have repeatedly fallen into this error.[12]

Another example:

> The Reformed paved the way for a new appreciation of the personal aspect of hearing and receiving the Good News. The Gospel of the forgiveness of sins, of acceptance by God, can be proclaimed and received in a direct personal way without the mediation of the Church. This emphasis has led to lasting renewal in both Church and society. But very often it also caused an underestimation of the equally imported insight that God's grace leads into the communion of the Church. Full of their own experience individuals have frequently disregarded the fellowship of the Church.

Furthermore,

> Aloofness from the Church as the fellowship which claims as a right the service of every individual member can only lead individual Christians with exceptional gifts of leadership to conclude too hastily that they are entitled or constrained to break away from the existing Church and form groups with like-minded followers. In many cases pioneers of private spiritual adventure have become the sponsors of Reformed division.[13]

Still another example:

> The Reformers attached great importance to the Church as local community. The whole body of Christ is fully present in each particular place which is the living or primary locus of fellowship with Jesus Christ. This fellowship becomes a reality where men and women are gathered together to hear the Word and break bread together. The universal Church is understood as a fellowship of local Churches which must constantly be rediscovering their unity. This emphasis, however, can easily be turned into an over-emphasis. The local or national Church can become closed to the universal fellowship of the church. The absence of a commitment on the part of the Reformed Churches to make visible and to take seriously the universal fellowship encourages and perpetuates many divisions.[14]

Here We Stand: Formulating an "Ecumenical Reflex" in the Twenty-first Century

Is the ecumenical movement a prophetic movement? This is open to debate.[15] But reminding the churches of their lack of unity has the characteristic of prophetic witness.[16] In light of solid ecumenical advances over the last century, if we have made some small break from the conflicts of the past, is it not also possible to move away from the unconscious tendency to divide, away from the "reformation reflex," away from the persistence of division, to an "ecumenical reflex"—a *conscious* urge and commitment, despite major problems, to continue the reconstitution of the unity of Christians which has been in process for a century?

The tragedy of Christian division is that it "openly contradicts the will of Christ, provides a stumbling block to the world, and inflicts damages on the most holy cause of proclaiming the good news to every creature" (*UR*, 1). Are we now ready in the twenty-first century to say "Here we stand" for the fullness of unity, not only of our own communion, but between the Christian world communions as well? "Here we stand" for unity for the sake of the gospel.

All of this is to say that an issue facing us today is: How do we now deal with the continuing reality of ongoing division? If we do not want our ecumenical achievements to wither away into irrelevance, or pale in face of ongoing division, we need to face the fact that uncontrolled division goes on. Do we have the courage to find a way to deal with it? Do we have the luxury or the right not to?

NOTES

1. Lesslie Newbigin, "Unity of 'All in Each Place,'" *Dictionary of the Ecumenical Movement*, 2nd ed., ed. Nicholas Lossky et al. (Geneva: WCC Publications, 2002), 1175–78.

2. Paul S. Minear, "The Conference in Context," in *The Nature of the Unity We Seek*, Official Report of the North American Conference on Faith and Order, September 3–10, 1957, Oberlin, Ohio, ed. Minear (St. Louis: Bethany Press, 1958), 23.

3. Ibid.

4. Ibid., 24.

5. Ibid., 25.

6. Decree on Ecumenism, *Unitatis redintegratio* (UR), available at *www.vatican.va*.

7. Rowan Williams, "To Work for His Kingdom," "Archbishop of Canterbury: Presidential Address at General Synod Focuses on the Communion Today," *Anglican-Episcopal World* (Eastertide 2007): 16.

8. Ibid., 17.

9. Ibid., 18.

10. *Mission in Unity*, Section II Discussion Paper for 22nd General Council of WARC, August 15–27, 1989, Seoul, Korea (Geneva: World Alliance of Reformed Churches, 1989), esp. 45–50.

11. Ibid., 48.

12. Ibid., 47.

13. Ibid., 48.

14. Ibid., 50.

15. Geiko Müller-Fahrenholz, "Prophecy," *Dictionary of the Ecumenical Movement*, 939.

16. Cf. ibid.

Chapter 14

KINGDOM CHAOS—
THE JOY OF FINDING UNITY:
AN EVANGELICAL PERSPECTIVE
ON THE FUTURE OF ECUMENISM

Kevin W. Mannoia

Any effort to provide a comprehensive explanation of anything dealing with *evangelical* would be an exercise in futility, at best, and foolishness, at worst. Probably the only way to truly get at *the* Evangelical perspective of unity would be to have all Evangelicals come to this meeting and speak their opinions. The one with the loudest voice would probably be the one most supported, until they got laryngitis and someone else's voice overpowered them. Of course, the real problem would be deciding who is an Evangelical and whether they should even be included.

At the same time, I realize that the Evangelical movement is a vital part of the church. It cannot be defined precisely, but neither can it be ignored or minimized. I tell pastors, denominational leaders, and students that movements are always messy. And they always create waves. The Evangelical movement is no exception. Those who try to codify it, organize it, define it, control it, direct it, or in any way manipulate it as a whole do so at their own peril.

There are a few of us who live and minister within this movement and who try to understand it as best we can within the larger work of God in the world. The word "evangelical" comes from the word *euangelion*. It is the Good news of salvation through Jesus Christ. Generally Evangelicals hold to a few important principles, although they are expressed and applied in multiple ways. Evangelicals hold strongly to the need for personal conversion in order to become beneficiaries of the saving work of God through Jesus Christ. The Scriptures are the trustworthy word of God, and their primacy is authoritative in matters of truth and life. Evangelism and discipleship characterize the activities of Evangelicals to the end that persons grow spiritually and in acts of charity. The community of believers is empowered by the Holy Spirit in pursuing the kingdom of God and adding to the church.

Now, this having been said, there are probably many more Evangelicals in this room than many Evangelicals may think. A bit confusing, perhaps. Yet therein lies the power and the genius of any movement, especially one that is fueled by the Holy Spirit. And in most cases I believe the Evangelical movement is a positive force of God in divine work in the world. In my humble opinion, any movement that can be explained, parsed, structured, organized, contained, or measured is not worthy of the Divine. Our God is beyond measure and is certainly not tame.

As we consider how such apparently disparate groups could ever come together in a commitment to unity, there are a few factors that I believe are important for consideration from an evangelical perspective. Let me outline some of these factors with full knowledge that this is a conversation that is dynamic. We all learn from one another and so pursue the mutuality of the kingdom in Christian community.

FEAR OF COMPROMISE

Perhaps it is due to the relative youth of the contemporary Evangelical movement; perhaps it is due to its relative poverty in economic standards; or perhaps it is due to the lack of a common, coordinating center. Whatever the reason, there generally exists within Evangelical circles a low-grade fear of compromise. The slogan "Cooperation without Compromise" is somewhat indicative of this fear. In fact, this phrase may be more suited as a declaration in an interfaith context where the tenets of the faith will more likely be threatened. In an ecumenical circumstance, where there is at least ambiguity over what is essentially evangelical and even more broadly Christian, such a posture presupposes an intransigence which itself mitigates the kingdom principle of being "mutually submitted to one another as unto the Lord" (Eph. 5:21). In other words, for those whose greatest fear is compromise, everything will be examined with a careful eye of suspicion. Lurking in the back of their mind is the constant warning to be on guard in case something sneaks up on them without realizing it, and compromise happens. A fortress mentality is the logical expression of this fear-based existence that leads to an enclave of exclusivism.

Probably the single most important area that drives this fear of compromise centers on the authority of the Bible. Of course, any threat to the authority of the Bible usually is discerned only when someone takes a position that breaches generally accepted thinking among those people who are considered to be sound Evangelical points of reference. So this fear of compromise often places Evangelicals in a reactive mode which then smacks of fundamentalism, which it is not. In reality the issue of the authority of the Bible is more a hermeneutical issue influenced by tradition, heritage, education, and church community.

Thankfully, increasing numbers of Evangelicals are recognizing the fact that while there are multiple hermeneutical approaches, the issue of the authority of the Bible is as much a matter of choice—perhaps faith—as it is a matter of the authenticity and accuracy of the written Word itself. Yet among Evangelicals at large, the vibrancy and effectiveness of the work of God in the world is closely tied to a high view of Scripture. Any threat to that means a potential compromise and loss of power.

IGNORANCE

Forgive my bluntness. Maybe you're not the ones I need to apologize to. Better yet, convey my apology to any Evangelical who hears about this and is offended by it. In reality, however, most Evangelicals and most Evangelical leaders have no idea what the Faith and Order Movement is. They do not know what Faith and Order is. They do not care. They will not go looking to find out. To them *faith* is good. That is belief in Jesus as savior and Lord. *Order* is okay, though somewhat suspicious. At best it means order of worship as in the church bulletin, or on the platform manager's clipboard to keep the service flowing, or the worship set of songs for the band in the service.

A few have come to realize there is a long-standing effort on the part of other Christians to bring centeredness to the diversity of the church, and Faith and Order is one of the organized efforts to that end. Though we would prefer the *life and witness* idea—since that has to do with personal vibrancy and action—we recognize that for our own good and maturity we must learn and grow in understanding the larger heritage, thinking, and Christian church that is our foundation, root, and source, whether we know it or not.

It is quite interesting that in the current unfolding of the Gen X mentality, and more significantly of the mosaic generation that is shaping the emergent church movement, these roots are becoming much more important. Many new church plants are exploring the history, tradition, icons, rituals, and thinking patterns that are foreign to most twentieth-century Evangelicals. They are not afraid of compromise. And they are determined to explore the power of the historic church, which has for decades remained hidden behind the curtain of ignorance.

I serve with four others on the board of one of the largest churches in America, and fastest-growing. The pastor has not a clue what I do in meetings like this one. He is ignorant to it, and quite honestly his intense focus is one of his greatest attributes, so I do not push it. But occasionally I drop a little story or open a small window describing someone in the mainline, Orthodox, or Catholic circles who is spiritually vibrant, passionate about Christ, and powerfully effective in ministry. Previously it was met with doubt and a glazed look. Gradually it has become a mild response of understanding punctuated with a comment that "there are great Christians in any institution." I am impressed with this pastor's increasing openness and desire to welcome such diversity. It is a reflection of his passion for the gospel as a unifying factor that transcends divisions.

Basically there is a general ignorance of the vibrancy and deep passion for spirituality that exists and may be building in mainline, Catholic, and Orthodox churches. Even in my description of this, I realize that I am probably exhibiting massive ignorance to any one of those circles of Christians, which underscores my point.

In most contemporary Evangelical circles, any mention of, say, the United Methodist Church (UMC) is accompanied by derision for the perception that the UMC has fallen prey to the slippery slope of liberalism. Yet I venture to say that a majority of UMC pastors are as Evangelical as the local Nazarene or Free Methodist pastor. Only in recent decades have Catholics in North America been blessed to be included by most Evangelicals in the circle known as *Christian*. And yet as I minister in an Evangelical university and in many diverse local churches, I find an increasing respect among people for the generous, grace-filled faith that is magnetic among Catholics on the faculty, staff, or in the community. As far as the Orthodox are concerned, well, there is still a journey. They are the mysterious ones. Most Evangelicals don't know what icons are. To them, the Orthodox church means incense, strange rituals, and long gray beards. Yet when I go to emergent church events among the mosaic generation of Evangelicals, they are mining the wealth of the deep traditions and historic stability of meaning in the Orthodox churches. Of course, the fact that most Orthodox people are relegated to the sidelines in the most heated theological discussions that pour from issues traceable to the Reformation helps them to remain above the fray and somewhat mysterious.

Evangelicals are coming to realize that the word "evangelical" is not another denomination. It is not a club, it is not an ecclesiastical delimiter—or at least it should not be. They are coming to see the word "evangelical" not as a noun, but as an adjective, a descriptor without institutional boundaries. Many are open to the vibrancy and passion for the kingdom and its Lord that knows no boundaries. They see themselves in all sorts of Christian traditions, and the veil of ignorance is beginning to be torn, from top to bottom.

LACK OF A CENTER

Contemporary Evangelicals trace their roots to a relatively recent past. They find their early formation in the energy of the modernist/fundamentalist debates of the late nineteenth and early twenieth centuries. Out of a hotbed of controversy over eschatology, and the nature and mission of the church, a group in the middle began to identify themselves as *not liberals* and *not fundamentalists*. Obviously this is a simplistic description of a complex mix of forces at work, but it helps to reveal the pattern of multiple streams in the one Evangelical movement all vying for a place and influence in shaping the life of the church.

At its root, the basis of identity is as a reaction to some other force. Evangelicals have largely been defined by what we are not. We are not liberals. We are not fundamentalists. Because of the inherently reactionary nature of the movement's identity, then, anything or anyone associated with "the other guys" immediately becomes a threat to be feared. Compromise is tantamount to capitulation. (I once had to decline being present at a significant meeting because of the possibility that it would appear that I had capitulated. Kindly, the director of the National Council of Churches [NCC] offered to take out ads in the *New York Times* declaring his hatred of me, thereby allaying any fears that I had become compromised.)

Anytime a movement attempts to define itself relative to another entity, it will ultimately become hostage to that entity and fail to become well-formed in its own identity. Thankfully a transition has begun in the periphery of Evangelical circles largely among the emergent generation, and from my perspective especially in the Wesleyan-Holiness segments of the academy.

I often describe the need among Evangelicals to move from bounded-set thinking to centered-set living. Rather than being defined by the perimeter of behaviors, positions, and actions that become a line demarcating in-ness or out-ness, we are being called to understand the center values from which behaviors proceed but which allow for diversity of appearance. The perimeter will always exist as long as we honestly seek to be classic Christians. The question is, however, where will we focus our eyes? On the outside edge of behavior to define ourselves, or on the centered values from which those behaviors proceed, and change? It is the same question I asked my daughter when I was teaching her to drive on the freeway entrance ramp. Where will you focus your eyes? On the inside of the curve—to stay close? Or on the outside of the curve—to stay away? The answer to that question determines our identity, to say nothing of our attitude toward others.

I further describe this thought in the book *Church 2K: Leading Forward*.[1]

An already complex mixture of thinking and actions has been exacerbated by having no magisterium to referee or guide the coalescing of the various streams. The Evangelical movement has no theology. And there is no central entity providing guidance to the orthodoxy, expediency, or heresy within its ranks. In essence the Evangelical movement is one big public conversation on the street corner of a rapidly changing city that is not completely attuned to the language or exclusivism it seems to portray as it stands in a circle talking to itself. Yet the city desperately needs the life, vibrancy, joy, and grace offered by the gospel that is central to its conversation. Thankfully, the passion in the conversation has motivated many to eschew the discussion in favor of single-mindedly penetrating the city in relevant, transforming ways that indeed make a big difference. Unfortunately by leaving the conversation, they can sometimes be driven by the passion of their mission to the exclusion of the tempering, deepening, and maturing effect that diversity and breadth afford. On occasion the conversation takes the form of graffiti that proffers truths on passing issues of politics, economics, social reform, or cultural commentary. This tagging becomes the mark of the Evangelical to the outside world, further compounding the perception of exclusive, reactionary, irrelevancy.

The Evangelical movement is not a theological movement as much as it is phenomenological. Having no theology, it only finds theological credibility when drilling into the various heritages or traditions commonly claiming a place in the movement. I realize I am biased, but the Wesleyan revival and theological method offer a wonderful place for the integrative thinking required to convene the streams of Evangelical thinking. Consider the breadth of theologies ranging from the Holiness movement, to the Alliance for Confessing Evangelicals, to renewal movements in the mainline denominations, to the charismatic Catholics and the upstart emergent movement. Each has a unique theological foundation. Yet in all of them the marks of an Evangelical movement can be found.

So what is *the* Evangelical movement? It belongs to no one—and everyone. It is *an* Evangelical movement among those within and without the established church, in multiple theological streams, fueled by the passion for God, the centrality and lordship of Jesus

Christ, and the empowerment of the Holy Spirit in renewing and transforming lives who then find unity and oneness of identity in the living Christ. If understood, this passion can be the unifying force that revitalizes our various traditions, restores our foundations as the Body of Christ, reorders our priorities, and reunites us as the people of God extending the work of the kingdom in the world.

MATURING EVANGELICAL COMMUNITY

This factor is somewhat more involved so I may not spend as much time discussing it. But for our purposes it is important to know that Evangelicals are still finding comfort levels among themselves. There is a diversity of positions in what some may assume to be a monolithic movement. With those positions come truckloads of issues and relationships all revolving around the question of trust and true effectiveness in Great Commission work.

Over the past few decades, those differences have manifested themselves in various ways across denominational lines. To name a few, they include what I call in *Church 2K: Leading Forward,* the Wars. Chief among them is the Scripture wars, including but not limited to the battle for the Bible in the seventies. Another was the more heated worship wars of the eighties and early nineties. Would the organ and piano give way to the drums and guitar? Would the choir give way to worship teams? Would the hymnal give way to the overhead projector, now the PowerPoint? Would folded hands give way to raised hands? And then there was the divisive war over gifts of the Spirit in which gifts given freely by God were used as trump cards to play spiritual one-upmanship. Structure and polity were also significant points of dispute, although much less publicly visible—also issues of general superintendency versus regional leadership, ecclesial authority versus constituted authority, general ordination or local licensing, CEO leadership or pastoral shepherding, visionary and prophetic leadership or facilitating managers.

A fairly significant, but often overlooked factor in the maturation of the Evangelical community is the balance of sodalic or modalic attitudes toward the church and its mission. This point fueled the rise of parachurch organizations created to meet a specialized, missional need that was perceived as not being met by the organized church. As these parachurch entities became successful in their singular mission, the gap became greater to the point of frustration and even disenchantment with ineffectiveness in local churches which appeared to have abdicated responsibility for mission to the sodalic, parachurch organizations.

The dynamic condition these circumstances create within the contemporary Evangelical movement have forced a maturation that is increasingly being formed as internal conversations and relationships are deepened and solidified. The result is a growing sense of identity that allows for broader conversations. It also is giving rise to greater recognition that those groups typically outside of the Evangelical circle may not be so bad after all.

LOW-CHURCH ECCLESIOLOGY

Generally Evangelicals do not see the church as a gift of God to be discovered. Rather it is an organization, created by God and constituted by those who respond to the call of God (*kaleo*) to be out of the world (*ek*). Grouping believers together is what comprises the church. The mystical nature of the Body of Christ is not in understanding ourselves as being the corporeal reality of Christ. It is the organization of the born-again ones into being the extension of Christ in the world as salt and light. The mystery, then, is not in being the church, but it is found in the way the Holy Spirit empowers otherwise ineffective people to be changed spiritually and to do things that surpass their human limitations. If the church is growing faster than we can effectively administer, it becomes a *God thing*. If the ministry is growing and finding effectiveness in expanding the church or touching lives well, it becomes *God is blessing the work*. If it is not growing and it is hard to measure, it becomes *God is doing something, we just do not know what it is yet*.

Ecclesiastical structures proceeding from this general ecclesiology incorporate democratic principles that begin with the assumption that salvation is an individual thing and the church is the corporate gathering of individuals, the net result of which is the Body of Christ. This congregational base of authority vested in the group of individuals immediately introduces the seeds of tension between the lowest level of the church and the governing judicatories and overseers. The result is a reticence on the part of so many leaders to speak for their church or denomination, much less for the larger Evangelical movement where they have no administrative authority whatsoever. And this also explains a growing mistrust of denominational leaders.

On the other hand, this has given rise to a significant sense of the body's life and emphasis on Christian community within churches. Right belief is important, but not without right living. In some cases right doctrine is secondary to the relationship among individual Christians that reflects what they have come to understand to be Christlike behavior.

At the same time, this ecclesiology has given rise to a heightened sense of pragmatism that often becomes the final point of evaluation. Does it work? If not, discard it. If so, then let us figure out how to incorporate it into our theology.

OUTCOMES-ORIENTED

A pragmatic emphasis is difficult to maintain without some form of measurable outcomes. Although no one has written the last word on what exactly those outcomes are for Evangelicals, many have tried. Titles of books that sound like menus, programs that list the easy steps to success, and prescriptive design steps for success capture the pragmatic emphasis of most Evangelical churches. My own book *15 Characteristics of Effective Pastors*[2] certainly contributes to this factor.

In short, if a church is not growing or having some measurable impact in some sphere, it is not considered to be effective. Usually the outcomes that are examined include but are not limited to conversions—how many people have received Christ personally; small groups—how many groups of believers meet regularly to "live out" their faith; spirit-filled—is there a sense of God's presence that is palpable in the services; political impact—does the church have influence in the community, region, or nation in ways that are noticed and generally for the good; issue-driven—is there a particular issue that has become the hallmark of that church and by which they are known; and, king of them all, weekend attendance at services.

In connectional forms of structures, these or similar points of accountability are the basis for evaluation, hire, and reputation among peers. It is not uncommon to observe the "pastoral dance" at pastors' conferences where each one is trying to find out how many the other had in church last Sunday without appearing to be too obvious, too unspiritual, too concerned, or too numbers oriented. (By the way, the church where I served as interim pastor has approximately 1,182 in attendance on Sunday morning; and the church I mentioned earlier, where I serve on the board, is thirty-second on the list of the top one hundred churches in America and with attendance reports for the last few months is about thirteenth largest—but who's counting!)

LANGUAGE

Getting saved, altar call, testimony meeting, witnessing, ecumenical, worship set, contemporary worship, emergent, Eucharistic, lay driven, staff led, apostolic succession, Faith and Order, personal savior, missions conference, executive pastor, icons, inner court/outer court, ushers, stewardship campaign, Book of Common Prayer, unity, spirit filled, chancel, acolytes, baptized in the Holy Ghost, praise team, lectionary, worship band, church growth: a cursory, incomplete selection of terms, phrases, and concepts that will not only confuse the most enlightened church statesperson but will tag, categorize, place, and mark anyone who uses them as a description of their faith journey. And you think it's confusing? Imagine the poor "Joe" who happens to show up at one of our churches seeking a spiritual experience only to be confronted with a thousand terms he has never heard before, much less understands. Or in some less sensitive, sectarian, zealous congregations, "Joe" may actually be quizzed to establish his qualifications for the privilege to attend and participate—When did you get saved? Do you know your power gift? We are a lay-driven church that expects the laity to be stewards of their ministry gifts for the witnessing of the kingdom through the empowerment of the Holy Spirit and authentic, inner court worship. Poor Joe!

There's a lifetime of discovery in that one phrase. And the words mean something different to each of us. Let us just take one such word: *unity*. I think that is the underlying premise behind the Faith and Order discussion, although even that may be incorrect given my own relatively recent exposure to the Faith and Order activities. Evangelicals by and large have no idea what Faith and Order is. And when it comes to discussing unity, there is disparity within Evangelical ranks about its meaning. How an Evangelical understands unity is determined by that person's ecclesiology, understanding of the mission of engaging the world, and the concepts of marketing the church in a neopagan culture. Unity is the casualty of the proliferation of denominations, styles, programs, and doctrines all foisted upon people with the claim that they are the truly Christian ones. In reality, it represents a confusion of terms.

Language is a major factor in considering anything to do with unity in the church. Somehow we have allowed ourselves to be commandeered by the multiplicity of traditions—each valuable—with their own set of words, phrases, and concepts. Over the course of time in our natural tendency for homogeneity we have confused the lines between our tradition and the kingdom. The drift allows for silos of independence to grow into competitive teams each claiming greater spirituality and closer proximity to the right hand of our Lord.

Evangelicals often have a hard time distinguishing between unity, unanimity, and uniformity. Merrill Tenney has helped me to categorize the differences.[3] The unity for which Jesus prayed has to do with the essential nature of our identity that is rooted in Christ, just as his identity proceeded from God. From this essential unity of nature we derive the doctrine of the Trinity—One Essence, three Persons. Within this Trinity there is both unity and diversity. Yet both are not possible unless there is some difference in category by which both may occur in perfect harmony. Unity in essence, identity, and nature, but diversity in manifestation (not modalism), person, role, and function. This is the unity which Jesus desires for his Body, the church. One river of God, flowing through a desert land bringing life wherever it flows.

Yet it is not uncommon for this call for unity to be misunderstood as a call for unanimity. Why can we not all agree?

Why are there so many doctrines? Why are there so many different expectations from different churches? Can we not all just get along? You see, unanimity presumes one-mindedness on the part of everyone in the circle. Where there is difference of opinion, there is no unanimity. This unanimity usually finds expression in the various denominational values, traditions, and polities that litter the ecclesial world. To the indiscriminate observer, this lack of commonality appears to be divisive. These people are ascribing to unity the definition of unanimity. To them, it is like multiple streams flowing in different directions and places, all claiming to be the real river.

To the still more exacting observer, and in some cases Evangelical leader, unity in the church should mean that we all look alike—a perfect definition for uniformity. To the propositional leader who sees success in terms of sameness, unity is only achieved when we all look alike, and do things the same way. And of course that's a euphemistic way of saying, "My way!" We should believe the same and talk the same in regard to the authority of the Bible, the nature of Jesus, the role of the church, the work of the Holy Spirit. Gradations of difference mean simply varying degrees of distance from the propositional truth. Uniformity in its positive manifestation can best be seen in the local church where there are common rituals, experiences, phrases, values, and behaviors that characterize real life together. Uniformity happens descriptively to people who walk the same path together and deal with the same issues as a group. It is kind of like being married; after a number of years they say we actually start looking like our spouse. You see, we tend to become like the people we spend time with. For the outside observer, this lack of uniformity means the church really does not have its act together and cannot agree. They try to define unity by descriptors that are only appropriate for uniformity. To them, it is like a side pool on the edge of a stream that has become isolated from the flow and begins to look the same—mucky, and act the same—stagnant, and smell the same—icky!

The church should manifest some measure of uniformity and unanimity, but mostly unity. At some level we should all look alike to people who are not part of the Body of Christ. And certainly there is a place where groups are of one mind and manifest the basic principles of the kingdom in common values that may be similar to family values and traditions. Most important, however, when people look at us, they should see some significant unity in spirit, essence, nature, character, identity. If not, then truly we have done a poor job of allowing the nature of Christ to so permeate our lives that our very DNA is altered to become like him. And this is the greatest concern I have—that we miss the transforming, unifying power of the resurrected Christ to bring unity.

CONCLUSION

In serving the Free Methodist Church as a superintendent and then as a bishop, I walked the painful road of trying to make sense of things.

- In suspending pastors for immoral conduct—How has the nature of Christ been thwarted in transforming their character?
- In confronting bureaucratic intransigence—How have we missed the passion for Christ and his Kingdom?
- In pleading for a more grace-filled response to people who were different from other denominations—Do these differences really matter?

I did not always find answers. And I still seek for understanding. But I did conclude and remain convinced that the unity of the church is not only possible, but is increasingly necessary as more and more Evangelicals seek deeper understanding and partnership in the cause of Christ in the world. This seems to be a huge challenge. It is almost tiring just to think of trying to find a path that would lead us to unity across so many lines, so many words, so many experiences.

It seems insurmountable. And that is the joy of it. It is impossible, for us. But for God, it is not. Our God is not ordered according to our patterns, not patterned in our image, not contained by our structures. In God there is chaos and energy that surpasses our ability to confine. In that I take hope. It is God's river, not ours. And Christ alone has the understanding of how each stream and side pool contribute to the larger flow of his Body, the church. This river moves through history making a difference and brings God's love, holiness, and presence into contact with dry and desperate lives and cultures. It is a river that we pray for, not a stream. And only God, in transcendent chaos, can bring the unity for which Jesus prayed. Were it possible to achieve on our own, there would have been no need for the prayer.

So, we too must pray and work. I ask that we hold loosely to anything but the Lord of the Church. May we apply ourselves with all diligence to finding that personal and corporate transformation that can only be traced back to the Holy Spirit. May we seek with all our energy to submit ourselves to one another as unto the Lord. May we passionately pursue the nature, the essence, the identity that only God can give through Jesus the Christ. May we in all our efforts truly seek to be one by the molding, shaping work of Christ in us. May we be the healthy, authentic, life-giving people that reflect Christ well. *Amen.*

NOTES

1. Kevin Mannoia, *Church 2K: Leading Forward* (Indianapolis: Precedent Press, 2007).

2. Kevin Mannoia and Larry Walkemeyer, *15 Characteristics of Effective Pastors: How to Strengthen Your Inner Core and Ministry Impact* (Ventura, CA: Regal Books, 2007).

3. Merrill C. Tenney, *John: Gospel of Belief* (Grand Rapids, MI: Eerdmans, 1976).

Chapter 15

VISION OF CHRISTIAN UNITY ON THE ECUMENICAL LANDSCAPE AND SOUNDSCAPE: A PENTECOSTAL ECUMENICAL ENGAGEMENT

David D. Daniels III

The ecumenical knowledge generated by the Christian communions within North America offer competing visions of Christian unity. These myriad visions depict Christian unity in terms of organic union, communion of communions, bilateral and multilateral theological agreements, *koinonia*, and mission. Some of these visions have caught the attention of Pentecostal communions like the Church of God in Christ.

Within the North American ecumenical landscape, various glimpses of Christian unity exist as grace-filled endeavors of the conciliar, Evangelical, and Pentecostal movements as three streams of the ecumenical movement. The ecumenical soundscape offers a complementary frame to explore Christian unity with its accent on the sonic dimension of the Christian faith expressed in the sounds of the faith found in the Christian liturgy and witness. The ecumenical landscape and soundscape provide two arenas to explore visions of Christian unity.[1]

The ecumenical landscape is marred by burrows that separate ecclesial communions into racial, regional, ethnic, and class sectors. Christians crisscross the terrain, bypassing congregations, to locate like-minded Christians whom they often resemble in terms of race, ethnicity, and class. The ecumenical soundscape is cordoned by sonic barriers that segregate ecclesial communions into sonic realms noted for their respective liturgical sounds.

The ecumenical knowledge generated by the Church of God in Christ (COGIC) draws from its encounters on the North American ecumenical landscape and soundscape. Its ecclesial heritage as a communion sought to counter the denominationalism and racial arrangement of Christianity that marked the ecumenical landscape of North America, to yoke apostolic faith and power that highlighted the transformative power of the gospel on the ecumenical landscape, and to craft a soundway that transcends the orality-literacy divide on the ecumenical soundscape.

MAPPING COGIC ON THE ECUMENICAL LANDSCAPE

> Lord, make us one
> Lord, make us one
> Lord, make us one, everywhere.
> Lord, make us one
> Lord, make us one
> Lord, make us one everywhere.

This chant rings out COGIC's yearning for Christian unity. It is a prayer that is sung to God requesting that God make the church everywhere one in the Holy Spirit. This pneumatological orientation is expressed in the additional refrain: "One in the Holy Ghost, One in the Holy Ghost, one in the Holy Ghost everywhere." Christian unity is a constant prayer of COGIC.

The Church of God in Christ is classified as one of the seven historic African American Protestant communions. A Pentecostal communion with congregations in the United States and Canada, its North American location is shaped by its affiliate jurisdictions (or dioceses) on four other continents and in nearly sixty countries. Beginning as a Holiness fellowship among African American Baptists in 1895 in the mid-South region of the United States, a faction of the fellowship led by Charles Harrison Mason in 1907 would join others in mounting the emerging Pentecostal movement.

Resisting the dominant racial arrangement of North American Christianity, COGIC has always had a white minority within its U.S. membership along with a smaller Latina/o membership.

Noted for being a bridge denomination on the contemporary U.S. religious landscape, its membership tends to be theologically conservative and politically liberal, and consequently holds in tension its social justice concerns with its conservative theology. As a North American Protestant communion, COGIC has included congregations in Canada since 1929.[2]

The ecumenical heritage of COGIC includes participation in various local and national ecumenical organizations since the 1930s. These include the National Fraternal Council of Negro Churches, the major ecumenical thrust among African American Christian communions and congregations of the mid-twentieth century that joined together the various Methodist, Baptist, and Pentecostal streams to Presbyterian, Episcopal, Congregational, and others. Also during the 1970s the Church of God in Christ became a charter member of the Congress of National Black Churches, the major black ecumenical organization of the late twentieth century.[3]

The COGIC is a part of an ecumenical venture in theological education spearheaded by the Interdenominational Theological Center, a consortium of seven seminaries located in Atlanta, Georgia. To strengthen cooperatively the theological education of African American Protestants, the ecumenical group of denominations sponsored the consortium, representing the National Baptist Convention, African Methodist Episcopal Church, Christian Methodist Episcopal Church, the Protestant Episcopal Church, United Methodist Church, and Presbyterian Church (U.S.A.), which group the Church of God in Christ joined in 1970.[4]

Within COGIC there has been a commitment to Pentecostal ecumenical ventures. For instance, COGIC had been instrumental in the Pentecostal/Charismatic Churches of North America (PCCNA), the first national interracial ecumenical council among Pentecostals, in 1994. A COGIC leader, Bishop Ithiel Clemmons, announced,

> PCCNA leaders are in continuing dialogue, in search of an ever-deepening understanding of the Biblical principle that All have equal access to God. Our goal is to create, encourage and intensify church-community based efforts to promote racial healing. We are calling upon churches and community leaders to speak out against

bigotry and violence whenever and wherever they occur, regardless of race, religion and ethnicity of the perpetrators, exposing the evils of racism and neo-racism. We envision that churches, colleges and other levels of Church-life address the problem of prejudice and that there be created projects that would send interracial teams into our society with the message of hope.[5]

"A Racial Reconciliation Manifesto" was drafted by PCCNA that called Pentecostals and Charismatics to commit themselves to confess the sin of racism, embrace radical repentance, combat institutional racism, affirm the racial inclusivity of the Body of Christ, and pray and "work for genuine and visible manifestations of Christian unity."[6]

COGIC has exhibited an interest in the wider conciliar ecumenical movement. COGIC participated in the 1954 Evanston Assembly of the World Council of Churches. Since 1990 COGIC has participated in the Faith and Order Commission. Recently, COGIC has been a participant in Christian Churches Together in the U.S.A. With establishment of an office of ecumenical affairs during the mid-1990s, the Church of God in Christ has begun to provide staff to support the ecumenical initiative. Among international bilateral and multilateral dialogues, COGIC participated in the fourteen-year international dialogue between Pentecostal and Reformed churches as well as the Pentecostal and World Council of Churches consultation.

While the Church of God in Christ has demonstrated a commitment to the ecumenical movement through its various ecumenical activities, vocal sectors in COGIC espouse a parochial vision of church. Some prefer to refrain from contact with non-COGIC churches; others prefer to limit ecumenical contact to African American churches; still others are only open to relating to Pentecostals.

A COGIC vision of Christian unity would most likely wrap itself around the pursuit of the "unity of the Spirit." Obviously, the pneumatological orientation of the unity of the Spirit would be appealing to COGIC but also its ecclesiological focus: the Holy Spirit unites the church. Yet COGIC gathers around the ecumenical table in faith and fear—in faith pursuing the "unity of the Spirit," and in fear that ecumenism misconstrued might distract us from God's work in the world.

From a COGIC perspective, how is Christian unity envisioned? My reflections bring together four marks of Christian unity:

Christian unity that transcends denominationalism on the ecumenical landscape

Christian unity that overcomes institutional racism and strives for racial justice on the ecumenical landscape

Christian unity that links apostolic faith with apostolic power on the ecumenical landscape

Christian unity that overcomes the orality-literacy divide on the ecumenical soundscape

These marks are meant to be partial and need to be expanded to envision a Christian unity that possesses theological and spiritual depth. These four marks have special significance within COGIC and Pentecostal memory, and are highlighted because of their peculiar North American, or maybe U.S., character. These four marks possibly expose the captivity of North American churches to denominationalism, modernity, and racism. COGIC would concur with H. Richard Niebuhr that the disunity of the church finds a basis in the social factors.

CHRISTIAN UNITY THAT TRANSCENDS DENOMINATIONALISM ON THE ECUMENICAL LANDSCAPE

COGIC and various Holiness and Pentecostal churches carry within their Christian memory a vision of the church that transcends denominations and denominationalism. The church of Jesus Christ is a community inaugurated out of the grace of God, through love of Christ, and by the power of the Holy Spirit. More than a denomination or a composite of all Christian denominations, the church is graced by God. COGIC envisions a church that transcends North American denominationalism.

COGIC leaders critiqued denominationalism on six accounts. First, the denomination as an ecclesial concept lacks a biblical basis. The inability to locate the concept of the denomination within Scripture makes the concept suspect. Second, the naming of Christian communions should refer to God and biblical ecclesial terms such as "Church of God" rather than forms of polity such a congregational, presbyterian, and episcopal; historical leaders such as Martin Luther, John Wesley, and Menno Simon; or liturgical practices such as baptism. Third, the denomination as a clustering of specific theological beliefs constructs theological systems that resist theological reform in light of Scripture. Fourth, the denomination as a clustering of Christian practices constructs liturgies and ways of the Christian life that resist the movement of the Holy Spirit. Fifth, the denomination promotes a polity or ecclesial organization that becomes more preoccupied with preservation, open to manipulation, and closed to the renewal that is God's mission in the world, thus bracketing off mission from the forefront of the denomination's purpose. Sixth, the denomination lacks the capacity to transcend nationalism and racism, and instead tends to reproduce societal structures.[7]

COGIC and other early Pentecostal institutions advocated nondenominationalism as their ecclesial choice. Nondenominationalism stressed the organization of congregations into councils, associations, fellowships, or brotherhoods (sibling-hoods). They advanced as ecclesial titles terms such as Church of God, Church of the Living God, Church of Christ, and Church of God in Christ. They sought to affirm the Bible as the paramount theological source while being aware of the historical development of Christian theology, highlighting the limiting role of creeds and confessions, and divergent ways of constructing doctrine from Scripture. They affirmed the call for the congregation and communion to be subject to the Holy Spirit in its worship, Christian practices, and polity. They acknowledged the tension between the quest for the freedom of the Spirit and for "doing things decently and in order." They recognized the tension between the biblical demand and sociological need for accountability structures on one hand and the inadequacy of organizational options. While they initially preferred to form councils of congregations, within one generation they moved toward polities with firmer lines of accountability that brought the groups closer to being denominations. They wrestled with responding authentically to the Holy Spirit in ways that challenged American nationalism and racism. This vision of Christian unity might be deemed insufficiently rigorous. However, it was an attempt to grapple with the limits of the denomination as an ecclesial understanding of the church.

Christianity in North America is structured, even misshaped, by denominationalism. While denominationalism has been in decline since the post-1970s era, according to sociologists and other scholars of religion, denominations still have been key factors in the structuring of North American Christianity during the early twenty-first century. Since the advent of the twentieth century, major Protestant missiologists, theologians, and ecclesial leaders have expressed frustration with the denomination being the organizing concept for churches. Their critiques of denomination often resonated with the critique of denominations by COGIC. According to H. Richard Niebuhr, "Denominationalism represents the moral failure of Christianity." He contended that the moral failure of Christianity in the United States was caused by the disunity of church, which denominationalism produced. Divisions were produced by "the accommodation of Christianity" to the societal structures of the United States. Niebuhr stated,

> It draws the color line in the church of God; it fosters misunderstandings, the self-exaltations, the hatreds of jingoistic nationalism by continuing in the body of Christ the spurious differences of provincial loyalties; it seats the rich and poor apart at the table of the Lord, where the fortunate may enjoy the bounty that they have provided while the others feed upon the crusts their poverty affords.[8]

Coupled with the lack of a biblical basis for the concept of denomination, some historians concluded that the denomination as a concept was a North American invention. Though not everything North American is unchristian, it is imperative to determine whether the concept of denomination and the reality of denominationalism hinders the quest for Christian unity.

Historically, the denomination as an institution provided a way to organize the Christian diversity of the United States. It blazed a way for the United States to function religiously without the establishing of a national church; in a sense, denominations collectively functioned like a national church with the direct legal support of the government and indirect support through taxation; denominations promoted social stability.[9]

While the concept of the denomination might have served a crucial purpose in the advancement of the Christian faith in the United States during the founding of the republic, does it serve the ecumenical church today? Has the concept of denomination fulfilled its purposes, and should it be replaced with a concept that will better advance Christian unity in the twenty-first century?

The denomination as a concept is elastic enough to accommodate an array of theologies and provide a "comprehensive organizational unity." Transcending any particular theology, liturgy, polity, or set of practices, it encompasses social norms that shape theological belief and practices such as corporate liturgy, hospitality, peacemaking, and personal prayer; property held by the congregation, presbytery, bishopric; religious authority and governance; and religious roles such as lay and clergy. The denomination structures what it means to be religious in the United States and contributes to the production of a shared religious culture.[10]

The shared religious culture provides social stability, contributes to the common good of the society through its religious and social activities, and strengthens the moral fiber of the society through its ethical grounding. As H. Richard Niebuhr argued, the denomination has reproduced class, racial, ethnic, and regional divisions.

Does the COGIC quest for a nondenominational structure for church offer the church an ecumenical trajectory worth re-examining? Does the postdenominational posture of a sector within the ecumenical landscape of North America provide ecumenical opportunities for a renewed quest of Christian unity that resemble the COGIC's ecclesial experiment with nondenominational structures?

CHRISTIAN UNITY THAT OVERCOMES INSTITUTIONAL RACISM AND STRIVES FOR RACIAL JUSTICE ON THE ECUMENICAL LANDSCAPE

The church as an inclusive community is marked by a Christian unity that overcomes racism and strives for racial justice. Sociologically, to be the church in the United States—maybe even in North

America—is to be an ecclesial community shaped by race. Theologically, to be the church in North America is to be a *koinonia* of Pentecost where the races are baptized in the Holy Spirit creating a new community. COGIC carries within its Christian memory visions of Christian unity that seek to overcome racism and strive for racial justice. How can COGIC share its visions of a racially inclusive Christian unity?

COGIC's interracial impulse found resonance within the racial inclusivity of the Azusa Street Revival, the leading founding event of North American Pentecostalism. A central figure within the revival recorded:

> There can be no divisions in a true Pentecost. To formulate a separate body is but to advertise failure, as a people of God. It proves to the world that we cannot get along together, rather than causing them to believe in salvation.... We are called to bless and serve the whole "body of Christ," everywhere. Christ is one and His "body" can be but "one." To divide it is but to destroy it.[11]

The COGIC apologetic of racial inclusion contends that the Christian God is against racism. They assert that the Christian gospel, as opposed to certain white Christian theologies, does not legitimate racism. In Christ, racial divisions are overcome. The Christian faith embraces interracialism. They affirm the goodness of God in the face of black oppression. Oppression is not a sign of divine disfavor; rather it is a product of the sin of racism. Others argue that the baptism of the Holy Spirit eradicates racial prejudice. Some theologians interject a liberationist agenda into ethics and the theology of salvation. "God is a God of justice who is deeply concerned about... the marginalized and the oppressed," they contend, who has demanded that "those who are entrusted with" God's gifts "must use such gifts to God's glory, in the cause of justice."[12]

Undergirding the theological vision of racial inclusion is that for approximately the first twenty-five years of the history of the Church of God in Christ, between 1907 and 1933, COGIC engaged in various interracial attempts to create a church that overcame the racial divide during the height of racial segregation in the United States. It participated in four attempts to bring black and white

Christians together within the same church, structuring an interracial religious body when most denominations were racially homogeneous or segregated. Surpassing the rhetoric of racial inclusion, they experimented with these four efforts of erecting an interracial religious body and creating an interracial "denominational" leadership. COGIC's structure attracted white clergy and congregations to a predominately African American religious body in an era when racial segregation was law in some states and the norm in most.

There was a black-led network of race-based networks. A black-led network of congregations and clergy created space for two white networks of clergy to coexist. Next, there was an experiment with an ecclesial structure where blacks and whites shared power and authority. The third attempt took its cue from majority Protestant denominations: establishing a racial minority conference. In COGIC's case, whites were the minority. During mid-1920s, white COGIC clergy proposed the formation of a white conference; this was a feeble attempt to retain white clergy and congregations in a predominately black church. The white COGIC conference continued until 1933 when it was disbanded. The fourth attempt has continued to the present wherein whites are welcomed as laypeople and clergy, and into the leadership without any special accommodations.[13]

At the heart of the ecumenical endeavor to overcome the racial shaping of the religious body was its 1917 statement on Christian unity and racial inclusion. They articulated their vision of Christian unity in these terms:

> Many denominations have made distinctions between their colored and white members. Some advised electing colored officials to preside over colored assemblies, while others have refused to elevate any colored elder to the episcopacy or any other office corresponding to it having equal power with white bishops. This has led to many misunderstandings and has caused the organizing of many separate colored denominations. The Church of God in Christ recognizes the fact that all believers are one in Christ Jesus and all its members have equal rights. Its Overseers, both colored and white, have equal power and authority in the church.[14]

Here they envisioned Christian unity cutting against the racial arrangement of their era. They constructed a polity that erased, or at least sought to minimize, racial distinctions as it shared power and authority without respect to race while recognizing race as an identifier. They fashioned a leadership cohort that crossed racial boundaries. When the advocates of racial justice as a mark of the church were even fewer than today, they sought to embody a different vision of church. The above quoted statement indicates their conscious effort to erect an ecclesial structure that reflects the oneness in Christ Jesus shared by black and white Christians.

COGIC approved and published its 1917 manual within the ecclesial, racial, and geopolitical context of the period. Included in the publication were pictures of the key black and white COGIC leaders, offering visual representation of the interracial impulse. The document codified COGIC's policy of integration against the backdrop of racial discrimination and segregation. It juxtaposed the COGIC polity of racial inclusion over against the segregationist polity of U.S. denominations. The statement presented two polities of racial subordination rejected by COGIC: an executive leadership system of racial subordination wherein whites supervised blacks and an executive leadership system wherein blacks supervised blacks, albeit within a hierarchy controlled by whites. The document identified these racial polities as a primary reason for the collapse of the interracial movement within American Protestantism and the formation of "many separate colored denominations." In opposing racial inequality in leadership, COGIC erected a structure that conferred "equal power and authority" to its black and white members and leaders. Such an achievement demonstrated the deliberative and prophetic stance of COGIC interracialism.[15]

The acceptance of white networks of clergy and congregations transformed COGIC into a racially inclusive network of networks. This attempt at the "Unity of the Spirit" by grappling with race as a church-dividing issue reconstituted the Church of God in Christ as a Pentecostal communion in North American and other continents.

A prominent white leader in COGIC of the post-1915 era was William B. Holt. A national officer within COGIC from 1916 to 1933, Holt served in various capacities: overseer (bishop) for a network of white COGIC congregations, superintendent of COGIC Spanish missions, general secretary, and national field secretary.

Holt and his other white colleagues identified with the interracial impulse. As well as affirming racial equality, Holt espoused social equality between the races. Holt publicly violated the racial etiquette of southern segregationists by greeting Mason and other black clergy with a holy kiss as well as hugging them, engaging in a "shocking display of interracial intimacy." Such intimate interracial behavior was reminiscent of blacks and whites embracing each other at the Azusa Street revival.[16]

While most COGIC congregations in North America were racially homogenous, there were congregations across the continent during the first generation that were interracial. By the 1920s, the communion began to debate the propriety of white members voluntarily withdrawing from interracial COGIC congregations to constitute a white COGIC congregation. Accommodating to the dominant racial arrangement of the United States, practical, ethical, and biblical arguments were mounted to address the challenge. First, the voluntary withdrawal of whites from interracial COGIC congregations was to be contemplated only under extraordinary circumstances such as local segregation laws. This would, then, preserve the peace of the congregation in a hostile racial environment. Second, the freedom of association must be honored; whites should not be forced to attend interracial congregations. While the spirit of racial division was to be denounced as unbiblical, it was appropriate for different races to have pastors of their own race.[17]

Interestingly, these racial debates and experiments with COGIC demonstrated the counterhegemonic discourse produced within this communion. Inverting the national racial conversation of the time, in COGIC the predominately African American religious body established norms about relationship of white clergy and congregations to this communion within the Black Church. They also produced norms about white members' withdrawal from interracial COGIC congregations.

Is there ecumenical value for experimenting with polities that foster these kinds of inter-/multiracial debates and structure during the dawn of the twenty-first century? Should there be the crossing of racial borders in ways that counter the dominant pattern of racial interaction? Can ecumenical knowledge be generated from African Americans, whites, and Latino/as within the first generation of COGIC that will aid in the overcoming of racial division and advance Christian unity? COGIC's ecumenical knowledge of racial inclusion could assist the changing racial landscape of American congregational life.

CHRISTIAN UNITY THAT LINKS APOSTOLIC FAITH WITH APOSTOLIC POWER ON THE ECUMENICAL LANDSCAPE

Christian confessions and communions offer different accents on apostolicity: creedal, episcopal succession, essential ordinances/sacraments and polity. COGIC adds a fourth dimension: apostolic faith and power. The church as an anointed community marked by apostolic faith and power embodies a vision of Christian unity that Pentecostals would recognize. The discussions and practice of apostolic power should join our theological studies of the apostolic faith. Apostolic power, in this context, refers to signs and wonders, the miraculous, and the gifts of the Spirit. Apostolic power demonstrates, in a way, the apostolic faith. The healing message and ministry were central to the work of Christ and are central to Pentecostal ecclesiology. The healing message and ministry are an expression of the good news of Jesus Christ, an avenue to connect with the vulnerable in society. Apostolic power points to the call to be a Spirit-filled church, a community that is open to and led by the Holy Spirit, a community that confesses to being surprised by the Holy Spirit. Apostolic power accents the exercise of the gifts of the Spirit in the life of the Christian community. It reveals the dependency of the Christian community on God in the practice of ministry, illustrating the role and need for the Holy Spirit in the operation of the so-called ordinary and extraordinary gifts of the Spirit. A commitment to apostolic power challenges the church to resist having a "form of godliness that denies the power thereof" and to embrace a "living and lively faith." Pentecostals have spoken of apostolic power in terms of "the outpouring of the Spirit." The church becomes the place "where Jesus Christ is lifted up, the Word of God is preached and obeyed, and where the Spirit's gifts are manifested in the lives of believers. The Spirit sovereignly bestows charisms upon the community and its members."[18]

Attention to apostolic power prods the church to go beyond the modern mind's inability to reconcile signs and wonders with reason and the postmodern theoretical openness to the gifts of the Spirit to an encouragement of the full exercise of the gifts of the Spirit in the contemporary church. Attention to apostolic power challenges the modern paradigm with its privileging reason over faith, science over theology, the routinized over the charismatic. The world becomes open to new possibilities and, maybe, a fuller Christian world.[19]

Attention to apostolic power might help us recover God as a subject, as an agent acting in history. Rather than a return to a pre-modern world or even the world of the ancients, it could become the opportunity for plunging or being plunged into the world of the twenty-first century.

Christian unity that links apostolic power with apostolic faith recognizes that the church is the community of the Spirit's gifts and acknowledges that "church is established and maintained by the gracious presence of the Spirit who gives gifts to the people of God." A focus on apostolic power affirms how indispensable the Holy Spirit and the Holy Spirit's gifts are to ministry and the life of the church. Apostolic power becomes a means to encounter the Christ who heals, speaks, converts, transforms, delivers, anoints, and empowers.[20]

Does the yoking of apostolic faith and power provide an expanded way both to dialogue about and encounter with apostolicity? By overcoming the binaries reproduced by modernity such as mind-body and rationality-emotionality, the yoking of apostolic faith and power can reconceive ecumenical engagement and the quest for Christian unity.

CHRISTIAN UNITY THAT OVERCOMES THE ORALITY-LITERACY DIVIDE ON THE ECUMENICAL SOUNDSCAPE

Ecclesial sounds shape the ecumenical soundscape. Distinct ecclesial sounds of the Southern Baptists, African Methodist Episcopals, Roman Catholics, Quakers, and Church of God in Christ mark the ecumenical soundscape in different ways. What are the sonic barriers to ecumenical engagement?

Walter J. Hollenweger was the first to attune the ecumenical movement to the orality of Pentecostalism: oral theology and liturgy. He argued that Pentecostal oral theology operated:

> not through the book, but through the parable
> not through the thesis, but through testimony
> not through dissertations, but through dances
> not through concepts, but through banquet
> not through a system of thinking, but through stories and songs
> not through definitions, but through descriptions
> not through arguments,
> but through transformed lives.[21]

Like other Pentecostals, COGIC performs oral theology and liturgy as well as produces written theologies. Oral theology and liturgy accent COGIC sound, which encompasses singing, music making, praying, preaching, and testifying in many quarters. As Daniel Albrecht contends, a "cacophony of sound" constitutes Pentecostal sound, a sound that includes musical and verbal "sounds that surround."[22]

During the emergence of COGIC and Pentecostalism, different cultural contexts thrived. In some cultural quarters, contesting modernity, the binary opposition of orality/aurality and literacy still existed; in other quarters, heralding modernity, orality/aurality was eclipsed by literacy; and, yet, in others, heralding folk sensibility, the binary failed to exist: sight complements sound.

On the ecumenical soundscape, the Church of God in Christ is recognized by its CDs, radio broadcasts, telecasts, and webcasts of choral arrangements, songs, testimonies, sermons, shouts, prayers, and praise. Its sound is noted for jubilance as well as sorrow. Attuning oneself to the cacophony of COGIC sound becomes an ecumenical task, sensing the sound, detecting the sounds.[23]

The ecumenical engagement of sound can be advanced by the employment of five terms: sonic, soundscape, sound, soundways, and syntax. The "'sonic environment' can be regarded as the aggregate of all sound energy in any given context," and soundscape is used "to put the emphasis on how that environment is understood by those living within it—the people who are in fact creating it." Sound in the singular refers to the ensemble of sounds. Soundways refer to the sonic paths. Syntax refers to the ordering of sounds.[24]

Engaging the ecumenical study of sound, the participants and dialogue teams could go beyond employing the binary of orality and literacy to explain Pentecostal difference. In some ecclesial contexts the focus is on literacy: printed liturgies, sermon manuscripts, published theologies; reason is deemed as a major source of religious authority. In other ecclesial contexts the focus is on orality: oral liturgies, sermons, and theologies; sound is deemed as a source of religious authority, a form of immediate revelation, a sense of truth, and a source of knowledge.[25]

Leigh Eric Schmidt and Richard Cullen Rath contend that a complex relationship exists between orality and literacy, sight and sound. Countering the "hierarchic, oppositional convention" of orality and literacy, Schmidt argued that sight and sound remained contestants during the Enlightenment and its aftermath. Challenging the hegemony of sight to sound, sound has been reshaped through its response to modernity as it functioned in a counterhegemonic manner in various quarters.[26]

In addition to the orality-literacy binary losing its explanatory value, Schmidt contends that the binary relies heavily on "racialized constructions of Western rationality and ecstatic primitivism." The orality-literacy binary plots the story of the triumph of literacy on "a hierarchy of the senses, with sight vastly ennobled and hearing sharply diminished" along with "a marked dichotomy between eye and ear cultures" wherein "'the African' lived in 'the magical world of the ear,' while modern Western 'typographic man' lives in 'the neutral visual world' of the eye." The world of vision produced historical progress while the world of sound was marked by magic. The historical challenge between the world of vision and the world of sound has been "the inability of oral and intuitive oriental culture," according to McLuhan, "to meet with the rational, visual European patterns of experience." What Schmidt deemed as "a larger racialized frame of comparison" would be a major problematic in the use of the orality-literacy binary in Pentecostal studies, especially the historiography that recognizes the multicultural, multiracial, and multinational character of Pentecostalism as a movement.[27]

COGIC sound is heir to the religious culture of the enslaved Africans. COGIC sound is "heir to the shouts, hand-clapping and foot-stomping, jubilee songs, and ecstatic seizures of the plantation 'praise houses.'" COGIC sound would remix this heritage in various ways over the last hundred years as it dealt with the interplay of orality and literacy. By the early twenty-first century, this COGIC, and larger African, sound entered the ecumenical soundscape through the soundways of COGIC, the Black Church, and American Pentecostalism and crossed over into the soundways of mainline Protestantism and Roman Catholicism through the charismatic renewal in the post-1960s and later through the contemporary worship movement.[28]

The change in the ecumenical soundscape of American Christianity can be surmised from the findings of the National Congregational Study. The study surveyed congregations within the Roman Catholic, mainline Protestant, Black Church, and Evangelical communions. In worship there has been a discernable change in the liturgical sound of congregations from 1998 to 2006–7, as indicated by an increase in:

- the offering of testimonies from 78 percent to 85 percent greeting or "passing the peace" from 78 percent to 81 percent
- the dialogical use of spontaneous saying of "Amen" from 61 percent to 71 percent
- the use of hand-clapping as means of applause from 55 percent to 61 percent
- the use of drums as a liturgical instrument from 20 percent to 33 percent
- the presence of speaking in tongues from 24 percent to 27 percent
- the presence of spontaneous shouting or jumping from 19 percent to 26 percent[29]

The changing soundways of the ecumenical soundscape introduce new challenges to Christian unity and supply an opportunity for fresh ecumenical encounters facilitated by an engagement of the ecumenical soundscape.

Sound can serve as a form of ecumenical knowing. In this sonic orbit, doctrines are deemed sound or unsound; they either sound right or wrong; they can either ring true or untrue; the discerning task entails sounding out the truth. COGIC seeks to preach sound doctrine. It adopts "religious ways of knowing that emphasize the aliveness of sounds, the power of scriptures to speak, the capacity of music to heal or inspire ecstasy." They cultivate "an especially fine-tuned ear for the voices, sounds and noises of the divine world" as well as the created order. Being called by God to perform certain activities and to prophesy becomes a soundmark on the Pentecostal soundscape. For early Pentecostals, the divine sound opens itself to the Pentecostal soundscape.[30]

Sound functions as a way of knowing, hearing, experiencing, and being in the world. Sound becomes a medium to express theology in song, speech, primal cries, ambient sounds, and music making. Through the choreography of sound, meaning is internalized. Sound becomes a hermeneutic, and its generation of knowledge supplements epistemology with acoustemology as a sonic way of knowing. Michael Bull ponders,

> If the world is for hearing, as Attali suggests, then there exists an unexplored gulf between the world according to sound and the world according to sight. Sound has its own distinctive relational qualities; as Berkeley observed, "sounds are as close to us as our thoughts." Sound is essentially non-spatial in character, or rather sound engulfs the spatial, thus making the relation between subject and object problematic. Sound inhabits the subject just as the subject might be said to inhabit sound, whereas vision, in contrast to sound, represents distance, the singular, the objectifying. Therefore aural relational experience might well differ from a more visually orientated one. This is not to suggest that they are mutually exclusive but merely to suggest that the relational nature of a technologically auditory experience differs epistemologically from an explanation that prioritizes the visual.[31]

Fran Tonkiss writes, "Hearing has its own relation to truth: to testimony, to spoken evidence, to placing trust in words rather than in images, to accepting things that are promised, even if they cannot be shown. Hearing likewise involves a special relationship to remembering and also knowing; admitting that something sounds credible." COGIC and other Pentecostals engage in "acts of making and hearing sounds" that make and hear a world. This "world of local knowledge" "is articulated as vocal knowledge." COGIC and other Pentecostals profess that hearing is believing or seeing is believing. As oft-quoted in the book of Romans scripture says: "Faith comes by hearing, and hearing by the word of God."[32]

Pentecostal soundings—primal cries, speech, ambient sounds, music making, testifying, preaching, prophesying, shouting—become a way to sound out suffering in community where the Holy Spirit redeems the suffering by transforming the sufferers and their circumstances. As Samuel Solivan proposes in the pneumatology of his Hispanic Pentecostal Theology project, "It is the Holy Spirit who is the transformer of the sufferer and the sufferer's circumstances into liberating *orthopathos*." He adds that "the Holy Spirit can liberate one's life, can turn one's suffering and oppression into hope and faith in spite of the evil social structures and, at times, even in spite of us." Solivan argues that *orthopathos* resonates with the pathos of God wherein *ortho-* refers to the liberating, redemptive, empowering character of *pathos*, with pathos as suffering. Possibly it could be described as a redemptive capacity of suffering enabled by the Holy Spirit.[33]

A COGIC vision of Christian unity wraps itself around the pursuit of the "unity of the Spirit." The Holy Spirit like the sound of a mighty rushing wind unites the church as sound itself is known to unite. Even as a still small voice, the Holy Spirit speaks life to the church, liberating the institutional church from its captivities. The ecumenical soundscape as a creation of the Holy Spirit is open to the blowing breath and wind of the Spirit.

The ecumenical soundscape emerges as a new arena for ecumenical engagement and the task of Christian unity. In a dynamic move, the ecumenical soundscape changes with the new developments in COGIC and other soundways generated by mainline Protestantism, Evangelicalism, and Roman Catholicism.

CONCLUSION

Possibly, there has emerged more visible Christian unity on the ecumenical soundscape than on the ecumenical landscapes, with the different Christian soundways in North America gaining greater resemblance in sound. The changes in the ecumenical soundscape that register across the three streams of the ecumenical movement are conciliar, Evangelical, and Pentecostal. The ecumenical landscape and soundscape would clearly be reconfigured by a Christian unity that transcends North American denominationalism, overcomes institutional racism and strives for racial justice, links apostolic faith with apostolic power, and overcomes the orality-literacy divide. This reconfigured ecumenical landscape and soundscape are informed by a quest for Christian unity that accents the unity of the Spirit.

The ecumenical knowledge generated by COGIC drawn from its encounters on the North American ecumenical landscape and soundscape offers visions of Christian unity that grapple with the critical issues that divide the church: denominationalism, institutional racism, and modernity. By seeking to transcend denominationalism and the racial arrangement of Christianity that still marks the ecumenical landscape of North America, the quest for Christian unity confronts a dilemma that limits the Christian witness. The yoking of apostolic faith and power highlights the transformative power of the gospel on the ecumenical landscape and moves beyond key binaries reproduced by modernity: mind-body, natural-supernatural. The crafting of soundways that transcend the orality-literacy divide exposes the significance of sound and of the ecumenical soundscape for the quest of Christian unity.

NOTES

1. As a metaphor, ecumenical landscape is navigated through the use of sight and the ecumenical soundscape is navigated through the use of sound. The latter recalls the navigating strategies of whales, for instance; for the three streams of ecumenism, see Jeffrey Gros, "Toward a Dialogue of Conversion: The Pentecostal, Evangelical, and Conciliar Movements," *Pneuma* 17, no. 2 (Fall 1995): 189–201.

2. "Follow Peace with All: Future Trajectories of the Church of God in Christ," in *The Future of Pentecostalism in the*

United States, ed. Eric Patterson and Edmund Rybarczyk (Lanham, MD: Lexington Books, 2007), 177–88.

3. Mary Sawyer, "The Fraternal Council of Negro Churches, 1934–1964," *Church History* 59 (March 1990): 51–64; C. Eric Lincoln and Lawrence H. Mamiya, *The Black Church in the African American Experience* (Durham, NC, and London: Duke University Press, 1990), 191–94; "African-American Pentecostalism in the 20th Century," in *The Century of the Holy Spirit: 100 Years of Pentecostal and Charismatic Renewal*," ed. Vinson Synan (Nashville: Thomas Nelson Publishers, 2001), 265–92.

4. "'Live So God Can Use Me Anytime, Lord, Anywhere': Theological Education in the Church of God in Christ, 1970–1997," *Asian Journal of Pentecostal Studies* 3, no. 2 (July 2000): 295–310.

5. "Memphis Miracle Revisited," *www.pctii.org/news/mayor.html;* "Memphis Mayor Touched with the Message of Reconciliation," Press Release 2, October 1, 1996.

6. "A Racial Reconciliation Manifesto" (1994), drafted by Ithiel Clemmons, Leonard Lovett, Cecil M. Robeck, and Harold Hunter.

7. David D. Daniels III, *The Cultural Renewal of Slave Religion: Charles Price Jones and the Emergence of the Holiness Movement in Mississippi, 1895–1905* (PhD dissertation, Union Theological Seminary, 1992), 37–38.

8. H. Richard Niebuhr, *The Social Sources of Denominationalism* (New York: Henry Holt and Co., 1929), 6.

9. Victor Nee, "Sources of the New Institutionalism," in *The New Institutionalism in Sociology*, ed. Mary C. Brinton and Victor Nee (New York: Russell Sage Foundation, 1998), 8.

10. Elwyn A. Smith, "The Forming of a Modern Denomination," in Russell E. Richey, *Denominationalism* (Nashville: Abingdon, 1977), 113.

11. Frank Bartleman, *Azusa Street* (South Plainfield, NJ: Bridge Publishing, 1980 [1925]), 68–69, cited in Allan Anderson, *An Introduction to Pentecostalism* (Cambridge: Cambridge University Press, 2004), 249.

12. George McKinney, "A God of Justice," *Reconciliation Justice* 1 (Summer 1998): 4; also see Leonard Lovett, *Kingdom beyond Color: Re-Examining the Phenomenon of Racism* (Philadelphia: Xlibris, 2007).

13. Lillian Coffey, complier, *1926 Yearbook of the Church of God in Christ* (n.p., n.d.), an April 6, 1926, letter with February 1924 as incorporation date on the letterhead along with name, "The White Churches of God in Christ."

14. William B. Holt, compiler, *A Brief Historical and Doctrinal Statement and Rules for Government of the Church of God in Christ* (n.p., circa 1917), 9.

15. Ibid.

16. Coffey, *1926 Yearbook* (n.p., n.d.), 125; Charles H. Pleas, *Fifty Years of Achievement (History) Church of God in Christ* (n.p., circa 1957), 12; Holt, *A Brief Historical and Doctrinal Statement*, 3, 5; Theodore Kornweibel Jr., "Bishop C. H. Mason and the Church of God in Christ during World War I: The Perils of Conscientious Objection," *Southern Studies: An Interdisciplinary Journal of the South* 26, no. 4 (Winter 1987): 277.

17. "Charles Harrison Mason: The Interracial Impulse of Early Pentecostalism," in *Portraits of a Generation: Early Pentecostal Leaders*, ed. James R. Goff Jr. and Grant Wacker (Fayetteville: University of Arkansas Press, 2002), 268–69.

18. "Word and Spirit, Church and World, Dialogue, 1996–2000; *http://www.warc.ch/dt/erl1/20.html*.

19. Hans Küng, *Christianity: Essence, History, and Future* (New York: Continuum, 1998).

20. Ibid.

21. Walter J. Hollenweger, "Pentecostalism, Growth and Ecumenism," *Pastoral Review* (April 1998).

22. Daniel E. Albrecht, *Rites in the Spirit: A Ritual Approach to Pentecostal/Charismatic Spirituality* (Sheffield, England: Sheffield Academic Press, 1999), 143.

23. For the studies in the history of sound, see Mark M. Smith, "Producing Sense, Consuming Sense, Making Sense: Perils and Prospects for Sensory History," *Journal of Social History* 40, no. 4 (Summer 2007): 841–58; R. Murray Schafer, *The Tuning of the World* (London: Random House, 1977); Leigh Eric Schmidt, *Hearing Things: Religion, Illusion, and the American Enlightenment* (Cambridge, MA: Harvard University Press, 2000).

24. Barry Truax, *Acoustic Communication*, 2nd ed. (Westport, CT: Ablex Publishing, 2001), 11.

25. Schmidt, *Hearing Things*, 18.

26. Ibid., 259, 22, 11, 8.

27. Mark M. Smith, "Making Sense of Social History," *Journal of Social History* 37, no. 1 (2003): 169, 171; Schmidt, *Hearing Things,* 21–22, 20, 21.

28. Cecil M. Robeck, *Azusa Street Mission and Revival: The Birth of the Global Pentecostal Movement* (Nashville: Nelson Reference & Electronic, 2006), 137; James R. Goff, *Close Harmony: A History of Southern Gospel* (Chapel Hill: University of North Carolina Press, 2002).

29. Mark Chaves et al., "American Congregations at the Beginning of the 21st Century: National Congregational Study" (2009), 23–24; also the raising of hands in praise has increased from 45 percent to 57 percent; guitars are used in 34 percent of the congregations surveyed.

30. Schmidt, *Hearing Things, Religion, Illusion, and the American Enlightenment*, 35, 5.

31. Michael Bull, "Soundscapes of the Car: A Critical Study of Automobile Habitation," in *The Auditory Culture Reader,* ed. Michael Bull and Les Back (Oxford: Berg Publishers, 2004), 361.

32. Fran Tonkiss, "Aural Postcards: Sound, Memory and the City," in Bull and Back, *The Auditory Culture Reader,* 307.

33. Samuel Solivan, *The Spirit, Pathos and Liberation: Toward an Hispanic Pentecostal Theology* (Sheffield, UK: Sheffield Academic Press, 1998), 62, 148, 61.

Chapter 16

ISSUES FACING ECUMENISM

C. Christopher Epting

I want to focus on three issues facing ecumenism today and to use lenses familiar to me as an Anglican and familiar to you as well. The three lenses are Scripture, tradition, and reason—the sources from which Anglicans have attempted to discern God's truth. I believe the way we handle those three sources, and how we deal with those who handle them differently, will eventually determine the future of our little Anglican experiment and also the future of the ecumenical enterprise.

How do we read and understand Scripture? What weight do we give to *the* Tradition (with a capital *T*), and how much of that Tradition are we really willing to listen to? What place does the uniquely human faculty of *reason* have to play in all of this? Since I know you would be disappointed if an Episcopal bishop did not speak about sex, I will look at our church's struggles around homosexuality through those three lenses because this is not only an issue for us, but for the whole church and therefore for the ecumenical movement.

For the sake of brevity and because they summarize decades (and even centuries) of ecclesiological thinking yet because they are also quite contemporary, I shall cite two main texts: the Lambeth Commission's 2004 work on Communion titled *The Windsor Report* and the Episcopal Church's formal response to that report, which we called *To Set Our Hope on Christ*.

SCRIPTURE

All Christian communions emphasize *the authority of Scripture*. However, as the *Windsor Report* points out,

> The common phrase "the authority of scripture" can be misleading.... Scripture itself, after all, regularly speaks of *God* as the supreme authority. When Jesus speaks of "all authority in heaven and earth" (Matthew 28:18), he declares that this authority is given, not to the books that his followers will write, but to himself. Jesus, the living Word, is the one to whom the written Word bears witness as God's ultimate and personal self-expression. The New Testament is full of similar ascriptions of authority to the Father, to Jesus Christ, and to the Holy Spirit. Thus the phrase "the authority of scripture" if it is to be based on what scripture itself says, must be regarded as a shorthand, and a potentially misleading one at that, for the longer and more complex notion of "the authority of the triune God, *exercised* through scripture."[1]

"The current crisis," the *Windsor Report* goes on to say of the contemporary situation in Anglicanism (and I would submit, also in many ecumenical situations),

> constitutes a call . . . to re-evaluate the ways in which we have read, heard, studied and digested scripture. We can no longer be content to drop random texts into arguments, imagining that the point is thereby proved, or indeed to sweep away sections of the New Testament as irrelevant to today's world, imagining that problems are thereby solved. We need mature study, wise and prayerful discussion, and a joint commitment to hearing and obeying God as he speaks in scripture, to discovering more of the Jesus Christ to whom all authority is committed, and to being open to the fresh wind of the Spirit who inspired scripture in the first place.[2]

Statements such as this, of course, invite the American authors of *To Set Our Hope on Christ* (which is a response to the *Windsor Report*) to point out that

> there has been considerable debate and discussion within both Judaism and Christianity about how to interpret the biblical texts that forbid same-sex relations. There are faithful scholars in both traditions who say that what the texts forbid is clear and that it applies today as it always did. On the other hand, there are faithful scholars in both traditions who believe that what the biblical texts describe is not as clear as it first appears and does not clearly apply in a very different cultural context. Because

the contextual situation of Leviticus, for example, is so different from our own, it would be inaccurate to assume that some of its texts are more binding on us today than all the other of its proscriptions that we, in fact, do not any longer follow.[3]

So, discussions on the authority of Scripture become inevitably discussions about the *interpretation of Scripture*. And the next question becomes, as the night follows the day, *who* interprets it? It is precisely here—in our current discussion within the Anglican Communion and so often in our ecumenical dialogues across the board—that we begin to hold up for consideration the second lens, tradition. How have the biblical texts been handled by the tradition? How have they been traditionally understood? And who gets to decide what tradition prevails?

TRADITION

Interestingly (and some would say, predictably) in the *Windsor Report* the section on "Scripture and interpretation" is followed directly by a section titled "The episcopate." Bishops in the "historic succession" are one important manifestation of the Christian tradition in Anglicanism. After a brief excursus on the English reformers' decision to retain episcopacy as the form of church government and its preservation in all thirty-eight provinces of the Anglican Communion today, the authors point out that "it is the bishop's role as teacher of scripture that is meant, above all, to be not merely a symbolic but a very practical means of giving the Church the energy and direction it needs for its mission and therefore the motivation and the groundwork for its unity."[4]

Not that all bishops have a completely magisterial function. For example,

> the Anglican Communion is thus bound together in a variety of ways, with scripture as the constant factor, the historic episcopate, the Instruments of Unity, and the synodical life of the Church as the practical means of living together under scripture, and with discernment and reception as the modes in which the Communion operates in relation to new proposals and the emergence of differences.[5]

Surely this is true across the wide spectrum of Christian communions today. The balance falls in different places with respect to the ministry of bishops, pastors, seminary faculties, and synodical bodies of all kinds, each of whom has a variety of roles to play in the interpretation of Scripture and the discernment of God's truth from age to age.

> One way in which unity has been maintained is by subjecting fresh developments within the Anglican Communion to a test of *reception*. In classic theological terms, "reception" was the process by which the pronouncements of a Council of the Church were tested by how the faithful "received it." The *consensus fidelium* ("common mind of the believers") constituted the ultimate check that a new declaration was in harmony with the faith as it has been received. More recently, the doctrine has been used in Anglicanism as a way of testing whether a controversial development, not yet approved by a universal Council of the Church but nevertheless arising within a province by legitimate processes, might gradually, over time, come to be accepted as an authentic development of the faith.[6]

Again, the authors of *To Set Our Hope on Christ* suggest at least two examples of such a reception process. In the first, they offer

> a reading of Acts 10–15, telling how early Christians came to believe that since God had already welcomed Gentiles and had poured out the Holy Spirit upon them, the followers of Jesus should welcome Gentiles into the Church without requiring them to become Jewish. The experience of one part of the Church (Peter and his companions) initially seemed to be in direct contradiction to God's word in Scripture and to the Church's present practices, so Peter and the others were rightly invited to explain themselves to the rest of the Church. As they told their stories to one another, and as they listened to one another with respect and patience, they reached an agreement that the Holy Spirit really was leading the Church—at first, part of the Church and, then, later, most of the Church—to include Gentiles as Gentiles and to welcome Gentiles as leaders of the Church.[7]

Later, in *To Set Our Hope on Christ,* the authors seek

> to describe the theological developments, over nearly four decades, by which some members of the Episcopal Church came to perceive (a) holiness in the lives of its members of same-sex affection, and (b) the potential for their covenanted unions to be open for God's blessing. In no way do we wish to minimize the sea-change in our understanding that this has represented. Indeed, we have only been able to conceive of what God might be doing in our midst by allowing the light of Holy Scripture to shine upon our experience and guide us to the living Word of truth. Thus have we prayed, and caught sight (in the Book of Acts) of Jesus' early followers struggling to understand the scarcely unimaginable wideness of God's mercy ... to overcome the most basic differences among members of the human family for the sake of a new and redeemed creation.[8]

Probably most Christians would agree that ongoing revelation, discernment of God's truth, and eventual reception of a new reality were operative in the case of the early church's inclusion of the Gentiles. Far fewer would agree today that the same process is at work in the Episcopal Church's decisions with respect to gay and lesbian persons and their place in the church. Perhaps this is the place to ask what role *reason* plays in all of this.

REASON

In Anglicanism, reason does not merely mean "the capacity for logical, rational, and analytic thought,"[9] but

> most fundamentally, reason is the capacity to think and talk about things—a fairly basic endowment of human beings, and one which seems to have a role in all kinds of human behavior, not excluding religion.... Reason is not to be identified simply with highly abstract and specialized activities like calculation or the construction of logical proofs of various sorts.... Reason is not less at work in musing and imagining, in reflective appreciation, and in purposive action. It is reason, after all, which sees and formulates the difference between "the God of the philosophers and the living God"—and which knows

that faith does not work in exactly the same way as scientific inquiry. . . . Faith alienated from reason would not be faith at all; for it would be blind and could not make sense.[10]

Reason, in this context, is understood in a classical sense as in Plato and Aristotle, as what might be called participatory knowledge. To know something is to experience it, to participate in something. At least this is the way Richard Hooker, the late sixteenth-century Anglican divine, would have understood it—as practical wisdom that informs and is informed by Scripture and tradition. As such, what we are talking about here is "Spirit-guided" wisdom.

The *Windsor Report*, in this writer's view, does not give enough attention to the role of reason in classical Anglicanism. Scripture and tradition stand almost alone in this text as ways of discerning God's truth. However, in a section titled "Discernment in communion and Reception," the authors do point out,

> As the whole Church, corporately and individually, gives attention to the reading and pondering of scripture, we are called to the specific unifying task of a common *discernment in communion*. We come from a rich variety of cultures, and each of us is called to read scripture within, and apply it to, our own particular setting—and to respect the fact that other churches face the same demands within their contexts. We cannot, therefore, confine our readings of scripture to our own setting alone. . . On the contrary, one of the ways in which we discern the limits of appropriate inculturation is by our rendering account to one another, across traditional boundaries, for the gospel we proclaim and the teaching we offer. One of the hallmarks of healthy worldwide communion will be precisely our readiness to learn from one another.[11]

Applying this human (and divine) faculty of reason to the process of discernment prompts the authors of *To Set Our Hope on Christ* to offer these reflections when considering biblical texts on homosexuality:

> Part of our discernment process, as we engage with any text of Holy Scripture, involves a thoughtful consideration of the contexts of the biblical writers and of ourselves. Is our situation like the situ-

ation of the biblical writers? Does a given biblical commandment or prohibition speak clearly to our own context?

This question will be helpful as we look at the biblical passages that prohibit same-sex relations. It seems very likely that there was no phenomenon in the time of the biblical writers directly akin to the phenomenon of Christians of the same gender living together in faithful and committed lifelong relationships as we experience this today. We most devoutly wish to stress the difference between this statement we are making—that our cultural context is different from that of a given biblical writer's context—and another statement that we sometimes hear but would emphatically disavow, "we today know better than the biblical writers." On the contrary, we affirm the wisdom and holiness of the Scriptures and assume, most gratefully, that we are to be instructed by them. Yet not every biblical norm is directly relevant to every situation in our own time. Discernment is required, through the direction of the Holy Spirit, in order to ascertain the Lord's will for us in every time and to follow in faith where Christ has led the way.[12]

In other words, reason (Spirit-guided wisdom) is necessary for us to understand and appropriate both Scripture and tradition. However, in order for these three streams and sources of authority to interact, to engage one another, indeed to correct for one another, there must be an environment—a container, if you will—inside of which the conversation can take place.

THE BODY OF CHRIST

That container is, of course, the Body of Christ. A great Episcopal ecumenist, William Reed Huntington, first proposed the four "walls" of that container for Anglicans—something that eventually came to be known as the Lambeth Quadrilateral:

1. The Holy Scriptures of the Old and New Testaments, as "containing all things necessary to salvation," and as being the rule and ultimate standard of faith.

2. The Apostles' Creed, as the Baptismal Symbol; and the Nicene Creed, as the sufficient statement of the Christian faith.

3. The two Sacraments ordained by Christ Himself—Baptism and the Supper of the Lord—ministered with unfailing use of Christ's words of institution, and of the elements ordained by Him.
4. The Historic Episcopate, locally adapted in the methods of its administration to the varying needs of the nations and peoples called by God into the Unity of His Church.[13]

The *Windsor Report*—itself citing the International Anglican Theological and Doctrinal Commission's "Communion Study"—suggests how these basic ingredients can be lived out: "The Lambeth Quadrilateral commits Anglicans to 'a series of normative practices: scripture is *read*, tradition is *received*, sacramental worship is *practiced*, and the historic character of apostolic leadership is *retained*.'"[14]

> Through such communion, each church is enabled to find completeness through its relations to the others, while fulfilling its own particular calling within its own cultural context. This does not mean, of course, that each church must accept every theological opinion, or follow every sacramental devotion or liturgical practice, characteristic of the other. Such a distinction, between essentials in which we agree and the non-essentials which do not inhibit communion, is a vital part of life within the Anglican Communion.[15]

Such an articulation surely finds resonance in ecumenical agreements entered into by the Episcopal Church. In *Finding Our Delight in the Lord: A Proposal for Full Communion between the Episcopal Church; the Moravian Church–Northern Province; and the Moravian Church–Southern Province*, it is said that,

> We understand full communion to be a living relationship between distinct churches in which they recognize each other as catholic and apostolic churches holding the essentials of the Christian faith, whereby the reconciliation, mutual availability, and interchangeability of ordained ministries is then fully possible. Full communion is not the same as organic unity or merger. Rather, it is widely recognized as a significant expression of the full visible unity of all Christians, which we do not yet discern but for which we pray. Within this full communion, we understand that the churches are

fully interdependent while remaining responsible for their own decisions. Full communion includes a commitment to establish, locally and nationally, recognized organs of regular consultation and communication in order to express and strengthen the fellowship and enable common witness, life and service. Striving to end our divisions but to preserve our diversity, neither of our churches seeks to remake the other in its own image, and each seeks to be open to the gifts of the other as it seeks to be faithful to Christ and his mission. Each church shall be open to the encouragement and admonition of the other church for the sake of the gospel.[16]

And *To Set Our Hope on Christ* finds this way to articulate that hope,

> The Gospel calls us into a great mystery, the reconciliation that Christ has won for us upon the Cross, and which can be wrought among us only by the grace of Christ. Learning to trust the faithfulness of those with whom we disagree can fuel the lifelong process of conversion for all. This mutual trust bears witness not only to the power of the bonds of unity, but also points quite beyond us to that mysterious power of divine grace at work in the Church's unity.... A unity-in-difference that reconciles divisions and holds out compassion to all can bear real witness to the power of Jesus' prayer that "we all may be one," which John's Gospel tells us was his fervent desire.... We pray that the struggles of our Episcopal Church may always be used by the Lord to exhibit the power of God's reconciling grace "so that the world may believe that" God sent the world's Redeemer.[17]

That is certainly my prayer: that my own communion will find ways to deal with these "Issues Facing Ecumenism." If we can, perhaps we can be a model for how we might deal with them together in the Body of Christ in the search for unity. If we cannot, perhaps you can learn from our mistakes. So that, eventually, we all may be one!

> O God, the Father of our Lord Jesus Christ, our only Savior, the Prince of Peace: Give us grace seriously to lay to heart the great dangers we are in by our unhappy divisions; take away all hatred and prejudice, and whatever else may hinder us from godly union and concord; that, as there is but one Body and one Spirit,

one God and Father of us all, so we may be all of one heart and of one soul, united in one holy bond of truth and peace, of faith and charity, and may with one mind and one mouth glorify you; through Jesus Christ our Lord.[18]

NOTES

1. *The Windsor Report: 2004* (London: Anglican Communion Office, 2004), 39.
2. Ibid., 42.
3. *To Set Our Hope on Christ* (New York: Episcopal Church Center, 2005), 19–20.
4. *Windsor Report*, 43.
5. Ibid., 46.
6. Ibid., 45.
7. *To Set Our Hope on Christ*, 17.
8. Ibid., 31.
9. *The American Heritage Dictionary,* 3rd ed.
10. Richard Norris, *Understanding the Faith of the Church* (San Francisco: Harper San Francisco, 1979), 4–5.
11. *Windsor Report*, 45.
12. *To Set Our Hope on Christ*, 19.
13. *The Book of Common Prayer* (New York: Oxford University Press), 877–78.
14. *Windsor Report*, 37.
15. Ibid.
16. The Official Text: Finding Our Delight in the Lord: A Proposal for Full Communion between the Episcopal Church; the Moravian Church—Northern Province; and the Moravian Church—Southern Province Called to Common Mission, Moravian Church—Southern Province website, *www.mcsp.org/resources/ecumenical/Finding_Our_Delight_Official_Text.pdf.*
17. *To Set Our Hope on Christ*, 43.
18. *Book of Common Prayer*, 818.

Chapter 17

HOW THE WORK OF CHRISTIAN UNITY RELATES TO INTERRELIGIOUS RELATIONS AND DIALOGUE: WHEN GOOD NEWS SOUNDS BAD

John Borelli

"It is fatuous to think that a 400-year-old wound can be healed overnight." So wrote John B. Sheerin on the front "editorial" page of *The Catholic* for the November 1957 issue. He was more annoyed with Catholics wanting a simple answer on the prospects for restoration of unity, after his attendance at the North American Faith and Order Study Conference in Oberlin, Ohio, September 3–10, 1957, than he was frustrated with the grand intentions of the planners of the North American conference itself. Before his comment on any hope for an ecumenical quick fix, Sheerin had pointed out that he preferred to say that he was impressed by the sincerity of the delegates and their return to biblical theology.[1] Paulist Fr. Sheerin and Jesuit Fr. Gustave Weigel attended as unofficial observers, and their presence at the conference was groundbreaking.

Under the heading of Faith and Order in the Context of Religious Pluralism, marking the fiftieth anniversary of those Oberlin events, I wish to offer observations on three topics: (1) the historical context for Catholic participation in North American Faith and Order, (2) the ecumenical dimension of interreligious relations, and (3) past deficiencies and how we need to proceed together.

THE HISTORICAL CONTEXT OF CATHOLIC PARTICIPATION

It is a temptation to spend all my time on the first topic because it is so very fascinating. The Paulist ecumenist John Sheerin and the Jesuit ecumenist Gustave Weigel authored a report, which I studied in Weigel's archives at the Georgetown University library.[2] Bishop John J. Wright, who headed the Catholic diocese of Worcester, Massachusetts, in 1957, had assured Sheerin and Weigel that if they were invited, the Vicar General of the Diocese of Cleveland would give them permission to attend. The permitting authority and vicar general was none other than Bishop John J. Krol, later cardinal archbishop of Philadelphia. The invitation to send Catholic observers came through Bishop John Wright's friends, Bishop Norman B. Nash of the Episcopal Diocese of Massachusetts, and Dr. Samuel McCrea Cavert, Presbyterian and noted ecumenist, then executive secretary of the U.S. Conference for the World Council of Churches.[3] Wright would soon afterward be transferred to head the Pittsburgh diocese and was destined to serve on the theological commission for the Second Vatican Council.

What made the Sheerin-Weigel attendance canonically possible in 1957 was the 1949 Instruction of the Vatican's Holy Office, forerunner of today's Congregation for the Doctrine of the Faith. Addressing the ecumenical movement and dated December 20, 1949, the document represented a somewhat mixed response to rapid developments after the first meeting of the World Council in Amsterdam in 1948:

> Now in many parts of the world, as a result of various external events and changes of views on the part of people, but especially in consequence of the common prayers of the faithful through the grace of the Holy Spirit, there has grown constantly in the minds of many persons separated from the Catholic Church the desire for a return to unity on the part of all who believe in the Lord Christ. To the children of the Church this is surely a cause of true and holy joy in the Lord, and at the same time an invitation to help all those who sincerely seek the truth, by earnest prayer to God imploring them the grace of light and strength.[4]

The instruction suggested that some initiatives, "though inspired by the best of intentions, are not always based on right principles, or if they are, yet they are not free from special dangers." Hence, Catholic bishops were instructed to become aware of what is being done through this "movement" in their dioceses. They were encouraged to designate well-qualified priests, who, according to the doctrine and norms prescribed by the Holy See, shall pay close attention to everything which concerns the "movement." Specifically mentioned for their instruction were the ecumenical, or perhaps I should describe them as the "pre-ecumenical," encyclicals of Leo XIII, Pius XI, and Pius XII—especially the latter's *Mystici corporis*.[5]

Despite the fact that the 1949 instruction warned against an "irenic spirit," indifferentism, and "vain desire for a progressively closer mutual approach among the various professions of faith," and notwithstanding the restraints it imposed on the participation in local ecumenical gatherings, the instruction allowed competent ecclesiastical authority, in all cases the ordinaries of place or local bishops, to send unofficial observers to ecumenical gatherings in their territories, especially when "there seems to be some hope of good results." An earlier *Monitum, cum compertum*, a severe warning on methodological grounds regarding Catholic participation in the inaugural meeting of the World Council of Churches, was issued on June 5, 1948, in advance of its foundational meeting in Amsterdam.[6] That warning remained in effect nine years later at the time of the Oberlin meeting; nevertheless, participation in mixed congresses was no longer forbidden.

This warning was good news, though it may not have seemed so at the time. Lukas Vischer, writing twenty years later even after the formal, positive steps of Vatican II in the direction of the ecumenical movement, judged the instruction's "main thrust was that of warning."[7] Thomas Stranksy's evaluation of the 1949 instruction was fuller and positive: "Although the RCC [Roman Catholic Church] still stood firmly in its ecclesiology of 'return,' it now accepted the basis for that dialogue-in-fellowship which had been serving of other Christians."[8] And so, Weigel and Sheerin went to Oberlin in 1957.

It was truly a delight to read their 1957 report in 2007. After more than sixteen years at the U. S. Conference of Catholic Bishops serving in ecumenical and interreligious relations, now I am affiliated with the first Catholic and Jesuit university in the United States, Georgetown University. It is my third Jesuit academic affiliation after undergraduate study in philosophy at St. Louis University and graduate study in history of religions and theology at Fordham University. I also serve as the National Coordinator for Interreligious Dialogue for the Jesuits in the USA and was privileged to have been tutored in ecumenism over the course of many years by Weigel's student, Jesuit Fr. John F. Long, SJ, who had served from 1963 to 1980 at the Secretariat for Promoting of Christian Unity. I am also working at the present time with Paulist Father Thomas F. Stransky, who set me on the course of ecumenism in 1981. We are shaping his four Georgetown lectures, delivered in 2006, into a book published by Georgetown University Press on *Nostra aetate*,[9] the declaration of Vatican II on interreligious relations. Stranksy staffed the initiative that would become *Nostra aetate* from 1960 until its promulgation in 1965. Among the first to serve on the staff of the secretariat, Stransky and Long were colleagues in that office from 1963 to 1970 and remained lifelong friends.

The report by Sheerin and Weigel was directed to the Most Reverend John J. Krol by "two Catholic priests who attended the North American Faith and Order Study Conference in your diocese."[10] They described their status as "unofficial observers," that is, "not representing anyone but our own individual selves." They reported their "completely passive presence" "with no privilege of the floor or of the vote." Yet they acknowledged that "the Oberlin Conference recognized us as unofficial observers of the Roman Catholic Church." As "recognized unofficial observers," their "completely passive presence" was not entirely passive, for they reported conversations between sessions when they corrected errors. These errors, they suggested, were made in good faith, as in the case of a phrase being gratefully corrected after John Sheerin pointed out what was wrong with it. To the delegates who asked, they explained that their abstention from fellowship in worship was not a sign of disdain or hostility but a matter of principle, as dictated in those pre–Vatican II years by the earlier noted disciplinary documents.

They reported several good reasons for a Catholic presence at this meeting though they were disappointed by a lack of doctrinal rigor and agreement on fundamental doctrines of Christ. They judged that Catholic participation in the World Council was quite impossible at this time, yet they identified many good reasons for attendance at its meetings to continue. A little over a year after Oberlin came the election of John XXIII in October 1958, and three months later, in January 1959, he disclosed that he was calling a general council of the church.

Another product of the 1949 Instruction of the Holy Office was the Catholic Conference for Ecumenical Questions, jointly managed by Johannes Willebrands and Frans Thijssen. Its members held nine study meetings from 1952 to 1963, at first engaging in simultaneous study of the theme for the 1954 Evanston Assembly so that they would be prepared for participation. The Holy Office left the matter of Catholic participation in 1954 to Cardinal Samuel Stritch of Chicago who forbad it, calling the WCC "some sort of man-made unity." Nevertheless, Evanston gave impetus to a U.S. group to begin Faith and Order discussions on this continent leading to the Oberlin Conference in 1957.[11] Weigel and Sheerin were to serve again in these circles, when they were named in August 1963 as "official Catholic observers" for the Secretariat for Promoting Christian Unity at the Central Committee meeting of the WCC in Rochester that year.[12]

THE ECUMENICAL DIMENSION OF INTERRELIGIOUS RELATIONS

By 1963 Msgr. Willebrands was secretary of the Secretariat for Promoting Christian Unity, in the midst of preparing a decree on ecumenism and related texts. After Vatican II, American Catholics would officially participate in Faith and Order structures of the WCC and the National Council of Churches of Christ in the USA (NCC), and by 1981, a Catholic, Bro. Jeff Gros, FSC, would head the Faith and Order office of the NCC. Here now, we draw the first connections between ecumenism and interreligious relations, for it was under Jeff Gros's guidance that the Faith and Order office of the National Council gave initial support to a Task Force on Christian-Muslim Relations. The task force received assistance for three meetings a year ably staffed by Presbyterian Bryon Haines and Methodist Marston Speight. Haines and Speight were located at the Duncan Black Macdonald Center for the Study of Islam and Christian-Muslim Relations, an institution dating back to 1893, the year of the Parliament of Religions at the Chicago Exposition. Though the parliament had an interreligious character, it was largely an ecumenical meeting.[13] The connection between ecumenism and interreligious relations dates also to the beginnings of the ecumenical movement. Is not the world missionary conference that met in Edinburgh in 1910 considered the beginning of conciliar ecumenism, and did it not bring together missionaries who had served among peoples of various religions throughout the world to ask the damaging question about the scandal of witnessing and propagating a disunited Christianity to the world of other religions? Haines and Speight, who staffed the NCC's task force on Christian-Muslim Relations decades later, had served as missionaries in Muslim lands, Haines in South Asia and Speight in North Africa. Catholic missionaries were key resource persons for the interreligious work at the Second Vatican Council.[14]

The Evanston meeting in 1954 was both ecumenical and interreligious, too. Evanston was a milestone for the number of Catholics present who had high theological credentials and ecumenical interests, but attended as journalists due to Stritch's unwillingness to allow any official observers.[15] Evanston was also significant for what it failed to do interreligiously. Fr. Edward H. Flannery, a priest of the Diocese of Providence and later the first to serve in Catholic-Jewish relations at the U. S. Conference of Catholic Bishops, reported that "on August 27, 1954, at Evanston, Illinois, the Second Assembly of the World Council of Churches voted 195 to 150 to strike from a statement on 'Christ—the Hope of the World' any reference to Israel's part in Christian hope."[16] In his analysis of the event, Flannery offered an overview of developments from the Amsterdam Assembly to the floor debate at Evanston. Lack of clarity on the place of the Jews, especially in reference to the Christian future, and insufficient preparedness worked against including several proposed references to the people of Israel in the final document. Flannery reports a twofold opposition: Arab Christians, including the Coptic Orthodox, the Antiochian Orthodox, and Evangelical churches of Syria and Lebanon, who feared political implications of the references; and a second group, mostly American churchmen, who in a spirit of goodwill did not want any attempt at a theological statement to jeopardize friendly relations with Jews. They were concerned that Jewish leadership might recoil at any Christian attempt to place Jews in relation to the movement for Christian unity. Today, ironically, Jews take pride in the fact that the Commission on Religious Relations with the Jews exists within the Pontifical Council for Promoting Christian Unity and not within the Pontifical Council for Interreligious Dialogue.

The irony of these joined forces of Philo-Semites and anti-Zionists at Evanston against a reference to the Jewish people was not lost on Flannery. He observed that neutral delegates were swayed by the emotional level of the arguments and thus found it easier to support no mention than to risk an early rift in the WCC. It is curious how this tension between doctrinal purity on the one hand and preserving religious relationships on the other continues today over, for example, Catholic and Jewish attempts to reflect on covenant and mission.[17]

The tension over whether a statement on the relation of the church to the Jews should be entirely theological in character and absent of any political content would be played out for the Catholic Church after Evanston at Vatican II. In 1964, when the shape of *Nostra aetate* was under discussion, there were three parties opposed to the council issuing a statement largely on the relationship between the church and the Jews: (1) Arab bishops and those living as minorities in Muslim lands who feared a statement on the Jews would be interpreted as an endorsement of the state of Israel; (2) bishops from Africa and Asia who preferred the church to address the religious majorities of their regions and not simply the Jews; and (3) a strongly conservative opposition who argued against departure from traditional teaching on the Jews and other religions.[18] As the conciliar process unfolded, the Vatican II statement expanded to address relations with all other religions, though relations with Jews remained the centerpiece of the final text in 1965. The opposition could muster fewer than 100 votes in the final, formal voting out of over 2,000 votes cast. Pope Paul VI wanted fewer than 400 opposing votes on any action regarding the draft, and the highest number of negative votes on any single item was 250.

The insight for us from parallel WCC and Catholic efforts is how ecumenical and interreligious issues and political and theological issues become naturally intertwined. Ecumenical and interreligious questions run together for several reasons, none of which are truly negative. The ecumenical movement and interest in interreligious dialogue emerged together, hand-in-hand as it were. Both employ dialogue as a major instrument for building consensus, trust, and mutual respect, and for providing reconciliation, mutual understanding, agreement on matters of faith and principle, and spiritual companionship. As long as the unique goal of building communion in faith and worship among Christians has the respect of the churches, interreligious relations and ecumenism should not be in opposition.

Mixing theological dialogue with political advocacy is risky and not always a good idea. In fact, I would suggest that it is seldom a good idea. This was true in 1954 at Evanston, in 1964 at Vatican II, and today in the era of the war on terrorism. Political concerns nearly scuttled *Nostra aetate*. The Central Preparatory Committee removed the initial draft, a mere forty-seven lines on the church and the Jews, from the agenda two months before the council was set to begin because the World Jewish Congress had announced that the Israeli official in charge of Christian relations would be its observer at the council.[19] In the first place, the only observers through all four sessions were Christians. In the second place, *Nostra aetate* was intended to be a theological statement and not a political one. Though political realities removed it from sight during the first session of the council, the intended purpose for a theological statement saved it through the combined efforts of Pope John XXIII and Cardinal Bea, the support of Paul VI, and the conciliar process.[20]

Today, when people speak of interreligious dialogue, and often when they specifically have in mind Christian-Jewish relations, it seems that political overtones are often stronger than theological ones. Christians from the politically charged lands tell us that theological dialogue with representatives of other religions is not possible because neither side is going to give up essential beliefs. For example, they will say that Muslims are not going to give up their understanding of the Qur'an and Muhammad and Christians are not going to abandon its Trinitarian and christological doctrines, so they quickly turn to public issues and abandon the theological discussion.[21] This is to confuse ecumenical dialogue, when Christians seek a language and agreement on doctrinal issues that separate them, and interreligious dialogue, which does not have the purpose of collapsing differences into a single religious unity. The sharing of faith in interreligious dialogue is for insight, edification, spiritual companionship, and opening depths of understanding, but not for replacing one's doctrine for another's.

Any honest Christian-Jewish discussion on theological grounds eventually needs to address the meaning of the state of Israel. Christian-Muslim dialogue needs to address attitudes regarding the relationship between political realities and religious realities, not just in our shared fourteen-hundred-year past, but today, in our world with its war on terrorism and questions of freedom and justice raised every day in the media. John Paul II was right when he wrote at the beginning of the new Christian millennium: "In the climate of increased cultural and religious pluralism which is expected to mark the society of the new millennium, it is obvious that this [interreligious] dialogue will be especially important in establishing a sure basis for peace and warding off the dread specter of those wars of religion which have so often bloodied human history."[22]

Theological dialogue is more difficult to initiate than dialogue on political and public issues, yet it is possible and necessary.[23] Christians and Muslims need to write the history of their relations together, but they also need to discern more clearly variations in their beliefs and theological explanations of revelation, prophecy, and scriptural exegesis, to name only three essential theological topics. We especially need, and in all these topics they can solicit the view of Jewish scholars and theologians too, to develop a hermeneutics of nonviolence and to communicate their findings to the young.[24]

Since the election of Benedict XVI, this mixture of the political and the religious in Catholic discourse has caused some confusion. Elsewhere, I have shown that with regard to ecumenism, Benedict strongly endorses theological dialogue; but in every reference to interreligious dialogue, though he calls it necessary and chartered by *Nostra aetate*, Benedict combines interreligious with "intercultural" dialogue or instead refers "civilizational" dialogue.

Much speculation followed his assignment of Archbishop Michael Fitzgerald as ambassador to Cairo and delegate to the League of Arab States. Fitzgerald had singular success in dialogues with Muslims and others as secretary and then president of the Pontifical Council for Interreligious Dialogue, but in his address to the Roman Curia at the end of 2005, Benedict interpreted interreligious dialogue in line with the public life of the church underpinned by *Dignitatis humanae*[25] and *Gaudium et spes*[26] calling for dialogue on public issues and not in light of *Lumen gentium*[27] and *Unitatis redintegratio*[28] and their vision of the communion of all humanity.[29] When he removed Archbishop Fitzgerald, giving him an important post in the Islamic world in Cairo, he did not appoint a successor. Instead, the pope named the head of the Pontifical Council for Culture, Cardinal Paul Poupard, to head the office for interreligious dialogue, too.

After his difficulties at Regensburg in September 2006, Pope Benedict quickly apologized to Muslims, but much of the damage control was handled by the Secretariat of State, rather than the Pontifical Council for Interreligious Dialogue, which had nurtured relations with Muslim leaders for decades. The Secretariat of State arranged a meeting of mostly ambassadors of Muslim nations for the pope at Castel Gandolfo. Putting the Council for Dialogue under the headship of the president of the Council for Culture, though Cardinal Poupard was a solidly Vatican II person and devoted to Paul VI, who had appointed him to the curia, raised the suggestion that the program in interreligious dialogue was left to die on the vine. But, several months later, Cardinal Tarcisio Bertone, the secretary of state, announced that they "were bringing interreligious dialogue back" with the appointment of a new president, the former "foreign minister" for the Vatican, Cardinal Jean-Louis Tauran. The new head for interreligious dialogue had displayed much interreligious sensitivity to the Balkan wars in the early 1990s and a Middle East policy appreciated by Christians and Muslims, but we see also in this appointment a continuing emphasis on public issues and not mutuality and theological discussion.

The mixing of public/political discourse with theological discourse leads to serious problems. A case in point is all this confusion over reciprocity. Definitely, in all discussions of justice, freedom, human rights and related topics, every human person has the right to demand reciprocity and equality. This should be the clear Christian message of the gospel. However, when it comes to interreligious dialogue as religious conversation, demanding reciprocity has no place. Courtesy dictates mutuality, but the Gospel impels us to hear the hopes and cries of others and to share the good news. We are courteous whether we are treated with courtesy or not. If one enters into interreligious dialogue making demands and with less intention to listen than to proclaim, then I doubt whether it will be a religious dialogue at all.

I want to avoid such an either/or approach when it comes to ecumenism and interreligious relations. First, given the tediousness of the task of Christian unity, some ecumenists may give it less attention and focus their efforts on interfaith activities as though they were saying, "Okay, it's impossible to please everyone in reaching full communion, let's do interreligious dialogue instead." Furthermore, some Christians, though they belong to churches fully engaged in the ecumenical movement, do not want full communion with certain other churches for one reason or another. Also, interreligious dialogue is still novel for most Christians in our land. Not only does it seem more interesting in some measures, its goals may seem less demanding. In actuality, one quickly discovers that interreligious dialogue is no less demanding than ecumenical dialogue, and the gospel impels us to both.

I fully concur with Cardinal Walter Kasper, when he said in his Prolusion at the 2006 plenary of the Pontifical Council for Christian Unity: "Even though inter-religious dialogue (which is theologically distinct from the ecumenical dialogue) has for understandable reasons taken precedence in public interest in recent times, ecumenism remains not simply the preserve of a few predisposed enthusiasts, it is the mandate which has been handed on to the church by Jesus Christ himself, and which she has irreversibly made her own through the Second Vatican Council."[30] I agree that the gospel impels us to restore unity so that the world may believe and that ecumenical dialogue and interreligious dialogue are not interchangeable. Both are necessary today.

Ecumenists are accustomed to reading the New Testament to support the restoration of unity, but the gospel also impels us to interreligious dialogue. When a Shi'ite leader in an annual Christian-Muslim dialogue in the Midwest tells his fellow Muslims that five-sixths of the New Testament they can accept, I know there is something evangelical to this Muslim's insight. This is little different from Jesus pointing out that "in no one in Israel have I found such faith" when the centurion confesses that he believes Jesus can heal his servant (Matt. 8:10/Luke 7:9). What happened to the centurion, or the Canaanite woman, or the Samaritan woman at the well, or Paul's Ephesian pagan interlocutors in Acts 19, who spoke up in his behalf, defended and protected him during a heated dispute on public religion and economy?

In the current Faith and Order Paper 198, *The Nature and Mission of the Church*, there is an ever so brief reference to the present Jewish people. It appears in the section on "people of God" and is among biblical insights for ecclesiology: "the Church remains related, in a mysterious way, to the Jewish people, even as a branch is grafted onto the rich root of an olive tree (cf. Rom. 11:11–36)."[31] Broader interreligious references are more numerous in the text, especially in the fourth part, "In and for the World." The text says, "There is no contradiction between evangelization and respect for the values present in other faiths."[32] Later, the text says that "Christians both can and should join together with the adherents of other religions ... to promote not only personal moral choices ... but also the social goods of justice, peace, and the protection of the environment."[33] This encouragement is expanded a little more in the next paragraph regarding public dialogue. Such references enrich our efforts at Christian unity.

Although the WCC failed in 1954 to mention the contemporary Jewish people at Evanston, it held a consultation on Christian convictions and attitudes in relation to the Jewish people in 1956.[34] That report, aided by other developments, led to some successful mention at New Delhi in 1961. We Christians committed to ecumenical unity need to make a renewed effort to express together in consensus our understanding of our relationship to Jews today.

Here in the United States, Christian-Jewish relations took off quickly in the 1960s at both the National Council and the newly formed National Conference of Catholic Bishops. Aside from our parallel efforts, which at times worked together in consultation, an earlier ecumenical past should not be neglected in our reflections on this occasion. I have in mind those first efforts to form associations with Jews that involved Protestants and Catholics and led to our initial testing of theological grounds for Christian-Jewish relations.

The National Conference of Christians and Jews came into being late in 1927,[35] not to promote dialogue but cooperation, to end anti-Semitism, racism, and other forms of public hate.[36] It was the anticipated candidacy of Al Smith, the first Catholic to be nominated by a major political party for president of the United States, that was the immediate concern, not unconnected with anti-Semitism. During that time, the KKK was experiencing resurgence, and Catholics and Jews were down the list of targets after African Americans. Later, in 1938, there was a shining moment of public ecumenical cooperation when Archbishop Edward Mooney, chairman of the National Catholic Welfare Conference, joined Rev. George Butterick, president of the Federal Council of Churches, and other Christian officials to denounce German atrocities against Jews.[37]

Structures similar to the NCCJ followed in Britain, Canada, and Australia. With the end of World War II, an effort to form a world body quickly came together in 1946 with the attempt to form the International Council of Christians and Jews in Oxford. More significant to our work was the meeting a year later in Seelisberg, Switzerland, when a large group of Christians and Jews, mostly from the Continent, Britain, and the United States, met again at the International Council of Christians and Jews. Commission 3 of that meeting produced the famous ten points of Seelisberg for ending Christian anti-Semitism and contempt for the Jews.[38] There were ecumenical gatherings with Catholics, Anglicans, Protestants, Orthodox, and Jews. There were subsequent meetings—some ecumenical and some of denominations—but the huge first step had been taken.

One of the participants, Professor Jules Isaac, who had served in the French Ministry of Education prior to the war and had escaped deportation though his wife, daughter, and son-in-law perished in the Holocaust, took the results directly to Pius XII in 1949. There was a Vatican advisory note that year that *perfidiis* could be translated as "unfaithful" or "unbelieving" instead of "perfidious." Nine years later, in 1958, Pius removed the anti-Jewish practice of *not* genuflecting at the Good Friday petition for the Jews, one of nine petitions offered at the service. Yet these could hardly be viewed as achievements.

Jules Isaac met with John XXIII on June 13, 1960, a few days after the pope had announced that among the preparatory commissions for the council would be a Secretariat for Promoting of Christian Unity. Isaac presented a file on the meetings, including the ten points of Seelisberg, and John assured him that he could hope for more than he expected.[39] Tom Stransky, who bases his judgment on conversations with Pope John's private secretary, believes firmly that before the visit of Isaac, it had not occurred to Pope John to suggest that the council address the relation of the church with the Jews, but after he met Isaac, he never gave up on the idea of that happening.

The line from Seelisberg to *Nostra aetate* is a clear line of development from idea to document, but much of what happened in Christian-Jewish relations in the twentieth century leading to *Nostra aetate* and the WCC's and NCC's statements occurred ecumenically or hand-in-hand with the development of fundamental ecumenical texts. This is our common Christian heritage.

The NCC was already progressing in Jewish relations and in Christian-Muslim relations by mid-decade in the 1980s, thanks to the task force mentioned earlier. It was at that time that Catholic bishops in the United States voted funding for a position in interreligious relations. That was in November 1986, not without some difficulty. Before I assumed the interreligious position at the NCCB in August 1987, Jay Rock and Marston Speight had already proposed to Eugene Fisher, the NCCB staff for Jewish relations, and then to me an ecumenical project. *Confessing Christian Faith in a Pluralistic Society*[40] was the result of that project, published and made available until recent changes through the Institute for Ecumenical and Cultural Research at St. John's University, Collegeville, Minnesota. It first met as a consultation in 1989, bringing together a range of Christians involved in dialogue and or missionary activity and asked the question of the relation between mission and dialogue. At first, we could show only a record of a conversation because there was insufficient consensus for issuing a text. It was another six years before we reconvened at Collegeville and produced a text in 1995 that has articulated for many various positions on these issues. This was a thoroughly ecumenical effort.

In the meantime, the National Council brought its work in Jewish relations and Islamic relations together into an Interfaith

Relations Commission, and among its several tasks was preparation of a statement for the National Council. Catholics advised on the preparation of the text, but this was largely a conciliar effort of representatives of the member churches. It was aided by Faith and Order, which had brought together a study commission on religious pluralism which met in 1994. S. Mark Heim edited the materials into the resource, *Grounds for Understanding: Ecumenical Resources for Responses to Religious Pluralism*.[41] The volume represents various understandings of the state of the question at the time, and in that way it is useful. Its use will be limited the further we move into the twenty-first century because for generations coming of age, religious pluralism is not a problem for Christian reflection but the reality of everyday experience. The policy statement was approved by the NCC in November 1999, and in the current configuration of the National Council, Interfaith Relations and Faith and Order are in a single unit.

PAST DEFICIENCIES AND THE ROAD AHEAD

I now turn to the third part of my reflections, namely, where we have been deficient and how we might proceed together in the future. Addressing religious pluralism and preparing a policy statement on interfaith relations are tasks that could become endless. Often, it is better to stop engaging in reflection on the process and the rationale and simply engage in dialogue. My colleague James Fredericks, who teaches at Loyola-Marymount University, has urged that we lay aside the task of theology of religions and take up the work of comparative theology instead.[42] Fredericks is a systematic theologian, who has acquired some of the tools necessary to study Buddhism. There is little nuance left to articulate how other religious traditions relate to our Christian faith, he feels, and it is better to befriend scholars and representatives of other traditions and work with them cooperatively and in dialogue to address the questions that arise when we study one another's traditions. In other words, we have had enough of internal reflection; it is time to get on with the dialogue and the hard work of research.

Comparative theology is not comparative religion. Comparative theology proceeds from theological conviction and with respect and care for what those of other religions have to say, so that by learning well their tradition in a comparative context with one's own tradition, a deeper understanding, interreligious understanding if you will, of one's own convictions is reached. To explain this point, I often cite from *Dialogue and Proclamation*, jointly prepared by the Vatican offices for dialogue, mission, and doctrine:

> Interreligious dialogue does not merely aim at mutual understanding and friendly relations. It reaches a much deeper level, that of the spirit, where exchange and sharing consist in a mutual witness to one's beliefs and a common exploration of one's respective religious convictions. In dialogue Christians and others are invited to deepen their religious commitment, to respond with increasing sincerity to God's personal call and gracious self-gift, which, as our faith tells us, always passes through the mediation of Jesus Christ and the work of his Spirit.[43]

We can talk topics to death among ourselves, yet we need to encourage more widely the experience of dialogue itself. Thus, in 1999 and in 2000, Jay Rock at the NCC and I at NCCB along with Patrick Henry, again at the Collegeville Institute, facilitated an interreligious consultation *Living Faithfully in the United States Today*.[44] The usual typology of dialogue follows the fourfold division, as given in *Dialogue and Proclamation* and elsewhere: the dialogue of life, the dialogue of social action and public works, the dialogue of experts, and the dialogue of religious experience. We tend to think of the dialogue of experts when we consider interreligious dialogue and the dialogue of religious experience as the one leading to the most profound experiences. *Living Faithfully in the United States Today* proved that the dialogue of life can be quite profound. The dialogue of everyday experience and conversation about our deepest concerns in this society by people of faith who practice and share their faith openly can be quite profound.

Speaking to the bishops gathered for the second of the four sessions of Vatican II, the newly elected Paul VI stated, "Look therefore beyond your own sphere and observe those other religions that uphold the meaning and the concept of God as one, Creator, provident, most high and transcendent, that worship God with acts of sincere piety and upon whose beliefs and practices the principles of moral and social life are founded."[45] My research with

Fr. Stransky in setting the record straight on the development of *Nostra aetate* has shown us that Pope Paul was not speaking in a vacuum when he uttered these words toward the end of his inaugural address to the assembled bishops as pope on September 29, 1963.

Paul first announced that he was adding the self-awareness of the church to the three goals already articulated by Pope John for the council: renewal of the church, the coming together of all Christians in unity, and dialogue of the church with the modern world. Paul tacked on engagement in interreligious activity to the dialogue of the church with the modern world. All things begin with our self-understanding as church, as *The Nature and Mission of the Church* stated in 2006.[46] Fifteen days prior to this address, Paul had announced that in due time there would be a Secretariat to relate to adherents of other religions. One council, one mission, and two secretariats; there is much for us to ponder just in the structure.

In Thomas Merton's Asian journal, one finds mention of communion among the notes for a talk titled "The Monastic Experience and East-West Dialogue," which he delivered in Calcutta in October 1968. On that occasion, Merton was analyzing the deeper meanings of communication, not unlike Pope Paul VI had done in *Ecclesiam suam*,[47] introducing dialogue and communion in relationship through a vision of the church. Merton writes about a level of interaction in interreligious dialogue that is "more than a simple sharing of ideas, of conceptual knowledge, or formulated truth." He notes, "The kind of communication that is necessary on this deep level must be 'communion' beyond the level of words, a communion in authentic experience which is shared not only on a 'preverbal' level but also on a 'postverbal' level." He further explains what he means when he calls this "communion": "I think it is something that the deepest ground of our being cries out for, and it is something which a lifetime of striving would not be enough."[48]

Thomas Merton was speaking from his experience in 1968, and others could do that as well. Where in our understanding of church as participation in the communion of God with all of humanity do we fit our relations with people of other faiths? Our understanding of the communion of the church will be enhanced by interreligious understanding. According to *The Nature and Mission of the Church*, the church is a creature of the Holy Spirit. I am reminded of the reflections of John Paul II after the first World Day of Prayer for Peace in Assisi:

> Every authentic prayer is under the influence of the Spirit "who intercedes insistently for us . . . because we do not even know how to pray as we ought," but he prays in us "with unutterable groanings" and "the one who searches hearts knows what are the desires of the Spirit" (Rom. 8:26–27). We can indeed maintain that every authentic prayer is called forth by the Holy Spirit, who is mysteriously present in the heart of every person.[49]

My sense is that we need to pay more careful attention to the implications of communion ecclesiology for understanding and promoting our relations with peoples of other faiths. This will not inhibit but will enhance our quest for Christian unity.

CONCLUSION

I began my presentation by quoting John Sheerin, an unofficial observer at Oberlin in 1957, when he wrote after that experience, "It is fatuous to think that a 400-year-old wound can be healed overnight." As we meet at Oberlin, fifty years later, we were reminded of the wounds of our disunity in another example that might even be a case of good news sounding bad. I refer, of course, to *Responses to Some Questions Regarding Certain Aspects of the Doctrine of the Church*, issued by the Congregation for the Doctrine of the Faith on July 7, 2007.[50] The answers are terse and the notes are profuse, including references to the *Decree on Ecumenism*[51] and to the encyclical on ecumenism, *Ut unum sint*,[52] which contribute to the good news of the text. Also, it is good news that *Responses* do not concur with the conclusions of an earlier attempt in an article prominently published to demonstrate that "subsists in" and "is" are equivalent.

Responses as an ecumenical text may sound bad because it repeats an interpretation of the conciliar position without any nuance from the last forty-five years of theological dialogues.

Further, it is a Catholic profile writ large, in contrast to the positions of others, demonstrating how the Catholic Church is wounded by the disunity among Christians. There are a number of other reasons why it sounds bad, reasons that theologians would take account of, on particular understandings of the conciliar record. Questions on the development of dogma, on degrees of difference on the elements that constitute the one church of Christ, and on variations of interpreting relevant conciliar passages remain in a form as though only ten years instead of fifty years have elapsed since Fr. Sheerin remarked about the four-hundred-year-old wound. The *Responses* text cites documents of the Congregation for the Doctrine of the Faith including *Dominus Iesus*[53] and the 1992 letter on some aspects of the church as communion.

I view these latter two texts on interreligious relations and on ecumenism respectively as very similar, much like I look upon the 1949 instruction that had the good effect of getting Sheerin and Weigel to Oberlin while Vischer and countless past and future partners in dialogue have viewed the instruction and these more recent texts as only warnings. While the instruction held powerful sway in 1957, it is a document largely for historical study today. The historical record stands and will be interpreted by all generations. In another fifty years, scholars may gather here to evaluate the long-term heritage of Oberlin. The conciliar record for Faith and Order and for the Catholic Church, and all our churches, will be there for them to study. *Ecclesiam suam*, *Lumen gentium*, *Unitatis redintegratio*, *Nostra aetate*, *Gaudium et spes*, *Redemptoris missio*,[54] the *Revised Ecumenical Directory*, and *Ut unum sint* are on the record, just as *Baptism, Eucharist, and Ministry*[55] and the *Nature and Mission of the Church* will be on that record, too. Historians will uncover what they intended to say and what they have affected in the past hundred years.

Before all these developments in ecumenical and interreligious relations, there was Pius XII's encyclical on the church, *Mystici corporis*. Toward the end of that letter, after talking about praying for the members of the church, Pius writes, "Likewise, We must earnestly desire that this united prayer may embrace in the same ardent charity both those who, not yet enlightened by the truth of the Gospel, are still without the fold of the Church, and those who, on account of regrettable schism, are separated from Us, who though unworthy, represent the person of Christ on earth."[56] The reference expands in the next paragraph where Pius says that he desires nothing more ardently than that "those who do not belong to the visible Body of the Catholic Church" "may have life and have it more abundantly." He asks each and every one of them "to correspond to the interior movements of grace and to seek to withdraw from that state in which they cannot be sure of their salvation." He continues, "Though by unconscious desire and longing they have a certain relationship with the Mystical Body of the redeemer, they still remain deprived of those many heavenly gifts and helps which can only be enjoyed in the Catholic Church."[57] What leaps off the pages to us enjoying this long Faith and Order heritage is the lack of a distinction between fellow Christians or those who are not Christian in these words of Pius XII.

The good news, as evidenced by the abundant record collected by the Congregation for the Doctrine of the Faith, is that this restricted view of membership in the Church and of elements of truth and grace as constituent to the churches and ecclesial communities not in full communion with the Catholic Church has undergone considerable development and change. We rejoice that a theology of communion, admitting of degrees of communion, makes such a reference to those outside the fold of the Catholic Church to include Christians and non-Christians obsolete in light of the layers of concentric circles of communion in *Ecclesiam suam* and *Lumen gentium*. I am not saying that fellow Christians enjoying the life of the church are not more advantaged than those who are not Christians. Yet the responses of 2007 refer to *Dominus Iesus*, and in its concluding paragraph, it cites this very text from *Mystici corporis* to support a rather ungenerous passage: "If it is true that the followers of other religions can receive grace, it is also certain that *objectively speaking* they are in a gravely deficient situation in comparison with those who, in the church, have the fullness of the means of salvation." One wonders how those compare who belong to churches and communities in which the fullness of the means of salvation does not subsist. The thought is unproductive, the passage in *Mystici corporis* is inappropriate to present discussion, and thus *Dominus Iesus* is flawed in this regard.

What is appropriate to present discussion is a passage in the CDF's letter on communion referenced by the responses and clearly implicit to the text of the responses, given the remarks of CDF officials. I am referring to paragraph 17.3. There the letter notes that since communion with the universal church, represented by Peter's successor, is an internal constituent of particular churches and is lacking in the venerable Christian communities of the East, their existence as particular churches is wounded. The letter continues to say that the wound is even deeper in those ecclesial communities of the West. Then, in the same paragraph, the letter says, "This in turn also injures the Catholic Church, called by the Lord to become for all 'one flock' with 'one shepherd,' in that it hinders the complete fulfillment of her universality in history." The good news sounds bad because we are reminded of how our disunity wounds us all.

For no other compelling reason than this fundamental incompleteness and how evangelization suffers from our wounds, our future interreligious relations need to go hand-in-hand with our ecumenical relations, particularly regarding our discussion of the core topics on the agenda of Faith and Order.

NOTES

1. John B. Sheerin, CSP, "The Sin and Agony of Disunity," *Catholic World* (November 1957): 81.

2. Georgetown University is fortunate to possess the archives of Gustave Weigel, John Courtney Murray, and John Francis Long—the three American Jesuits who worked on projects of the Secretariat for Christian Unity at the Second Vatican council (1962–65). Given the fact that Sheerin's archives and those of Thomas F. Stransky, another Paulist who served as ecumenical staff at the Council, are across town in Washington, DC, at St. Paul's College, which itself is next door to the U.S. Conference of Catholic Bishops and its archives, the nation's capital has become the place for research on the origins and early years of Catholic participation in the ecumenical movement and interreligious relations.

3. Gerald F. Fogarty, *The Vatican and the American Hierarchy from 1870 to 1965* (Wilmington, DE: Michael Glazier, 1985; first published in 1982), 388.

4. Translation available in *Instruction on the Ecumenical Movement,* the official English translation of the "Instruction to Local Ordinaries about the 'Ecumenical Movement,'" issued by the Supreme Sacred Congregation of the Holy Office, December 20, 1949, Commentary by Rev. William Conway, JCD, Unity Studies 1, Pamphlet 11–1 (Garrison, NY: Franciscan Friars of the Atonement, 1952).

5. Pope Pius XII, "The Mystical Body of Christ," *Mystici Corporis Christi,* Encyclical given at Rome on June 29, 1943; Online Papal Archive, the Holy See; *www.vatican.va.*

6. Ruth Rouse and Stephen Charles Neill, eds., *A History of the Ecumenical Movement: 1517–1948* (Philadelphia: Westminster Press, 1968), 689.

7. "The Ecumenical Movement and the Roman Catholic Church," in *A History of the Ecumenical Movement,* vol. 2, *1948–1968,* ed. Harold E. Fey (Philadelphia: Westminster Press, 1970), 316.

8. Nicholas Lossky et al., eds., *Dictionary of the Ecumenical Movement,* 2nd ed. (Geneva: WCC Publications, 2003), 997.

9. Pope Paul VI, "The Relation of the Church to Non-Christian Religions," *Nostra Aetate,* Proclaimed October 28, 1965; Online Vatican Resource Library, Documents of II Vatican Council, the Holy See; *www.vatican.va.*

10. John B. Sheerin, CSP, and Gustave A. Weigel, SJ, "Report of the Oberlin Conference," September 1957, in The Rev. Gustave A. Weigel, SJ, Papers, Box 8, Folder 354, Lauinger Library Archives, Georgetown University.

11. Notes from a letter from Thomas Stransky, Tantur Ecumenical Center, March 12, 2007, to John Borelli, Georgetown University.

12. National Catholic Welfare Conference News Service, "Two U.S. Priests to Represent Vatican Body at World Council's Central Committee Meeting," August 5, 1963.

13. See Richard Hughes Seager, *The World's Parliament of Religions: East/West Encounter, Chicago, 1893* (Bloomington: Indiana University Press, 1995).

14. For example, Joseph Cuoq, MAfr, first served at an Islam desk in the Congregation for Oriental Churches in 1961, a year before Vatican II opened; Georges Chehata Anawati, OP,

consulted on the preparation of a paragraph on Muslims for *Nostra aetate* and had given a public lecture hosted by Cardinal Tisserant on November 29, 1963, on Islam at the time of the Council, a Prolegomena to an Islamic-Christian Dialogue; and Josef Neuner, SJ, provided expertise on Hindu-Christian relations in the preparation of *Nostra aetate*.

15. George H. Tavard, *Vatican II and the Ecumenical Way* (Milwaukee: Marquette University Press, 2006), 33.

16. Edward H. Flannery, "Hope and Despair at Evanston," *The Bridge: A Yearbook of Judaeo-Christian Studies*, vol. 2, ed. John M. Oesterreicher (New York: Pantheon Books, 1956), 271.

17. In 2002 the dialogue between the U.S. Conference of Catholic Bishops and the National Council of Synagogues issued a report titled "Reflections on Covenant and Mission." One can find a whole array of responses and counterresponses on the Dialogika website at *www.ccjr.us/index.php/dialogika-resources.html*. See my article, "Troubled Waters," *America* (February 22, 2010).

18. See Mauro Velati, "Completing the Conciliar Agenda," in *History of Vatican II*, vol. 5, ed. Giuseppe Alberigo and Joseph A. Komonchak (Leuven: Peeters; Maryknoll, NY: Orbis Books, 2006), 211–21.

19. John W. O'Malley, *What Happened at Vatican II* (Cambridge, MA: Harvard University Press, 2008), 220.

20. Giovanni Miccoli, "Two Sensitive Issues: Religious Freedom and the Jews," in *History of Vatican II*, vol. 4, ed. Giuseppe Alberigo and Joseph A. Komonchak (Leuven: Peeters; Maryknoll, NY: Orbis Books, 2003), 137ff.

21. See John Borelli, "The Dialogue of Truth," *America* (May 12, 2008), 10–11.

22. John Paul II, "At the Beginning of the New Millennium" (*Novo Millennio Ineunte*), 55.

23. See Archbishop Alexander Brunett, "What Dialogue Means for Catholics and Muslims," *Origins: CNS Docmentary Service* 30, no. 41 (March 29, 2001): 660–61.

24. See John Borelli, "Christian-Muslim Relations in the United States: Reflections for the Future after Two Decades of Experience," *The Muslim World* 94, no. 3 (July 2004): 321–33; "U.S. Catholic-Muslim Dialogue," *Origins: Catholic News Service Documentary Service* 36, no. 35 (February 15, 2007): 558–63.

25. Pope Paul VI, "The Right of the Person and of Communities to Social and Civil Freedom in Matters Religious," *Dignitatis humanae*, *www.vatican.va*.

26. Pope Paul VI, "On the Church in the Modern World," *Gaudium et spes*, Promulgated on December 7, 1965; Online Vatican Resource Library, Documents of II Vatican Council, the Holy See; *http://www.vatican.va*.

27. Pope Paul VI, "Dogmatic Constitution on the Church," *Lumen gentium, www.vatican.va*.

28. "Decree on Ecumenism," *Unitatis redintegratio, www. vatican.va/archive*.

29. See John Borelli, "Judgment at Regensburg," *New Theology Review* 20, no. 3 (August 2007): 44–54.

30. Cardinal Walter Kasper, "Ecumenism in Transition," Prolusio of the President, *Information Service*, Pontifical Council for Promoting Christian Unity, 123 (2006/3–4), 98; also published in *Origins: CNS Information Service* 36, no. 26 (December 7, 2006): 407–14.

31. Faith and Order Paper 198, *The Nature and Mission of the Church: A Stage on the Way to a Common Statement* (Geneva: World Council of Churches, 2006), par. 18.

32. Ibid., par. 110.

33. Ibid., par. 114.

34. "Christian Convictions and Attitudes in Relation to the Jewish People," *Ecumenical Review* 9, no. 3 (April 1957): 303–10.

35. *New York Times,* December 11, 1927.

36. The reaction of Leo XIII and curial officials to Catholic participation in the World's Parliament of Religions brought disciplinary order from Rome to the American hierarchy to avoid all forms of dialogue. See James F. Cleary, "Catholic Participation in the World's Parliament of Religions, Chicago, 1893," *Catholic Historical Review* 55 (January 1970): 585–629.

37. "U.S. Christians Join in Reich Protest," *New York Times,* December 24, 1938, 6.

38. See Christian M. Rutishauser, "The 1947 Seelisberg Conference: The Foundation of the Jewish-Christian Dialogue," *Studies in Christian-Jewish Relations* 2, no. 2 (2007): 34–53; *Sens. L'Amitié Judéo-Chrétienne* (1998/10). Entire issue devoted to Seelisberg and After: Acts of a Colloquium at Strasbourg with contributions by

Y. Chevalier, L. Landau and others; William Simpson, "The Ten Points of Seelisberg: A Significant Anniversary," *SIDIC* 10, no. 1 (1977): 21–25.

39. J. O. Beozzo, "The External Climate," in *History of Vatican II*, vol. 1, ed. Giuseppe Alberigo and Joseph A. Komonchak (Leuven: Peeters; Maryknoll, NY: Orbis Books, 1995), 393–97. One caution about this reference: the date of the meeting between John XXIII and Jules Isaac was June 13, 1960, and not June 3, as the English edition of vol. 1 indicates.

40. *Confessing Christian Faith in a Pluralistic Society*, Ecumenical and Interfaith News Network—PCUSA; *http://www.eif-pcusa.org/documents/cllgvll-confessingchrist.pdf.*

41. S. Mark Heim, ed., *Grounds for Understanding: Ecumenical Resources for Responses to Religious Pluralism* (Grand Rapids, MI: Eerdmans, 1998).

42. James Fredericks, "The Catholic Church and the Other Religious Paths: Rejecting Nothing That Is True and Holy," *Theological Studies* 964, no. 2 (June 2003): 252–54. He develops this in *Buddhists and Christians: Through Comparative Theology to Solidarity* (Maryknoll, NY: Orbis Books, 2004).

43. Pontifical Council for Inter-Religious Dialogue, *Reflection and Orientations on Interreligious Dialogue and the Proclamation of the Gospel of Jesus Christ: Dialogue and Proclamation,* the Roman Curia Online; Pontifical Councils; Inter-religious Dialogue, §40; *www.vatican.va.*

44. *Living Faithfully in the United States Today* (Collegeville, MN: Institute for Ecumenical and Cultural Research, 2001).

45. Published among numerous places in *Interreligious Dialogue: The Official Teaching of the Catholic Church from the Second Vatican Council to John Paul II (1963–2005)*, ed. Francesco Gioia (Boston: Pauline Books and Media, 2005), 157. The excerpt was the opening speech of Pope Paul VI for the second session of the Second Vatican Council, September 29, 1963.

46. *The Nature and Mission of the Church: A Stage on the Way to a Common Statement,* Faith and Order Paper No. 198 (Geneva: World Council of Churches, 2005), par. 10.

47. Pope Paul VI, "On the Church," *Ecclesiam suam,* Encyclical issued on August 6, 1964; *www.vatican.va.*

48. See *The Asian Journal of Thomas Merton*, ed. Naomi Burton, Brother Patrick Hart, and James Laughlin (New York: New Directions, 1973), 315–16.

49. *Interreligious Dialogue: The Official Teaching of the Catholic Church from the Second Vatican Council to John Paul II (1963–2005),* 405. This quotation, dated December 22, 1986, John Paul II later incorporated into his encyclical on mission, *Redemptoris missio* (29)

50. Published in *Origins, CNS Documentary Service* 37, no. 9 (July 19, 2007): 134–39.

51. See n. 27.

52. Pope John Paul II, "On Commitment to Ecumenism," *Ut unum sint, www.vatican.va.*

53. Congregation for the Doctrine of the Faith, "On the Unicity and Salvific Universality of Jesus Christ and the Church," *Dominus Iesus, www.vatican.va.*

54. Pope John Paul II, "On the Permanent Validity of the Church's Missionary Mandate," *Redemptoris missio*, issued December,7, 1990; *www.vatican.va.*

55. *Baptism, Eucharist and Ministry: 1982–1990*, Faith and Order Paper 149 (Geneva: World Council Publications, 1990).

56. See n. 5. *Mystici corporis,* par. 102.

57. *Mystici corporis,* par. 103.

Chapter 18

CHRISTIAN ECUMENISM AND THE ABRAHAMIC FAITHS

Lewis S. Mudge

> Portions of the argument and material of this paper are found in greater elaboration in Lewis S. Mudge, *The Gift of Responsibility: The Promise of Dialogue among Christians, Jews, and Muslims* (New York and London: Continuum, 2008). The original paper that was delivered at Oberlin II is printed here with permission.

We citizens of the early twenty-first century live with a growing awareness of the ambiguous portents of religious pluralism in our midst. On the one hand, faith communities, and particularly the Abrahamic ones, Judaism, Christianity and Islam, find themselves locked in various forms of both internal and interfaith conflict. Either we are violently acting out anticipations of our own eschatological narratives or allowing ourselves to be caught up in the ambitions of competing national, cultural, or economic interests. On the other hand, a deepening understanding of pluralism's peaceful potential has encouraged exceedingly numerous attempts to bring our faiths together for serious interaction and forms of mutual commitment. Thus we have an apparent paradox: rising levels of angry confrontation coexist with deepening dialogical relationships, if not always exactly at the same time or place or with the same participants, to create situations both urgently threatening and remarkably promising. It is hard to name any previous historical epoch in which such a combination of impulses has been so salient. The same religious traditions living in the same global world at the same moment of time are producing both violent and peacemaking versions of themselves. Two distinct, yet possibly interconnected, narratives are being acted out on the world stage. Which story is the *real* story? Which is more likely to sway the long-term human future?

If one consults the media, the violent story wins out. Reporters and editors prefer news of lurid events to accounts of patient efforts to foster mutual forgiveness, trust, and solidarity among the faiths. But constructive relationships among Jews, Christians and Muslims are being built in some of the same venues where conflict is at its worst. A signal example has been the city of Jerusalem and Israel-Palestine in general. Here, to name just one example, an umbrella organization calling itself the Interfaith Encounter Association headed by a rabbi of Russian origin, Yehuda Stolov, sponsors a vast array of dialogues, debates, shared activities, public manifestations, and the like. Such gatherings go on virtually every day of the year throughout this territory, involving persons and organizations of all three faiths (plus the Druze). The numbers of these events greatly exceed the number of reported terrorist incidents and retaliatory air strikes. Which story is the *real* story? And what does it *mean* that such efforts go on in the midst of violence, not only in Israel/Palestine, but all over the Middle East?

The question of meaning is crucial. Do such constructive efforts have a force of history behind them? The overwhelming majority of these peacemaking activities are not self-interpreting. That is, their leaders and followers generally do not pause to ask what is going on in an upstream sense. They are too busy following the advice of Tariq Ramadan, a Swiss-born Muslim scholar now teaching at Oxford—in effect, "Don't ask too many questions. Just act!" But it is important to raise the fundamental issues. In a world-historical sense, what is going on here? Do these peacemaking activities and others have any purchase on the future? Are they, in the end, the *real* story of our times, or are they not?

But one *must* ask questions about what is going on when we act in these ways. What fundamental background assumptions are needed to make these relationships in the face of violence feasible? I will argue that such commitments as those described can arise only if those involved are gifted and motivated by some sense of shared responsibility to one another and to the world. In the case of the Abrahamic faiths, this means responsibility *to* a covenantal promise of blessing to humanity, of the sort described in Genesis

12:1–3, with its scriptural parallels and echoes. Members of each of the three faiths living in mutual relationships are able to *recognize* such a gift of responsibility to covenant in the lives and traditions of those of the other faiths. In no way am I speaking of agreed theological formulae. I am speaking of a mutual recognition of a certain resonance across cultural and religious difference that is a sign of the presence of such a gift of responsibility that each can understand in his or her own way just as the different "families of the earth" come to "be blessed," or "bless themselves," in ways corresponding to their traditions of faith. The fact that these three faiths are historically interrelated and look to overlapping scriptures strongly suggests that there is potential, some of it already beginning to be realized, among them for something new, for what Hannah Arendt calls a "novum," to arise on the stage of history. Already many Jews, Christians, and Muslims are working in various ways to bring this about. The implications for Christian ecumenism could be significant. But can we from our present vantage point say what these implications are?[1]

MOVING FROM HERE TO THERE

How does one move from where one lives theologically by heritage and training to take on a question such as this one? I am a Christian theologian, and I intend to remain one. Furthermore I reaffirm my long-standing commitment to Christian ecumenism, the shared effort of the churches together to rediscover and affirm the meaning of Christian faith for the world through a shared recovery of unity and purpose. This personal history and these commitments obviously color what it is possible for me to do with the inter-Abrahamic dimension. But the question is by now unavoidable. The question of inter-Abrahamic relationships is about to become, if it is not already, a divisive issue *within* the Christian ecumenical conversation itself. In fact it could soon become the central issue. We ecumenists had better be ready for this encounter. Indeed I suspect that the fact that interreligious issues have been in the room for some time, yet insufficiently recognized programmatically up to now,[2] accounts in part for the sense of theological and organizational malaise one feels across the Christian world. We have not truly seriously approached the challenge of religious pluralism in a common search for understanding. The inquiry we are making with this Oberlin panel could help lead to what I have elsewhere called "the next ecumenism." This would mean not merely a new subject matter for ecumenical conversation but an approach to what Christian theology in a pluralistic world now needs to *be* and seems at present so ill-equipped to become.

One asks just where one's own faith tradition, conventionally understood, begins to seem inadequate to the challenges around it. The situation just described is one in which familiar formulas seem less and less persuasive. Musing on these things, I remember a byword spoken years ago by my former mentor, the Scripture scholar W. D. Davies: "When you find yourself stuck, try enlarging your categories." This was the advice that W.D. would give his students as we struggled to find our way through the complexities of biblical interpretation. When insights cease to come, he would say, when arguments seem to be losing their traction, we should suspect that the paths being followed are too narrow for us to avoid muddy patches and ruts, whether inherited or of our own making. We should consider reframing our projects in larger landscapes.

Whether certain Christian ecumenical projects today literally qualify as stuck is for those involved to say. Some are and some are not. But it does seem that we Christians are almost paralyzed by a number of diversionary internal debates that seem to defy resolution. Too many of our fields of contention seem bogged down in political and cultural polarization. To suggest enlarging categories to take in new horizons may in fact be an unwelcome suggestion to many battlers who draw energy from their current struggles and do not want to see them end too soon. And I certainly do not think that seeking a responsibility covenant among Abrahamic communities will solve many, if any, of the problems wracking our communities from within. Many of these internal questions are, after all, worth contesting because they are theologically and humanly important. But the initiative I am suggesting might nevertheless divert the attention of some of the combatants to wider horizons for pursuing their concerns. It could certainly raise new points of contention, leading to still more comprehensive struggles between those willing to entertain proposals such as this one and those abhorring the very idea. The resulting fracas could help resolve many of today's dilemmas simply by dwarfing them. It could also help dramatize what is truly at stake as we struggle to understand what it means to be people of faith in a world such as ours.

One reason we are stuck with our present debates may be that we Faith and Order types have lost touch in this generation with the broader theological task of connecting with the burdens and possibilities of contemporary humankind.[3] Faith and Order work seems of late to be insufficiently engaged with the problems of modernity in a religiously pluralistic world: one in which much that is vital to faith itself is radically threatened. Reaching out to and deciphering the evidence for this, we find that Jews and Muslims—they at least but others, too—are grappling with many of the same issues that face us as Christians. The forms taken by these questions are inevitably diverse, but not mutually incommensurable or incommunicable. Facing similar dilemmas about the nature of their being-in-the-world, these communities, particularly the Abrahamic ones, have so much in common that it becomes inconceivable that they would willingly continue to wrestle in isolation. It is time for the different religious traditions to reach out to connect together with the human condition in each particular situation where they live, and, in doing so, to connect with one another.

What kind of a common theological project would this likely be? It would not be a simple matter of accommodating our thinking to the spirit of the age. Nor would it be a simple theological postmodernism either, determined to undermine secular certainties in the interest of letting every flower, including theological flowers, bloom. Rather it would be a shared effort to bring newly recovered and appreciated traditions to bear on modernity's self-betrayals without seeking to translate religious messages totally into modernity's categories. Postmodernism has placed theology in a position to do this, as long as we do not forget that modernity is still with us as a material and spiritual culture that has deeply shaped our identities and continues to do so.

For two centuries and more, most religious responses to modernity have been either self-protective or apologetic in nature. Nearly all of these responses have been worked out within the limits of particular religious traditions struggling to survive the onslaughts of secularism, either intellectually or institutionally or both. But today these relationships have changed. Religion as such, whether or not defined in ways that please us, has made a significant comeback in the public world, even as religious communities are being forced to recognize the reality of radical pluralism among themselves, even as different faiths jostle for position and preferment in myriad public arenas. And modernity as such, having ridden high, is now deeply troubled as its economic engines fuel divisive political ambitions and broadly ignore the welfare of persons and cultures.

Yet modernity has helped to bring Western religious consciousness to a point at which serious interaction between faith traditions is conceivable. Historical-critical method has saved many of us from fundamentalism and exclusivism. This same method has helped us see the appropriate response to the scriptural promise of universal blessing as at least in part a human enterprise subject to the false starts, mistakes, and distortions of all things earthly. Entering responsibly into the actual history of responses to this gift convinces us that we in our generation need to enter this process alongside Abrahamic companions who are now trying to do the same thing. Such a perspective, of course, now includes the use of human-science resources—those of sociology, anthropology, political philosophy, and the like—to illumine the character of our religious origins and our religious prospects. Many prophetic oracles and Gospel parables, for example, take on new meaning when they are studied with a knowledge of ancient Near Eastern agricultural economics and the debt system of Palestine in the time of Jesus. Modern hermeneutical attitudes, moreover, illumine the ways in which texts take on new meanings in their passage through different conditions and cultures on their way to contemporary readers.

The postmodern critique of Western consciousness has in turn liberated such texts and their interpretations from having to justify themselves before the secular thought-police. Religious affirmations can now be what they want to be, while simultaneously exercising the inner freedom to reach out toward the affirmations of other faiths. Critical methods—perspectives that have helped us see our interpretative responsibilities as fallible historical beings—are now subject to questioning about their own pretensions to finality. The claims of human language to be able to grasp reality independent of itself have themselves been called into question. Modernity's achievements for human well-being are being justly celebrated even as its secular certainties and absolutist reasoning styles are under challenge. This means that scriptural narratives have their own validity simply by being what they are, without submitting to any extraneous logical or epistemological claims.

This paper's argument displays a number of these modern and postmodern traits. It stands apart from modernity to find leverage for helping to save modernity from itself. It sees religious texts not merely as products of social-historical circumstances, but also as worlds of discourse within whose unique logics we can come to live and act. It puts a premium on practices rather than propositions as carriers and conveyors of religious truth. It learns from Emmanuel Levinas that faith resists ideological "totalization" and that ethics is "first philosophy."

Yet, all this said, we continue to live in the epoch we call modernity, our name for the stage of history we are all passing through. I mean by this the whole material and cultural civilization that has followed on the Enlightenment, now more obviously religiously pluralist than ever before. Modernity does not look the same everywhere, but its manifestations are linked together economically and communicatively so that, for better or worse, it is rapidly creating a single global civilization. The achievements of modernity are great, but its injustices and other shortcomings are enormous as well, so much so that the latter threaten to undermine the very conditions of religious freedom and flourishing, not to speak of broadly shared human well-being. We need to criticize this modernity simultaneously with defending its best features. This is a project not only for Christian ecumenism but for the Abrahamic faiths and others to pursue together.

ENLARGING TRADITIONAL CATEGORIES OF ECUMENICAL THOUGHT

But, to grasp such a possibility, religious leaders and scholars will truly need to enlarge their categories. The proposed shared inquiry into presuppositions in the hope of finding an agenda will inevitably pose a challenge to each faith to rethink the *way* it holds its animating beliefs, including core affirmations. Such rethinking of the manner of believing for our time is already happening. Many responsible religious leaders and thinkers (I think of Rabbi Jonathan Sacks) now seem ready to reframe at least one core presupposition: the application of the Platonic-Aristotelian law of contradiction where religious language is concerned. More and more of us refuse to believe now that if our own formulations of faith are "true," all formulations that appear to say something different must then be "false." Some of us are abandoning religious exclusivism not only as contrary to the nature of faith language as such (powerfully symbolic and metaphoric, not literally descriptive) but also as contrary to the substantive convictions that our faith languages seek to express.

In 1999 a group of Asian Christian missionary leaders issued a report that included (albeit buried in the middle of a long paragraph in the middle of a long document) this disarming question: "Can we understand the reign of God as religiously plural?"[4] The question, so expressed, is not further explored in the report in question. But it represents the sort of simple yet profound query whose answer is now being taken for granted by many religious progressives, and even by some of the more conventionally minded. The answer, in whatever context we ask the question, must be "yes." But what does this "yes" mean? Where does it lead? It is one thing to be genially open to any and all religious expressions while sending vague good wishes to the human race. It is another to deal responsibly with such a conviction—concerning, of all things, the "reign of God" in human affairs—within the central precincts of each of our traditions of faith that have, over the years, shown the world more than a small streak of religious exclusivism.

It makes a huge difference how such questions are asked and answered, how such a thing is done. This paper proposes a certain way of understanding what it means to do these things. It offers a theological argument for a responsible sort of "yes" to a religiously plural vision of God's rule in human life and in the unfolding of historical events. It seeks to make this affirmation seriously within a Christian perspective, as this is rethought collaboratively with scholars of Judaism and Islam. Its purpose, further, is to do this in a manner potentially open to other religious traditions.

Along this way, we face three questions of fundamental importance. First, what is the nature of what has recently been called God's mission to the human race? Not our own confessional or institutional religious mission to other people, but rather the mission of God to all of us human beings, the communication to us, by the final Power with whom we have to do, what Karl Barth called God's self-determination for us, the members of the human race. That mission may not be adequately articulable in today's conventionally religious languages.

Second, what kind of need does each tradition of faith have for the collaboration of other faiths in answering such questions while maintaining its own authenticity? The underlying issue here concerns the sort of space that needs to be made by each faith, at the heart of its own self-understanding, for the religiously Other. Is this not a hospitable space of Other-welcoming needed for the full and genuine expression of each faith in a world of many faiths?

And finally, what, in the economy of God, are we as believing human beings responsible for? What is our human role in meeting the obligations that come with the gift of life and faith? Speaking in Christian terms, the issue is the perennial one of nature and grace. We are not responsible for achieving our own salvation. But by saving grace we are *given* the responsibility of making the world ready for the coming of God's rule. Combining the word "gift" with the word "responsibility" and the word "blessing" seems to me to catch that basic nuance. From here I see the idea of a gift of responsibility for conveying God's blessings ramifying into many different applications. Among these is the idea that if the Abrahamic faiths were together, in all their diversity, to appropriate such a responsibility, that would be a stupendous peacemaking gift to the rest of humankind. Hence the question: what are we Christians therefore to do?

Such questions would not have been even formulable at the heart of Christian (or any other) faith without years of history-of-religions scholarship, interreligious information-sharing, and exchanges of friendship. But such a query clearly makes a new demand on us. This demand constitutes the essence of the critical moment in which we now live and to which we need to be alert. As Henry David Thoreau wrote in *Walden*, "No day dawns save the one to which we are awake." Our common consciousness of certain realities allows a day to dawn whose meaning we can work together to discern and act out.

PROGRAM PLANNING FOR FAITH AND ORDER

What, programmatically, might all this mean? Broad insights are not always easily captured in institutional programs. But it would seem obvious that Faith and Order could usefully take steps to carry on its work *in a living context of* enhanced awareness of, and practical exposure to, the ongoing Abrahamic (and trans-Abrahamic) dialogues going on all around us today. Especially if we ask, as a fundamental question for our current critical moment, What is the role of organized, visible, ecclesiastical bodies in God's pursuit of God's mission to the human race? We need to assume that our own ecclesiastical traditions and institutions are, as Jürgen Moltmann says, "indispensable," but yet only "provisional," instruments of the divine mission in relation to which we human beings, as a planetary society, are to *become,* through unspeakable historical travail, an image of God in the universe. God has "other sheep that do not belong to this fold" (John 10:16). Presumably many of these sheep are Jews, Muslims, Buddhists, and members of other faiths, as well as religiously unaffiliated persons of spiritual depth and conviction. We need to pursue our own continuing concerns as Christians for visible unity and worldly witness as foci of a specific concern relevant to a wide range of concerns about deep human well-being on this planet. At this point we have a stake alongside other faiths that share the same concerns, if not the same ways of articulating them.

How might we go about this programmatically? Many possibilities exist. One might simply be to organize a study in which Faith and Order representatives would work with the NCC Interfaith Relations Commission in order to help frame the Abrahamic question, or a broader question, in Faith and Order terms, or, alternatively, to enlarge our Faith and Order categories in order to see them in Abrahamic perspectives. Such a study could well mimic structurally the WCC ecclesiology and ethics project of the 1990s carried out jointly by WCC Faith and Order and the WCC department for Justice, Peace, and the Integrity of Creation.[5]

But however such a study might be organized and whoever might be involved, the still more interesting question concerns the topics and perspectives that could be included. The remainder of this paper offers some thoughts on the latter question, the question of substance. In no case do I mean to suggest any sort of syncretism. The project is always to discover insights about our own faith, and to contribute insights about other faiths, so that all, living together but yet distinct, can be instruments of God's self-commitment to humanity.

THE GIFT OF RESPONSIBILITY FOR ABRAHAMIC BLESSING AS PIVOTAL CATEGORY

I have already introduced the idea that the new relationships among the Abrahamic faiths can be understood in the light of a shared, if incompletely expressed, presupposition: that they have a common gift of responsibility to a shared covenantal promise to one another and to humanity. It will be well to dwell for a moment more on what I take this to mean. What, in a world created, redeemed, and being brought to its fulfillment by God, is it the responsibility of human beings to be and to do? Scripture sees this capacity for responsibility as a gift before it is a task, as a gift in order for it to be a calling. But this word has a great variety of meanings in common use needing to be sorted out before we can be clear what is meant by it here.

The notion of responsibility has been seen by some as the threshold of ethics generally. To be responsible is first of all to identify ourselves with our own acts or deeds: to own up, as the saying goes. But there are other definitions. An enormous literature exists on this subject.[6] But a few indications can be given now. "Being responsible," for example, sometimes is taken to mean endorsing social gradualism, going slow, having patience, conforming to common wisdom, acceding to entreaties from authorities not to rock the boat. It also sometimes is taken to mean planning the lives of people deemed incapable of caring for themselves (e.g., "taking on the white man's burden"). Or it sometimes represents a demand that others shape up, that is, reasoning that people are poor because they do not manage their lives better than they do, and insisting that they do so before being helped (i.e., self-reliance as a conservative mantra). Or a notion of responsibility may be derived from its often-forgotten tie to human rights, as when one speaks of rights and responsibilities. This thought can turn rights into something one *earns* by being responsible, whatever that means, instead of something God-given with the evolutionary emergence of self-conscious personal agency. Or one can say that being responsible is being accountable to humankind for wrongs that have been done in the name of religion through the ages. This last insight comes closer to my point.

The core of the responsibility theory at work in this proposal derives from the story of a particular actor, Abraham, the patriarch of all three Abrahamic faiths. The notion of Abrahamic, rather than mere arbitrary, responsibility is an example of enlarging the usual categories of ancient thought and of our own thinking as well. Abraham is the model of responsibility before God in ways that go beyond the usual meanings of the word—that is, doing one's assigned tasks, being accountable, bringing one's integrity and competency to handling complex challenges. Abraham does all this, but in addition he undertakes responsibilities never before given in any job description for a nomad chieftain of the ancient Middle East. He extraordinarily helps foreign monarchs and tribal leaders make peace with one another. Furthermore, in Genesis 22 (the *Akedah* or binding and unbinding of Isaac) he comes to grasp that his responsibility is not to obey what he can only see as a sheer, irrational command but responsibility to a gift: the gift of a promise to him and his descendants. And hence he comes to know that true obedience to God requires him responsibly to exercise the gift of discernment. He must ask himself what is the real nature of this gift, and what it calls on him to do.

As Walter Brueggemann puts it, obedience to "the demand of YHWH" confers on Israel "a responsibility, given in the same breath, given in this initial utterance of generosity." This is the *gift of responsibility* to be discerned at the origin of all three Abrahamic faiths. Taking on such responsibility is included in the scope of appropriate human response to the divine command. We are summoned to do those things that make us free to be instruments of the promise of *blessing* extended to all human beings. In this vision extended and developed lies the theological possibility that the three Abrahamic faiths can come to compatible interpretations of the gifts of worldly responsibility they have received, while maintaining their own traditional understandings of the divine authority that has given them such a gift. The exercise of this divine gift of responsibility is the appropriate in-depth response to God's summons.

Among the implications of Abrahamic responsibility is the need to responsibly interpret our sources, words, and actions in the presence of one another. Abrahamic responsibility becomes the key constant or touchstone of this interpretative process. Much more is involved than the interpretation of *written* texts. Scholars such as Paul Ricoeur and Clifford Geertz, as well as semioticists such as Roland Barthes, have shown that our words, actions, cityscapes, monuments, and all the rest are textlike: subject to interpretations that have consequences. Our behavior with one another and toward the human world depends very much on how we read one another's words and actions, and on how we present our own actions to be interpreted. The opportunities for mutual misinterpretation are enormous, and we have responsibility as human beings to get it right.

It makes a difference, for example, if we are interpreting our own texts alongside others who are interpreting their texts in relation to ours. Such a situation demands a higher than usual demand for integrity and attention to the consequences of what we say our Scriptures mean. The mere fact that interpretation is done together with mutual responsibility for integrity and attention to consequences is vital to our argument. We need also to admit the difficulties we encounter, to acknowledge to one another the lines of argument that do not work. I try to use the notion of parallel and interactive hermeneutics (or theories of interpretation) of ancient texts and of contemporary patterns of symbolic communication among our three faiths as a conceptual resource for reconstructing the ancient scriptural notions of covenant. To live in covenant is to live in a community of mutually communicated expectations, including God's expectation for all. I am well aware that it has different meanings in the different religious traditions. I am also aware that its signification differs in different parts of my own Christian tradition.[7] I cannot make my argument rest on any supposed or given univocity of sense for this or any other leading idea, such as gift, responsibility, promise, blessing, or otherwise. Indeed this argument has the audacity of trying to *lend* such words commensurable meanings across traditions and situations by projecting what inter-Abrahamic discourses may come to be. Such terminology can gain shared meanings in the very process of the discourses this paper describes and seeks to understand.

We exercise our responsibility for understanding one another, I say, in the context of responsibility to the covenantal promise of *blessing* to humankind. I am speaking of responsibility here in the sense implied in Adam and Eve's responsibility for the Garden, the promise inherent in the call to Abraham and Sarah, Hagar and Ishmael, to bring through their descendants a covenantal *blessing*. In both these deeper senses, looking back and looking forward, responsibility rests on the gift of a promise giving it both depth and direction. Abrahamic dialogue in a religiously troubled world needs to bring forth an agenda based on this gift, discerning its meanings today and the tasks to which it leads. Such a shared-responsibility agenda could even help modernity save itself from its injustices, its false modes of reasoning, and its perverse uses of power.

If responsibility is a question of identifying ourselves with our deeds, then it is a question of expressing ourselves, and discovering the intentions of other selves, through our interpretations of our actions and deeds, seeking to align all actions or deeds with the promise of blessing. Loyalty to the scriptural promises gives us a way not to let ourselves be used by political, economic, or ideological forces to recruit support for violent reactions to the world's provocations. Such cooptation happens particularly where eschatological texts and traditions—for example, Armageddon and all that precedes and follows it—are concerned. Allowing such texts literally to lead us to bring death rather than life to humankind is to deny the gift of responsibility for interpretation—in the presence of, before the face of, the Other—that is intrinsic to the covenant promise. And, in turn, such responsible-to-promise interpretation by Jews, Christians, Muslims—not to speak of members of other religious communities—is a *gift of responsibility* to humankind in another sense: a gift of the presence of people whose behavior brings blessing rather than curse.

Responsibility to promise means loyalty to what we, as a religiously diverse community of interpreters of overlapping scriptural promises, can see as signs of that promise. We take on an ethic of discernment where we identify ourselves with the promissory signs we can identify in the world about us. Reading together about these things is only adequate as reading when we become ourselves indicators and bearers of promise.

This responsibility agenda thus summons Abrahamic scriptural interpreters into the center of today's debates over human purposes and meanings. Those who live by the conviction that their responsibility to humanity is a divine gift could possibly make the difference between a modernity apparently bent on self-destruction and a modernity purged and preserved to bless us on the way to the achievements of tomorrow.

THE THEME OF BLESSING AS DEEP WELL-BEING BEFORE GOD

Our discussion of Abrahamic responsibility has repeatedly made reference to the theme of blessing for "all the families of the earth" (Gen. 12:3). I believe that this theme has great potential for a Faith and Order discussion in the context of an Abrahamic dialogue. It is worth saying a few words about this potential.

By "blessing" our Scriptures mean, in their various ways, deep human well-being before God, or in the sight of God. It is this, according to Genesis 12:3 and other similar passages, that we have a common gift of responsibility to foster for the human race as a whole. Blessing or blessedness is an ethical category, applicable both to individuals and to communities, a category that the Abrahamic faiths can share without danger of syncretism or anything close to it. On the one hand, as we will see, blessing stands close to several central formulations of our faiths. But, on the other hand, it is not a politically sensitive category and is theologically relatively undeveloped. Thus it can function to name a common concern while remaining rooted in the separate religious traditions.

Both the Hebrew and the Arabic terms for blessing are based on the root *b-r-k*, whose core meaning is "to kneel," as one (or a camel) kneels to drink at an oasis in the desert. Here is powerful visual imagery. We have a shared covenantal gift of responsibility for making the whole human habitation livable and fruitful. Each faith can rethink its own structures and inner nature in relation to this common worldly responsibility. By placing Faith and Order concerns within this wider set of considerations, we can begin to see anew what tradition of religious self-understanding now looks like and needs to accomplish to be instrumental to God's mission.

A project of sharing responsibility for universal covenantal blessing also addresses itself directly to issues with which religious ethicists are now wrestling. These scholars tend to believe that questions of "the good" for humanity cannot be solved with allegedly universal (but usually Western) moral principles. Cultures and situations differ too much for that. Certain broad assumptions about behavioral "decency" do seem to exist in our society. But secular ethical reasoning has not produced any consensus about the grounds for these common assumptions. There is much of value in specialized moral codes, as in medical ethics, legal ethics, business ethics, and so forth. We need to explore what we have in common with such assumptions and codes. Unspoken social and religious traditions very likely underlie arguments that are persuasive to people, including ourselves. Mere logic is not persuasive unless underlying cultural or religious tradition makes it so.

Is there, then, a biblical frame of reference for moral reasoning that engages the current debates and the real-life dilemmas that people face? How can we today map such a frame of reference or conception for the household of life in which human beings live? How do we argue from that frame of reference to rules for the human household? How do Christians, acting alongside others, see the whole context of human life in which specific decisions of all kinds need to be made?

I do not think that any simple formula suffices to grasp what a Christian ethic of human well-being should mean. The history of Christian faith exhibits many such formulas. Often these have emerged in the midst of controversy. The ethical yield of the law/

gospel combination is often elusive, especially today. Yes, we know that neither law nor gospel is sufficient without the other. We know we need *both* justice *and* love. But it is hard to hold both these values in mind at the same time, or to act in ways that simultaneously express both of them. We tend to say: on the one hand this, and on the other hand that. But what do justice and love, law and gospel, mean in concrete terms that we, as believers in Jesus Christ and members of his church, living alongside those of other faiths, should *do*? In face of modern moral dilemmas, that is not always easy to say.

I propose the notion of conferring God's blessing as one way of addressing these dilemmas. So far as we know, the terminology of blessing has not often been used for what the specialists call theological anthropology, or the study of human nature in the sight of God. But it seems an obvious choice today. Not only, as we will see, are our Scriptures drenched in this idea, but it has the further advantage of being a very common word that large numbers of people can understand. Without knowing much theology, most people know what is meant by being thankful for blessings. Before meals, we "ask the blessing." We know what is meant by "mixed blessings" or "blessings in disguise." Using this word, we define human nature and value not in terms of minimum capabilities but in terms of a very widely understood symbol of human satisfaction and fulfillment. We are what, in God's sight, we *can* be.

"Blessing" thus means many things: life itself, family, friendships, material sufficiency, worthwhile purpose in life. Above all, it means carrying God's gift of deep well-being with us in all we do and say, ministering that well-being to the lives of others. Blessing is both word and deed. We experience blessing as a calling to exercise the gift of moral responsibility to God's promises in the midst of life, aligning our actions with God's ministry to the human race. By being in Jesus Christ we are able to see that this is true, not only for ourselves, but for our world. God's creative power *and* grace are already at work in both the natural order and the social order, bringing the promise of blessing to human life. Blessing is thus grounded in what some Christians have called "common grace." It is there for all. It thus becomes a key moral category: the gift that unites our different faiths with possibilities in common human experience. It is the possibility of being blessed and of becoming an agent of God's blessing that dynamically constitutes for us the lived-out nature and value of human life.

We are justly allergic to oversimple formulas, yet we cannot resist offering one that seems to sum up what we have said. An ethic of covenantal responsibility to the promise of Genesis 12:1–3 as affirmed by the gospel might, for Christians, go something like this: "So act and speak that the promise of God's blessing in Jesus Christ to all families of the earth is responsibly received and handed on to others in all you do and say." In other words, strive for words and actions that bring blessing, that act as channels for God's favor, to humankind.

This is to say that the nature of human (i.e., not merely biological) life is an inherently covenantal gift from the beginning. The condition of life is responsibility for tending the garden where life has first emerged. Human nature is to have this responsibility, and its value is to be an instrument of God's blessing. We are called to fulfill both by being responsible to God's creating and covenanting promise of blessing to us Christians as believers in Jesus Christ, and through us to "all the families of the earth" (Gen. 12:3). Our witness in the world as regards issues concerning the nature and value of human life rests on our reading-into-action of that covenant promise.

The word of God in which we find this promise gives rise to fresh insights in every age. Each new situation calls forth new perspectives on that familiar story. That is why it is so important, in our own global human situation, to read it again, this time with an eye to what that story means by such words as "responsibility" and "blessing." Created and called by God, we are gifted with responsibility to help shape human affairs so as to bring forth the blessing— the deep well-being—that God intends for God's children, for every family, for every culture, for every nation. And we are called to confront every life issue we meet with an eye to finding the way to receive and pass on that blessing: that gift of deep well-being.

PARALLEL AND INTERACTIVE HERMENEUTICS: SOME ILLUSTRATIVE SCRIPTURE PASSAGES

One of the practices that can deepen our relationships with those of other faiths is the practice of reading related Scriptures together.

I offer commentary here on a few passages seemingly suitable for this purpose, setting forth the gift of responsibility we share for fostering blessing among earth's many tribes and families.

I have already alluded several times to Genesis 12:3 and its parallels. It is not necessary to do so again. But subsequent passages in Hebrew and Christian Scripture refer back to the Abrahamic account, if only to illustrate its centrality. Generation after generation through the Hebrew Scriptures the promise of blessing is renewed, contingent on acceptance of the gift of responsibility. Fathers lay hands on the heads of sons to pass it on. Sons (yes, the perspective is very patriarchal) vie with one another to receive these blessings. Their identities, their whole lives, their reasons for being are at stake.

Genesis 49 gives a vivid impression. Here the aging Jacob-Israel is blessing his sons, the ancestors of the "twelve tribes." These blessings are biographically specific, sometimes embarrassingly so. The ones blessed are in fact families or tribes, each one different in character, each blessed "with a suitable blessing." Blessing here does not mean induction into a single rigid expectation, but into many different expectations, depending on the person or tribe involved. What is blessing to one may not be blessing for another. Each son of Jacob-Israel (including, of course, their descendants) is blessed to be *himself* in his way of being responsible for his life.

Reuben is "as unstable as water" and he "shall no longer excel" (v. 4). "Simeon and Levi are brothers; weapons of violence are their swords... cursed be their anger" (vv. 5, 7). "Issachar is a strong donkey" (v. 14). "Naphtali is a doe let loose" (v. 21). "Benjamin is a ravenous wolf"(v. 27). And so forth. But the blessings given two sons are very different. Judah shall bear the scepter "and the obedience of the peoples is his" (v. 10). And finally the blessing of Joseph in Genesis 49:22–26 rings lyrical changes on the scriptural idea of blessing, given to be passed on to others. Read carefully. These not-very-well-known biblical words are powerful.

> By the God of your father, who will help you,
> by the Almighty who will bless you
> with blessings of heaven above,
> blessings of the deep that lies beneath,
> blessings of the breasts and of the womb.

> The blessings of your father
> are stronger than the blessings of the eternal mountains,
> the bounties of the everlasting hills;
> may they be upon the head of Joseph,
> on the brow of him who was set apart from his brothers.

These words are remarkable. They convey a sense of deep well-being reflecting the powers of the very orders of being: "heaven above," the powers of "the deep," the powers of "breasts and womb." Such foundational favor transcends even the "blessings of the eternal mountains" or the "bounties of the everlasting hills." This blessing is something fundamental that brings with it the empowerment that comes from God through creation and nature and into covenantal history itself.

Much goes wrong with the implementation of the Abrahamic calling over the generations of the life of Israel, and of our own lives as well. Israel's kings forget the promise and try to be like the kings of the nations around them, obsessed with grandeur and military power. The prophets again and again call Israel back to the covenant, and foresee a messiah who will put things right. Jesus Christ is the One who fulfills the covenant promise. Behold the Man: the one who heals the wounds of creation by his woundedness, taking on himself all the wounds of all human beings. The English word "to bless" is in fact derived from an Old English word *bledsian*, which means to consecrate with blood, hence too the French *blesser*, "to wound." Yet this French word is a false cognate: it does not correspond to the English word "bless." For that, the French say *benir* or *benediction*. All this is suggestive, but these connections seem not to have existed for the Hebrew and the Greek.

Whatever the linguistic data may show, the story of Jesus' words and work is drenched in the idea of blessing. At his baptism by John in the Jordan (Matt. 3), Jesus is affirmed (the actual term "blessing" is not used, but the words are tantamount to that) by God in his identity as God's son, given his identity as the one who brings blessing to Israel and the world. "This is my beloved son, with whom I am well pleased." The baptism narrative refers to the children of Abraham (v. 9), so proud of their family identity. Jesus nonetheless calls them a "brood of vipers." The axe will be laid to the root of the tree that does not bring forth good fruit. This passage, in which Jesus receives a blessing from God that defines his obedience and therefore his unique responsibility to the covenant promise, parallels Genesis 12:1–3, in which Abraham receives the blessing recounted at length above. What is conveyed in these acts comes close to having the same meaning as salvation, and the responsibility for passing it on.

The Gospel accounts of Jesus' life and preaching are full of echoes of this theme of covenantal blessing. The Beatitudes in Matthew 5 come immediately to mind: "Blessed are the merciful. Blessed are the peacemakers. . . . Blessed are those who are persecuted for righteousness' sake . . . ," and so forth. Here the Greek word translated "blessed" is *makarios*, a different term from that used in the Greek version of Genesis 12:3. Yet we are dealing here with a close synonym. Using the English word "blessing" or "blessed" for both does not mislead. Compare Matthew 23:13–39, where Jesus' words of blessing are countered by his words of woe upon people of a very different kind: "woe to you, scribes and pharisees, hypocrites!" (v. 13). The same words are repeated in verses 16, 23, 25, 27, and 29, each time adding details to the indictment. There are no blessings here, but only curses. The imprecations pile up, until at the end we read, "For I tell you, you will not see me again, until you say, 'Blessed is the one who comes in the name of the Lord'" (v. 39).

An interesting question is whether the Beatitudes simply say that those who are merciful, peacemakers, and so forth will live lives of well-being rather than woe, or whether these words in effect *grant* or *confer* blessing upon all these sorts of righteous ones. Are these clauses in Matthew 5 *acts* of blessing like those of Israelite fathers of old? Is Jesus here giving gifts of responsibility to be what these words say, commissioning these sorts of people to fulfill their identities in this way? The words are important not only for their intrinsic sense but because they introduce the Sermon on the Mount, where Jesus speaks of not destroying the law of Moses, but of fulfilling it.

And look at the parables of the sheep and the goats in Matthew 25:31–46. This, too, is a parable about blessing (see v. 34). Here the word is *eulogemenoi*, the same word used in the Greek of Genesis 12:3. Taking the parable as referring only to individuals who may or may not have had compassion on "the least of these," we forget that those concerned are called the "nations." Of course there were no nation-states in the modern sense in biblical times. The Greek word is *ethne*, from which we derive the word "ethnic." So the meaning is "peoples," however organized politically. The issue is whether the peoples (or families or tribes) practice social justice, whether they order their lives so as to bring blessing to the least privileged of the "families of the earth." To those people who have done so, giving human life its true value in the public dimension, the king (or "Son of Man" as in verse 31) will say, "Come, you that are blessed by my Father, inherit the kingdom prepared for you from the foundation of the world" (Matt 15:34). The words "you that are blessed by my Father" clearly refer to those whose lives with one another have fulfilled the responsibility laid on them by having received God's blessing (Gen. 12:3). The question here is whether the responsibility to "the least of these" engendered by "blessing" has or has not been fulfilled. The presence of the Son of Man and his followers and the way they are treated generates a kind of litmus test as to whether the nation concerned has taken on the gift of responsibility for engendering blessing or deep well-being. This is the covenantal context in the sight of God that gives human life its nature and its value.

The theme of Abrahamic blessing also occurs in New Testament passages *about* Jesus, where we have the beginnings of what the church has called Christology. Peter's sermon at the Beautiful Gate of the Temple represented in Acts 3 lays down one of the church's earliest expressions of witness to Jesus' identity. It is a sermon about blessing in the sense of healing, in this case the healing of a lame man. It is striking that this sermon, so definitive of some central themes of early Christianity—servanthood, crucifixion, resurrection—ends with verses that bring us straight back to the covenantal blessing of Abraham in Genesis 12:3. It is this promise of blessing, Peter tells his audience, that Jesus Christ fulfills in his church.

> You are the descendants of the prophets and of the covenant that God gave to your ancestors, saying to Abraham, "And in your descendants all the families of the earth shall be blessed." When God raised up his servant, he sent him first to you, to bless you by turning each of you from your wicked ways. (Acts 3: 25–26, NRSV)

"Blessing" here takes on a decidedly ethical meaning. It is turning us away from our wickedness, toward the fulfillment of our covenantal identity.

Many more New Testament passages ring the changes on similar themes. See Matthew 11:6; Luke 6:28; Acts 20:35; Romans 15:27, 15:29; 1 Corinthians 4:12; 14:16; Titus 2:13 Revelation 7:12; 14:13. It seems to follow from passages such as these that the people of God have responsibility not only for inheriting blessing (salvation, grace, well-being) for themselves but for seeing to it that God's intention that all earth's families are blessed is carried out.

Above all there is Galatians 3. What is the relation here between "blessing" and "grace"? Are these near synonyms, or are they not? My impression is that "blessing" links the grace of God through Abraham to the common human experience of Gentiles, even if the latter are not aware of it. See verses 8 and 9: "And the scripture, foreseeing that God would justify the Gentiles by faith, declared the gospel beforehand to Abraham, saying 'All the Gentiles shall be blessed in you.' For this reason, those who believe are blessed with Abraham who believed." The passage seems almost to equate "justification by faith" with "blessing." This blessing seems identified with what is elsewhere called salvation. See verse 14: "that in Christ Jesus the blessing of Abraham might come to the Gentiles, so that we might receive the promise of the Spirit though faith."

The word "blessing" seems associated with the Gentiles in particular. It would seem that this term is made in Scripture to carry the weight of the idea that God's grace is already at work in "those who believe" whose faith is not yet (and may never be) explicitly "Christian." Believers are then to join hands with this sort of blessing at work in common human experience, and in the experience of other faiths.

A program of shared reading of such passages and others, including Qur'anic parallels, by representatives of the different faiths, could well be part of a Faith and Order program of enlarging our categories. Already this is being done in many situations not formally connected with the Christian ecumenical movement. Our task would be to illumine the common responsibility of Abrahamic faiths for addressing today's human condition, a task in which the notion of God's blessing upon the earth's families, in part through us, could play a significant role.

LEWIS S. MUDGE

A PROPOSAL FOR BEFORE, OR AFTER, THE WAR?

Some shifts of theological consciousness come about only when violence or plague sweep a former world away. That may be the case for the proposal in this paper. With many others, I take for granted that we are headed for events that will make a major historical break in the human condition as we have known it since the dawn of modernity. What might such a break consist of? A global financial collapse? The use of nuclear weapons by terrorists and nuclear replies by the United States, Britain, France, or Israel? Or merely a more contemporary version of Spengler's *Decline of the West*, in which the United States would cease, out of its own folly, to be a superpower and other powers would inevitably become realigned? One can pray for the latter sort of break. It would risk violence, but would not need to become violent. It could be a good thing for us and for humanity.

    The first duty of those who believe that religious communities might yet have some influence in the world is to do their best to help humanity come to the softest landing possible, much as happened in South Africa in the nineties when most were expecting a bloodbath. But proposals such as this one may not (to say the least) be able to head off a catastrophe. They may not come into their own until some global paroxysm has brought the human race, or what is left of it, to its knees, or its senses. A lesson comes from a history I know well (others could give their own versions of it). From 1937 onward, as war in Europe drew near, theologians and church leaders met repeatedly to gather up what they had learned from the preceding half-century of nascent Christian ecumenical effort, with the idea of launching a bold new initiative. Nearly simultaneously, theological writings were under way that were later to become enormously influential. Dietrich Bonhoeffer was already at work on his *Ethics*, Reinhold Niebuhr was giving the Gifford Lectures in Edinburgh, afterward published as *The Nature and Destiny of Man*. (German soldiers were marching into Poland as he reached his conclusion in September 1939.) Ecumenical thinking and planning continued underground, and in safe locations like Geneva.

Little of this activity was to bear fruit openly until after the war, with the formation of the World Council of Churches at Amsterdam in 1948 and a renaissance of theological studies in the West. These developments, of course, followed closely on the formation of the United Nations and the adoption of the Universal Declaration of Human Rights. No one in that postwar dawn could but be aware that in the conflict just concluded "Christian nations" had opposed one another in the skies, on the seas, and in the trenches. Christian combatants on each side had fought against equally committed Christians on the other, just as Sunnis and Shi'ites are doing in Iraq now. The mood at the war's end in 1945 was to say "never again." A network among the churches needed to be built that could remain intact across whatever new political and ideological chasms might open in the future. The interreligious dimension was, for the most part, not yet on the horizon.

Now, in the year 2007, much has changed, but much is also hauntingly familiar. Christian ecumenism has accomplished much. But many of its major goals remain unfulfilled. Adherents of the Abrahamic faiths are already fighting one another in Palestine, Afghanistan, and Iraq. Such struggles threaten to ignite yet another global conflagration: financial, biological, nuclear, or otherwise. And once again we need to lay plans together, this time on an interreligious basis, that we pray will bear fruit in time to head off such a tragedy. Perhaps our efforts will turn out to have been already too late for that. Perhaps our present thinking will turn out to mean more when the next war—this time an intercultural and interreligious war—is over, and once more we say to each other "never again." And again we try to weave a network of trust, solidarity, and responsibility, this time among our three faiths and other faiths, a tissue of relationships that we hope can resist all ideological and political forces that seek to tear it apart.

NOTES

1. Some will ask, why not include faiths other than the Abrahamic ones? I am well aware of the riches for humankind offered by the Hindu, Buddhist, Confucian and many other religious cultures. I do not mean to denigrate any of them by omission.

But the three Abrahamic faiths have characteristics that urge us to ask what their new relationships might mean and what they might do together for such a world as this. These faiths have been among the worst religious troublemakers through the centuries. Just to achieve a world without their involvements in religio-political violence would be more than well worth doing.

2. The World Council of Churches has for years had a department dealing with interreligious issues, headed by such excellent scholars as Stanley Samartha and Hans Ucko. But the council has repeatedly failed to give such matters any serious programmatic centrality. The recent Ninth Assembly of the WCC (Porto Allegre, 2006) failed to take any action on the subject despite the enthusiasm of the then-moderator of the Central Committee, Catholicos Aram I of Cilicia, Lebanon, where interreligious issues are a part of daily life. The current reorganization of the Council appears to be further subordinating these concerns.

3. The WCC ecclesiology and ethics project brought Faith and Order into contact with ecumenical social ethics, but there seems to have been a reversion to Faith and Order business as usual afterward.

4. *The People of God among All God's People: Frontiers in Christian Mission,* Report from a Theological Roundtable Sponsored by the Christian Conference of Asia and the Council for World Mission, ed. Philip L. Wickeri, Hong Kong, November 11–17, 1999, 28.

5. See the report of this study, Thomas F. Best and Martin Robra, eds., *Ecclesiology and Ethics: Ecumenical Ethical Engagement, Moral Formation, and the Nature of the Church* (Geneva: WCC Publications, 1997).

6. For a most helpful treatment of the theme of responsibility in relation to Christian ethics in particular, see William Schweiker, *Responsibility and Christian Ethics* (New York and Cambridge: Cambridge University Press, 1993).

7. The term "covenant," like other terms used in this argument, is by no means uniformly received even among different Christian groups. Most of the preponderant "catholic" (small "c") traditions—Roman Catholic, Orthodox, Anglican—give greater centrality to the idea of sacramental imagination. These traditions will likely find the notion of "covenant," as this paper sees it, less

than compelling. To capture a greater part of Christianity's content, one needs to speak, as Rosemary Ruether and many others do, of covenant and sacrament. I myself represent the Reformed or Calvinist tradition, with its distinctive covenantal emphasis. I choose the notion of covenant for this argument not only because it is part of my own theological upbringing but because it is at least present in all three Abrahamic faiths, while the notion of "sacrament" is not. It is even possible that "covenanting" will appeal to Christian "catholics" as an inter-Abrahamic bridge category precisely because it does not directly engage their sacramental theologies. But I know full well that talk of covenantal responsibility will not gather all Christians in, any more than it will engage all Muslims or all Jews. I am grateful to Larry Rasmussen for pointing this out and for also passing on an anecdote. He remembers a long-ago comment by Roger Shinn concerning an exchange with a Muslim scholar. The latter said, citing his preference for Calvinism among the Christianities he had met, "It's the Christian version of Islam!"

Chapter 19

THE BUDDHIST-CHRISTIAN ENCOUNTER IN THE UNITED STATES: REFLECTIONS ON CHRISTIAN PRACTICES

Amos Yong

> After being presented at Oberlin II, this paper was originally published in *Border Crossings: Explorations of an Interdisciplinary Historian—Festschrift for Irving Hexham*, ed. Ulrich van der Heyden and Andreas Feldtkeller (Stuttgart: Franz Steiner Verlag, 2008), 457–72. It is reprinted here with permission from the author and Franz Steiner Verlag.[1]

The Christian encounter with Buddhism stretches back perhaps fifteen millennia to when Nestorian missionaries first traveled the Silk Road and arrived in East Asia.[2] Along the way, Christians have engaged in a wide range of practices in their interactions with Buddhists. Some missionaries and apologists have debated with Buddhists while others have adopted what we today might call more a dialogical approach that resulted in "Buddhistic" forms of Chinese Christianity.[3] Both strategies, as well as others, can be seen in the Christian encounter with Buddhism in America.

My goals in this essay are twofold, corresponding to the two parts that follow: first, to provide a broad historical overview of the various ways in which Christians and Buddhists have interacted in America, and second to reflect theologically and missiologically on Christian practices vis-à-vis American Buddhism in particular and the Christian encounter with other faiths in general. My thesis is that Christian interreligious practices have perennially been multifaceted, in various ways shaped by the many situations and contexts in which Christians find themselves in relationship to people of other faiths. In this paper I will seek to illustrate this thesis by looking specifically at the history of the relationship between Buddhism and Christianity in America.

THE BUDDHIST-CHRISTIAN ENCOUNTER IN AMERICA: A BRIEF OVERVIEW

The first Buddhists to arrive in America were Chinese and Japanese workers and immigrants in the mid-nineteenth century.[4] Yet for most of these families and individuals, Buddhism did not function as a religion in their lives as Christianity might have for Christians. Rather as with many East Asians throughout history, Buddhism has been interwoven with strands of Daoism, Confucianism, and local religious practices so that it is unidentifiable as a distinctive religious identity. Further, the fact of the matter is that without access to temples or prior to the establishment of the Sangha, Buddhist practices were more or less individualized if maintained at all. It would not be until 1899 that the first Jodo Shinshu missionaries from Japan (representing the Pure Land Buddhist tradition) would arrive in San Francisco in order to specifically establish that branch of Buddhism in North America.[5]

Yet during the nineteenth century, Caucasian Americans also began to discover Buddhism. This American fascination with Buddhism can be traced back to intellectuals like Emerson, Thoreau, Whitman, Bronson Alcott, Edwin Arnold, and many others. Thomas Tweed has described this as the encounter between Victorian culture and Buddhism on American soil.[6] In his account, while overall initial American images of Buddhism were fairly negative—in terms of its passivity, its atheism, and its impersonalism, at least in some readings—the Buddha and his Dharma did find a hearing among a small group of intellectuals. Those in pursuit of esoteric religious and philosophical ideas found in Buddhism lofty and yet intriguing ideals on the one hand, as well as a new way of understanding the traditional Christian idea of the immortality of the soul (in terms of karmic reincarnation) on the other. Others who were drawn to the Romantic movement saw in Buddhism a naturalistic worldview that was a congenial alternative to traditional theism. Still others found in Buddhism a rational philosophy that did not necessarily require the rejection of Christianity but helped to stabilize theism on a more secure foundation in the face of higher criticism, Darwinism and modern science, and the emerging discourse of comparative religion. For many, Buddhism was compatible with Victorian cultural themes, especially with regard to how the Buddhist articulation of a noble personal ethic fit with the Victorian emphasis on self-reliance. Ironically, as Tweed's portrayal shows, it was Buddhist ideas that in a sense rescued the theistic faith of some of these interreligious explorers, albeit while providing further religious and philosophical rationale for late-nineteenth-century American values like individualism, activism, and cultural optimism.

These nineteenth-century developments culminated at the World's Parliament of Religions (WPR) held alongside the World's Columbian Exposition Fair in Chicago in 1893.[7] Representatives of all the major religious traditions of the world had a platform to present their ideas. Speaking on behalf of Buddhism were Anagarika Dharmapala (1864–1933) from Theravada Ceylon and the Japanese Zen master Shaku Soen (1859–1919). The former focused on the commandments of (Theravada) Buddhism while the latter spoke on the laws of cause and effect, arguing for the compatibility of Buddhism with the world of modern science.[8] As their ideas were accessibly presented, the WPR communicated the impression that Buddhism had by now secured its place on the stage of world religions. These speakers were careful, however, as well-behaved guests, to neither overemphasize the major differences between Buddhism and Christianity, nor insist too blatantly on Buddhism's superiority to Christian faith.

In the wake of the WPR, Dharmapala, Soen, and other Buddhists traveled throughout the United States introducing Buddhism to interested audiences. Soen's personal secretary at the WPR, D. T. Suzuki (1870–1966), would carry on his teacher's work into the next century.[9] Widely published both at the scholarly and lay levels,[10] Suzuki has perhaps done more than anyone else to demystify Buddhism in general and Zen Buddhism in particular for Americans. By the mid-twentieth century, his students had emerged as leaders of the movement to Westernize Zen Buddhism in the American context. Chief among these were Dwight Goddard (1861–1939), whose *The Buddhist Bible* (1938) was to leave a lasting impression among Christian inquirers into Buddhism;[11] Alan Watts (1915–73), a onetime Episcopalian priest whose initial exposure to Buddhism was through the lectures and writings of Suzuki;[12] and, later, Beat generation figures like Allen Ginsberg (1926–97), Jack Kerouac (1922–69), and Gary Snyder (b. 1930).

Given these developments, it would be unsurprising to find that those in the Zen Buddhist tradition have been the most eager to engage in the more formal scholarly dialogues between Buddhists and Christians in the United States. Yet at the same time, the broad spectrum of Buddhist and Christian traditions was represented in the emerging American dialogue scene.

With the abolishment in 1965 of the national-origins quotas limiting immigration from Eastern Hemisphere countries and the development of religious studies programs and departments in American colleges and universities shortly thereafter, the academic study of Buddhism took on the task of interpreting Buddhism not just as an Eastern religious tradition but also as a dynamic and flourishing form of American religiosity.

In this context, the first International Buddhist-Christian Conference was called and held at the University of Hawaii in 1980, organized by scholar-practitioners David W. Chappell and George Tanabe Jr. Out of this and subsequent meetings, the Society of Buddhist-Christian Studies was formed (with its annual journal *Buddhist-Christian Studies*) and other dialogical conferences were envisioned and then held. Out of these conferences, one especially vibrant set of interchanges that occurred on various occasions over the course of two decades (1984–2004) was the International Buddhist Christian Theological Encounter Group cochaired by Zen Buddhist philosopher Masao Abe and Christian theologian John B. Cobb Jr.[13] By the time of the first meeting, the latter had already published a major book on Buddhist-Christian dialogue, engaging specifically with the Japanese tradition of Pure Land or Amida Buddhism, while Abe was on the verge of becoming a household name in Buddhist-Christian dialogue circles with many of his books and essays translated into English during and since that time.[14]

While it is beyond the scope of this paper to go into the details of these dialogues,[15] allow me to briefly summarize some of their key features. First, given the breadth of Christian and Buddhist traditions represented at the dialogue, participants deployed a wide range of philosophical, hermeneutical, and theological perspectives and methods in their approaches; this range was even further expanded when Jewish thinkers were invited into the conversation.[16] Second, proselytism and apologetics were a secondary concern at best, especially since individuals were found on both sides of the dialogue table that had begun in one tradition but by now either had converted to or were in the process of negotiating dual religious identities. In either of these cases, the other side knew just as much if not more about the two religious traditions as their conversation partners. Often, participants came out of the dialogues even more deeply committed to their own tradition, although certainly also having been transformed variously in the process of engaging the discussion. Finally, the dialogues involved theologians, philosophers, and scholars who were also practitioners of their respective religious traditions. Hence the dialogues were engaged at a high academic level, but were at the same time deeply informed by confessional commitments and practices.

This confluence between dialogue and practices has been the central feature in discussions between Christian and Buddhist monastics. In these encounters, there are often scheduled periods of personal and group meditation, with the latter sometimes involving members of both traditions meditating together in silence, rotating between formal and informal dialogue sessions.[17] Of course, since Protestant churches lack a developed contemplative tradition, most of the Christians involved in these monastic dialogues with Buddhist practitioners come from the Roman Catholic tradition. In any case, while similar to the academic conversations in which mutual understanding and exploration are prioritized over proselytism or apologetics, the monastic interreligious encounters are different in that the goals of personal transformation are much more central and pronounced because of the commitment to meditative practice. But in the midst of the alternating silence and conversation, there is a deep sense of communion testified to by participants from both traditions. There is something that happens when sitting together that nurtures this kind of affinity which does not happen when engaged in the more formal academic exchanges of paper presentations and responses.

Yet these developments on the monastic front mirror developments "on the American ground." Most non-Asian and non-immigrant laypeople who may or may not be formal converts to Buddhism come from across the sociopolitical and economic spectrum of American society and are inevitably drawn to especially the Buddhist practice of meditation. And since the 1960s, meditation centers from across the Buddhist spectrum can now be found all over the country. Yet as adaptations of the various Tibetan, Nepalese, Tantric, Theravadan (also known as Vipassana or insight meditation), and Ch'an/Zen traditions, what may be unique in the American context is the hybridity that continually shapes Buddhist meditative practices. Practitioners and their instructors and teachers are less likely to insist that there is the unique or pure form of Buddhist practice; rather, a blending of Buddhist traditions with psychotherapeutic strategies, medicinal and health-care prescriptions and recommendations, and, to a growing extent, socially aware and engaged practices are increasingly the norm.

Mention of socially Engaged Buddhism in the West requires further comment.[18] Buddhist mindfulness and compassion, its practitioners insist, produces an engaged rather than detached Buddhist disposition. Whether it be the Buddhist Peace Fellowship, Prison Zen Practice, International Network of Engaged Buddhists, the Benevolent Organization for Development, Health and Insight, the Free Tibet Movement, the Friends of the Western Buddhist Order, or others, Engaged Buddhists recognize the interdependence that characterizes life on this planet and therefore are committed to addressing important issues related to the flourishing of all people as part of their practice. As with other forms of American Buddhism, Engaged Buddhists hail from the wide range of Buddhist traditions, often combining insights and practices from various streams of Buddhism in their lives. And as is increasingly the case with socially mindful movements, Engaged

Buddhists are generally nonsectarian, seeking alliances with any and all, including those in other faiths, who are willing to work with them on issues of common concern.

I now wish to turn our attention back to 1965 when, as mentioned previously, immigration and naturalization laws were liberalized to reopen America's doors to Asia. With the influx of Asian immigrants came not only the Hare Krishnas and Hindu gurus of all stripes, but also the masses of East Asians (Chinese, Korean, and Japanese) whose identities have been shaped over time by various traditions of Buddhism. Further, refugees from Tibet, Sri Lanka, and Southeast Asia (including Vietnam, Laos, and Cambodia) have brought with them varying forms of Buddhist belief and practices as well. The result is that over the course of the last generation, immigrants from across the Asian continent have erected temples, built educational institutions of different types and sizes, and established transnational Buddhist networks.[19] The concerns of these immigrant Buddhists, of course, are much different from those of nonimmigrant and non–Asian American practitioners and converts to Buddhism. The former are worried about assimilation and adaptation, as well as about linguistic, social, and economic factors that do not impinge in the same way on the latter. Yet the Buddhist commitments of Asian immigrants are perhaps for these reasons all the more intense, to the point that Buddhist missionaries are now arriving on Western shores in greater numbers than ever before. Their motivations have been not only the pastoral care of the growing Buddhist diaspora but also the commitment to seeking American converts.[20]

This explosion of Buddhism resulting from Asian immigration to America raises many interesting issues regarding the present and future of Buddhism in this country.[21] I note the following rather generalized comparisons and contrasts:

1. Whereas Asian immigrant Buddhists are almost always ethnically constituted, American Buddhists were at one point almost all white, but now are increasingly diversified.

2. Whereas Asian Buddhist traditions have generally viewed the monastic life as a higher vocational calling, Asian American and American Buddhists tend to emphasize lay expressions of the tradition.

3. Whereas Asian Buddhist traditions have tended to be hierarchical and authoritarian, American Buddhism has been much more democratic and egalitarian.

4. Whereas Asian Buddhism has generally been patriarchal, American Buddhist traditions have been much more open to the participation of and leadership by women.

5. Whereas some Asian Buddhists have focused either on the centrality of the Enlightenment experience and others on the ceremonial aspects of the tradition, Asian American and American Buddhists are much more focused on everyday life and experience.

6. Whereas Asian Buddhism has emphasized the doctrinal elements of the Dharma, American Buddhism has been much more focused on the practical expressions of the Dharma.

7. Whereas traditional Buddhism has evolved a number of highly standardized and ritualized forms, American Buddhism has been more exploratory, innovative, and experimental in its approaches.

8. Whereas ethnic Buddhism in America has retained a palpable Asian sensibility, the Americanized version of Buddhism has a distinctively "Protestant" character (e.g., there are now Buddhist "Sunday schools," churches, and ministers).

9. Relatedly, whereas ethnic Buddhism is generally sectarian, American Buddhism is generally ecumenical, less concerned about maintaining proper boundaries, and more open to intra- and inter-Buddhist cooperation.

Now I should also be quick to emphasize that these are broad generalizations that mask continuities amidst the apparent discontinuities and vice versa. At the same time, these observations highlight the important issues confronting American Buddhists of all stripes. Perhaps most important of these may be two major questions: that which concerns the transition between the first and second generations of ethnic or immigrant Buddhism in America and that which concerns American Buddhist identity overall. With regard to the former, the issues are familiar. Demographic changes have produced more diffused patterns of immigration, meaning that there may be either more temples (and as a result, stiffer competition) or fewer temples (and as a result, lack of accessibility in order to sustain ties to the Buddhist community). Further, the costs of building, maintaining, and perhaps later expanding physical structures are usually greater than immigrant communities can bear.[22] Finally, and most importantly, the second generation usually does not have the same religious commitments as their parents. More often than not, Americanization involves a process of assimilation and accommodation that leaves the "religion of the parents" less attractive to those who were born or grew up in America.[23]

Interestingly, however, this question of the second generation affects not only immigrant or ethnic Buddhist communities but also the white baby-boomer generation that embraced Buddhist meditational practice and then got married and began raising children. Generations X and Y (also known as the Millennial group) are usually not brought up in self-consciously Buddhist homes or environments and often are left to find their own way.

All of these issues open up what may be an obvious question: what does it mean to be an American Buddhist, or what is the definition of American Buddhism? From the viewpoint of immigrant Buddhists, at least those from East and Southeast Asia (in contrast to South Asia), the Buddhist identity is never defined in any distinctive manner. Rather these Asian identities are complex wholes of interwoven strands drawn deeply from various religious, philosophical, and ritual traditions. It is perhaps among some white converts to Buddhism that the taking of the Three Refuges—in the Buddha, the Dharma, and the Sangha—provides the basis for a distinctive Buddhist identity. But just as many if not more white practitioners of the Buddhist path go so far as to say that to embrace a Buddhist identity requires no formal doctrinal commitments whatsoever.[24] And finally, there are also American Buddhists who do not consider Buddhist practice to be exclusive of other religious ways of life.[25] A common testimony among these converts is the ironic admission that for them, "Buddhism was also a gateway [back] to Christianity."[26] How should Christians respond in the face of this fluid and dynamic American Buddhist landscape?

TOWARD A CHRISTIAN THEOLOGY OF INTERRELIGIOUS PRACTICES IN DIALOGUE WITH BUDDHISM

The preceding overview of Buddhism in America has been succinct in the extreme and does not do justice to the complexities of the American Buddhist experience. Nevertheless my interests as a Christian theologian are to simply sketch what might be called the lay of the land with regard to American Buddhism in order that we might chart some ways forward for the Buddhist-Christian encounter in the twenty-first century. In the remainder of this essay I suggest that Christians should learn from the history of Buddhism in America that a wide range of postures, attitudes, and practices are essential for a vital interchange. This includes at least three overall approaches that I call *social engagement*, *interreligious dialogue*, and *evangelical apologetics*. I proceed to discuss these in order.

There are at three aspects to the Buddhist-Christian encounter at the level of *social engagement*: the interpersonal, the communal, and the sociopolitical. With regard to the interpersonal dimension, I am thinking specifically about refugee Buddhist communities. Insofar as American Christians have been and remain hosts to a large number of Asian Buddhists who are forced refugees from their land of birth, to that same degree our primary obligation is to demonstrate what I have elsewhere called the hospitality of God.[27] Motivated here by the parables of the Good Samaritan and of the Sheep and the Goats, I suggest that Christian hospitality to the stranger, the naked, the hungry, and poor must include religious others who are also refugees, exiles, and immigrants of various types. Whether it is enabling their setting down new roots, learning new languages, adapting to new social customs, or simply obtaining needed employment or other forms of relief and assistance, the Christian task is to meet the needs of their (new) neighbors, when it is in their means to do so.

This level of interpersonal engagement leads naturally to a discussion about community building. What I have in mind here is the kinds of local projects such as housing developments, institutional formation, and social networking that are essential for any new community to find its bearings in a strange land. The focus here, however, is in specific local communities so that the level of engagement is midway between that of merely interpersonal relationships and that of overly cumbersome bureaucratic structures. Projects at this level might include Christian contributions to the development of community centers and even religious sites. This is the praxis of what might be called communal hospitality.

A third level of social engagement, however, might be that involving Christians and Buddhist, forging alliances (that may not be exclusive of those in other faiths) to address common social, political, and economic concerns. We have already discussed the emergence of Engaged Buddhism (above). These are individuals committed to a compassionate engagement with social issues because they are drawn to the ideal of the Bodhisattva's vow to desist from entering into Nirvana so long as there remain any suffering sentient beings. At this level, then, social engagement focused on alleviating poverty, injustice, crime, and war, among other social ills, requires the goodwill of many people working patiently and persistently across religious boundaries.[28] Here Christians can, should, and must join forces with all whom God might raise up—and this would include their Engaged Buddhist coreligionists—to realize the peace, justice, and righteousness that anticipates the eschatological kingdom of God.[29]

A second level of Christian engagement with American Buddhism is what I call "interreligious dialogue." Now of course, social engagement cannot proceed without dialogue of some kind. But socially engaging dialogue may or may not turn to explicitly religious—explicitly Christian or Buddhist—concerns. The interreligious dialogue I am now discussing, however, is focused precisely on religious matters. In the following, I flesh this out in terms of academic dialogue, the dialogue of spiritual practices, and the dialogue of religious ideas. (Before doing so, however, I want to specifically identify, and reject, any notion that what I am calling "interreligious dialogue" in this discussion is understood merely instrumentally to serve the purposes of religious conversion. I believe there is a place for religious conversion, but I call the kind of dialogical engagement directed toward conversion "evangelical apologetics." We return to that topic momentarily. Here, however, our focus is on interreligious dialogue for the many reasons other than that designed to produce religious conversion.)

The academic encounter generally involves experts from both traditions interacting from out of their research and scholarship. The goals at this level, as already mentioned (above), are to achieve mutual understanding. Academics, of course, do what they do for many reasons, not the least of which is intellectual curiosity, the love of teaching, or a predisposition to scholarly activity. In each of these cases, then, the purposes of interreligious dialogue between Christian and Buddhist scholars and academics would have as many different rationales as participants. But there is a specific domain of academic interreligious dialogue that I think needs further comment: that involving the scientific disciplines.[30] While Christians and Buddhists can gather around the dialogue table representing a wide range of perspectives from the humanities, there is a growing realization that their religious perspectives belong in the dialogue with the natural and human sciences. In this case I am referring not just to Christians in dialogue with scientists or Buddhists in dialogue with scientists, but rather Christians and Buddhists and scientists interacting in what might be called a "tri-logue."[31] Of course, such a tri-logue is exponentially more complex than any dialogue because adding a conversation partner to the dialogue table multiplies the conversational directions. However, Christians have much to learn from how Buddhists are engaging the sciences and vice versa,[32] even as the sciences have much to benefit from a more inclusive encounter with the world of many religions. And insofar as we live in a world dominated by science, technology, and modern medicine, and inasmuch as there are urgent matters demanding our attention such as global warming, the environment, and ethical issues surrounding our use (and possible abuse) of science, to that same extent the tri-logue between Christianity, Buddhism, and science is not a luxury but a necessity.

The interreligious dialogue also includes, I suggest, the dialogue of spiritual practices. Here I am referring not only to the monastic interreligious dialogue that we have already seen but also the dialogue between lay practitioners of meditation. In fact, at the lay level, many people who consider themselves Christians are avid advocates of Buddhist meditation practices,[33] even as there are also those who reject either the Christian or Buddhist label but have found much that is valuable in the contemplative traditions of both Christianity and Buddhism. In the latter case, meditators find themselves in group situations in which the interreligious dialogue revolves around the spiritual practices concomitant with, informed by, and supportive of meditation.[34] Here again, the reasons for dialogical engagement vary according to the reasons for embracing the practice, and these range from health and lifestyle concerns to dealing with anxiety to deeply spiritual motivations. Inevitably, however, meditators are less inclined to dwell on doctrinal, theological, or philosophical matters if these fail to illuminate practice in some way.[35] For many of these, interreligious dialogue is both intrapersonal (involving the depths of their own beings) as well as interpersonal (involving other dialogue partners).[36] Many Buddhist practitioners interested in dialogue would consider dialogue itself to be a form of spiritual practice.[37]

This leads to a third level of interreligious dialogue, often the most controversial one: that involving religious ideas, including the doctrines, theologies, and philosophies of both Christian and Buddhist traditions. The reasons for the controversy have something to do with the (alleged) similarities and dissimilarities between Christian and Buddhist traditions. Those concerned about the similarities may be worried about religious syncretism or may just be interested in pursuing the question of how to understand such similarities and what their implications might be.[38] The dissimilarities, however, are just as controversial since they raise the question about how to define Christianity, Buddhism, and religion. Further, they also challenge the sometimes superficial assumptions about the possibility of Christian dialogue with and understanding of Buddhism, and vice versa. Finally, of course, there are the question of truth claims and the fundamental claims regarding salvation and damnation on the Christian side, and regarding suffering, greed, ignorance, karmic consequences, and enlightenment on the Buddhist side. Which tradition has the greater explanatory power and why? These are very complex matters, and I am convinced we are still at the very beginning stages of the Buddhist-Christian dialogue and that we will need much more time before being able to identify the appropriate comparative categories through which we can properly engage the issues.[39]

Finally, I want to discuss what I call the "evangelical" approach to the Buddhist-Christian encounter. By this, I mean a posture that prioritizes evangelizing religious others because of the conviction that the Christian gospel or the Buddhist Four Nobel Truths are indeed "good news" (hence: "evangelical") for all people and not only for those who are already Christians or Buddhists. Again, there are at least three aspects of this evangelical approach to the encounter: that related to religious freedom, that related to evangelistic strategies, and that related to apologetics. I treat these in reverse order.

To begin, evangelical apologetics is but the flip side, I would argue, of interreligious dialogue.[40] By this, I mean that any genuine dialogical encounter must involve religious representatives who have sufficient understanding of and commitment to their own faith tradition so that something is at stake in the discussion. Without involvement of such individuals, no dialogue ensues; rather a monologue of agreeing voices actually covers up what is really taking place. But given the presence of what I am calling "evangelical apologetics," an authentic context of interreligious exchange emerges whereby the explanation of one's religious position at some point in the dialogic process is actually also an apology for that position.[41] Ironically, the greatest interreligious apologists are those who know other faith traditions just as well as their own.[42] In these cases, one is engaged not only in what might be called "negative apologetics" that defends one's position against the criticisms of others but also "positive apologetics," wherein one critically interacts with the other tradition on its own terms. It should also go without saying, I hope, that evangelical apologetics is a two-way street: Christians who insist on having their turn on the proclamation and apologetic side of the dialogue must also be ready to listen.

A related task of evangelical apologetics is a kind of dialogical engagement that seeks to understand the religious faith of others for the purposes of facilitating smoother interreligious interactions focused on religious conversion. This is what some missiologists have called "contextualization" or "inculturation." The key principle here is that evangelism and mission must be sensitive to the thought forms (worldview), practices, and values of the receiving culture in order to minimize misunderstanding and maximize the possibility of reception. This is a part of all interreligious processes designed to establish, sustain, and perpetuate a religious tradition in a foreign context. We have seen that Buddhist missionaries, immigrant Buddhist communities, and American converts to Buddhism have wrestled with precisely this set of questions, and it may even be possible that Christians can learn from the experiences of their Buddhist interlocutors on this issue. What I want to warn against, however, is any kind of approach to interreligious dialogue that is not honest about the evangelical motivations for engaging the dialogue. Of course, our dialogue partners are usually able to see through our motivations and identify other purposes that bring us to the dialogue table. I am not saying that dialogue focused on missionization and evangelization is unacceptable. I am simply saying that if that is our objective, it should not be hidden, and that we should not step up to the interreligious dialogue table involving science, academics, monastics, and so forth, and pretend to be there for the purpose of fostering mutual understanding leading perhaps to mutual transformation, if in fact we are not. There is a time and place for everything, and it is important to be honest about the intentions behind our presence at the dialogue table.

This raises questions about the strategies for evangelical approaches to the interfaith encounter in general and to the Buddhist-Christian encounter in particular. Of course, evangelical apologetics needs to be engaged civilly and respectfully. But there are at least two sides to such an imperative: first, that such respect is earned in the give-and-take of dialogue borne out of deep commitments, and second, that such respect needs to be accorded up front to the dialogue participant as a matter of common human courtesy. Yet this element of common human courtesy and decency should apply not only in the case of evangelical apologetics but also in any evangelical approach to religious others. Here I have in mind specifically any and all forms of evangelization and missionization that may be deployed in approaching people of other faiths. I would insist that all forms of coercive proselytism—including making promises regarding financial or material reward in exchange for conversion, or the more subtle forms of manipulation that might be applied to people in vulnerable existential situations, or the structural forms of pressure that impinge on refugee populations, and so on—do not respect the integrity of people as religious agents.[43]

Evangelical approaches must guard against adopting unfair tactics aimed at generating converts. Of course, this cuts both ways and applies to evangelical agents in all traditions. At the same time, the principle has its own consequences: genuine conversions are usually more lasting, whereas those who convert because of other (nonreligious) motivations do not remain.

But, finally, conversions themselves are certainly appropriate when evangelical approaches respect the religious freedom that the American Constitution protects and upholds. Going back to the 1893 Parliament of World's Religions and beyond, people of all faiths have been free to practice in America. Dharmapala, Soen, and Suzuki were Buddhist "evangelicals" who spread the Dharma far and wide and in the process convinced many Christians (nominal or otherwise) to consider Buddhist beliefs and practices. On the other side, of course, committed Christians have borne witness to the gospel to their Buddhist neighbors, coworkers, and friends; Christian evangelists have held rallies, crusades, and revival meetings inviting people of all or no faith; and Christian denominations have developed specific mission strategies to evangelize Buddhist immigrants to the United States.[44] The nature of religious faith is such that it invites sharing. Christians and Buddhists alike will be driven to share their beliefs and practices if their faith is vibrant. From the perspective of the Buddhist-Christian encounter in America, it would seem that nonrefugee immigrant Buddhists would be the most open to Christian conversion, not only because they have chosen to come to America to begin with, but also because they would be the most committed to assimilating into American life. These social dynamics invite the Christian mission to Asian American Buddhist communities, as long as Christian evangelical agents approach their mission with sensitivity, compassion, and integrity.

CONCLUSION

Robert A. F. Thurman, Jey Tsong Khapa Professor of Indo-Tibetan Buddhist Studies in the Department of Religion at Columbia University and longtime Buddhist practitioner, at one point wrote that American Buddhism may be destined to play a key role in the evolution of Buddhism as a world religious tradition.[45] On the one hand, he is convinced that Buddhism must go beyond Buddhism in order to accomplish its American mission, since it should do so precisely in terms of bursting the category of religion altogether in the most pluralistic nation on earth. On the other hand, in the process, American Buddhism will temper the individualism and egocentrism of American life and in that way serve as the therapeutic mechanism that it is. If American Buddhism can do this, then it will continue to be the countercultural force it has been since its emergence in caste "India" in the sixth century BCE.

Similarly, I want to suggest, Christianity can play a number of interesting roles in the ongoing evolution of Buddhism in the American context. On the one hand, Christianity can be a prod that challenges, inspires, and even motivates the transformation of Buddhism on American soil. We have already seen how this might happen in the lives of American converts to Buddhist traditions in America: inevitably, their Christian religious experiences have influenced their Buddhist practices. On the other hand, if Christianity is able to do this in any positive sense for American Buddhism, it will have to be at its best: sensitive to the dynamic complexities that characterize American Buddhism on the ground and capable of deploying the wide range of practices needed to engage the varied Buddhist traditions in their various stages of evolution. In these cases, the Christian contribution to the ongoing vitality of Buddhism in America will itself be what is required to sustain the plausibility and vigor of Christianity itself in a world of many faiths. Hence, the diversification of Christian mission practices spells not the waning of Christian faith, but precisely its intensification.

Ironically, then, the Buddhist mission to America would in turn have contributed in its own way to the transformation of American Christianity. In this reading, the Buddhist-Christian encounter in America will have been mutually transformative for both traditions. Such is exactly what happens when religious people are serious about their faith in a pluralistic world.[46]

NOTES

1. I was delighted to have been invited to participate in this festschrift for Professor Irving Hexham. I met Irving in the fall

of 2000 at a conference organized at Regent College, Vancouver, BC, where we were both invited to present papers that were then published in John G. Stackhouse Jr., ed., *No Other Gods before Me? Evangelicals and the Challenge of World Religions* (Grand Rapids, MI: Baker Book House, 2001). Irving then later wrote a very nice commendation for my book, *Beyond the Impasse: Toward a Pneumatological Theology of Religions* (Grand Rapids, MI: Baker Academic, 2003). I have always appreciated his scholarship on new religious movements, and used his texts when I taught on that subject while on the faculty at Bethel University (St. Paul, Minnesota). It is with gratefulness that I present this essay as a token of my appreciation and respect for his scholarly contributions.

2. On the Nestorian mission to China, see P. Y. Saeki, *The Nestorian Monument in China* (London: SPCK, 1916), esp. 118–61; John Foster, *The Church of the T'ang Dynasty* (London: SPCK, 1939); David Bundy, "Missiological Reflections on Nestorian Christianity in China during the Tang Dynasty," in Frank K. Flinn and Tyler Hendricks, eds., *Religion in the Pacific Era* (New York: Paragon House, 1985), 14–30; and Li Tang, *A Study of the History of Nestorian Christianity in China and Its Literature in Chinese: Together with a New English Translation of the Dunhuang Nestorian Documents*, European University Studies, Series 23, Asian and African Studies 87 (Frankfurt and New York: Peter Lang, 2002).

3. On medieval Christian apologetics, see David Scott, "Medieval Christian Responses to Buddhism," *Journal of Religious History* 15, no. 2 (1988): 165–84; Richard Fox Young, "*Deus Unus* or *Dei Plures Sunt*? The Function of Inclusivism in the Buddhist Defense of Mongol Folk Religion against William of Rubruck (1254)," *Journal of Ecumenical Studies* 26, no. 1 (1989): 100–137; Hans-J. Klimkeit, "Christian-Buddhist Encounter in Medieval Central Asia," in G. W. Houston, ed., *The Cross and the Lotus: Christianity and Buddhism in Dialogue* (Delhi: Motilal Banarsidass, 1985), 9–24; and Dale T. Irvin and Scott W. Sundquist, *History of the World Christian Movement*, vol. 1: *Earliest Christianity to 1453* (Maryknoll, NY: Orbis Books, 2001), chaps. 25 and 35. For Chinese Christian sutras that summarize the gospel in Buddhist terminology, see John W. Coakley and Andrea Sterk, eds., *Readings in World Christian History*, vol. 1: *Earliest Christianity to 1453* (Maryknoll, NY: Orbis Books, 2004), 247–51.

4. This story is told by Rick Fields, *How the Swans Came to the Lake: A Narrative History of Buddhism in America* (Boulder, CO: Shambhala, 1981), esp. chap. 5.

5. See Kenneth K. Tanaka, *Ocean: An Introduction to Jodo-Shinshu Buddhism in America* (Berkeley, CA: Wisdom Ocean Publishers, 1997), chap. 4.

6. Thomas A. Tweed, *The American Encounter with Buddhism, 1844–1912: Victorian Culture and the Limits of Dissent* (Bloomington and Indianapolis: Indiana University Press, 1992).

7. A centenary assessment of the WPR's significance is provided by Richard Hughes Seager, *The World's Parliament of Religions: The East/West Encounter, Chicago, 1893* (Bloomington: Indiana University Press, 1995).

8. Their speeches have been published in numerous venues—e.g., John Henry Barrows, ed., *The World's Parliament of Religions*, 2 vols. (Chicago: Parliament Publishing Company, 1893), 2: 29–31 and 862–80; and Richard Hughes Seager, ed., *The Dawn of Religious Pluralism: Voices from the World's Parliament of Religions, 1893* (La Salle, IL: Open Court, 1993), chaps. 52–53.

9. For the significance of Suzuki's contributions to spreading the Buddhist Dharma across North America, see Francis Haar and Masao Abe, *A Zen Life: D. T. Suzuki Remembered* (New York: Weatherhill, 1986).

10. Suzuki's historical and textual scholarship is primarily in Japanese, although some of these works have been translated into English. A selection from his books and many essays is in William Barrett, ed., *Zen Buddhism: Selected Writings of D. T. Suzuki* (New York: Doubleday/Image, 1996).

11. See Dwight Goddard, ed., *A Buddhist Bible* (1938; reprint, Boston: Beacon Press, 1994).

12. See Alan Keightley, *Into Every Life a Little Zen Must Fall: A Christian Philosopher Looks to Alan Watts and the East* (London: Wisdom/Elements Books, 1986).

13. Rita M. Gross, "The International Buddhist-Christian Theological Encounter: Twenty Years of Dialogue," *Buddhist-Christian Studies* 25 (2005): 3–7.

14. See John B. Cobb Jr., *Beyond Dialogue: Toward a Mutual Transformation of Buddhism and Christianity* (Philadelphia: Fortress Press, 1982), and—representative of Masao Abe's work—Abe, *Zen*

and Western Thought, ed. William R. LaFleur (Honolulu: University of Hawai'i Press, 1985).

15. Those interested can consult Whalen Lai and Michael von Brück, *Christianity and Buddhism: A Multicultural History of Their Dialogue* (Maryknoll, NY: Orbis Books, 2001), 219–34.

16. The multireligious character of the dialogue is seen most clearly in one of the main publications out of the Cobb-Abe group: Christopher Ives, ed., *Divine Emptiness and Historical Fullness: A Buddhist-Jewish-Christian Conversation with Masao Abe* (Valley Forge, PA: Trinity Press International, 1995).

17. Representative volumes from these dialogues include Donald W. Mitchell and James Wiseman, OSB, eds., *The Gethsemani Encounter: A Dialogue on the Spiritual Life by Buddhist and Christian Monastics* (New York: Continuum, 1999), and Bruno Barnhart and Joseph Wong, eds., *Purity of Heart and Contemplation: A Monastic Dialogue between Christians and Asian Traditions* (New York: Continuum, 2001). See also *Monastic Studies* 19 (1991), which entire issue is devoted to "Buddhist and Christian Monasticism," as well as the *Bulletin of the Monastic Interreligious Dialogue* at *http://monasticdialog.com/bulletins.php.*

18. There is a growing literature on Engaged Buddhism in general, especially focused on Asian Engaged Buddhist movements. For Engaged Buddhism in the Western Hemisphere, see Fred Eppsteiner, ed., *The Path of Compassion: Writings on Socially Engaged Buddhism,* 2nd rev. ed. (Berkeley, CA: Parallax Press, 1988); Thich Nhat Hanh, *Interbeing: Fourteen Guidelines for Engaged Buddhism,* 3rd ed. (Berkeley, CA: Parallax Press, 1998); Christopher S. Queen, eds., *Engaged Buddhism in the West* (Boston: Wisdom, 2000); and Christopher S. Queen, Charles Prebish, and Damien Keown, eds., *Action Dharma: New Studies in Engaged Buddhism* (London: RoutledgeCurzon, 2003), esp. essays in parts 2 and 3. Sallie B. King's *Being Benevolence: The Social Ethics of Engaged Buddhism* (Honolulu: University of Hawai'i Press, 2005), focuses on Asian Engaged Buddhists; we await her analysis of Western Engaged Buddhism.

19. For the dizzying shape of immigrant Buddhism in America, see Richard Hughes Seager, *Buddhism in America* (New York: Columbia University Press, 1999), part 2; and Charles S.

Prebish and Kenneth K. Tanaka, eds., *The Faces of Buddhism in America* (Berkeley: University of California Press, 1998).

20. See Linda Learman, "Introduction," in Linda Learman, ed., *Buddhist Missionaries in the Era of Globalization* (Honolulu: University of Hawai'i Press, 2005), 1–22.

21. Here, I follow especially Lama Surya Das, "Emergent Trends in Western Dharma," in Al Rapaport and Brian D. Hotchkiss, eds., *Buddhism in America* (Rutland, VT, Boston, and Tokyo: Charles E. Tuttle, 1998), 543–54, and Charles S. Prebish, *Luminous Passage: The Practice and Study of Buddhism in America* (Berkeley: University of California Press, 1999), esp. chap. 2.

22. These issues are brought out nicely in Wendy Cadge, *Heartwood: The First Generation of Theravada Buddhism in America* (Chicago and London: University of Chicago Press, 2005), 199–201.

23. An interesting case study is George J. Tanabe Jr., "Grafting Identity: The Hawaiian Branches of the Bodhi Tree," in Linda Learman, ed., *Buddhist Missionaries in the Era of Globalization* (Honolulu: University of Hawai'i Press, 2005), 77–100.

24. See, e.g., Stephen Batchelor, *Buddhism without Beliefs: A Contemporary Guide to Awakening* (New York: Riverhead Books, 1997).

25. See the essays in part 1 of Rita M. Gross and Terry C. Muck, *Buddhists Talk about Jesus, Christians Talk about the Buddha* (New York and London: Continuum, 2000).

26. Helen Tworkov, *Zen in America: Five Teachers and the Search for an American Buddhism*, 2nd ed. (New York, Tokyo, and London: Kodansha International, 1994), 181.

27. See my "Guests, Hosts, and the Holy Ghost: Pneumatological Theology and Christian Practices in a World of Many Faiths," in David Jensen, ed., *Lord and Giver of Life: A Constructive Pneumatology* (Louisville, KY: Westminster John Knox Press, 2008), and "The Spirit of Hospitality: Pentecostal Perspectives toward a Performative Theology of the Interreligious Encounter," *Missiology: An International Review* 35, no. 1 (2007): 55–73; cf. also Yong, *Hospitality and the Other: Pentecost, Christian Practices, and the Neighbor*, Faith Meets Faith Series (Maryknoll, NY: Orbis Books, 2008), chaps. 4–5.

28. Hence the refrain of Hans Küng that there can be "No world peace without peace between the religions." See Küng,

Global Responsibility: In Search of a New World Ethic, trans. John Bowden (New York: Continuum, 1993), xv.

29. Christian theologians like Paul Knitter have thus argued for a liberationist theology of religions for precisely this reason; see Paul Knitter, *One Earth, Many Religions: Multifaith Dialogue and Global Responsibility*, and *Jesus and the Other Names: Christian Mission and Global Responsibility* (Maryknoll, NY: Orbis Books, 1995 and 1996, respectively).

30. Christians have long been involved at the interface of religion and the sciences. Increasingly, Buddhists are making their presence felt in this arena as well; see my "Trinh Thuan and the Intersection of Science and Buddhism: A Review Essay," *Zygon: Journal of Religion and Science* 42, no. 3 (2007): 677–84.

31. I attempt to provide one model for such a tri-logue in my "Christian and Buddhist Perspectives on Neuropsychology and the Human Person: *Pneuma* and *Pratityasamutpada*," *Zygon: Journal of Religion and Science* 40, no. 1 (2005): 143–65.

32. As laid out in Paul O. Ingram, *Wrestling with God* (Eugene, OR: Cascade, 2006).

33. As witnessed to in a book that is now a classic: William Johnston, *The Still Point: Reflections on Zen and Christian Mysticism* (New York: Fordham University Press, 1970).

34. See Terry C. Muck and Rita M. Gross, eds., *Christians Talk about Buddhist Meditation, Buddhists Talk about Christian Prayer* (New York: Continuum, 2003).

35. There are also, of course, many other forms of spiritual practices around which Christians and Buddhists might dialogue. I discuss, for example, the rite of exorcism in Christianity and Buddhism in my "The Demonic in Pentecostal-Charismatic Christianity and in the Religious Consciousness of Asia," in Allan Anderson and Edmond Tang, eds., *Asian and Pentecostal: The Charismatic Face of Christianity in Asia* (London: Regnum International; Baguio City, Philippines: Asia Pacific Theological Seminary Press, 2005), 93–127.

36. Raimundo Panikkar, *The Intrareligious Dialogue* (New York: Paulist, 1978).

37. See Stephen C. Rowe, "A Zen Presence in America: Dialogue as Religious Practice," in Donald W. Mitchell, ed., *Masao Abe: A Zen Life of Dialogue* (Boston: Charles E. Tuttle, 1998), 354–60.

38. A recent book with a fascinating title that is on my reading list is Brian J. Pierce, *We Walk the Path Together: Learning from Thich Nhat Hanh and Meister Eckhart* (Maryknoll, NY: Orbis, 2005).

39. For sophisticated discussions of the difficulty and yet necessity of identifying appropriate comparative categories in the interreligious conversation, see the various essays on these topics in Robert Cummings Neville, ed., *The Comparative Religious Ideas Project*, 3 vols. (Albany: State University of New York Press, 2001).

40. See William R. Burrows, *Redemption and Dialogue: Reading Redemptoris Missio and Dialogue and Proclamation* (Maryknoll, NY: Orbis Books, 1993).

41. See Paul J. Griffiths, *An Apology for Apologetics: A Study in the Logic of Interreligious Dialogue* (Maryknoll, NY: Orbis Books, 1991).

42. Here I am thinking about Buddhist apologists like Anagarika Dharmapala (mentioned above) as well as, more recently, Gunapala Dharmasiri, *A Buddhist Critique of the Christian Concept of God* (Antioch, CA: Golden Leaves, 1988).

43. Here the discussion of J. D. Van de Vyver, ed., *The Problem of Proselytism in Southern Africa: Legal and Theological Dimensions* (Atlanta: Emory University School of Law, 2000), is valid, even though the case studies focus on the South African context. See also John Witte and Richard C. Martin, eds., *Sharing the Book: Religious Perspectives on the Rights and Wrongs of Proselytism* (Maryknoll, NY: Orbis Books, 1999).

44. E.g., *Suffering and Redemption: Exploring Christian Witness within a Buddhist Context* (Chicago: Division for Global Mission of the Evangelical Lutheran Church in America, 1988).

45. Robert A. F. Thurman, "Toward an American Buddhism," in Rapaport and Hotchkiss, *Buddhism in America,* 450–68.

46. I thank Ann Riggs for the invitation to participate in this historic gathering. I am also grateful to my graduate assistant, Doc Hughes, for his feedback on a preconference version of this paper.

Chapter 20

OBERLIN 2007: THE NEED FOR AN EXPANDED METHODOLOGY?

John T. Ford, CSC

>Following its presentation at Oberlin II, this paper was originally published in *Ecumenical Trends* 38, no. 8 (2007): 5/117–8/120, 15/127 and is reprinted here with permission from the author and *Ecumenical Trends*.

Oberlin 2007 was a notable ecumenical event in multiple ways.[1] The conference—whose theme was "On Being Christian Together: The Faith and Order Experience in the United States"—commemorated the golden anniversary of the first Oberlin conference in 1957; at least five people—"57ers"—who had been present at "Oberlin I" returned to celebrate a half-century of expanding ecumenical commitment.

"Oberlin II," however, differed from its predecessor in two notable ways: first, there were over a hundred young people present, and second, there was much greater diversity among the participants in terms of denomination, gender, race, and ethnicity. The continued participation of young people is essential if a commitment to ecumenism is to be passed on to the next generation. Similarly, greater diversity is also necessary if ecumenism is to engage all Christians, not just those of "mainline" churches.

Among these newcomers, two questions repeatedly surfaced: (1) What are they—the speakers and ecumenical veterans—really talking about? (2) How does Faith and Order relate to me and my ministry? The first question was inevitable: newcomers to any discussion can hardly be expected to be familiar with the details of previous conversations—especially one that has been ongoing for fifty years. Nonetheless, the newcomers had a valid point: veteran ecumenists have a habit of using "ecu-speak" in general and "ecu-anagrams" in particular. For example, while ecumenists may be conversant with the Lund Principle, how is a newcomer to know what it is?[2] Similarly, while ecumenists habitually speak of *BEM* in reference to the Faith and Order report on baptism, Eucharist, and ministry—why expect a newcomer to know about it?[3]

The confusion occasionally created by such ecumenical shorthand was sometimes compounded further by the use of denominational vocabulary, ecclesiastical terminology, and theological citations. The result, from a newcomer's perspective, was occasionally an ecumenical tower of Babel, rather than clarity in communication. In this respect, the newcomers provided a wholesome reminder that the message of ecumenism not only can be but will be misunderstood—if not completely ignored—unless it is clearly and cogently communicated. In other words, "ecu-speak" and "ecu-anagrams" easily become conversation stoppers for ecumenical novices.

The second question—how does Faith and Order relate to us and our ministry?—is equally helpful. While the conference presentations raised significant issues in regard to church-dividing issues, sometimes new participants were left wondering about the significance of these issues for their ministries. Even when questions were precisely delineated from a theological perspective, sometimes participants wondered what speakers really felt: Were the speakers simply expressing their denomination's position, or were these issues really a matter of personal concern?

Once again, the newcomers provided a healthy reminder that the message of ecumenism needs to be relevant to people in the pews. And to be relevant, an ecumenical message must be presented not only in understandable terms but also in energizing language. In other words, ecumenism needs to be more people-relevant and people-engaging than it has been in the past.

AN ECUMENICAL JANUS?

For much of its history, the modern ecumenical movement has unfortunately had an uncanny resemblance to the Roman god

OBERLIN 2007: THE NEED FOR AN EXPANDED METHODOLOGY?

Janus—the double-faced deity, who looked in opposite directions and so was presumably capable of speaking in two different ways.[4] The ecumenical counterpart on the one hand is the Faith and Order Movement, whose emphasis has been on the resolution of doctrinal issues and the reconciliation of ecclesiastical structures as the means to achieving Christian unity. On the other hand is the Life and Work movement, whose emphasis has been on common witness and collaborative work as the most feasible way to bring Christians together.[5]

Life and Work proponents customarily point out that "doctrine divides while work unites." This dictum has validity insofar as the Faith and Order comparison of official doctrinal statements is quite useful in pointing out areas of agreement and disagreement; however, such comparative dogmatics usually fails to provide a path to resolve fundamental disagreements. In terms of results, when comparative dogmatics is used in Faith and Order discussions, participants are usually able to clarify where they agree and disagree, but are often left with the task of determining whether there is a sufficient amount of agreement for unity—presuming that their areas of disagreement are not so fundamental as to be major barriers to unity. However, comparative dogmatics is usually unable to discover a path whereby areas of disagreement can be transcended.

Given such a limitation, the approach of Life and Work seems at first sight to be ecumenically more promising: surely Christians can find ways of working, living, and worshiping together. Such an approach to visible unity has often proved highly successful in practice. Numerous are the examples of interdenominational cooperation on such diverse projects as civil rights, disaster assistance, environmental concerns, equal opportunity, food distribution, housing assistance, and so on.

Nonetheless, practical unity without a theological basis can be problematic insofar as divisive issues of Faith and Order—of doctrine and discipline, of belief and morals, of church teachings and church structures—can and do surface. For example, while current neuralgic issues include denominational stances on abortion and homosexuality, in the past, such issues as gambling and public funding of church-related schools have also been church-dividing.[6] Without theological undergirding—as provided by

Faith and Order discussions—Life and Work projects can collapse because of unexpected conflicts.

What the newcomers at Oberlin 2007 seemed to sense was a Janus phenomenon: theological discussion going in a theoretical direction, while issues of Christian evangelization and witness were heading in a practical direction. If not necessarily traveling in opposite directions, these two conversations were not always intersecting. Accordingly, what seems to be needed in current ecumenical dialogue is a way of overcoming such bidirectionality: Faith and Order seemingly speaking in one direction, with Life and Work apparently acting in another direction. Is there a way of balancing the intellectual/theological discussions in Faith and Order with the activist/programmatic projects of Life and Work?

Notional and Real

The resolution of the bidirectionality of Faith and Order/Life and Work might be assisted by John Henry Newman's distinction between *notional* and *real* assent.[7] On the one hand, *notional* assents deal with abstractions and generalities, with theories and laws—in short, with what is proposed as logically demonstrable and generically, if not universally, true. On the other hand, *real* assents deal with the singular and the concrete, with specific people and particular places—in effect with particularity in all its confusion and complexity, with individuals in all their rich diversity and creativity.

Both types of assent are necessary in life, and each type has validity in its own sphere. Nonetheless, both types of assent have limitations: *notional* assents tend to be abstractions that are intellectually defensible, but may be so divorced from reality that it is hard to see how they apply in concrete situations. *Notional* arguments may take on a life of their own and so may seem logically irrefutable; yet, as Newman remarked, the chain of logical conclusions "hangs loose at both ends."[8] On the one end, a logical system initially depends upon suppositions that are not demonstrable; when suppositions are not shared, a conversation usually grinds to a halt.[9] On the other end, a logical conclusion is often not readily applicable to a concrete situation. *Notional* assents may not have any concrete exemplification; indeed, they may result in apparent contradictions.[10]

In contrast, *real* assents involve the concrete realities of life ranging from the trivial—our daily choices of food, clothing, entertainment, and so on—to the most important—love and family, occupation and religion, life and death, and so on. *Real* assents, however, are never absolutely certain; they always carry an inescapable element of risk: we may eat what is tasty, but unhealthy; we may take the wrong turn, either on a vacation trip or in life as a whole. In fact, *real* assents can be so powerful that they go counter to the evidence: such is the case of a thoracic surgeon who performed numerous operations for lung cancer, but adamantly refused to give up smoking. *Real* assents can run counter to logic.

Real assents are usually far stronger than notional, since they involve our most important life decisions; for example, literally millions of people have resolutely sacrificed their lives for their Christian belief, but one is hard pressed to find martyrs for the Pythagorean proposition even though its logic is definitively demonstrable.[11] In effect, real assents tend to have a strong personal grip on a person, while notional assents—though logically coherent and convincing—usually lack a deep personal hold. Nonetheless, notional assents are important to every discussion, since they are the means for making a case, for presenting an argument, for explaining an issue, for resolving theoretical problems, and so forth. Notional assents speak to the head. And people like to be intellectually persuaded before making real decisions.

This strength of notional assents is also their inescapable weakness: notional assents may operate on the intellectual level, but not necessarily on the personal practical level. For example, debates usually function on the notional level; a winning debate team is usually able to argue either side of a case—even the side that the team members find personally distasteful. Members of a good debate team can usually argue either side of case, since their task is notional, not real. When it comes to their personal viewpoints, however, debaters tend to tilt to one side or the other—based not only on their understanding of the notional arguments in the specific case, but much more on the basis of their real experience.

However, the goal of most discussions is not simply to speak at a notional level; the goal is to present new insights that will result in new convictions; in other words, the goal of most discussions is to change the hearts and minds of people, to convert discussion into action. In fact, notional assents can be changed into real assents.[12] Indeed, for notional assents to be personally efficacious, they need to be changed into real assents.[13]

IMPLICATIONS FOR ECUMENICAL DIALOGUE

To date, much of the discussion in Faith and Order has involved notional assents; for example, what is the official teaching of your church? How does your church's teaching compare with the teaching of my church? Where do our churches agree? Or disagree? A major strength of the traditional Faith and Order approach has been its analytic approach, its ability to sort out issues, especially its specification of where churches agree, where they disagree, and where they simply do not understand each other.[14] In effect, much of the success of Faith and Order has been on the notional level.

In contrast, much of the activity in Life and Work involves real assents: What can we as Christians do to help these unfortunate people? How can we, working together as Christians, bring about peace and goodwill in the world in which we live? The strength of the traditional Life and Work approach has been its ability to respond to urgent needs, to recognize concrete problems, and to marshal the resources—material and personal—to address these concerns. In effect, Life and Work functions on the real level.

One should then credit both Faith and Order and Life and Work for doing exactly what they were designed to do. In fact, given the obstacles and limitations that both movements have faced, both Faith and Order and Life and Work have been extraordinarily successful.[15] Yet some of the new voices at Oberlin detected a disconnection in these efforts, a disjuncture between the doctrinal/structural endeavors of Faith and Order on the notional level and the pragmatic/evangelizing efforts of Life and Work on the real level.

In life, the notional and the real go together: the notional without the real tends to be speculation, while the real without the notional tends to be superficial.[16] If so, as an ecumenical corollary, Faith and Order and Life and Work need to be more engaged as ecumenical partners.

AN ECUMENICAL ITCH

Historians of the ecumenical movement have pointed out that one of the unexpected contributions of the Third World Conference on Faith and Order which met in Lund, Sweden, in 1952, was a methodological shift away from "comparative dogmatics" to an approach that sought a "Christological synthesis."[17] Five decades and five years later, the discussions at the second Oberlin Conference suggest that a new ecumenical methodology is now needed.

Although the Oberlin participants generally recognized the need for the visible unity of the churches and thus the need to resolve the doctrinal questions and structural differences that are presently obstacles to Christian unity, some participants also felt that many Faith and Order discussions just do not seem to relate to them nor to the actual life of their churches. As one participant remarked in down-home fashion: "Faith and Order is not scratching where it itches."

Where is the itch? One suspects that it may be the bidirectionality of Faith and Order/Life and Work. Faith and Order, by opting for the study of doctrines and structures, may have inadvertently tended to isolate itself on the notional level. Life and Work, in its concern for Christian witness through compassionate care, may have unconsciously tended to restrict itself to the real level. What some voices at Oberlin seemed to be saying is that the two levels need to meld, if not merge.

Yet, if the "itch" can be described, the task of "scratching" is much more difficult. The first difficulty is personnel: the theologians involved in Faith and Order are adept at analyzing problems on the theoretical level; the pastoral people involved in Life and Work projects are proficient in addressing practical problems. Many people are simply not gifted with both types of expertise or experience.

The second difficulty is methodology. Methodology is notoriously difficult to teach—as any professor who has directed doctoral students knows all too well. Even more difficult is the challenge of devising new methodologies—since they usually are not designed in advance. Perhaps they are not always predesignable—but emerge from concrete circumstances via the proverbial method of trial and error. Indeed, this may be a new challenge that the ecumenical movement needs to face in the twenty-first century: the elaboration of a new ecumenical methodology.

AN EXPANDED METHODOLOGY?

The methodology that was used in the discussion groups at Oberlin has been employed by the Faith and Order Commission of the National Council of Churches during the past decade.[18] This method has three components:

1. *Resonance:* Where do we fundamentally agree, even though we may use different terms to express our belief?

2. *Dissonance:* Where do we basically disagree, even though we may be using similar language?

3. *Nonsonance:* Where is our language so different that we do not really understand what each other is saying?

One advantage of this method is that it allows participants to identify areas of agreement, disagreement, and lack of understanding from their own perspective; participants may voice their own views without relying on the categories of others.[19]

Yet one major drawback to such a method is that it allows participants to remain on the notional level without requiring them to implement their areas of agreement or resonance. Thus, the Achilles' heel to this method is that it is a case of logic being loose at the concluding end. While participants using this method necessarily have to sort out their suppositions—otherwise, they are unable to identify areas of agreement and disagreement; the method as such does not push them far enough—they may fail to come up with a real course of action. Their dialogical answers then remain on the notional level—even when the participants have found resonance. An additional dimension is needed:

4. *Ordinance:* How can our agreement be put into practice at every level?

The choice of ordinance as an addition to this ecumenical methodology is motivated in part by a desire for rhyme and mnemonics to facilitate use. However, ordinance also seems appropriate in terms of its derivation from the Latin: *ordinare* = "to put in order." Thus, the proposed dimension of ordinance is intended to complete the notional process of Faith and Order with a proposal for real implementation in the manner of Life and Work. In other words, how can resonance—our areas of ecumenical agreement—be put into practice? In effect, the agreements found in pursuing the question of resonance should not remain simply notional; such findings need to be translated into the realm of the real. Resonance needs to be complemented with ordinance.

From a theoretical viewpoint, perhaps the ecumenical movement would benefit by borrowing an insight from Newman.[20] His distinction between notional and real seems to resemble the disconnection between Faith and Order on the one hand and Life and Work on the other. Yet, while Newman was willing to grant both notional and real their appropriate domains of discourse, he also emphasized the need for their interaction, indeed their cooperation: if the real is to be effective, then it needs to be solidly supported by what is understandable and reasonable; if the notional is to be relevant, then it needs to address practical issues of implementation. Similarly, the discussions of Faith and Order need to be implemented via Life and Work.

Although it may be premature to attempt to devise a completely new methodology for Faith and Order in the immediate wake of Oberlin 2007, perhaps a modest beginning can be made by expanding the triad—resonance, dissonance, and nonsonance—to a quadrilateral that includes ordinance.

NOTES

1. For information about the conference, see the official website of Oberlin 2007 at *www.ncccusa.org/faithandorder/oberlin2007/*; also see the comments that appeared at *www.xanga.com/alumnipresident/605644574/reflections-of-oberlin-2007-ncc-faith-and-order.html.*

2. The "Lund Principle" refers to the challenge posed by the Third World Conference on Faith and Order at Lund, Sweden, in 1952: "Should not our churches ask themselves whether they are showing sufficient eagerness to enter into conversation with other churches, and whether they should not act together in all matters except those in which deep differences of conviction compel them to act separately?"

3. *Baptism, Eucharist, and Ministry (BEM)*, Faith and Order Paper 111 (Geneva: World Council of Churches, 1982); see online *www.oikoumene.org/index.php?id=2638.*

4. Incidentally, the month of January owes its name to Janus, the god of gates and doorways, of beginnings and endings.

5. For a historical overview of Faith and Order and Life and Work and the formation of the World Council of Churches, see Willem Visser 't Hooft, *Genesis and Formation of the World Council of Churches* (Geneva: World Council of Churches, 1988).

6. Such was the experience of one bilateral dialogue when the Roman Catholic participants supported the legalization of bingo to support parochial schools, while their Protestant dialogue partners objected to gambling as immoral.

7. This distinction is discussed in detail in chapter 4 of Newman's *An Essay in Aid of a Grammar of Assent*; hereafter cited: *Grammar; www.newmanreader.org/works/grammar/index.html.*

8. Newman, *Grammar,* 284: "As to Logic, its chain of conclusions hangs loose at both ends; both the point from which the proof should start, and the points at which it should arrive, are beyond its reach; it comes short both of first principles and of concrete issues."

9. The absence of shared suppositions is often difficult to diagnose during an actual dialogue; one indicator, however, is when a conversation seems to meander and when the participants seem unable to find a common focus. Such a conversation is often

simultaneously fascinating in its diversity and frustrating in its apparent lack of direction.

10. Mathematics furnishes a number of such examples: (a) the square root of [–a] has no real counterpart; (b) it seems contradictory to speak of different types (cardinalities) of infinity; yet both these examples are notionally valid in mathematics.

11. Pope John Paul II, in the opening paragraph of *Ut unum sint,* extolled the "courageous witness of so many martyrs of our century, including members of Churches and Ecclesial Communities not in full communion with the Catholic Church."

12. The reverse is also true: real assents can become notional; for example, friendships that were so important while in school are often neglected after graduation and subsequently fade away.

13. For example, in chapter 5 of his *Grammar*, Newman went to great lengths to show how a Christian can assent to the Trinity, not merely notionally, but really.

14. See John T. Ford, "Learning the Language of Ecumenism," *Ecumenical Trends* 26, no. 9 (October 1997): 11–13.

15. For example, among the many recent studies produced by the Faith and Order Commission of the National Council of Churches is *Ancient Faith and American-Born Churches: Dialogues between Christian Traditions*, ed. Ted Campbell, Ann K. Riggs, and Gilbert W. Stafford (New York/Mahwah, NJ: Paulist Press, 2006); hereafter cited: *Ancient Faith and American-Born Churches.*

16. See *Grammar*, 34: "Each use of propositions has its own excellence and serviceableness, and each has its own imperfection. To apprehend notionally is to have breadth of mind, but to be shallow; to apprehend really is to be deep, but to be narrow-minded."

17. See Robert McAfee Brown, *The Ecumenical Revolution: An Interpretation of the Catholic-Protestant Dialogue,* rev. and exp. ed. (Garden City, NY: Doubleday Anchor–Image Book, 1969), 40–43.

18. The methodology was presented by John T. Ford, "Theological Language and Ecumenical Methodology," in *Ancient Faith and American-Born Churches,* 15–23; *www.ncccusa.org/unity/fandoford.html.*

19. See R. Keelan Downton, "Beyond Discussion Questions: Reflections on Teaching Ecumenical Method in Anticipation of Oberlin 2007, "*Ecumenical Trends* 36, no. 6 (June 2007): 1–5.

20. For a detailed proposal to use Newman's *Grammar* as a vehicle for dialogue, see Frederick D. Aquino, *Communities of Informed Judgment: Newman's Illative Sense and Accounts of Rationality* (Washington, DC: Catholic University of America Press, 2004).

Chapter 21

THE FLAME OF ECUMENISM: STUDENT RESURGENCE AND AN EMERGING ECUMENICAL MODEL

Juliana M. Mecera

At Oberlin II, celebrating Faith and Order in the U.S.A. from 1957 to 2007 gave occasion to much reflection about ecumenism's status in North America at the beginning of its next fifty years. How alive and well is the ecumenical movement? And by what standards do ecumenists measure its health?

Oberlin II was foremost a celebration of Faith and Order's achievements, but many participants acknowledged that, in comparison to the ecumenical happenings of the 1960s, '70s, and '80s, in more recent decades ecumenism seems to have been experiencing a type of winter (chap. 12, Downton). Even so, the presentations and panel discussions were thoughtful, creative, and timely topics for the twenty-first century.

During the conference, attendees spent time reflecting upon the postmodern times—and what this concept signifies within ecumenism. Ford, champion of what has become the traditional ecumenical method of study (in which differences, similarities, and confusing aspects of each other's traditions are discussed), proposed an additional step to his methodology: determining what concrete practice can be implemented based upon discovered similarities. In the breakout group in which I participated, we openly expressed the desire that new ecumenical processes be established and utilized soon for the well-being of the next fifty years. We discussed focusing on small-group discussion and study, the importance of bilateral dialogues, and interactive presentation styles at conferences.

The large number of students who were sought out and present was one prominent aspect of Oberlin II, suggesting that the ecumenical movement's strength and vigor is growing once again. Informed and inspired by the first Faith and Order leaders and their accomplishments, younger leaders (between the ages of eighteen and thirty) are seriously engaging their local communities, and their local and national ecumenical bodies, in unique efforts to further the next fifty years of Faith and Order and of ecumenism broadly.

CATCHING THE FLAME: LESSONS FROM THE FIRST FIFTY YEARS

As a student just entering the ecumenical scene, I mark Oberlin II as my initiation into the ecumenical movement. Beyond gathering knowledge about ecumenical history, learning some "ecu-speak," and becoming familiar with prominent WCC assemblies and the significant turning points of ecumenical history, I learned the practice of ecumenical work by observing Faith and Order members in action. I noticed that participants from a cross-section of various denominations were not only colleagues but were longtime friends with respect for each other and each other's scholarship. I was encouraged that the unity of the Christian churches—an imposing and sometimes abstract goal—looked promising on a personal level. Members from my church explained that one expectation of ecumenical work is that participants knowledgeably represent their own tradition, since the first step of dialogue is to comprehend each other's beliefs as much as possible. Sometimes participants disagreed, but I found that disagreement is not discouraged in ecumenical culture since disagreement can be productive if participants have listened and gained insight from one another. I was encouraged to see that theology, faith, and worship practices were taken seriously. Criticisms and hopes for progress were thoughtful, constructive, and sincere. Goodwill, well-earned pride for Faith and Order, and a positive outlook on the future prevailed.

I was especially inspired and instructed by Cecil "Mel" Robeck Jr.'s address. Robeck is a Pentecostal Christian who told his story of having sacrificed some respect among fellow Pentecostals because of his dedication to ecumenism, which has been seriously questioned by his communion. As an Orthodox Christian, this tension between my enthusiasm for ecumenism and my communion's hesitations is part of my experience as well. Though the initial urging to form an organization like the World Council of Churches came from the Ecumenical Patriarchate, Orthodox theological perspectives (e.g., in ecclesiology) mean that Orthodox Christians proceed very cautiously in ecumenical endeavors because of the seriousness that the Orthodox Church ascribes to unity. As Faith and Order USA makes a commitment to expanding dialogue and projects to underrepresented Christians, Robeck is an important example of one who shared his communion's gifts and thereby advanced the movement.

Robeck's story provides an ecumenical typology of sorts in which support and challenge were both represented. A standing ovation at the end of his remarks indicated that the ecumenical movement can at times function as a "family" that offers encouragement and support. However, the amount of time and effort that Robeck had devoted to ecumenical projects coupled with a resulting lack of respect from some parts of his communion demonstrated the essentiality of a mature faith that can engage both serious work and spiritual challenges. Faith and Order requires confronting brokenness and seeking reconciliation, wherever that brokenness may be—within our own communions and without. When ecumenism compels us to talk and work with those with whom it is most difficult—as Paul encouraged the Jews and Gentiles to do (1 Cor. 8)—it forces our focus on Jesus Christ instead of on ourselves and increases our capacity for love and wholeness as people and as church. The model of grappling with brokenness is one of the greatest lessons that Faith and Order in its first fifty years has passed on to current leaders.

Now Ford urges ecumenists to continue on the journey of Faith and Order by taking action to implement practices informed by discovered similarities among Christian communions. The student participants at Oberlin II and young ecumenists across the United States have been taking on this challenge since (and even in the few years immediately preceding) Oberlin II. The themes explored at Oberlin II have been central to their work.

JULIANA M. MECERA

KINDLING THE FLAME: BRINGING STUDENTS TO OBERLIN 2007

The 2007 fiftieth Anniversary Celebration placed special emphasis on students and the generation of rising ecumenists through a self-consciously forward-thinking mind-set. As a result, over one hundred students were brought to Oberlin on scholarship and integrated into the conference as full participants. They read conference papers ahead of time, attended plenary sessions, asked presenters questions from the floor, participated in worship, and were assigned to discussion groups integrated with all other attendees. Oberlin II conveners also provided the students specialized opportunities for ecumenical formation with an orientation session, networking opportunities, and structured reflection time. At this critical time in the ecumenical movement, Faith and Order capitalized on young people, considering them one of its vital strengths, and this investment has yielded increase. A resurgence of vision and action has been initiated and carried out within the ecumenical movement by many dedicated, theologically educated young leaders.

FANNING THE FLAME: YOUNG ADULT ECUMENICAL DEVELOPMENTS

Outreach to students at Oberlin II and other similar efforts has helped fuel significant growth in the ecumenical movement in the form of young adult ecumenical events and organizations over the last decade. These young adult programs and groups include, but are certainly not limited to, Ecumenical Advocacy Days, affiliated with the NCC, which advocates for justice concerns each year in Washington, DC; the Young Adult Ecumenical Task Force established out of the WCC; Ecumenical Young Adult Ministry Team; and the Student Christian Movement USA's renewal. Additionally, the formation of a website (*www.FaithConnectsUs.org*) and New Fire are two other specific developments that have arisen from outreach to students that deserve to be highlighted.[1]

History/Background

The *New Fire Concept Paper* (2010) records that from approximately 2004 to 2008 an unprecedented number of young adult ecumenical initiatives flourished from the vision of a group of young leaders in the U.S. Conference for the World Council of Churches who were planning U.S. involvement in the WCC Decade to Overcome Violence in 2004 and the Ninth Assembly of the World Council of Churches in Brazil in 2006. They envisioned a website for networking and the formation of the position of young adult ecumenical formation coordinator. Young adult initiatives, such as the Young Adult Ecumenical Forum and specifically young adult programming at Ecumenical Advocacy Days and Christian Churches Together, sprung up and grew in number. Furthermore, the National Council of Churches, the U.S. Conference for the World Council of Churches, and the World Student Christian Federation (WSCF) also increased and strengthened their own initiatives for young adults. The WSCF relaunched its North American region by hiring a North American regional secretary. The NCC Young Adult Ecumenical Ministry Team gained higher attendance as well at their yearly event, "Come to the Feast." The vast number of specifically young adult gatherings and events that were taking place and being formed both independently and through established ecumenical bodies and assemblies solidified the need for coordination and intentional networking.

A Multifeatured Networking Website: www.FaithConnectsUs.org

In response to the Young Adult Task Force and strong young adult leadership, the *www.FaithConnectsUs.org* website and the New Fire Coordinator staff position were inaugurated in 2007 through joint efforts of the WCC and NCC to efficiently connect young ecumenists and their programs. The website is a front door to ecumenism for young adults in North America and throughout the world. (Over 50 percent of the hits on *www.FaithConnectsUs.org* are international.) Through this website, fundraising campaigns are run, upcoming events are publicized, and job openings are posted. Press releases from dozens of ecumenical organizations make *FaithConnectsUs.org*. the go-to place for all young adults involved in ecumenism. *FaithConnectsUs.org* also has a blogging feature that has allowed individuals to tell their personal ecumenical stories to build community and to encourage others. Directly underneath news stories about specific events, those who were participants can blog about their personal reflections and share anecdotes. Capitalizing on these creative ways of building connection is essential for young leaders since their colleagues, many of whom have not met in person, are spread across states and continents.

New Fire Coordinator and the Formation of the New Fire Network

Oberlin II intentionally brought together young people interested in ecumenism in a way that would allow them to begin to build collegial relationships, share ideas, and take on ecumenical responsibilities. In continuity with these efforts and in attempts to further relationships previously begun at ecumenical gatherings such as Oberlin II, the New Fire coordinator and the New Fire Network have connected young adult leaders to each other and thereby have helped these leaders to collaborate on ecumenical projects. The first New Fire Gathering was held in 2008 in Denver, Colorado, just prior to the NCC/CWS General Assembly, with the goal of revitalizing the younger generation's participation in the church and coordinating the many new young adult ecumenical initiatives that had recently sprung up. This first gathering brought together young ecumenical leaders from across the country and from over a dozen diverse ecumenical groups to learn about each other's initiatives and to begin coordinating projects and interests by setting common goals and initiating action plans. Through this first gathering, continued tele-meetings, and an expansion of the groups and denominations that New Fire participants represent, the New Fire Network has become a clearinghouse for young adult ecumenical programs and a strategic planning think-tank. Its goals include the following:

- To coordinate all young adult ecumenical efforts
- To eliminate duplication of efforts
- To resource local and grassroots ecumenical groups

- To envision short-term and long-term plans for the well-being of the ecumenical movement
- To fundraise to become self-sustaining

The New Fire coordinator, most generally, facilitates the convening and carrying out of projects of the New Fire members. She or he networks throughout all the known young adult groups and gathers representatives together from each group to collaborate on projects, to aid the groups in coordinating their goals, and to help ensure no duplication of efforts or competition for funding. The coordinator assists with fundraising through grant writing, creates partnerships with other ecumenical organizations by building relationships, assesses the needs of young adults in their communities, and aids in developing programmatic resources and promotional materials specific to New Fire's objectives. The New Fire coordinator also convenes and coordinates annual New Fire gatherings and throughout the year chairs regular conference calls among New Fire members and partners across North America.

Reception: A Hallmark of Young Ecumenical Efforts

At Oberlin II, discussions occurred about whether young adults play a unique role in the ecumenical movement. Most young adults—based upon personal interactions with New Fire members and other ecumenical experiences—believe they bring gifts and leadership to ecumenism based on their individual propensities rather than as a function of their age. Young adults take on as many different types of positions as any other category of ecumenist does. However, amidst the range of projects run by and leadership positions held by young adults, reception is one particular concept discussed at Oberlin II that New Fire (and other young adult organizations and events) has directly addressed. "Reception" refers to the ways that national ecumenical projects and studies, such as the research of the Faith and Order Commission, are incorporated into the lives of local congregations, pastors, and the faithful. Through ecumenical projects and dialogues in local communities the NCC's work is concretely bridged to the faithful and vice versa. For example, the video series shown at Oberlin II visually contextualized the ways that local groups were conceiving of ecumenical work. Reception was frequently a driving concern behind questions on the plenary floor. As evidenced by its goals (stated in the section above), through its networking model, New Fire aims to address reception by being an intersection of national ecumenical efforts and local ecumenical engagement.

GROWING THE FLAME: AN EMERGING ECUMENICAL MODEL

As Faith and Order begins another fifty years of work for Christian unity, Oberlin II has acted as one catalyst for initiating new models of doing ecumenical work. The New Fire network, in its formation and work, demonstrates an emerging ecumenical model, complete with its own objectives (as noted above), processes and methods, and already-realized successes. The New Fire model is neither completely grassroots nor is it a strictly top-down arrangement. Rather, New Fire draws upon the strengths of both structures. For example, the concept of a network such as New Fire originated in young adult programs of the WCC and NCC, and New Fire is housed in the NCC. Futhermore, a significant portion of New Fire's tasks require networking with national partner organizations. Thus, New Fire is firmly planted within formal ecumenical structures, and at the same time has embraced a working model that devotes much energy to communicating and working with local bodies. In turn, New Fire then connects local leaders to regional and national ecumenical structures.

RECEPTION: A KEY TO THIS NEW ECUMENICAL MODEL

The way in which New Fire carries out its vision can serve to further illustrate this ecumenical model. New Fire envisions a church and ecumenical movement in which youth from all corners of North America participate in ecumenical events and take ownership of ecumenism. Thus, to effectively realize more local, lay, and congregational involvement in ecumenism, New Fire directly engages local bodies and leaders. Once connected locally, New Fire members help implement ecumenical programs based on unique local needs. To do so they rely on support from bodies such as the National Council of Churches to further these efforts on the ground with resources such as books, curricula, and national opportunities for ecumenical service projects. The program "Faith Forum" is one such resource at the NCC's Faith and Order Commission that assists congregations to engage in ecumenical dialogue with others at nearby churches. New Fire's work such as this in local settings directly impacts reception, extending the reach of the ecumenical movement to directly impact individual Christian communities and enriching the various communions through understanding and collaboration. In turn this work also strengthens the regional and national councils by tying them to a broader range of constituents who implement their ecumenical initiatives on the ground.

THE METHODS AND PROCESS OF THIS NEW ECUMENICAL MODEL

New Fire's methods by which it carries out its tasks are another unique aspect of this emerging ecumenical model. The process in which young adults carry out their ecumenical work is characterized primarily by national and international telecommunication and Skype meetings, email networking, grassroots startups, local dialogue, and community projects. Through teleconferencing, young leaders pray with and for each other, offer support, and connect each other with materials and local leaders or organizations. Email and Google Documents convey important information, aid in the development of materials, and serve as the primary means for communicating about new projects and implementing them in New Fire members' own contexts. When New Fire members are together in person, interactive PowerPoint presentations and Youtube videos are readily employed. Storytelling and filming are also popular for promotion or sharing about events.

New Fire's method is not unique only because it capitalizes on these technologies and local connections, but rather because

New Fire's method and objective themselves are shaped by these processes and rely solely on them to enable New Fire to be a successful network that stretches from California, Alberta, and Texas to Nebraska, Washington, DC, and Connecticut. A method built around Internet software applications such as Skype and Google Docs, processes that rely on technology and that conform to local needs, and a main goal of spreading ecumenism's reach to lay people in the pews are all integral parts of what constitutes this emerging ecumenical model that young ecumenists are using to revitalize and promote the ecumenical movement.

SUCCESSES OF NEW FIRE'S MODEL

Thus far, the success of New Fire has led to two New Fire gatherings held preceding the NCC/CSW Assemblies in 2008 and 2009, and the formation of the formal New Fire Task Force in 2010, which is charged with spelling out specific goals and carrying out action plans. New Fire has also already produced greater connectivity of young adults and their efforts—as evidenced by stories shared online at faithconnectsus.org, Facebook groups, frequent communication via Skype, commitment to conference calls, and periodic meetings. New Fire's vision and its range of projects are producing concrete success on the local level as well.

In early 2010 four local ecumenical projects were implemented through a New Fire Seed Grant Program supported by the Ecumenical Young Adult Ministries Team of the NCC. Students in Boston, Massachusetts, developed an ecumenical, monastic-style, monthly prayer service and used a seed grant to further enrich their worship, which draws upon a variety of liturgical traditions and attracts mostly young adults. Congregations in Omaha, Nebraska, entered into common study and relationship about hospitality throughout Lent 2010 and gathered their youth together to lead a culminating presentation on Palm Sunday. In Minneapolis, Minnesota, young adults served on an interfaith panel highlighting young adult leadership for social justice. The panel drew college student and community participation from the greater St. Paul–Minneapolis area and served to empower young leaders in their peace and justice work by naming them as community leaders and by giving them an opportunity to network and share ideas as authoritative voices. In Winston-Salem, North Carolina, young adults used their grant to host two ecumenical dialogues about combating HIV/AIDS among university and seminary students at Wake Forest. The program encouraged young leaders to take action in their local churches and throughout their community.

Additionally, a New Fire film screening project was recently implemented across the United States. In September and October 2010, New Fire, in partnership with three organizations, hosted four screenings of documentaries in a series called *Have You Heard from Johannesburg* by acclaimed filmmaker Connie Field, which chronicles the involvement of faith communities and local movements in ending apartheid in South Africa. New Fire capitalized on these screenings as an opportunity to bring together in dialogue congregants from different communions. The film screenings were intended as an opportunity for neighbors to begin relationships with each other and to demonstrate the power that ecumenical work can have in bringing about justice. The screenings were also an opportunity to resource local people with ecumenical materials and connections that a network like New Fire can offer, spreading the spirit of unity.

This model of working with national bodies and local communities has been shown to be effective in its ability to be replicated by anyone doing ecumenical work. As just one example, students at Yale Divinity School met in the spring of 2010 to discuss the implications that the new interim Eucharist-sharing agreement between the Episcopalian Church and the United Methodist Church has for preparing worship services. Students also sponsored a Lutheran-Methodist Eucharistic service with engagement from a New Haven, Connecticut, church and held fellowship following worship.

The New Fire Network has become the organizing network of young adult ecumenical groups designed to further ecumenism and revitalize the church with increased young adult engagement and leadership. Their work is inaugurating a new, successful ecumenical model that both capitalizes on the resources and organizational connections of national ecumenical bodies and solidly invests in the contribution of young leaders to spread reception of ecumenism.

JULIANA M. MECERA

FEEDING THE ECUMENICAL FIRE AND WATCHING IT SPREAD

Oberlin II was one among many significant catalysts that helped to spark the formation and growth of New Fire and other young adult ecumenical organizations, which have come into being over the last decade. New Fire and the fiftieth Anniversary Celebration of Faith and Order in the U.S.A., in particular, crossed paths and influenced each other. Oberlin II chose to intentionally respond to the resurgence of young adult activity within the ecumenical movement at that time and encouraged young adults to take the flame of ecumenism that was sparked by the first fifty years of Faith and Order and to run with it into the next fifty years. Now, young adults across North America are connecting more people, especially younger Christians, to the ecumenical movement, spreading the gift of unity that God already gives.

Oberlin 2007, "Becoming Christian Together," was visionary in bringing together a large group of students to learn and grow together as part of the Faith and Order celebration. As these young people went forth from Oberlin, they took their experience and knowledge back to their campuses, congregations, and ecumenical groups. Many of them are now collaborating with each other and new colleagues, formulating and implementing new models for ecumenical work, and strategically planning for the future of the ecumenical movement. These young adult efforts represent an effective new model for doing ecumenical work, focused on reception, and they have already seen the beginnings of success. The ecumenical winter seems to have begun to thaw.

NOTE

1. I am grateful to Rev. David Fracarro and Shantha Ready Alonso for their leadership as New Fire coordinators. They were invaluable in providing many of the details, the facts, and the historical timeline about *www.FaithConnectsUs.org* and New Fire discussed in this section.

OBERLIN II: CONTRIBUTORS

Dr. Antonios Kireopoulos is the associate general secretary for Faith and Order and Interfaith Relations at the National Council of Churches USA. Previous to this portfolio, he was associate general secretary for International Affairs and Peace. He received his PhD in theology from Fordham University (2003) and has spent most of the last twenty years engaged in ecumenical and interfaith dialogue. From 1999 to 2003 Kireopoulos served as executive director of Religions for Peace–USA. He serves as chair of the board of United to End Genocide.

Ms. Juliana M. Mecera interned with Faith and Order as the Elenie K. Huszagh Orthodox Intern from 2008 to 2010. Mecera received her MA in Theology from St. Vladimir's Seminary in 2009 and continued her theological and ecumenical studies in the STM program at Union Theological Seminary in New York City, where she wrote her thesis titled "Orthodox Women Priests: Concepts of Priesthood, Ordination, and Theological Anthropology at Stake" (2010). She is a member of the National Council of Churches' New Fire task force for young ecumenists.

Dr. John Borelli directed religious studies at the College of Mount St. Vincent, New York City, for eleven years (1976–86), and served more than sixteen years as associate director of the Secretariat for Ecumenical and Interreligious Affairs, U.S. Conference of Catholic Bishops (1987–2003) and as a consulter to the Vatican's Pontifical Council for Interreligious Dialogue (1991–2007). Currently Borelli is special assistant for interreligious initiatives to Dr. John J. DeGioia, president, Georgetown University, and in that capacity serves as national coordinator for interreligious dialogue and mission for the U.S. Jesuit Cconference.

Rev. Dr. David D. Daniels III is th e Henry Winters Luce Professor of World Christianity at McCormick Theological Seminary, where he has taught since 1987. Daniels is the author of various articles on the history of Christianity, and he serves as a member of various organizations and research projects relating to U.S. religious life. An ordained minister in the Church of God in Christ since 1980, he received his doctorate in church history from Union Theological Seminary in 1992.

Dr. Donald W. Dayton is now retired after thirty five years of seminary teaching in a variety of traditions. He has served as president of the Wesleyan Theological Society (recently honored with the society's lifetime achievement award) and the Society for Pentecostal Studies. He has had extensive ecumenical experience, including a quarter of a century as a comissioner on Faith and Order. A layman in the Wesleyan Church of America, he received his PhD from the University of Chicago. Among his writings are *Theological Roots of Pentecostalism* (Scarecrow, 1984) and *Discovering an Evangelical Heritage* (Harper & Row, 1976).

Dr. R. M. Keelan Downton served as the Faith and Order postdoctoral fellow at the NCC from 2005 to 2007 and is currently a research professor of theology in the Micah Institute at New York Theological Seminary and Communications and Public Relations Specialist for the Woodstock Theological Center at Georgetown University. He is an ongoing participant in the emerging church conversation through the lens of Wesleyan, Anabaptist, and Pentecostal theological traditions with research interests in narrative theology, ecumenism, and peace studies. Downton is author of *Authority in the Church: An Ecumenical Reflection on Hermeneutic Boundaries and Their Implications for Inter-Church Relations* (2006).

Avery Cardinal Dulles, SJ, held the Laurence J. McGinley Chair in Religion and Society at Fordham University from 1988 until September 2008. He was widely acclaimed for his groundbreaking 1974 work *Models of the Church*—one of twenty-five books published under his name—in which he defined the church as institution, mystical communion, sacrament, herald, servant, and community of disciples, and critiqued each. In 2002 he was made a cardinal of the Roman Catholic Church. Dulles remained a notable friend of Faith and Order until his death in December 2008.

The Rt. Rev. C. Christopher Epting, DD, served as the Episcopal bishop of Iowa from 1988 to 2001. Epting recently retired from duties as the deputy for ecumenical and interfaith relations of the Episcopal Church, where he was responsible for facilitating interdenominational and interfaith dialogue with religious bodies around the world.

The Rev. Dr. John T. Ford, CSC, is professor of theology and religious studies, coordinator of Hispanic/Latin programs, and area director for historical and systematic theology at the Catholic University of America, Washington, DC. A Roman Catholic, he is currently chair of the ecumenism committee of the Washington Theological Consortium, as well as a member of the Faith and Order Commission of the National Council of Churches of Christ, USA.

Brother Jeffrey Gros, FSC, was the first Roman Catholic director of Faith and Order and served in this role for ten years. Gros is former associate director of the Secretariat on Ecumenism at the U.S. Conference of Catholic Bishops. He is well known in the ecumenical movement for broadening the reach of ecumenism through writing, editing, and speaking. Gros is Distinguished Professor of Ecumenical and Historical Theology at Memphis Theological Seminary.

The Rev. Dr. Jione Havea is a native of Tonga, ordained by the Methodist Church of Tonga, and now lives in Australia, where he teaches at United Theological College and the School of Theology, Charles Sturt University. He is interested in cultural modes of thinking, reading, and behaving, as those relate to, and are driven and coerced by, biblical and popular texts. Havea has published multiple books in Tongan and is published in English as well, including chapters in *Christian Worship in Australia* (2009) and *The Bible and the Hermeneutics of Liberation* (2009). He has edited *Out of Place* (2010) and *Talanoa Ripples: Across Borders, Cultures, Disciplines* (2010).

The Rev. Dr. Diane C. Kessler is an ordained minister in the United Church of Christ. Kessler is coauthor of *Councils of Churches and the Ecumenical Vision* (World Council of Churches, 2000) and editor of *Together on the Way: The Official Report of the Eighth Assembly of the World Council of Churches*. She served as the executive director of the Massachusetts Council of Churches from 1988 to 2007.

The Rev. Dr. Sarah Heaner Lancaster is the Professor of Theology in the Bishop Hazen G. Werner Chair of Theology at the Methodist Theological School in Ohio and an ordained elder in the United Methodist Church. She received her PhD from Southern Methodist University (1996), and her areas of expertise include systematic theology, Wesleyan studies, United Methodist doctrine, and the authority of Scripture.

CONTRIBUTORS

The Rev. Joseph A. Loya, OSA, is associate professor in theology/religious studies at Villanova University in Pennsylvania. He attained his PhD from Fordham University and specializes in Eastern Christianity. Loya has served as editor for Christian resources for the *Journal of Ecumenical Studies* from 1994 to the present.

The Rev. Dr. Kevin W. Mannoia is professor of ministry and serves as the graduate and faculty chaplain at Azusa Pacific University. Mannoia has served as bishop of the Free Methodist Church and president of the National Association of Evangelicals. He is author of *Church Planting: The Next Generation; Century 21 Church Planting Manual; The Integrity Factor: A Journey in Leadership Formation; Church 2K:Leading Forward; 15 Characteristics of Effective Pastors* and *The Holiness Manifesto*.

The Rev. Dr. Lewis S. Mudge Jr. was considered a leading ecumenical theologian and theological ethicist in America and abroad. Dean of San Francisco Theological Seminary in San Anselmo, California, until 1995, he was also the Robert Leighton Stuart Professor of Theology until 2000. Simultaneously and until his death in 2009, he taught as a core faculty member of the Graduate Theological Union in Berkeley. Mudge published over twelve books, most recently, *The Gift of Responsibility: The Promise of Dialogue among Christians, Jews, and Muslims* (Continuum, 2008).

Dr. Aristotle Papanikolaou is associate professor of theology and the cofounding director of the Orthodox Christian Studies Program at Fordham University. His research interests include contemporary Orthodox theology and Trinitarian theology. Papanikolaou authored *Being with God: Trinity, Apophaticism, and Divine-Human Communion* (Notre Dame, 2006) and most recently coauthored and edited *Thinking through Faith: New Perspectives from Orthodox Christian Scholars* (SVS Press, 2008) and *Orthodox Readings of Augustine* (SVS Press, 2008).

Msgr. John A. Radano served on the Vatican's Pontifical Council for Promoting Christian Unity from 1984 to 2008. Having returned to the United States, he now teaches at Seton Hall University. He has authored many articles on ecumenism. His book *Lutheran and Catholic Reconciliation on Justification* was published by Eerdmans in 2009.

Dr. Cecil M. Robeck Jr. is professor of church history and ecumenics and director of the David J. DuPlessis Center for Christian Spirituality at

Fuller Theological Seminary. A longtime participant in Faith and Order in the United States and international ecumenical circles and a spokesperson for Pentecostalism, in 2000 Robeck offered a course on "Global Pentecostalism and the Ecumenical Challenge" at the Ecumenical Institute in Bossey, Switzerland, the first time a Pentecostal had been invited to offer a course there. Robeck's historical research centers on the Azusa Street Mission and Revival.

Dr. Michael Root is professor of systematic theology at Lutheran Theological Southern Seminary in Columbia, South Carolina. Root is a member of the U.S. and international Lutheran-Catholic dialogues and has served on the U.S. Lutheran–United Methodist dialogue, the Anglican-Lutheran International Working Group, and the Anglican-Lutheran International Commission. He served on the drafting teams that produced the Lutheran–Roman Catholic Joint Declaration on the Doctrine of Justification and Called to Common Mission, which established full communion between the Evangelical Lutheran Church in America and the Episcopal Church.

Dr. Amos Yong is J. Rodman Williams Professor of Theology and the Director of Doctor of Philosophy Program at Regent University School of Divinity in Virginia. His research interests include Buddhist-Christian dialogue, global Pentecostalism, liberation theology and theology of disability, political theology, theology and science, and the theology of religions and the interfaith encounter. Yong recently authored *Hospitality and the Other: Pentecost, Christian Practices, and the Neighbor* (2008) and edited (with Barbara Brown Zikmund) *Remembering Jamestown: Hard Questions for Christian Mission, 1607–2007* (2010).

Dr. Barbara Brown Zikmund is a retired historian of American religion who served as president of Hartford Seminary (Hartford, CT) from 1990 to 2000. In the 1980s she served on the NCC Commission on Faith and Order; in the 1990s she was a member of the WCC Programme on Theological Education; and from 2000 to 2007 she chaired the NCC Interfaith Relations Commission. She is ordained in the United Church of Christ, and one of her most recent scholarly works has been as general editor of a seven-volume collection of UCC materials titled *The Living Theological Heritage of the United Church of Christ* (1995–2005).